The Complete Codex Zouche-Nuttall

MIXTEC LINEAGE HISTORIES AND POLITICAL BIOGRAPHIES

By Robert Lloyd Williams

Foreword by Rex Koontz

UNIVERSITY OF TEXAS PRESS   AUSTIN

This book is a part of the Latin American and Caribbean Arts and Culture publication initiative, funded by a grant from the Andrew W. Mellon Foundation.

Requests for permission to reproduce material from this work should be sent to:
Permissions
University of Texas Press
P.O. Box 7819
Austin, TX 78713–7819
http://utpress.utexas.edu/about/book-permissions

∞ The paper used in this book meets the minimum requirements of ANSI/NISO Z39.48–1992 (R1997) (Permanence of Paper).

Library of Congress Cataloging-in-Publication Data
Williams, Robert Lloyd.
The complete codex Zouche-Nuttall : Mixtec lineage histories and political biographies / by Robert Lloyd Williams ; foreword by Rex Koontz.
    p.   cm. — (The Linda Schele series in Maya and Pre-Columbian studies)
Includes bibliographical references and index.
ISBN 978-0-292-74438-7 (cloth : alk. paper)
1. Codex Nuttall.   2. Manuscripts, Mixtec.   3. Mixtec Indians—Kings and rulers.   4. Mixtec Indians—Kinship.   5. Mixtec Indians—Politics and government.   I. Title.
F1219.56.C62532W556   2013
972′.7401—dc23   2012042789

doi:10.7560/744387

This volume is dedicated to the great Mixtec people of Oaxaca, past and present; to the memory of Zelia Maria Magdalena Nuttall and Linda Schele; to David Schele, my parents, and Professor Frank Kent Reilly III.

Contents

Foreword

The Codex Zouche-Nuttall is one of a very small group of indigenous books that have been fundamental to our understanding of Ancient American history and thought. Although the picture writing used by the ancient scribes is in many ways meant to communicate effectively across time and language, there are difficulties in the reading that have long troubled scholars and made whole passages of the book opaque. The commentary presented here by Robert Williams proposes solutions for some of the thorniest problems, but more importantly it is the most complete reading of the codex available in English.

The Mixtec culture that gave us the Codex Zouche-Nuttall is one of several literate pre-Columbian cultures that flourished in what is now the state of Oaxaca, Mexico. Many Mixtec princes at the time of the Spanish Conquest traced their genealogy to a great hero of five hundred years earlier named Eight Deer Jaguar Claw. In his commentary on the reverse of the Zouche-Nuttall, Williams synthesizes what we know of that manuscript's version of the hero's life and deeds. The story of the young noble who becomes the greatest ruler the Mixtecs had known is told through a careful reading greatly aided by Williams's attention to the narrative details employed by the brilliant author(s) of this section. By providing the detailed narrative context of this paradigm of Mixtec rulership, Williams contributes something that is important to scholars and advanced students of this manuscript, of pre-Columbian writing, and of Ancient Mixtec history and culture. It is in locating much of the best recent scholarship on Mixtec history and culture in the narrative details of the Zouche-Nuttall that this section finds its center and its strength.

Crucial to the link between the Zouche-Nuttall and larger questions of Mixtec history and culture is a careful attention not only to narrative details but also to narrative strategies and structures and what they may tell us about fundamental aspects of the text. Williams argues that it is possible to decipher many of the more imagistic passages because the particularly iconic writing used in these codices lends itself to understanding regardless of the language the reader speaks. In this aspect, Williams is inserting himself into some of the more interesting and sophisticated discussions on Mesoamerican writing in the last two decades.

Further, Williams embeds his reading in ideas of performance, or performative reading, an established and sophisticated approach to the decipherment of these texts. While Williams is sensitive to the linguistic analogies and analyses used by recent scholars on specific passages in the book, he finally argues that it is the image system itself that allows for a fuller accounting of detail, and his close reading is able to pick up on such detail.

Williams pays equally close attention to scribal strategies in his reading of the Zouche-Nuttall obverse. The author is able to straighten some crooked chronologies and untie some narrative knots that have long bedeviled scholars of this section. He is also able to show us how the later scribes who composed this section were in dialog with the heroic life and genealogy of Eight Deer Jaguar Claw told on the other side of the manuscript. The reader can only see this panorama of Mixtec history, culture, and politics by following Robert Williams through the entire Codex Zouche-Nuttall, a journey well worth taking for all of us who value pre-Columbian history and thought.

REX KOONTZ
School of Art
University of Houston

Preface

In the early 1990s, two colleagues and I attended a public lecture by a formidable scholar of Mixtec codices. We were astonished to hear that scholar say that everything that could be done with these fascinating artifacts had already been accomplished and that no one else need bother with them. These remarks reminded me that in the late nineteenth century a distinguished English physicist declared the study of physics was—from that point forward—a "rote" subject because all that could be done with it had been done.

Subsequently, Linda Schele directed me to found the Mixtec Codex Workshop at the spring break Maya Meetings (University of Texas at Austin), and after the first year of its existence, John M.D. Pohl signed on as codirector. He and I taught the Mixtec Codex Workshop for the next twelve years until it was mysteriously dropped from the curriculum in the early twenty-first century, after Linda's death. However, shortly after the workshop's founding, John Pohl and his colleague Bruce Byland published *In the Realm of 8 Deer: The Archaeology of the Mixtec Codices* (University of Oklahoma Press, 1994) and gave generous testimony thereby that the study of Mixtec codices was anything but finished; in short, the study itself was not (pardon my phrase) "a closed book." Work on the same subject in Europe (notably by Maarten Jansen) reinforced this concept.

My graduate work began in 2004 at Texas State University with Professor Frank Kent Reilly III. He and the other members of my committee, James Garber and John M.D. Pohl, approved my thesis, which was subsequently published as *Lord Eight Wind of Suchixtlan and the Heroes of Ancient Oaxaca: Reading History in the Codex Zouche-Nuttall* (University of Texas Press, 2009). It covered the first eight pages of Codex Zouche-Nuttall (obverse) and also featured supporting essays.

Then, as I continued my graduate work at the University of Texas at Austin with Professor Brian Stross as chair, Professor Kent Reilly as cochair, and

Professors Fred Valdez, Martha Menchaca, and John M.D. Pohl as committee members, my dissertation presenting the narrative structure of Codex Zouche-Nuttall (obverse) was approved. This present effort is that dissertation greatly expanded to include substantial interpretation of the mysterious and delightful Codex Zouche-Nuttall (obverse) document (Pages 1–41). So as to complete the codex's presentation, a commentary on the reverse document (Pages 42–84) was written and included.

The Codices

The Mixtec pictogram manuscripts, or codices, are painted sequences of pictogram tableaux. Theme, chronology, personnel, places, and events visually connect the tableaux. This style of pictogram writing encoded oral traditions to stimulate the memories of bards who knew the complete narratives, as do modern motion-picture production storyboards. As well, the codices were performance documents to be sung, danced, and enacted at elite functions. They were unfolded and situated along walls as minimurals. Ceramics, cloth garments, and full-size murals contained codex scenes. The scribes had a variety of techniques available to them, so no two codex presentation formats are exactly alike.

The five major codices (Selden, Bodley, Zouche-Nuttall, Vindobonensis Mexicanus I, and the Colombino-Becker I fragments now called Codex Alfonso Caso) encode seven manuscripts. Codex Zouche-Nuttall Manuscript One (museum-numbered Pages 42–84) is the older of the two sides of the Zouche-Nuttall and is now called the "reverse" of the document. The "obverse," or Manuscript Two (museum-numbered Pages 1–41), is the most recent of them. In Codex Vindobonensis Mexicanus I, the oldest document is its "obverse" (museum-numbered Pages 52–1 in Arabic numbers), and the most recent document is the "reverse" (Pages I–XIII in Roman numerals added by Europeans, probably when the codex arrived in Europe). Thus, there are seven documents among five major codices.

The culture that produced these manuscripts is now archaeological, although at this time several hundreds of thousands of Mixtec Indians live in the northwestern part of Oaxaca and in some areas of Puebla. There are Mixtec speakers in the Mexican state of Veracruz, and their territory dates from antiquity.

The pre-Hispanic history recorded in the Mixtec codices consists of chronologically marked interconnected themes: political/religious events, biographies, and genealogies. After the Spanish Entrada (entry) into Oaxaca in AD 1521, the stories were remembered and, in the case of Codex Selden (ca. AD 1556), recorded in the native pictogram writing style for purposes of establishing royal genealogies and thus ownership of properties. All codices and their related documents, such as Colonial Period *lienzos*, agree on dates for almost all major founding events and genealogies, although there are exceptions to this last statement.

However, by the seventeenth century, the old oral traditions degraded, as is evidenced by the 1607 creation folk tale surviving in Spanish in the monastery at Cuilapa (Williams 2006). It blends and confuses two origin "histories," the first concerning the birth and deeds of the god Nine Wind Quetzalcoatl (Codex Vindobonensis Mexicanus I, Pages 52–47) and the second those of the aforementioned lineage founder Lord Eight Wind Twenty of Suchixtlan (Codex Zouche-Nuttall, Pages 1–8).

The Mixtec codices are intensely political documents because the kingdoms/city-states and their dependencies rivaled one another and were not far distant from one another geographically. They interconnected by complex marriage alliances granting lucrative trade routes to intermarried elites. The formative era of Mixtec complex independent society occurred in the Late Classic Period and extended into the early years of the Postclassic Period, during an era I call the Mixtec Epiclassic (ca. AD 935–1063). With the collapse of the grand, mysterious megacity Teotihuacan and the subsequent decline of Zapotec Monte Albán (which dominated the Mixtecs), the Mixtec elites seized the historical opportunity to re-form their society independent of Zapotec dominance.

This turbulent period saw the rise of the great lineage founder Lord Eight Wind Twenty of Suchixtlan (b. AD 935), the War from Heaven (AD 963–979), and the establishment of a dominant female line of descent from Lord Eight Wind Twenty ruling at Jaltepec, a major city-state. The founding of an enduring male line of descent came with Lord Eight Deer Jaguar Claw of Tilantongo (b. AD 1063), a contemporary of Lady Six Monkey of Jaltepec.

Each polity produced codex manuscripts reflecting its own history and political point of view. Codex Selden is the royal document of Jaltepec. As such, it occults certain historical information in favor of its own political points of view. The other Mixtec codices painted elsewhere favored various city-states, such as Tututepec, Tilantongo, Achiutla, Teozacoalco, and Chalcatongo, but are ambiguous as to the exact locality that produced the documents. However, these manuscripts include the histories (or at least parts of them) omitted by the Jaltepec scribes and occult their own particulars according to political interest. The topic of this occultation is presented in a later chapter, as is a summary of Mixtec history that I call "the four voices."

Methodology

The authors of Codex Zouche-Nuttall have been dead for at least six hundred years. Their language—Mixtec—survives, yet their history is encoded in a-linguistic sequences (tableaux) of pictograms, neatly painted on fanfolded books made of gesso-covered leather. To paraphrase myself from a previous work (Williams 2006), the Mixtec histories chiefly employ iconic symbols. Therefore, they are linguistically unavailable but symbolically accessible and available for study because they literally still tell their stories. The manuscript writings are stated in icons, symbols like language but sans phonemes and grammar. They are provocateurs of image, religious and environmental symbols imbued with meaning that can communicate across cultures separated by time. I, now or recently so, can have the phenomena they represent affect me, but I as native informer's subject must be affected by them in a manner as close to the ancient sense as possible, somehow discovering the original meaning and appreciating its transformation and translation across time within myself. They—in a sense—write the observer, because the observer's meaning is empowered with a new consciousness transmitted from antiquity. Words spoken or written are deleted in one genre (codices), impelled by a different genre (communication to an observer), but the experience of original songs and impulses is conveyed and created by unusual evocation in yet another (interpretation by the observer). Stephen Tyler's correlation of ethnography and poetry is insightful: "Ethnography is a cooperatively evolved text consisting of fragments of discourse intended to evoke in the minds of both reader and writer an emergent fantasy" (1986:125).

The Mixtec manuscripts are discourse. Non-Mixtec observers are empowered to share the native cultural system of meaning and integrate it with their own. This transaction is both effective ethnology and divorced from it as original native narrative experience becomes contemporary in content and context. The Mixtec fanfolded books explain ancient Mixtecs to those who will listen with their eyes.

In a real sense, the codices can never be finally analyzed because they represent kinetic ongoing story outlines in the process of being performed. We have limited access to the original performances, and what remains for our codex interpretation is almost literally what is painted on the pages—perhaps five to ten percent of their original, memory-encoded information.

Acknowledgments

This study began as an assignment given to me by Professor Linda Schele in 1990. Her memory has been a constant inspiration. Professor John M.D. Pohl has provided continuous encouragement and motivation from 1992 to the present day, and it has been my privilege to learn from him for at least ten years.

My undergraduate studies were shaped and promoted by Professor James Neely and Professors Thomas Hester, James Denbow, and Pauline Turner-Strong. Professor F. Kent Reilly III was the major force in my education on Mesoamerican cultures, beginning in the fall of 2004 with my master's studies at Texas State University-San Marcos for which he was the thesis chair. He was aided and abetted by Elizabeth Erhart, Richard Warms, and James Garber. I owe an additional debt of gratitude to the students who taught me in my various Mixtec codices classes and seminars at the University of Texas and Texas State University. I am grateful to John Fielding, a friend and fellow student of many years, who willingly undertook the task of proofreading this manuscript, crunching the numbers, and asking questions—many questions.

Theresa J. May, Editor-in-Chief at the University of Texas Press, Austin, has been not only an inspiration in the completion of this present book but also a model of patience and understanding—to which she has brought her professional wisdom and experience. I am deeply grateful to her.

Susan Snyder, Head of Public Services at the Bancroft Library, University of California, Berkeley, graciously granted permission to utilize the library's copy of Zelia Nuttall's photograph for this publication. She also graciously tolerated my e-mail communications and responded with helpful goodwill.

Underscoring all of this is the spirit of my Cherokee grandfather, John Lloyd Gray, whose love and constant concern for me did not cease with his death in 1966.

The Complete Codex Zouche-Nuttall

1   The First Historian of the New World

Peter Martyr d'Anghera: General Remarks

The documentation of New World native books and their arrival in Europe remains controversial, as does the interpretation of those that may survive in museum and library collections. Part of the controversy is fueled by the unusual nature of native New World writing itself. While some examples are what scholars call "true writing" or "closed writing," tied to systems from which specific languages can be recovered—such as Classic Period Maya inscriptions—many are examples of another technique of writing called "open writing" and bound to no language while containing elements of their mother tongues. These open-writing texts are pictography. They communicate by producing a narrative sequence of juxtaposed static images. Still other Mesoamerican writings seem to combine both systems. Elizabeth Hill Boone recently elucidated this distinction between open and closed writing systems by defining the former as "alternative literacies" written in pictogram tableaux (2000:28–35).

However, the appearance of these types of native books in Europe was a source of both curiosity and wonder. One of the earliest extensive commentators we have on them is Peter Martyr d'Anghera, whose family name is lost and whose town of origin, Anghera in northern Italy, is variously spelled in the literature (i.e., Anghiera, Angleria). His biographer and translator, Francis MacNutt (D'Angleria 1912, 1:30), gives his epitaph, wherein is stated that he is from "Mediolanum," the district of modern Milan.[1] Considering that Peter Martyr's work is prototypal, commentary must begin with him and then proceed to a limited number of modern scholars whose work advances this present study.

As was true of Christopher Columbus, the scholar-priest known as Peter

Martyr d'Anghera (born February 2, 1457; died September 23 or 24, 1526) was born on the Italian peninsula, lived in Spain, and worked for the Spanish Crown. He was not a martyr but was baptized with the name of the Dominican Peter the Martyr of Verona (d. 1252), whose cult was popular, even fervent, in Italy at the time of Peter's birth.

In 1511, he was appointed by the Spanish emperor Charles V to the post of historiographer and set about writing the official history of the discovery and conquest of the New World, thus he was substantially the New World's first historian. MacNutt (D'Angleria 1912, 1:17) calls him "the first to herald the discovery of the new world, and to publish the glory of his unknown compatriot [Columbus] to their countrymen." He wrote serially from the documentation of Columbus and then from Hernán Cortés as well as their compatriots. Between 1516 and 1587 (many years after his death), a series of publications of Peter Martyr's work appeared, all broadcasting the achievements of Spaniards and glorifying the triumphs of their empire. Because Peter Martyr addressed the clergy and wrote in Latin, his works were not confined to Spain but found audiences all over Europe. There were at least twelve publications of his volumes, and, therefore, his *Of the New World* (*De orbe novo*) was the sixteenth and seventeenth centuries' equivalent of a bestseller. His work literally informed Europe of the New World and advertised its wonders and financial possibilities.

Although Peter Martyr held an ecclesiastical appointment to an institution in Jamaica, he never visited the New World, and thus there is a temptation to regard him as an armchair ethnographer or merely as one who culled facts (Moreno García and Torres Santo Domingo 2008:5). Some sources (*The Catholic Encyclopedia*, 1913; Wikipedia; etc.) remark that although Peter Martyr d'Anghera never visited the New World, he financed construction of the first stone church in Jamaica. He did finance a stone construction on the island, but according to the Jamaica National Heritage Trust:

> When the Spanish settlement of Sevilla la Nueva was moved from the coast to higher ground, construction of a cut stone Church was started in 1534 by Abbot Peter Martyr of Angleria, Italy. Only the Church walls were built as in 1534 the Spanish centre of Government was moved to Spanish Town.

We know that Peter Martyr d'Anghera died in 1526, but overlooking that, the church remains unfinished even to this present day. The Jamaica National Heritage Trust (cited above) quotes English historian Hans Sloane as follows:

> the Church was not finished. . . . [It was] built of a type of stone between free stone and marble, taken from the quarry about a mile up the hill . . . the west gate of the church was very fine work and stands entire, standing seven feet wide and as high before the arch began. Over the door in the middle was Our Saviour's head with a crown of thorns.

The unfinished building was known as Peter Martyr Church, and as early as 1770 the British were criticized for allowing the unfinished, high-quality structure to fall into ruins. In 1925, the estate owner deeded title to five acres containing the Peter Martyr Church site to the Roman Catholic bishop. Subsequently a fund-raising campaign resulted in a new church building, finished in 1943. Located next to the ruins of the original Peter Martyr Church, the new edifice is named Our Lady of Perpetual Help Church.

As to the cognomen of "armchair ethnographer," Peter Martyr d'Anghera's Latin prose accounts gave Europeans their first impressions of New World peoples, customs, and events. He vividly described the spectrum of New World discoveries ranging from peoples, to animals, to plants.[2] As well, he records the enslavement of New World indigenous peoples by Christopher Columbus, the local beliefs on human origins (1:105), and the European introduction of animals such as swine (1:113). As a commentator, Peter Martyr managed to convey the freshness and excitement of the original contacts between the Spaniards and the new exotic peoples they encountered.

His accounts of these fascinating new peoples are not demeaning. To him, they were truly "new people" with new customs and offered new adventures and, of course, business opportunities. Peter Martyr decried local customs such as human sacrifice and cannibalism. In short, although addressed to Roman Catholic cardinals and at least one pope, his writings, initially and later, found a wide audience in general consumption. Their assignment to Spanish and Roman Catholic royalty added to their luster as official documents.

Peter Martyr d'Anghera on Indigenous New World Writing

The subject of indigenous writing, however, is mentioned only once in Peter Martyr's first volume, in Book X (1:237–238).

> A learned lawyer called Corales, who is a judge at Darien, reported that he encountered a fugitive from the interior provinces of the west, who sought refuge with the cacique. This man, seeing the judge reading, started with surprise, and asked through interpreters who knew the cacique's language, "You also have books? You understand the signs by which you communicate with the absent?" He asked at the same time to look at the open book, hoping to see the same characters used among his people; but he saw the letters were not the same. He said that in his country the towns were walled and the citizens wore clothing and were governed by laws. I have not learned the nature of their religion, but it is known from examining this fugitive, and from his speech, that they are circumcised. What, Most Holy Father, do you think of this?[3]

To our point, however, Peter Martyr d'Anghera describes native books in Volume 2, Decade 4, Book VIII, pages 39–41 (addressed to Cardinal Egidio Antonini, Legate of Pope Leo X). The first type of book "on which the natives write" was made of thin tree-bark-like palm leaves:

> We have already stated that these natives possess books. The messengers sent from the new country of Colhuacan brought a number of these books amongst other presents. The pages on which the natives write are made of the thin bark of trees, of the quality found in the first, outer layer. It may be compared to those scales found not precisely in the willow or the elm, but rather in the edible palm leaves, in which tough filaments cross one another in the upper layer, just as in nests the openings and narrow meshes alternate. These membranes are smeared with tough bitumen, after which they are limbered and given the desired form; they are stretched out at will and when they are hardened, a kind of plaster or analogous substance is spread over them. I know your Holiness has handled some of these tablets, on which sifted plaster similar to flour was sprinkled. One may write thereon whatever comes into one's mind, a sponge or a cloth sufficing to rub it out, after which the tablet may be again used. The natives also used fig leaves for making small books, which the stewards of important households take with them when they go to market. They write down their purchases with a little point, and afterwards erase them when they have

been entered in their books. They do not fold the leaves into four but extend them to a length of several cubits: they are square-shaped. The bitumen that holds them together is so tough and flexible that, when bound in a wooden cover, they appear to have been put together by the hand of a skilled binder. When the book is wide open, both pages covered with characters are visible, and these first two pages conceal two others, unless they are pulled out to their whole length; for although there is one single leaf, many such leaves are fastened together.

Peter Martyr notes that a smaller type of book was employed by stewards of important households to take to market, write down their purchases "with a little point," and afterward erase them when the data were entered into a more permanent record. These were actually seen in Europe, a happenstance both interesting and evocative.

A second description (page 41) seems to indicate two types of books by contents, although Peter Martyr is not careful to distinguish between the two types except by description of use. These other books are not four-folded like napkins as large sheets would be[4] but rather extended "to a length of several cubits: they are square-shaped." It is best to reproduce the description in its entirety instead of fragmenting it. Thus, he continues:

The characters are entirely different from ours, and are in the forms of dice, dots, stars, lines, and other similar signs, marked and traced as we do our letters. They almost resemble the hieroglyphics of the ancient Egyptians. Among the figures may be distinguished those of men and animals, especially those of kings or great lords. Thus it is permissible to assume that they report the deeds of each king's ancestors. And do we not in our own times see engravers of general histories or fabulous stories draw pictures of what is told in the volume? The natives are also very clever in manufacturing wooden covers for the leaves of these books. When these books are closed, they seem to differ in no respect from our own. It is supposed that the natives preserve in these books their laws, the ritual of their sacrifices and ceremonies, astronomical observations, and the precepts of agriculture.

In this passage, Peter Martyr d'Anghera therefore describes two types of Indian manuscripts. The first kind appears to be larger sheets (he calls them "tablets") and smaller ones used for everyday purposes and easily erased and reused.[5] In fact, according to his text, several had been sent to Europe and examined by Cardinal Antonini. The second type (actually two types by contents) of native books is clearly the well-constructed fanfold histories and augural manuscripts (books of fate). In this latter type, Peter Martyr notes the "dice," which are very likely a series of squares or rectangles with circle-date numbers and other illustrations that are known to be indicative of augural codices, such as those in the Borgia group.

He describes another, fourth type of book also. In Volume 2, Book V, Decade 10, page 206, he cites Ribera about them:

> I have already often said that they have books, of which a number have been brought here. Ribera states that these books are not written to be read, but are various collections of designs the jewelers keep to copy in making ornaments, or decorating coverlets and dresses. . . . I hardly know what to believe, because of the great variety one observes in these books, but I think they must be books whose characters and designs have a meaning, for have I not seen on the obelisks in Rome characters which are considered letters, and do not we read that the Chaldeans formerly had a similar writing.

In summary, then, this popular, busy writer indicates to us that the natives of the Spanish New World had four basic kinds of books: erasable notebooks for daily casual use, augural books, history books, and books of patterns and designs for the trade. Yet even the latter he surmises "must have a meaning."

It was not difficult for Peter Martyr d'Anghera to deduce that the native books he had seen were used to record history; as he has it, "it is permissible to assume that they report the deeds of each king's ancestors." Slightly more than three hundred years later, the American traveler, diplomat, and author John Lloyd Stephens explored the solemn and mysterious Classic Period Maya city of Copan. His companion artist, Frederick Catherwood, meticulously drew the monuments and architecture they found deep in the Honduran jungle. Catherwood used a camera lucida for accuracy. Stephens recognized that many of the monuments contained hieroglyphic writings, and it was not difficult for him to speculate (correctly) that they recorded the history of the place and the deeds of the great lords and kings there. As he says (1969[1841]:159–160): "One thing I believe, that its history is graven on its monuments. No Champollion has yet brought to them the energies of his inquiring mind. Who shall read them?"

The subject of Native American recording of history, despite support for the concept in the testimonies of two seminal authors widely separated

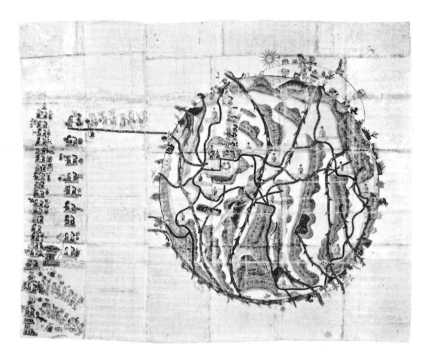

Figure 1.1. El Mapa de Teozacoalco. The Benson Library, University of Texas at Austin.

in time, has been controversial. In fact, the very idea of Native American writing was itself fraught with controversy. This subject is revisited in the next chapter on historiography and native history with the presentation of the efforts of a few prominent late-nineteenth through twentieth-century commentators. Their studies deal primarily with fanfold manuscripts called codices, but also with later Colonial Period documents such as the cloth Lienzo de Zacatepec and the paper Map of Teozacoalco.

Figure 1.2. Cover of *De orbe novo*. Internet image.

2 Historiography and Native History

Six contemporary authors and their work are presented here to provide a contextual background for the Codex Zouche-Nuttall and for their important contributions to historiography and native history: Zelia Nuttall and her introduction to the published codex bearing her name (1902); Alfonso Caso; Otto Adelhofer's (1974) "History and Description" of the Codex Vindobonensis Mexicanus I (called Codex Vienna), which introduces the Akademische Druck- u facsimile; Lauran Toorians's two essays on the history of the Codex Vienna in Europe (1983, 1984); Jill Leslie Furst's commentary on Codex Vienna (1978a) and her article about Codex Zouche-Nuttall Pages 1–7 published in that same year (1978b); and John M.D. Pohl.

Zelia Maria Magdalena Nuttall (1857–1933)

Zelia Maria Magdalena Nuttall was born in San Francisco, California, on September 6, 1857, and died at Casa Alvarado, Coyoacán, Mexico, on April 12, 1933. Hers was a privileged family, and when but a child, her mother gave Zelia a copy of Lord Kingsborough's monumental work on ancient Mexico. Her father (originally from an old Lancashire family and born in Ireland) took his family to Europe in 1865. She was educated in France, Germany, Italy, and England, where she studied at Bedford College in London. The Nuttalls returned to San Francisco in 1876 when Zelia was nineteen or twenty.

Zelia Nuttall was for forty-seven years a noted "Americanist" and Honorary Assistant and Fellow in Mexican Archaeology at the Peabody Museum of Harvard University. Her publications were many, and in 1901 she published her largest work, *The Fundamental Principles of Old and New World Civilizations*. However, Alfred Tozzer notes in his obituary for her (1933) that despite her many talents and contributions to her chosen field of work, she is remembered most for her talent for finding lost or forgotten manuscripts and bringing them to the attention of scholars. She learned of the codex that now bears her name entirely by accident, and her pursuit of it and its subsequent deposition in the British Museum is legendary. She hired two British artists to copy the fanfold manuscript and arranged for its publication by the Peabody Museum, Harvard.

Zelia Nuttall's introduction to the 1902 Peabody Museum artist's reproduction of the manuscript, now called Codex Zouche-Nuttall, gives brief mention to the arduous investigation and labor she undertook through several years to bring the codex to public attention and place it in the hands of scholars. Her labor is the darling of historiographers, and Nancy Troike details it in her introduction to the 1987 (pages 17–22) Akademische Druck- u. Verlagsanstalt facsimile published in Graz, Austria.

Although Nuttall considered the manuscript Aztec (her eulogist, Alfred Tozzer, considered it Zapotec) and fails to mention that the 1902 Peabody Museum edition contains a major pagination error (page 42, the first page of the reverse side, appears as the last page of the obverse side), she is adamant in referring to codices Zouche-Nuttall and Vienna as "sister" documents (1902:4, 9–11). She even believes the same artist painted both codices and, though erring in that conclusion, correctly intuits that they are concerned with the same "contemporaneous facts and circumstances" (1902:9a). In this latter remark, she very likely refers to the genealogies of the Vindobonensis reverse as reflecting the genealogies of Tilantongo recorded on the Codex Zouche-Nuttall obverse, as well as other similarities in personnel. Even if this is the case, it remains difficult to see how she could not notice the difference in artistic quality between the Vienna obverse (which is superb) and reverse (which is not) and the excellence of the Zouche-Nuttall codex in its entirety. Years ago, a noted Mesoamerican scholar remarked to me that, obviously, a lesser artist painted the Codex Vienna reverse (Michael Coe, personal communication, ca. 1990).

Nuttall discounts the later glosses written in Spanish and Italian as worthless but seems to consider it evidentiary that just because a later annotator writes in Italian on the codex pages that it is in Nahuatl, it is therefore an Aztec document (1902:9b). In fact, she notes, all glosses seem to be erroneous except when it comes to identifying specific years as Reed, Rabbit, House, or Flint Knife.

Despite this, Zelia Nuttall conducts an accurate description of the manuscript. Her linkage of it with Codex Vienna and her assessment that both were in the library of Montezuma II and were subsequently those two "native books" mentioned in Cortés's manifest of 1519, although discounted by some later scholars, remain of interest.

Alfonso Caso Andrade (1896–1970)

In his introduction to the posthumous publication *Reyes y reinos de la mixteca*, Alfonso Caso (1984:1–39) makes no mention, thus no speculation, on the arrival of various Mixtec manuscripts in Europe. He does so, however, in his introductions for his interpretations of Codex Bodley 2858 (1960:11a–b) and, to some extent, for Codex Selden 3135 (A.2) (1964:61), but he is silent on the arrival in Europe of Codices Vindobonensis Mexicanus I and Zouche-Nuttall. In his description of Codex Colombino (1966:115b), he does mention glosses in Codex Zouche-Nuttall and records his impressions of one of them:

> Next, a blank page which I call F, another page which I call G, on which someone believed it necessary to leave us evidence of his vandalism:
> "Storia Mejicana
> 92 pages. Aug. 1919 C.J.C.
> Examined by C.J.C."

Caso was, however, the first scholar to accurately identify the manuscripts as Mixtec in origin. His work will be examined in more detail below.

Otto Adelhofer

Otto Adelhofer's introduction to the Akademische Druck- u. Verlagsanstalt edition of Codex Vindobonensis Mexicanus I is interesting. Although our knowledge of and classification of Mesoamerican writing systems has advanced since Adelhofer wrote, he makes two salient points (admittedly among many) that catch our attention for this present work: (1) the mnemonic nature of the Mixtec pictogram documents and their use in the transmission of historical knowledge, and (2) his notation that the Mixtecs inhabited not only the modern territories assigned to them but also, from antiquity, an area in Veracruz that he regards as very likely their homeland—called the Mixtequilla. Adelhofer believes it possible that the Mixtequilla explains how two Mixtec codices could come into the hands of Hernán Cortés, thus he does not discount Zelia Nuttall's original assertion per se, omitting only reference to Montezuma II. He mentions (1974:10b) that it is commonly accepted that the two native books mentioned by Cortés in the 1519 manifest are Codices Zouche-Nuttall and Vienna.

At least forty-six publications about the Mixtequilla have come out since 1974 (the era of Adelhofer's essay), and at least eight theses and dissertations have been written on the topic from 1990 to 2003. A prominent investigator of the area is Barbara Stark, whose Proyecto Arqueológico La Mixtequilla (an Internet site maintained by Arizona State University) notes cultural development there beginning about 900 BC. Besides the distinctive nature of local cultures, Stark notes: "Highland people settled in the region about C.E. 1200, approximately at the time of striking disruption of Classic period cultural traditions."

Adelhofer makes another assertion that is important for those who wish to consider the ages of the remaining Mixtec manuscripts. None seem very old, that is, predating the fourteenth century. Codex Selden was composed in 1556, well after the conquest. Taking his cue from Alfonso Caso, Adelhofer notes that under Phillip II of Spain in 1580, Europeans took extreme interest in native aristocracy. As Adelhofer says:

> The result was, among other things, complete family trees of the Mixtec noble houses of Tilantongo and Teozacoalco, two once powerful towns in present-day Oaxaca. If the records prepared under Spanish supervision are compared with the old pictographic manuscripts of the Mixtecs, striking correspondences are soon noticed. (1974:8a)

Two such native documents produced during this time of European interest in Native American royal genealogy besides Codex Selden are the Lienzo de Zacatepec that traces descent from Lord Four Wind (who also appears in codices such as the Bodley, Zouche-Nuttall, Selden, and the Colombino-Becker I fragments—now called Codex Alfonso Caso) and the Mapa de Teozacoalco, tracing descent from the lords of Tilantongo, notably Lord Eight Deer Jaguar Claw. Eight Deer appears in every major Mixtec codex. The Lienzo is a painted cloth document and the Mapa is made of European paper glued together and painted in the native style of the day.

Lauran Toorians

Codices Manuscripti (the Austrian National Library) published two interesting articles by the scholar Lauran Toorians that provide the most valuable of all things for the historian of Mexican and Central American codices in Europe, namely, a paper trail. The first of these articles was "Some Light in the Dark Century of Codex Vindobonensis Mexicanus I" (1983), and in the second of them, "Codex Vindobonensis Mexicanus I, Its History Completed" (1984), Toorians detailed the vagaries of this manuscript's European ownership. These data are also utilized in Maarten Jansen's (1990) paper, "The Search for History in Mixtec Codices." According to Toorians, the European owners/custodians of the manuscript were:

1. 1521, King Manuel I of Portugal;
2. 1521–1534, Giulio de' Medici, aka Pope Clement VII;
3. 1534–1535, Ippolito dei Medici, nephew of Clement VII (Zelia Nuttall thinks that about this time the "sister" manuscripts were placed in the Medici Palace Library in Florence. If so, the Zouche-Nuttall was transferred to the Florentine Library of San Marco, and the Vindobonensis, to Austria, Bavaria, etc.);
4. 1535–1537, Nikolaus von Schönberg;
5. 1537–1557, Johann Albrecht Widmanstetter;
6. 1558–1579, Albrecht V of Bavaria;
7. 1579–1597, Wilhelm V of Bavaria;
8. 1597–1632, Maximilian I of Bavaria;
9. 1632–1662, Wilhelm IV of Saxe-Weimar;
10. 1662–1678, Johann Georg I of Saxe-Eisenach;
11. 1678–1705, Leopold I of Habsberg;
12. 1705 to present, the Imperial Library of Vienna, now the Austrian National Library.

The interval between Hernán Cortés's acquisition of the two codices in 1519 until King Manuel I of Portugal received Codex Vienna is the only lacuna in this list of dates. Also unresolved is the issue of the source of Cortés's acquisition of the manuscript: as a gift from the ill-fated last Aztec emperor or from a Mixtec tribal king in Veracruz.

Jill Leslie Furst

In 1978, Jill Leslie Furst published an article titled "The Life and Times of ♂ 8 Wind 'Flinted Eagle': A Commentary on the First Seven Pages of the 'Obverse' of *Codex Zouche-Nuttall*." She notes that in AD 1519, Hernán Cortés mentioned two native books in his first letter from Mexico to Charles V, later described by Peter Martyr as books "such as the natives have."[1] The books are described as square and painted on native paper made of fig-tree bark. Furst remarks that the scholars Zelia Nuttall, Alfonso Caso, and Otto Adelhofer believe these books to be the Codices Zouche-Nuttall and Vindobonensis Mexicanus I.

According to Furst, this identification is insecure because the codices in question are neither square nor painted on fig-bark paper; furthermore, the manuscripts are neither books nor codices but screenfolds. Yet she concludes that Peter Martyr's identification may have been imprecise as to material and shape, thus a generic description. Therefore the theory of the identification of the two Mixtec manuscripts under discussion cannot be discounted.

The important question of exactly how Mixtec manuscripts came into Cortés's possession on the eastern Mexican coast (a question raised by Adelhofer) is a thorny one. As to Codex Vindobonensis Mexicanus I: the obverse document is substantially a map of the Mixteca region as revealed by Lord Nine Wind Quetzalcoatl, then divided into districts, each associated with diverse gods and, at times, also various ceremonies and divinatory dates; the codex is therefore also associated with lineages and dynasties. Arguments over land ownership in the Mixteca were frequently noted in colonial times and, as Furst remarks (1978b:3a), are not infrequent today. It is possible, therefore, that the Vindobonensis Mexicanus I codex might have been conveyed to Tenochtitlán to resolve such conflicts and then to the Gulf Coast, where it came into the possession of the conquistador.

Furst seems to have difficulty relating a similar course for Codex Zouche-Nuttall because (as she says) it is primarily a genealogical document. She remarks: "Why Zouche-Nuttall should have been sent from the Mixteca to the Gulf Coast or to Tenochtitlán is a mystery, unless it also figured in the hypothetical land dispute" (Furst 1978b:3b). However, the genealogical content of the manuscript is precisely why it would have accompanied Codex Vindobonensis Mexicanus I, namely, because it gives an accounting of ruling genealogies on its obverse side, and on the older, reverse side provides the political biography of Eight Deer Jaguar Claw of Tilantongo. The ruling families of the past extend into the present as those who rule in contemporary times; therefore, by virtue of such a document, one may know who rules which district and who pays tribute to overlords such as the Aztecs.

Another positive rationale accounting for the presence of Codex Zouche-Nuttall in Tenochtitlán is Lord Eight Deer Jaguar Claw himself. He initiated an alliance with the Toltecs (see Codices Bodley, Zouche-Nuttall, and Colombino-Becker I). Eight Deer wore a Toltec nose ornament, and that same type of ornament appears in some name glyphs for the last Aztec emperor, Montezuma II, including on his stone monument in Chapultepec Park (Aguilar-Moreno 2007:17). The affinity of two rulers separated by nearly four hundred years for the same royal insignia is suggestive. Although inconclusive, a rationale is established for the presence of both documents in the Aztec capital, and the similarity of their importance for documenting native royalty may also account for their subsequent conveyance together to the Mexican Gulf Coast.

In her dissertation, Furst addresses the European appearance of both manuscripts—Vindobonensis Mexicanus I and Zouche-Nuttall—on page 1. She notes that at least Codex Vindobonensis appears to have arrived in Europe shortly after the Spanish Entrada because of an inscription in it stating that King Manuel I of Portugal owned it. That inscription dates the king's acquisition of it as AD 1521, the year Pedro de Alvarado entered Oaxaca. Therefore, if Vindobonensis was one of the two manuscripts mentioned in the Cortés manifest, it would have been acquired earlier than 1521, thus prior to the Spanish Entrada into Oaxaca. This suggests that Codex Vindobonensis Mexicanus I was acquired from somewhere other than Oaxaca.

While acknowledging J. Eric S. Thompson's doubt about the codices being the two documents sent to Europe by Hernán Cortés in 1519 because they did not fit the description by Peter Martyr d'Anghera as being square, Furst concludes that D'Anghera's description was probably generic, not specific. Then, prudently, she leaves the discussion at that. Lacking that prudence, I have noted in Chapter 1 that D'Anghera did exactly describe such square native books when he talked about erasable tablets or notebooks made of netlike fig bark and covered with tough bitumen. Peter Martyr also tells us that such types of native books had been seen in Europe and examined by Cardinal Antonini. The telling factor that remains, however, is the 1521 date and the inscription stating that the king of Portugal owned Vindobonensis Mexicanus I.

John M.D. Pohl

John M.D. Pohl's work is prolific, determinative, and definitive. Beginning with his dissertation, *The Politics of Symbolism in the Mixtec Codices* (1994), and continuing through many articles, television documentaries, and especially a 1994 publication coauthored with Bruce Byland (*In the Realm of 8 Deer: The Archaeology of the Mixtec Codices*), Pohl almost single-handedly established the paradigm for modern research in the United States on these Native American manuscripts, and his scholarship represents a turning point in the study of these graphic artifacts. His website on FAMSI (Foundation for the Advancement of Mesoamerican Studies, Inc.), John Pohl's Mesoamerica, remains extant and serves to contextualize the Mixtec manuscripts in the broader context of Mesoamerican pre-Columbian civilizations. In short, because of John Pohl's extensive experience with visual media as well as his experience as an anthropologist/archaeologist working in the field, his many publications in the area of indigenous communication systems of the Americas establish him as a primary source for all subsequent scholars.

Discussion and Summation

Zelia Nuttall wrote an accurate description of the artifact that now bears her name (1902). However, this brilliant and insightful investigator considered the manuscript to be Aztec in origin, narrating the conquests of Aztec or possibly Texcocan warriors. With this cultural misidentification in place, it was impossible to conduct an accurate study of this codex or of other Mixtec manuscripts surviving in Europe and the one known fragment remaining in the New World (Codex Colombino). Cooper Clark, writing in 1912, considered these codices to be Zapotec in origin. In 1926, Richard C. Long made the first attempt to determine the narrative structural contents of the Codex Zouche-Nuttall. He divided it into five sections and proposed a chronology of 478 years for the manuscript.

In 1944, Alfonso Caso attended a history conference convened in Guadalajara, Mexico (Dirección de Estudios Geográficos de la Secretaría de Agricultura), because several Colonial Period district maps, native documents of Jalisco, were displayed there. He was delighted to discover that the map of Teozacoalco, Jalisco, was really the sixteenth-century map of Teozacoalco,

Oaxaca, and was indeed the missing map from the Relaciones Geográficas for the town. This map (see Figure 1.1), subsequently housed in the Benson Library at the University of Texas, Austin, allowed Caso to identify the kings and queens displayed on it as royal Mixtec ancestors. He therefore concluded that the corpus of major Mixtec manuscripts mentioning those rulers (Codices Selden, Bodley, Zouche-Nuttall, Vindobonensis Mexicanus I, and the Colombino fragment) were neither Aztec nor Zapotec, but Mixtec.

Subsequently, in his watershed work, *El mapa de Teozacoalco* (1949), Caso correctly identified the cultural assignment for these mysterious and magnificent artifacts. However, Caso also made another contribution to the study, one that continues to affect scholars of later generations. It was a comment he made about written native history:

> It is very common when speaking about the history of America to say that it began with the (European) conquerors and the first Spanish chroniclers and that the Indians have no written history; [implying] therefore, that the surviving written accounts that refer to the remote past of native peoples were recorded only when the Indians learned to write in Spanish after the Conquest. We will demonstrate that this opinion is completely false. The Indians not only of Mexico, but from the whole of Mesoamerica, possessed a true historical vocation, and they told and wrote history. (1998:1)

It may be added to Alfonso Caso's elegant tirade that the conquerors burned most native books and then denied that indigenous peoples could even write.

In the 1960s, Caso published commentaries (or "translations") of Codices Selden, Bodley, and Colombino to accompany facsimiles of those ancient manuscripts in a series issued by Sociedad Mexicana de Antropología, Mexico. He also published a commentary on the reverse of Codex Vindobonensis Mexicanus I in 1950. In his commentary on the Colombino fragment (1966), Caso was the first to identify the document as part of the Colombino-Becker I complex, thus one manuscript had been separated into two fragments, with Colombino remaining in Mexico and Becker I located in the Austrian National Library.

In his introduction to the 1975 Dover edition of Zelia Nuttall's original 1902 publication, *The Codex Nuttall: A Picture Manuscript from Ancient Mexico*, Arthur Miller remarks that prior to Caso's death in 1970 he had completed a "translation" of Codex Zouche-Nuttall. He cites part of it on pages xvi(a)–xvii(a) of the Dover publication. However, there is no mention of the commentary in Miller's "References Cited." The conclusion remains, then, that it was at this time an unpublished work and, perhaps, unfinished.

Considering the enormous scope of Alfonso Caso's life work, the Mixtec elements mentioned above alone suffice to qualify him as the "father" of Mixtec studies. Anything written before him is historiography, and anything after is heavily dependent on his precise in-depth analyses of the Mixtec manuscripts. However, although his knowledge of ancient Mexican use of the native calendar was encyclopedic (Caso 1971), he mistook the usage of it in Mixtec manuscripts and recorded many incorrect pre-Hispanic dates for the historical events in them. See the discussion under "The Calendar as Memory" in Chapter Three.

Conclusions

Despite Peter Martyr d'Anghera's statement that native codices were not necessarily uncommon in Europe, the arrival of the "sister" codices there is ambiguous for Codex Zouche-Nuttall but less so for Vindobonensis Mexicanus I. Some scholars (such as Thompson) conclude that there is no evidence for these two manuscripts based on early European sources, but others, such as Toorians, demonstrate that there is indeed evidence for at least one, Vindobonensis Mexicanus I, and, by inference, that particular evidence can be extended to the other (Codex Zouche-Nuttall). Zelia Nuttall's speculations are insightful and dedicated. Adelhofer's references to the Mixtequilla people in Veracruz also remain of interest.

The subject remains an appealing mystery. When it comes to Codex Zouche-Nuttall, documentation may never emerge, and its connections to its sister document remain inferential. Their relationship is enhanced because one can be used so easily to cross-reference personnel and events in the other. For this reason the mystery of the manuscripts' arrival in Europe will always be relished.

Are these books those read and owned by Montezuma II and seen by Cortés? Are these artifacts those once present (even if only as minor background props) during that terrible, magnificent era when the world changed forever? If so, then they partake of a sublime historical grandeur. How did such delicate objects manage to survive an ocean voyage and the vicissitudes of their treatment when in Europe—especially since so many remained behind and even some in Europe did not? While in some cases speculation can be demeaning, in the case of the two sister manuscripts it adds a certain cachet to the environment surrounding their study and appreciation.

Concerning the Zouche-Nuttall Screenfold Manuscript

The original manuscript has been in the possession of the British Museum for over a century. It was part of the original Robert Curzon (the fourteenth Baron Zouche of Harynworth, England) collection of ancient manuscripts. The collection, including the codex, was placed in the care of the British Museum upon his death in 1876. Upon the death of Curzon's last heir, Darea Curzon, in 1917, the museum became owner of the entire collection. The Codex Zouche-Nuttall was kept in the Museum's Department of Manuscripts until 1926 and then, after a brief stay in the Museum of Mankind, was housed in the British Museum's Department of Ethnography, its present location.

The artifact is composed of sixteen strips of animal-hide leather. The ends are overlapped somewhat and glued together to form a continuous piece measuring 11.41 meters in length. The individual skins were carefully trimmed and are approximately 18.4 centimeters in width. Both sides of this strip were covered in white primer (gesso) and then scored to make the fanfold panel-pages. These panel-pages vary in length from 23.3 cm to 25.05 cm.

The older side of the document is now called the reverse in common parlance and in this present study. Examination of the original manuscript under low-power magnification shows that paint from the obverse seeped through small holes and cracks and overlaid painted figures in the reverse. Therefore, the reverse was painted first and is the older. The mottled front cover of the manuscript was also examined under low-power magnification, and the brown mottling was deduced to be glue with geometric shapes and feather shapes impressed into it. It must have been beautifully decorated and apparently had no wooden cover, as does its "sister" manuscript, Codex Vindobonensis Mexicanus I.

The Codex Zouche-Nuttall has been published in its entirety several times. The first edition of it was a color lithograph set published by the Peabody Museum, Harvard University, in 1902. Each codex page was individually traced and colored by British artists, and the Peabody edition reproduced the original format by placing the pages sequentially over cloth-covered stiff paper. Six hundred prints were made of the pages, three hundred of them bound fanfold and the remaining three hundred sold with loose-leaf binding. A bound fanfold copy was the first reproduction of Codex Zouche-Nuttall I studied, and it had the first page of the reverse (Document 2, Page 42) as the last page of the obverse (Document 1)—an error unmentioned in the Dover reprint.

The Librería Anticuaria Guillermo M. Echániz issued twenty-five hand-colored copies in 1939 in Mexico. I have a hand-colored copy of Codex Borgia by this same publisher in my collection, with the issue date of 1937. As is the case with the 1939 edition of Zouche-Nuttall, it is not in the original fanfold format but bound in red leather boards secured by two metal posts on the left side. The title page is elegantly calligraphed and reads

> Manuscrito pictórico mexicano que se conserva en la
> Biblioteca de la Congregatio Propaganda Fide en Roma.
> Edición limitada de 25 ejemplares numerados. Librería
> Anticuaria.
> G. M. Echániz. México. D.F. Donceles 12. Apdo. Post
> 499.

It is beautiful, and I can only imagine what this publisher's hard-to-find edition of Zouche-Nuttall must present to the reader.

La Estampa Mexicana published three thousand copies of a reproduction of the 1902 Peabody Museum edition in 1974, but they were bound as regular books, not as fanfolds. Dover Publications published the 1902 edition in 1975, but, sensitive to the original format as a fanfold or screenfold, bound it to read from back to front, though still in the format of a regular book. A facsimile of the original codex was published in the original format in 1987 by Akademische Druck- u. Verlagsanstalt, Graz, Austria, in its Codices selecti phototypice impressi series as Volume 84. Nancy P. Troike wrote the introduction and description of the manuscript for that edition. Troike's introduction is the source for the publication and descriptive data used in this section, excepting information concerning the Echániz edition of Codex Borgia.

The Fondo de Cultura Económica in Mexico City issued a boxed publication of the Codex Zouche-Nuttall in original fanfold format in 1992. The commentary was by Ferdinand Anders, Maarten Jansen, and Luis Reyes García.

The Nature of Mixtec History

Except for known Colonial Period documents such as Codex Selden 3135 (A.2) and others such as the Lienzo de Zacatepec, the pre-Hispanic manuscripts were written to be read and performed but not written specifically for us to read. Thus, the history they preserve is according to a uniquely local Native American worldview that varies in detail and mode of expression from culture to culture. This type of history recording tells stories of ancestors and provides extensive genealogies of royalty. The story-histories are themselves the basis of culture and encode memorized traditions that are often conflated and episodic, as befits devices for encoding memorized oral traditions. Specifically, Mixtec history as recorded in the codices consists of biographies, genealogies, religious and political events, and the founding of royal dynasties. However, these classifications are not separate: a biography is a religious event or a series of them, as are genealogies, political doings, dynasty founding, and so on. The pictography works by presenting to the reader a sequence of juxtaposed static images that, when taken progressively, create a story.

Dennis Tedlock (1985:64) calls the Maya version of Mesoamerican history telling and writing "myth history." By virtue of this designation, Tedlock provides a profound insight into indigenous history, although he does not phrase it that way; namely, there was no sharp dividing line in the minds of those native peoples between the physical and metaphysical. I extrapolate this to native Mesoamerican cultures in toto. Perhaps, therefore, theirs was a larger interactive universe, one in which beings of all spheres of existence—over world, the world of human beings, and the underworld—interacted to effect and affect not only cosmic purposes but human life itself. In short, religion and daily life were mutually interactive states.

In his respectful and reverent description of contemporary and ancient Maya spiritual and cultural practitioners, Tedlock makes still another valuable contribution to our understanding of the communication of native history: it is composed of performance stories, designed to be sung and danced while recited. This type of cultural format implies the poetic element added to historical preservation, for poetry can move hearers beyond the mundane and into allusions, metaphors, and substances that are essentially transcendent, thus implying the spiritual. This numinous transcendence can infuse the ordinary in human experience with the extraordinary and create a product unlike prose. From Edna St. Vincent Millay:

The world stands out on either side
No wider than the heart is wide;
Above the world is stretched the sky,—
No higher than the soul is high.[2]

In the Mixtec codices, we see this kind of expression of history in a lyrical, alternative, nonalphabetic writing: we see it in pictures represented as sequences of interrelated, episodic tableaux presented in brilliant colors. In fact, we can (and do, whether we realize it or not) think of the codex images and tableaux as "juxtaposed pictorial and other images in deliberate sequence, intended to convey information and/or to produce an aesthetic response in the viewer" (McCloud 1993:9).[3]

This type of alternative literacy (alternative as opposed to alphabetical, language-bound writing [Boone 2000:4]) is not alien to our contemporary culture. The insightful social scientist John M.D. Pohl has likened it to a movie storyboard. Drawing his analogy from a Colonial Period description that he cites from Francisco de Burgoa, Pohl writes (Byland and Pohl 1994:9):

> ... they [codices] were presented or "read" as a storyboard is used in the development of an animated film today. In the performance of a storyboard an actor dramatizes the action, while an animator . . . reads the images on the board. Musical accompaniment . . . provides dramatic effect and ambience. The director . . . ensures that the performance communicates the story effectively on film.

Continuing the analogy of a motion picture, the sequential progression of images in a Mixtec codex represents motion through time but in a linear fashion. A motion picture projects each image/frame onto exactly the same space but progresses (advances or regresses) them sequentially in time. Static codex images are juxtaposed, usually side by side in static spatial relationships, but that juxtaposition advances or regresses them in time sans kinetic motion (McCloud 1993:7).

The storyboard format so effectively described above by Pohl has a significant drawback for those of us who work to understand the ancient manuscripts and tell their stories today. We have no director to ensure effective communication of the entire performance. The codices are mnemonic texts recording the highlights of the history/myth/stories they encode, but the connecting narratives supplied by a performer of the memorized stories are missing.

Occasionally a conflated highlight pictogram tableau in one codex can be augmented with concordant data relating the same event more completely in another. If we had only Codex Zouche-Nuttall Page 44a–c that shows a young Lord Eight Deer Jaguar Claw at Chalcatongo with the equally youthful Lady Six Monkey of Jaltepec, we would have no idea of Lady Six Monkey's identity or importance. Codex Selden, the royal document of Jaltepec, however, supplies the supportive data for this monumental historical event and tells us the pertinent elements of her royal biography (Williams 2009). If only Codex Selden existed, then we would know Eight Deer Jaguar Claw of Tilantongo only as the father of two princesses who married the sons of Lady Six Monkey and Lord Eleven Wind, the king of Hua Chino. The political rivalry between the two polities (Tilantongo and Jaltepec) is implicit.

When Codex Zouche-Nuttall begins the story of the War from Heaven on Page 3, the narrative starts with events in AD 963. The very next tableau records events in AD 965. The events in AD 964 are entirely absent and, unless they can be found in another codex for that same calendar cycle, are lost to us. Obviously, the study of Mixtec history from original manuscripts is never confined to one document because one always seeks concordant narratives from all of them.

The first part of this present study treats the histories as they appear in one document, the Zouche-Nuttall obverse, Pages 1–41, as though the combining of myth and history creates a unified history encoding the broader reality of the people who composed it and for whom it represented their cultural identity. Concordant references from other codices are kept few except when necessary. The main focus of this study is to elucidate the narrative layout of the document in question and describe the contents of the various sections and their pages. Necessary interpretation is presented herein under sections called "Discussion" and also appears appropriately in the discussed narrative formats.

Figure 2.1. Zelia Nuttall. The Bancroft Library, University of California, Berkeley.

3 Reading Techniques

The five major Mixtec manuscripts referenced herein—Codices Selden, Bodley, Vindobonensis Mexicanus I, Zouche-Nuttall, and the Colombino-Becker I fragments (Codex Alfonso Caso)—are fanfold documents written in colorful pictogram text. This text is composed of diverse tableaux connected by chronological markers in the Mesoamerican calendar (year calendar/day calendar). Utilizing sequential juxtaposition of static images, the tableaux can depict all or some of the following: places (toponyms), dates, actors, and events. The texts are of two basic kinds: historical/religious events and royal genealogies. Religious ceremonies are, however, also historical events. Lists of toponyms are the equivalent of native maps. Though varying somewhat, the texts proceed according to a pattern observed in earlier Classic Period Maya inscriptions: date, event, personnel, and place. Although there are basic techniques used by the ancient scribes, no two codices proceed in exactly the same manner, and they employ visual techniques selectively, not consistently. This means that every codex document differs slightly from the others in narrative structure and narrative procedure.

The fanfold documents are made of strips of deer hide glued together, trimmed, and primed with a gessolike medium. Each prepared strip is then scored to make panel-like pages that can be folded one on top of the other to make a compact, continuous manuscript, which is called here for convenience *codex* in the singular, *codices* in the plural; although, strictly speaking, the manuscripts are neither books, scrolls, nor codices (Furst 1978b:3b).

Commonly, each distinct panel-page is divided into either vertical columns or horizontal bands by red lines that direct the reader's eye either up and down or horizontally across the pages. This vertical or horizontal linear text moving from side to side or from bottom to top and top to bottom is called *boustrophedon*, a Greek word meaning "as the bull plows." Boustrophedon is not always used, however, as some pages have no red lines.

To serve the purposes of this study, columns or bands that appear on Codex Zouche-Nuttall pages are referred to with lowercase letters, for example: Page 3a indicates the first column of pictogram text on Page 3. If a reference indicates more than one band of text, an en dash (–) is inserted, for example: Page 3a–c. This is contrary to the older procedure of using Roman numerals to indicate bands or columns of text, as in 3-I or 3-I-II. I abandon the older form for Codex Zouche-Nuttall because the obverse of it (Document 1) is seldom analyzed so completely and, when analyzed at all, only partially so. The use of lowercase alphabet characters to refer to bands and columns seems less cumbersome and clearer. The older use of Roman numerals is retained in examples from Codices Bodley, Selden, and Vindobonensis Mexicanus I simply because there is more literature available concerning them that uses that style.

As a general rule, complete codex manuscripts that read from right to left begin reading in the lower-right column or tableau of the first page. This is the case with Codices Zouche-Nuttall (both documents) and Vindobonensis Mexicanus I (both documents). Complete manuscripts that read from left to right begin in the lower-left tableau column of the first page. This is the case with Codex Bodley obverse. Codex Selden (A.2) is a Colonial Period palimpsest written over an older document. It unfolds from bottom to top and reads from the lower-right column of page one upward from page to page in ascending horizontal bands that are unvarying throughout. Codex Vindobonensis Mexicanus I, both documents, initiates reading in the lower right of each first page and then reads progressively from right to left, with the reverse document format first ascending across one page and then descending across the next page; thus the reverse document is written in two-page format. This is unvarying throughout all reverse pages of Vindobonensis Mexicanus I (Pages I–XIII).

However, the codex scribes had a variety of techniques available to them whereby they could represent the remembered stories in their res gestae, fact- or event-driven texts (Boone 2000:70–77). For this reason, the reading order might not be a linear boustrophedon at all but a roughly comma-shaped one (as on Codex Zouche-Nuttall Pages 11b–13), or red lines might not be used at all (Codex Zouche-Nuttall Pages 1–2, Page 14, Double-page 19, and Page 22). In the case of Codex Zouche-Nuttall Pages 36–39, only two red lines are used. A footpath leading the reader from event to event indicates the direction and progress of action.

A lack of red lines can create frustrating ambiguity for a modern interpreter of the Mixtec manuscripts. In the case of Zouche-Nuttall Pages 1–2, I successfully elucidated the reading orders elsewhere, and they will be demonstrated again in this text in the appropriate sequence (Williams 1991, 2006, 2009). Page 14 remains without a clear reading order for its six tableaux; but the ambiguous Pages 19 and 22 do have a reading order progression that will be elucidated in the appropriate place.

Full-page-length red lines—either vertical and straight or roughly vertical zigzag—occasionally separate sections of text within distinct sections of the manuscript. These divisions are noted in the description of the Zouche-Nuttall obverse (Document 1) contents.

Chronology also directs the linear movement of the eye to recover the pictogram stories as they progress forward or backward in time. From antiquity, throughout Mesoamerica and regardless of culture, the indigenous peoples employed a single type of calendar, although it had diverse cultural applications. It is found in the Monte Albán I phase, dating from about 600 BC; on Stela C from Tres Zapotes, and on the El Baúl Stela in Guatemala. Caso (1971:333) notes that at the time of the Spanish Entrada,

> . . . the calendar was used among Aztecs and other Nahuatl-speaking cultures such as Texcocans, Tlaxcaltec, Cholultec, and the Nahua-speakers of Puebla and Veracruz; among the Otomi and Matlatzinca, Tarascans, Huastec and Totonac, the various groups of Oaxaca (Mixtec, Zapotec, Cuicatec, Mazatec, Popoluca), the Tlapanec of Guerrero, and the Nahua of southern Veracruz.

The calendar combined two basic parts or calendars: a 365-day vague solar year (for recording years) and a 260-day divinatory augural calendar (for recording days). The two began concurrently in Year 1 Reed on Day 1 Alligator and restarted at that point 18,980 days later after the lapse of 52 vague solar years running concurrently with 73 augural/divinatory cycles of days. As to the actual Mixtec calendar usage, it appears that the ancient scribes used events to find dates, not dates to find events. Therefore, dates sometimes appear secondary to events, and sometimes dates for events do not appear at all; my assumption in this later case is that the reciters could simply add the appropriate dates in their performances according to local tradition. Virtually all the major codices agree on dates for major events such as founding stories. There are occasional exceptions for dated events within the stories themselves, and this very likely reflects diverse local oral traditions regarding the histories.

The Calendar as Memory

The Maya employed a Long Count system to fix events securely in time from cycle to cycle, but other cultures—including the Mixtec—did not. The Mixtec remembered the sequence of historical events from 52-year cycle to 52-year cycle by memorizing data, which was then reinforced by the codex tableaux. Therefore the codices in which they recorded their histories are mnemonic devices intended to jog the memories of reciters and performers of the pictogram stories. For this reason, when the Spaniards invaded and conquered Oaxaca in 1521, the sequence of calendar cycles in progression was lost, despite the fact that on colonial foundation stones European Julian calendar dates (the modern Gregorian calendar was not introduced by the papacy until 1582) and Mixtec dates were both inscribed.

The task of assigning modern European calendar dates to Mixtec recorded dates has been problematic. This conundrum was magnified when modern scholars interpreted Mixtec historical events in the codices either incorrectly or as metaphorical expressions only. In Alfonso Caso's commentaries on Codices Selden (1964), Bodley (1960), and Colombino (1966), every Colonial Period date and the native dates for the 52-year cycle immediately preceding the Spanish Entrada into Oaxaca are correct, and virtually every other pre-Hispanic date is wrong.

This problem was successfully mitigated by the work of Emily Rabin (1979). By applying her new reading of Mixtec chronology, which unfolded in several articles, to a seminal event recorded in two major codices, namely, the War from Heaven, she provided a template that resulted in a projected chronology of Mixtec recorded history by later scholars, chiefly Byland and Pohl (1994) and, to some extent, Jansen and Pérez Jiménez (2005).[1] Using these chronological tools, then, students of the Mixtec histories can more securely progress and regress Mixtec dates according to the modern (Gregorian) European calendar and produce historical studies that bring Native American history into the realm of world history.

Despite this available chronological precision, the Mixtec scribes employed dates to fulfill purposes other than merely establishing progressive or regressive counts of years and days. Days in the 260-day calendar had augural meanings, and the majority of those meanings are lost, yet the Mixtec employment of them remains to confuse us from time to time. A significant example, which I define as an augural use of dates, occurs in Codex Selden in the historical biography of Lady Six Monkey of Jaltepec. On Page 6, Bands

Table 3.1. The AD Eras of Mixtec History

Cycle 1: 883–934	Cycle 8: 1247–1298
Cycle 2: 935–986	Cycle 9: 1299–1350
Cycle 3: 987–1038	Cycle 10: 1351–1402
Cycle 4: 1039–1090	Cycle 11: 1403–1454
Cycle 5: 1091–1142	Cycle 12: 1455–1506
Cycle 6: 1143–1194	Cycle 13: 1507–1558
Cycle 7: 1195–1246	Cycle 14: 1559–1610

(*Source*: Byland and Pohl 1994)

III and IV, the year is 5 Reed and the name of Lady Six Monkey's betrothed is Lord Ten Wind. However, to be in sequence with other events established in the Selden narrative, the year must be 6 Reed, and the very next page of the document correctly lists the bridegroom as Lord Eleven Wind. The use of "5" and "10," though inappropriate for exact historical data, very likely had augural/divinatory meaning. When events such as this occur in the Zouche-Nuttall obverse document, the correction will be listed in parentheses, such as Lord Ten(Eleven) Wind or Year 5(6) Reed.

Chronology and Occultation: Time's Arrow

In most cases, the Mixtec scribes progressed events by calendar years, that is, with Time's Arrow moving from past to present to future. We see this especially in Codex Zouche-Nuttall Document 2 (reverse). However, that is not always the case for the obverse manuscript, particularly the stories that begin each major section. It may be, as has been stated elsewhere (Monaghan 1990), that structural arrangement of the narratives is related to performance, considering the manuscripts essentially as scripts, but that chronology guides, augments, or influences recitation.

Otherwise, chronology can interpret occulted data, as is the case in the ambiguous reading order for Pages 1–2 of Zouche-Nuttall and Pages 48–47 of Codex Vindobonensis Mexicanus I. These two pages of Codex Zouche-Nuttall can be read in two ways according to the needs of performers. If the performer of the document wanted to include the War from Heaven on Pages 3–4, then reading the tableaux by similarity of dates connects the last date in that sequence on Page 2 (Year 3 Reed) with the first date (3 Reed) on Page 3. However, if the reader wished to either omit the War from Heaven on Pages 3–4 or elaborate the biography of Lord Eight Wind of Suchixtlan, then, when interpreted in sequential years according to the 365-day calendar, the four surviving tableaux and five dates on Zouche-Nuttall Pages 1–2 reveal a roughly circular reading pattern that determines those pages to be an introduction to the hero's biography. They are highlights of the first fifty-two years of his long and amazing life—literally a cycle of the first fifty-two years of it. Pages 3 and 4 interrupt this biography with the War from Heaven events, and, if omitted, then Page 2 connects with the Lord Eight Wind biography that resumes on Page 5, which then progresses sequentially. A similar situation concerns Pages 48–47 of Codex Vindobonensis in that sequencing the dates progressively reveals a different reading order from the one recorded linearly.

The occulted data on Codex Vindobonensis Mexicanus I Pages 48–47 encode a complex ideology involved with the god Lord Nine Wind Quetzalcoatl putting the sky above an area of the Mixteca now called "The Place Where the Sky Was." Few dates appear on the preceding pages, but beginning on Page 48-II through Page 47 there is a cluster of dates, some ten in number (one is repeated three times). Once these dates are sequenced, the occulted ideological statement emerges, namely, that Rain God Hill (Yucuñudahui) is the center of the world. The sequenced series of pictograms says literally, "Yucuñudahui is the center beneath the four skies." It is literally the fifth direction lying at the crux of east, west, north, and south. Considering the nature of these two "sister" documents, Zouche-Nuttall and Vindobonensis Mexicanus I, together they make an ideological statement regarding Yucuñudahui, Lord Nine Wind Quetzalcoatl, and Lord Eight Wind Eagle Flints (Lord Eight Wind Twenty) of Suchixtlan, which is, in brief: Lord Nine Wind Quetzalcoatl put the sky above the Place Where the Sky Was and Yucuñudahui became the fifth direction, or center of the world beneath the sky. Then, in Codex Zouche-Nuttall, Page 2 (see Figure 4.3), Lord Eight Wind Eagle Flints rises from a cave opening at the top of Yucuñudahui, he conducts a prototypal ordering ceremony for the place and district, the War from Heaven begins there, and Lord Eight Wind remains on site until one year after the war ends—at which time he goes to Apoala and becomes one of the new ruling Lords of the Tree.

Corrections and Erasures

Corrections and erasures in pictogram text are not uncommon. When examined under various light frequencies, high-resolution images from the British Museum of Codex Zouche-Nuttall Page 1 show a lacuna in the text on the top left-hand side where an entire figure was erased (see Figure 4.2).

Other minor erasures and corrections occur occasionally in the text of both Zouche-Nuttall documents, but the older reverse side of the codex (Document 2) has erasures on Page 47a–b, black line uncolored pictograms on Page 49c–d, an erased date subsequently redrawn and moved up slightly on Page 50d, a black-and-white but partly colored toponym on 60c–d, a circle intended to be a shield but uncolored on Page 64c, and an uncolored personal name on that same page and band. In fact, many erasures exist on the reverse. While the subject of this study, the obverse document, Pages 1–41, is complete, the political biography of Lord Eight Deer Jaguar Claw on Document 2 (Pages 42–84) is unfinished and sometimes gives the impression of being a work in progress. It may be that material subsequent to that recorded on Page 84 was erased.

The actual number of erasures and subsequent replacements of data in Codex Zouche-Nuttall Document 1 gives the impression that those details could be altered at will to suit various needs over time. Also, one gets the idea that occasionally the Mixtec scribes simply made mistakes in text that remain uncorrected—for whatever reasons.

Subtle Techniques

The Mixtec scribes also used a variety of subtle "fine points" to establish their rules of reading and recitation. Page 24b of Zouche-Nuttall displays the last king of Tilantongo's first dynasty, Lord Two Rain Twenty Jaguars, standing atop a toponym that completely occupies the width of the column, thus blocking it and, for those who recited the story, indicating that his reign had ended. Page 20a lists the leaders of the Wasp Hill lineage clans, Lord Twelve Wind Smoke-Eye from the Sky and Lady Three Flint Younger, sitting atop a masonry substrate that completely separates them from the list of thirteen destroyed clans that follows afterward. Thus the seated founders are clearly marked as being apart from those whom they rule and not among those destroyed in the War from Heaven. An event or toponym can also occupy or "bleed over" parts of two columns, as is the case on Page 21a–b. This signifies that the events portrayed in each column are not fully separate, but related in some way.

When, for some reason, it was not practical or useful to use a full-length red line to divide one page and its events and actors from a following page, the scribes employed a subtle discontinuity of reading order between the two pages. That is, a page can end at the bottom of its last column, but the next page begins at the top of its first column. For example, this technique serves to indicate that Pages 15–16 and 17–18 of Codex Zouche-Nuttall are related but individually paired and subtly distinct from one another. Further, just as the reading order for Pages 1–2 (the introduction to the biography of Lord Eight Wind of Suchixtlan) is roughly circular in format, the same is true for Double-page 19, Page 22, and Page 41. Scribes can also indicate continuity from page to page by having part of a scene or tableau appear directly across a page fold from its continuation. This technique is employed in Zouche-Nuttall reverse, Pages 42–84, for certain tableaux. It is especially noted on Pages 45d–46a, 49d–50a, and 50d–51a.

The amount of space devoted to a tableau or a subject in a series of sequential tableaux indicates the importance of it. On Codex Zouche-Nuttall Pages 1–2, Page 2 is the dominant tableau, and the three tableaux on Page 1 are secondary. On the reverse of that codex, in the story of Lord Eight Deer Jaguar Claw of Tilantongo, almost fourteen complete pages are devoted to the conference held by Lord Eight Deer and his older half brother Twelve Motion with 112 tribal lords. The entire reverse document is approximately forty-three and one-half pages, so these fourteen pages constitute a significant portion of the manuscript and leave no doubt as to the importance of the conference.

A series of sequential tableaux can be separated from following tableaux by having the actors in the first of them face against reading order and then the following actors in the next sequence face toward the reading order. This occurs on the reverse of Zouche-Nuttall on Pages 42–43 that detail Lord Five Alligator's two families. Perhaps the most obvious use of this technique occurs in the Colonial Period Codex Selden. The narrative concerning the reign of Jaltepec's first dynasty and its Lord Ten Reed (Pages 3-I to 4-III) ends when the personnel (including Lord Ten Reed) are shown facing against the horizontal ascending boustrophedon reading order. A second narrative relating Lord Ten Reed's history then begins and, without explanation, the first dynasty ends on Selden Page 5-III.

Folding Out to Omit Data

Codex Zouche-Nuttall obverse employs a technique that seems unique to it. Those double pages telling the War from Heaven (3–4, 20–21) can be omitted from the narrative by "folding out." The rigid in-fold/out-fold nature of the codex permits these pages to be omitted, and in the first case, Pages 1–2 would then connect to Page 5 and produce a continuous story of Lord Eight Wind of Suchixtlan. In the second instance, Page 19 can be connected to Page 22 and display a format similarity between the destroyed lineage of Wasp Hill (Page 19) and the first lineage/dynasty of Tilantongo (Page 22). This implies a continuity that will be discussed subsequently in the text.

Dates and Names

Individuals have formal names, and these are the days on which they were born or named after birth, for example, Lady Three Flint, Lord Eight Deer, and Lord Two Rain. These personal day names are written out in text, as above. Dates, on the other hand, are expressed in numerals: 3 Flint, 8 Deer, 2 Rain, or Year 1 Reed Day 1 Alligator, and so on.

Figure Numbers

Figure numbers indicate that the figures are placed at the end of chapters and listed as Figure 1.1, Figure 1.2, etc., sequentially from first to last.

Narrative Structure of Codex Zouche-Nuttall Obverse, Pages 1–41

Pages 1–41 of Codex Zouche-Nuttall have a distinct graphic layout that divides the whole document into three main parts with subsections in each part. Each major part (I, II, III) consists of a story or stories followed by a genealogy or genealogies. This is the simplified outline of Document 1:

I. Part I
    A. Narrative 1, Pages 1–8: Lord Eight Wind
    B. 1st genealogy (genealogies), Pages 9–13

Living with the Dead

Both Zouche-Nuttall documents (obverse and reverse) contain major historical/religious events involving communication with the dead, specifically mummies. On Zouche-Nuttall obverse, Pages 7–8a, Lord Two Rain, the six-year-old boy-king of Tilantongo, consults with the mummy of his great-great-grandfather, Lord Eight Wind of Suchixtlan, in Year 4 House on Day 1 Rain (AD 1081). The mummy is shown seated in a temple as though alive. Immediately thereafter, but four years after the death of Lord Two Rain (in AD 1096), Two Rain's mummy is shown in a temple as though alive and speaking with Lord Eight Deer Jaguar Claw. This second mummy conference is a restatement of the same event shown in the older reverse document on Page 82; however, on Page 82, the mummy is passive. Also, on the codex reverse (Page 44a–b), the Oracle of the Dead at Chalcatongo (Lady Nine Grass) addresses the mummy of the deceased Lord Three Lizard. This occurs during a conference with Eight Deer Jaguar Claw (at age twenty) and Lady Six Monkey of Jaltepec (at age sixteen).

Each of these mummy events precedes pivotal events in Mixtec history; that is, the consultations with the deceased significantly influence subsequent Mixtec history. Those who communicated with the deceased ancestors are either priests authorized to do so (*yaha yahui* priests) or the Oracle of the Dead. On Zouche-Nuttall Page 44a–b, it is the Oracle who conducts the consultation. On Page 82, it is the *yaha yahui* priest Lord Eight Deer of Tilantongo; however, on Page 8b, the active role is given to Lord Two Rain's mummy, who is shown with Eight Deer's personal name (a jaguar claw) attached to the mummy's sleeve on his "speaking" (gesticulating) hand.

Apparently the ability to communicate with the dead was a two-way street: it could be initiated by the living or by the dead, and the interaction was bilateral.

4 Document 1 (Obverse), Part I, Pages 1–13: Lord Eight Wind

Part IA, Pages 1–8: Synopsis

Pages 1–8 include the history of Lord Eight Wind Eagle Flints of Suchixtlan, the War from Heaven in the northern Nochixtlan Valley, and events in the time of Lord Eight Deer Jaguar Claw. Pages 1–2 provide an introduction to the highlights of Lord Eight Wind's first fifty-two years. Pages 3–4 record the War from Heaven (which occurred at the beginning of Eight Wind's career) in the northern Nochixtlan Valley. The war has two basic campaigns: the War with the Stone Men (Page 3) and the War with the Striped Men (Page 4). The final tableau of Page 3 and Page 4 is the ceremonial resolution of the war for both phases, and that resolution occurs at Apoala in Year 13 Rabbit. Pages 5–6a return to Lord Eight Wind and provide his history after the war, detailing his three marriages. Pages 6b–7a list his offspring and provide a transition to the time of Lord Two Rain of Tilantongo and Lord Eight Deer Jaguar Claw of Tilantongo (Page 8b).

Pages 1–2: Lord Eight Wind's Introduction (Figures 4.1, 4.2, 4.3)

Lord Eight Wind's biographical introduction: the first fifty-two years.
  Page 1, Tableau 1: Eight Wind born at Cavua Colorado.
  Year 1 Reed Day 1 Alligator (AD 935)
    +28 years
  Page 2, Tableau 2: Lord Eight Wind at Yucuñudahui.
  Year 3 Reed Day 4 Flint (AD 963)
    +17 years
  Year 7 Flint Day 1 Motion (AD 980)

Page 1, Tableau 3: Lord Eight Wind at Apoala.

Year 7 Flint Day 1 Motion (AD 980)

    +7 years

Page 1, Tableau 4: Lord Eight Wind at Suchixtlan.

Year 1 Reed Day 1 Alligator (AD 987)

Page 1, Tableau 5: Erased figure.

Discussion: Description and Purpose of Pages 1–2

The reading order of the codex obverse is right to left, therefore the sequence begins in the lower-right corner of Page 1 with Tableau 1; moves to the dominant tableau, Tableau 2, which is the entirety of Page 2, along with two dates; then back to Page 1, Tableau 3, at Apoala; then to Page 1, Tableau 4, at Suchixtlan. The reading order is circular, beginning in the lower right of Page 1; moving left to Page 2 (reading from bottom to top); then right, back to Page 1 (pictogram on the bottom left); and ending at the upper right of that same page with Tableau 4 directly above the beginning tableau. This circular reading order is also displayed on Page 19, Page 22, and the final page (41), so this format occurs at the beginning, in the middle, and at the end of Codex Zouche-Nuttall obverse.

While the reading order described above is the occulted reading order, the obvious reading order intended to be used if the War from Heaven episodes on Pages 3–4 are elaborated in the narrative was described in an article published previously (Williams 1991). In that article—as well as another archived at the University of Texas at Austin, in the website CHAAAC—I demonstrate reading order by similarity of dates. That is, Page 1, Tableau 1 in Year 1 Reed Day 1 Alligator; to Page 1, Tableau 4 in Year 1 Reed Day 1 Alligator; to Page 1, Tableau 3 in Year 7 Flint Day 1 Motion; to Page 2, Tableau 2 in Year 7 Flint Day 1 Motion, then to Tableau 2 in Year 3 Reed Day 4 Flint.

The idea of similarity of dates to establish reading order seemed popular at the time and is now the accepted notion about reading these pages, but, as demonstrated above, it is only the obvious reading order, not the occulted one that exists by chronological progression. In this regard, the reading order seems at first ambiguous due to chronologically irrelevant dates, but progression according to Time's Arrow makes the dates relevant by rendering them historically progressive. The clue is this: Pages 1–2 record five dates and only one of them (Year 3 Reed Day 4 Flint) is not repeated. The Year 3 Reed on Page 2 in Tableau 2 is repeated, however, on Page 3 as Year

3 Reed Day 6 Dog. This repetition of Year 3 Reed establishes a visual connection between Page 2 and Page 3.

Tableau 1, Page 1, is Year 1 Reed Day 1 Alligator, or AD 935. Tableau 2, Page 2, has two dates. The first is Year 3 Reed Day 4 Flint, or AD 963. This same year is the first date on Page 3 that shows the beginning of Eight Wind's appearance at Yucuñudahui and also the beginning of the War from Heaven on Day 6 Dog (22 days before Year 3 Reed Day 4 Flint or 236 days after it) at Yucuñudahui. The reason for this variability is that both days—4 Flint and 6 Dog—occur twice in Year 3 Reed.

The second date of Tableau 2 is Year 7 Flint Day 1 Motion, or AD 980— one year after the War from Heaven ends. The date recorded in Tableau 3 on Page 1 is also 7 Flint 1 Motion, and the tableau displays Lord Eight Wind appearing from the cave at Apoala. Tableau 4 on Page 1 is dated Year 1 Reed Day 1 Alligator and is fifty-two years after the first recording of the date in the first tableau on Page 1. It is AD 987, or fifty-two years after Lord Eight Wind was born from the earth in Tableau 1. This two-page introduction is a synopsis of the important events in the first fifty-two years of Lord Eight Wind's life, from birth in the Cavua Colorado district, to rulership at Yucuñudahui just before and/or during the War from Heaven, to his journey to Apoala for important dynastic events (as seen in Vindobonensis Mexicanus I obverse), and, finally, his rule at Suchixtlan.

An erased figure in the upper-left section of Page 1 (see Figure 4.1) is deduced from detailed examination of a high-resolution photograph of Page 1 supplied by the British Museum. Johann Sawyer at Texas State University-San Marcos undertook examination of the page in various light spectra at my request. Determination of an erasure is the result of that investigation. Otherwise, little can be said about it. The entire left-hand portion of the page seems to have been extensively reworked and produces the lacuna where the figure was. The lacuna stands out precisely for the absence of artwork—both Pages 1 and 2 are very "busy" with figures and actions, except for the blank area on Page 1.

Lord Eight Wind of Suchixtlan and the Sacred Plants

The first two pages of Codex Zouche-Nuttall obverse are an introduction to the protagonist of the manuscript's first narrative (Pages 1–8). He is Lord Eight Wind Eagle Flints (of Suchixtlan), and his introduction highlights the first fifty-two years of his life in four tableaux. However, of the four tableaux and five dates on Pages 1 and 2, the second tableau comprises an entire page and contains two dates indicating a seventeen-year span for the events encoded within it. The year date span (Year 3 to Year 7 Flint) is exactly the same interval recorded in Codex Vindobonensis Mexicanus I, Pages 18–17b, for one of nine ordering rituals that sanctified the Mixtec landscape (Furst 1978a:233–256). The sanctification of places by various deities involves, among other things, a generally ubiquitous component, namely, the raising of a bundle of powerful sacred plants above or before the area to be sanctified or "ordered." These plants were originally acquired after the Vindobonensis sacred mushroom ceremony (Page 24b) when Lord Seven Wind Two Faces descends beneath the lineage river at Apoala and retrieves them from the underworld.

I have proposed (Williams 2006) that the authors of Zouche-Nuttall obverse claim that the Page 2 event is the prototype of this sacred ceremony because: (1) the chronology of events in the Zouche-Nuttall tableau precedes the Tree Birth ceremony at Apoala shown in Vindobonensis Mexicanus I, and (2) the protagonist (Lord Eight Wind Eagle Flints, shown rising from the earth) is displayed as the literal source of several sacred plants. At least one of them, the maguey, seems to grow from his throat. The other plants are either found as components of his costume or grown from Yucuñudahui at Eight Wind's appearance there for the ordering ritual. Although stylized plants in the codices differ somewhat from document to document, at least one of the nonmaguey plants in the Zouche-Nuttall tableau under discussion appears in Vindobonensis Mexicanus I, namely, a stalk with paddle-shaped or spade-shaped leaves. In the Zouche-Nuttall Page 2 tableau, it is situated at Eight Wind's feet directly behind him. It may be tobacco.

An interesting plant-related component of this scene and many others in all Mixtec codices is the use of a round woven grass mat and grass knot in bird-decapitation ceremonies. These sacrifice ceremonies are typically performed when an individual passes from one level of being (over world, middle world, underworld) to another. The ordering ceremony at Yucuñudahui shows Eight Wind appearing from a cave there with associated sacred plants as the bird for decapitation sacrifice is being presented.

The mat itself is frequently used today in the Mixteca when the Catholic Church celebrates feast days for local saints. Several mats are placed around door arches at the church entrances and possibly symbolize passage from one world to another. It may also be that the grass mats are woven to resemble an even more ancient vegetation prototype, namely, a horizontal section through an ear of corn.

Lord Eight Wind was a revered ancestor and, as such, is displayed on Pages 1–2 as doing amazing things. All of those things are religious/ceremonial in nature, and all have dynastic, political implications. The Mixtecs and their often-hostile neighbors, the Zapotecs, were ancestor worshippers. Therefore, great ancestors had supernatural abilities. In the case of Lord Eight Wind, he embodied the power of the sacred plants and is displayed in the pictogram tableaux as traveling through the earth, specifically through caves, to journey from one place to another. This is highlighted in Tableaux 2 and 3 where he is shown in the same year and on the same day journeying from Yucuñudahui to Apoala. He emerges from a cave at Yucuñudahui and seventeen years later from a cave at Apoala. This last cave—Serpent's Mouth Cave—is also very important in the final narrative sequence of Zouche-Nuttall Document 1, Pages 36–39.

The Sequence of Events on Pages 1–2

The very fact that there are two possible reading orders for Pages 1–2 of Codex Zouche-Nuttall Document 1 indicates the flexibility of the performance narrative. There were, in reality, two ways of "seeing" these pages. Folding out Pages 3–4 (discussed below) produces a performance narrative focused entirely on the biography of Lord Eight Wind of Suchixtlan as the lineage founder of one of the most important dynasties in the Mixteca. Including Pages 3–4 adds dramatic narrative concerning Lord Eight Wind's role at Yucuñudahui, such as the beginning of the all-important lineage reorganization war (War from Heaven), the institution of new lineage dynasties at Apoala (the Birth Tree event), a truce with the original inhabitants of the northern Mixteca, and the initiation of Lord Eight Wind as both an earth-born and a Tree-born noble. Pages 1–2 show Lord Eight Wind going to Apoala one year after the termination of the War from Heaven, and Pages 3–4 demonstrate why he did so.

Pages 3–4: The War from Heaven (Figures 4.4, 4.5)

Page 3: War with the Stone Men in the Northern Nochixtlan Valley at Yucuñudahui

Tableau 1. Year 3 Reed Day 5(6) Dog (AD 963). The battle begins there. Lord Eight Wind enters a cave. Stone Men attack and capture Lady Eight Monkey.

Tableau 2. Year 5 House Day 7 Snake (AD 965). Lady Six Eagle defends Yucuita, and the god Lord Seven Snake attacks a Stone Man.

Tableau 3. There are three dates indicating a fourteen-year span of time: Year 5 House (AD 965), Year 12 Flint (AD 972), and Year 5(6) Reed (AD 979). During this time, Lord Seven Motion sacrifices Stone Men. The last year of the War from Heaven is AD 979.

Tableau 4. Year 5 House Days 4 Dog, 4 Wind, 8 Wind. The capture of Stone Men by Lord Seven Wind and Lady Eight Deer.

Tableau 5. The Year 5 House is assumed. A male identified as Seven Wind is displayed in full eagle attire. Since this attire and the face paint are identical to those used for Lord Eight Wind, this scene is assumed to show Eight Wind perambulating. His destination is Apoala, shown in Tableau 6. The second part of this tableau shows the males Seven Dog and Six Dog capturing a Stone Man.

Tableau 6. There is no associated date, but I associate it with the Tree Birth ceremony at Apoala in Year 13 Rabbit Day 2 Deer (AD 986). This is a maguey goddess ceremony (Furst 1978a:233) and is a part of the complex ceremony associated with the new lineage founded at Apoala.

Page 4: The War with the Striped Men in the Nochixtlan Valley and the Resolution at Apoala

Tableau 1. Year 12 Flint (AD 972) with a one-day interval from Day 7 Alligator to Day 8 Wind. This year was first encountered on Page 3, Tableau 3. The antagonists are Striped Men who emerge from a cave opening in the sky and descend to earth. The sky has the day names of two gods, Two Alligator and Seven Flower. The three descending Striped Men have meteorological attributes: one is thunder, one is lightning, and the third to the far right is rain. Blue color in this text has faded to gray.

-3 years

Tableau 2. Lord Four Snake, brother of the deity Lord Seven Snake seen on Page 3, Tableau 2, and Lord Seven Motion seen on Page 3, Tableau 3, capture Striped Men. They stand on a year sign for 10(9) House (AD 969), three years before Tableau 1, thus this scene is a retrospective. Tableaux 1 and 2, therefore, cover three years of events in the War from Heaven.

+3 years

Tableau 3. Year 12 Flint Day 12 Motion (AD 972). Lord Four Snake, brother of Seven Snake, sacrifices a bird named One Jaguar. The god-name Two Alligator that appeared in Tableau 1 in the sky is repeated here. Ceremonial bird sacrifices are typically by decapitation; however, this sacrifice is by cardiac excision, which leads me to believe that we are seeing the sacrifice of a human being named One Jaguar transformed into his nagual, or spirit animal.

-6 years

Tableau 4. Year 6 Rabbit Day 2 Motion (AD 966). This is the mummy-bundling ceremony for Lords Four Motion and Seven Flower. It occurred three years after the war began in AD 963. These mummy lords appear again in the Ballcourt of Death in Tableau 6.

+20 years

Tableau 5. Year 13 Rabbit Day 2 Deer (AD 986), the year of the Tree Birth at Apoala. This scene occurs across the top of Page 4 from right to left and spans two columns of pictogram text. Three nameless lords and Lord One Wind face left and venerate the Stone Man, Lord Five Flower, who faces them. Lord Five Flower was last shown on Page 2 venerating Lord Eight Wind at Yucuñudahui. Directly below him, the Lords Ten Death and the Rain God (or an individual dressed as the Rain God) hold a conference with Lady Eight Monkey. She was last seen being captured at Yucuñudahui on Page 3, Tableau 1.

Tableau 6. Year 13 Rabbit Day 2 Deer (AD 986). The location is the Ballcourt of Death and Eleven Alligator Place, both last seen on Page 3, Tableau 6. This tableau is a séance wherein Lady Eight Monkey and Lady Seven Wind are seated at Eleven Alligator Place. The deceased, mummified Lords Seven Flower and Four Motion (last seen on Page 4, Tableau 4) are here shown alive in the Ballcourt of Death.

Discussion: Description and Purpose of Pages 3–4

These two war pages are a second-stream story inserted into the mainstream biography of Lord Eight Wind. It can be omitted by taking advantage of the rigid infold/outfold structure of the codex and connecting Page 2 to Page 5, thus producing a continuous biography of Lord Eight Wind.

The story of the War from Heaven is told twice in Codex Zouche-Nuttall obverse. This first telling concerns the initiation of the war in the northern Nochixtlan Valley as is evidenced by the initial battle at Yucuñudahui. This northern segment of the war is bifurcated; that is, Page 3 concerns the War with the Stone Men (the original inhabitants of the Mixteca), and Page 4 concerns the battle with the Striped Men from the Sky. Both Pages 3 and 4 have final tableaux (each the sixth tableau of their respective pages) that record the resolution of the war in ceremonies at Apoala, although these tableaux are ambiguous until corresponded with explanatory narratives in Codex Vindobonensis Mexicanus I, obverse Pages 38c–35. It is important to recall that when we see ceremonial events in codices or stone-carved texts, we see only a moment or conflated moments of ceremonies. As a result, it is not unexpected that one codex or even different parts of the same codex record different stages of one ritual performance.

Pages 5–7c: Lord Eight Wind the Lineage Founder (Lord Eight Wind's Family) (Figures 4.6, 4.7, 4.8)

Page 5 has five tableaux, and Page 6, Tableau 1, is an extension of Page 5, Tableau 4. There are seven dates on Pages 5–6a, spanning forty years.

Pages 5-6a: Lord Eight Wind the Lineage Founder

Tableau 1. Year 1 Reed Day 1 Alligator (AD 987). Lord Eight Wind at Little Yellow Man Temple. This date is the same Year 1 Reed 1 Alligator shown in Tableau 4 on Page 1 of Pages 1–2.

+17 years

Tableau 2. Year 5(6) Flint Day 7 Flower (AD 1004). Lord Eight Wind and the Rain God. Lord Eight Wind is sixty-nine years old (born AD 935). This scene initiates a lengthy ceremony involving the Rain God.

+ 5 years

Tableau 3. Year 9(10) House Day 1 Eagle (AD 1009). Lord Eight Wind and the Rain God. Lord Eight Wind spent three years at the Rain God Place.

-1 Year

Tableau 4. Year 9 Flint Day 5 Flower (AD 1008). Lord Eight Wind marries Lady Ten Deer.

+6 years

Tableau 5. Year 2 Rabbit Day 13 Grass (AD 1014) is the birth date of their first son, Thirteen Grass. This tableau also lists some of Lord Eight Wind's

Table 4.1. Chronology of Pages 5–6a

Page	Date	Event
5a	1 Reed 1 Alligator (AD 987)	Eight Wind at Little Yellow Man Hill
5a	5(6) Flint 7 Flower (AD 1004)	Rain God ceremonies
5b	9(10) House 1 Eagle (AD 1007)	End Rain God ceremonies
5c	9 Flint 6 Flower (AD 1008)	Eight Wind's 1st marriage
6a	11 Rabbit 3 Eagle (AD 1010)	Eight Wind's 2nd marriage
6a	12 Reed 9 Deer (AD 1011)	Eight Wind's 3rd marriage
5c	2 Rabbit 13 Grass (AD 1014)	Birth of ♂ Thirteen Grass
5c	2 Reed 2 Reed (AD 1027)	Eight Wind dies at age ninety-two years
	Total = 40 years	

other children, but by no means all of them. The other children listed are: twin sons named 3 Lizard (for one of them, see Codex Zouche-Nuttall reverse, Page 44b) and two daughters, named Two Snake and Six Reed. It also displays Year 2 Reed Day 2 Reed (AD 1027). The reed/dart of the year bearer points to Lord Eight Wind, and I interpret this as his death at age ninety-two. Year name "Reed" is also used as a pointer on Page 9c and Page 20c. On this latter page, two Reed years are indicators of the death dates of two males.

Page 6a

Tableau 1. In Year 11 Rabbit on Day 3 Eagle (AD 1010), Lord Eight Wind married his second wife, Lady Five Grass. In Year 12 Reed on Day 9 Deer, he married his third wife, Lady Ten Eagle.

Combined with Pages 1–2, Pages 5 through 6a complete the biography of Lord Eight Wind as a living man. He appears again on Page 7d after his death and 145 years after his birth. The chronology of Zouche-Nuttall Pages 1–6a spans years AD 935 to AD 1027, or the ninety-two years of the life of Lord Eight Wind Eagle Flints of Suchixtlan.

Pages 6b–7c

Pages 6b–7c are undated. Page 6b is composed of seven individuals in columns b–d all facing right toward the children of Lord Eight Wind and Lady

Ten Deer. They are likely the children of his second marriage, to Lady Five Grass in Year 11 Rabbit on Day 3 Eagle. One of them, Lady Nine Monkey (Page 6c) is shown again on Page 10b as the wife of Lord Two Lizard.[1]

Page 6e begins a series of twelve individuals extending through Page 7c. They face left toward the events on Pages 7d–8a, the scene with Lord Eight Wind's mummy and the boy-king Lord Two Rain of Tilantongo. These persons are probably the children of Lord Eight Wind's third marriage, to Lady Ten Eagle in Year 12 Reed on Day 9 Deer.

The function of all these persons is mysterious, but they constitute, in effect, a transition from the death of Lord Eight Wind on Page 5c to his post-mortem appearance on Page 7d in the era of his great-grandson Lord Two Rain Twenty Jaguars. I have proposed (Williams 2006, 2009) that since Lord Eight Wind would be 145 years old at the time of this conference with his 6-year-old great-grandson, he is a mummy here, though shown living and communicating with the living—as mummies in Oaxaca are known to do from time to time.

In this case, the procession of mysterious persons could be considered the escorts of Eight Wind during this temporal transition from the time of his actual death until the era of his ancestor Lord Two Rain—who lived in the time of Lord Eight Deer Jaguar Claw but died before Eight Deer's reign ended. One of the females displayed on Page 6—Lady Nine Monkey—also appears on Page 10b as a bride. Therefore, it is likely that these mysterious individuals are some of Lord Eight Wind's large family and that Lady Nine Monkey is one of his daughters. Possibly, the codex tells us by this list of persons that Lord Eight Wind's family survived to the time of Lords Two Rain and Eight Deer Jaguar Claw.

Pages 7d–8: The Eight Wind/Two Rain/Eight Deer Events, or The Parliament of Mummies (Figures 4.8, 4.9)

Pages 7d–8

In Year 4 House on Day 1 Rain (AD 1081), the last king of Tilantongo's first dynasty, the 6-year-old Lord Two Rain, consults with the mummy of Lord Eight Wind (who, if alive, would be 145 years old). The concordant scene that explains this conflated tableau is Codex Selden Page 6b–d.

According to the Codex Selden narrative beginning on Page 6, column "b," in Year 4 House on Day 4 Wind (three days after Day 1 Rain when the mummy-consultation ceremony took place), Lord Two Rain Twenty

Jaguars conducted a cave ceremony, and his great-grandfather's son, Lord Three Lizard, attacks Jaltepec (Lady Six Monkey's town). Lord Ten Eagle of Tilantongo—husband of Lady Six Monkey's mother, Lady Nine Wind, who was the daughter of Lord Eight Wind Eagle Flints and his wife Lady Ten Deer (but not shown in Codex Zouche-Nuttall) and thus the sister of Lord Three Lizard—successfully defends Jaltepec and kills Lord Three Lizard. After Tilantongo (Lord Two Rain's town) loses the war, a series of events occur (Codex Selden, Page 6c–d) that culminate with the Oracle of the Dead (Lady Nine Grass) reassigning the marriage alliance from defeated Tilantongo to Lord Eleven Wind of a town called Red-and-White Bundle (now commonly called Hua Chino).

It is possible to interpret Codex Zouche-Nuttall Pages 7d–8a (the meeting of Eight Wind's mummy with boy-king Two Rain) as the same cave ceremony shown in Codex Selden and the subsequent failed battle as the result of advice for war coming from the consultation. That is to say, the marriage alliance between Tilantongo and the prosperous town of Jaltepec failed, Tilantongo attacked Jaltepec and lost, and subsequently the marriage alliance was reassigned, joining Jaltepec to Hua Chino. This action on the part of Jaltepec and the Oracle of the Dead at Chalcatongo produced an enduring conflict that Lord Eight Deer Jaguar Claw would resolve by destroying Hua Chino; sacrificing its king, Lord Eleven Wind, and Eleven Wind's sons by a previous marriage (to Eight Deer's half sister); and sacrificing Eleven Wind's present wife, Lady Six Monkey. This information ties directly to the final tableau on Codex Zouche-Nuttall Page 8b.

Page 8b: Lord Two Rain's Mummy and the Soldiers of Lord Eight Deer of Tilantongo in Year 10 Flint Day 2 Flint (AD 1100)

According to Codex Bodley, Lord Two Rain died by suicide in AD 1096, so this is indeed a postmortem event. This event connects to the political biography of Lord Eight Deer Jaguar Claw of Tilantongo that is the subject of the codex reverse, Pages 42–84. Specifically, this obverse Page 8b event connects to the reverse Pages 80b–82, which depict a scene in which Lord Eight Deer Jaguar Claw of Tilantongo consults with an unnamed mummy, who is now identified by this correlation as being that of Lord Two Rain. Two Rain's mummy is shown here as alive, seated in a temple, and his gesticulating hand and arm display a jaguar-claw ornament known to represent Lord Eight Deer's personal name.

On the reverse Page 82, Lord Eight Deer Jaguar Claw is emphasized. Two

Rain is an unnamed passive mummy decorated with an ornamental mask and garment. On the more recent obverse Page 8b, Lord Two Rain's mummy is not passive at all, but shown alive and seated in a temple, as was Lord Eight Wind's mummy in the previous scene of the conference with six-year-old Two Rain. The obverse Page 8b minimizes the role of Eight Deer—who is the major actor on the reverse Page 82—by showing only his personal name as a jaguar-claw ornament attached to the sleeve of Two Rain's speaking hand. Thus, on Page 8b, Two Rain is shown postmortem speaking to passive Jaguar Claw. Between reverse and obverse scenes, the roles of the actors are reversed. One almost gets the impression that while Lord Eight Deer Jaguar Claw initiates the mummy consultation tableau on Page 82, Lord Two Rain the mummy initiates it on Page 8. Therefore both narratives—reverse and obverse—provide us with an interesting diversity of perspectives on the same eventful story tradition.

A full-length red line on the left side border of Page 8, running from top to bottom, indicates that this section is now ended. The events depicted on codex Pages 1–8 span 165 years (AD 935–AD 1100).

Part IB, Pages 9–13: The First Genealogy (Figures 4.10–4.14)

Several subdivisions of text occur within each larger part of Document 1, and, generally, the codex obverse reads from right to left, although there are exceptions to be found on Pages 11, 12, and 13. These pages follow a two-page format that permits the text to be read, sung, recited, or otherwise performed in two-page sections. Genealogies may also include narrative content, and each genealogy begins with an introduction that may be brief or expanded by elaboration.

The older reverse document, comprising Codex Zouche-Nuttall Pages 42–84, reads in a boustrophedon manner from right to left. Unlike the obverse document, there are no exceptions to reading order on the reverse. Page 75 (introduction to the Battle in the Sky) is linear in format, with two basic lines of text proceeding from right to left. This linear style is also noted on obverse Pages 14 and 36–41.

The chronology recorded on the reverse is progressive by years, proceeding from the earliest to the latest events. A forward progression within each story or narrative of the chronology is also assumed for the obverse, but apparently for reasons of literary form or performance presentation, the year dates are occasionally shuffled and have to be reordered to establish progressive reading according to Time's Arrow. This is particularly true for the narrative sagas—which I call stories—but not necessarily true for the genealogies.

Zouche-Nuttall obverse contains a mysterious series of genealogies on Pages 9–13 as well as the genealogies of the first and second dynasties of Tilantongo (Pages 22–27 et seq.). These Tilantongo dynasties are recorded—sometimes in a more elaborate form—on the reverse of Codex Vindobonensis Mexicanus I. The introduction of the first dynasty of Tilantongo, on Zouche-Nuttall obverse Page 22, is displayed as a panel map and terminates the preceding narrative by introducing the succeeding genealogy. The preceding dynastic territory of Wasp Hill on Double-page 19 is also a map, but elaborated across two pages that I call 19a–b.

The genealogies following the story of Lord Eight Wind Eagle Flints Twenty of Suchixtlan, the War from Heaven, and events in the time of Lords Two Rain and Eight Deer Jaguar Claw, depicted on Pages 1–8, begin on Page 9 and end on Page 13. The founder of the genealogy is Lord Nine Rain. He is either born at or comes from Olla River in what Caso calls "a mythical date" (1984:425a–426a) of Year 1 Reed Day 1 Alligator. As mentioned previously, this year and day statement, besides being an actual date, is also a metaphor for either "beginning" or "it happened long ago."

Pages 9–10: Introduction to the Dynasty and Ceremonies

Tableau 1. Year 1 Reed Day 1 Alligator. Year and day are both number 1 in the calendar. The day occurs in Tonalpohualli 1.

Lord Nine Rain emerges from Olla River clapping his hands. Lady Six/Seven Rain, who is assumed to be his spouse, greets him: therefore, they are the founders of this dynasty.

    +30 years

Tableau 2. Year 5 House Day 7 Snake. The year number is 31 and the day 7 Snake occurs twice within it, as days 55 in Tonalpohualli 43 and 315 in Tonalpohualli 44.

The Caso (1984) interpretation of this tableau is confusing. According to appearances, Lord Four Water, the companion of Lord Nine Rain below, emerges from a round, cogged circle, "Cerco amurallado del quetzal" (Caso), singing and holding powdered tobacco. Lady Nine Rain, who is presumably his wife, greets him. Caso names this couple in the date Year 5 House Day

7 Snake as the founders of this genealogy and the date of its founding. However, this interpretation is in error. See "Discussion" below.

+33 years

Tableau 3. Year 12 Rabbit Day 13 Vulture. Year 12 Rabbit is number 12, and Day 13 Vulture occurs twice within it, as day 41 in Tonalpohualli 16 and day 301 in Tonalpohualli 17.

A holy tree with a male figure in it rises from a river in which is seated a kneeling nude woman with a sacrificial flint knife at her crotch. It is tempting to identify this unnamed female as Lady One Eagle, the goddess of rivers and lakes, but it is not she. Seven currents of water flow from this female's right hand, one current of water flows from her left hand, and she faces a curved colored band. She appears to sit on four currents of water within the river, and in all, thirteen flows of water are associated with her and flow outward from her.

Caso's accurate interpretation of this passage is rendered with his usual decisiveness (1984, 2:165b–166a):

> We interpret this passage in the following way: on Day 13 Vulture of Year 12 Rabbit, the [Lady] Five Deer was bathing in the river, when there appeared the God of the Sun [probably (Lord) One Death] in a tree and fertilized it.

By "it," Caso means the river and thus the woman. The Sun God in the tree is certainly pointing downward at both, and he stands on a ray descending from the solar disc. Caso continues:

> Consequently, in the same year but on Day 3 Reed—this is at the beginning of the 9th lunar month of 29.5 days each after the fertilization—is born male Three Reed, and his mother, Lady Five Deer, presents/displays him to his father the Sun "Shoots with a War Arrow" in Culhuacan at the Quetzal Temple.[2]

Regarding this description, see Tableau 4, below.

Tableau 4. No date. Lady Five Deer kneels and presents a male child named Three Reed before a red-painted male seated in a temple atop the hill at Descending Quetzal. This temple is flat-topped with five crenellations, each in a different color—from left to right, they are colored red, green, yellow, blue, brown—the same colors as the curved colored band faced by the female in the river in the preceding tableau. A warband arrow is directly behind the seated male and outside the temple. A jeweled circular object with an image of the Rain God in its center is directly beneath Lady Five Deer.

Caso notes (1984, 2:165a–b) that Lord Three Reed is a mythical person who seems to be the son of the Sun God Lord One Death and the goddess Lady Five Deer. He then remarks that in Year 12 Rabbit on Day 13 Vulture, when Lady Five Deer was bathing in the River of the Tree, it (the tree) received the sun and was fertilized. Then Three Reed was born and his mother presented him to the sun at Quetzal Hill.

+35 years

Tableau 5. Year 8 House Day 4 (eroded) Jaguar. The year is number 47. The adult Lord Three Reed and another male, Lord Ten Vulture Golden Eagle, conduct an animal sacrifice, probably a coyote or a dog. At this point, I depart from Caso's interpretation.

Although the day date, 4 Jaguar, is connected to Lord Three Reed's foot by a black line, this does not indicate that his name is Four Jaguar; rather, it merely indicates that Lord Three Reed (whose name is directly above him, with the reed/arrow pointing directly at him) performs the sacrifice ceremony on that day. As mentioned above, some confusion exists (Caso 1984, 2:395a–b) regarding the relationship between these two males and the identity of Lord Three Reed in this particular tableau. Caso thinks they are twin brothers (or a pair), since Day 4 Jaguar occurs immediately after Day 3 Reed. Indeed, both days occur only once in Year 8 House, and thus both are in the Tonalpohualli 66. However, the mystically impregnated mother, Lady Five Deer, presents only one son, Lord Three Reed, to his father the sun. It would seem that if both were sons of the sun, both would have been presented and, as well, both would have the same day names, as do the twin Lords Three Lizard seen on Codex Zouche-Nuttall Page 5c.

Directly above the coyote/dog sacrifice ceremony is Descending Quetzal Temple, although somewhat different from the one displayed in Tableau 4 on Page 9b. This temple has a white tied bundle in it and a thatched roof topped with a white curling crest. Alfonso Caso (1984, Plate 8) describes it as "templo con techo cónico; un quetzal desciende" (temple with a conical roof; a quetzal descends). It is the location of the ceremony directly below it on Page 9c.

Page 10a–b: Final Ceremonies

Tableau 1. No date. On Page 10a, reading from the top right downward, two black-painted males are seated before the unnamed Sun God seated on the jaguar throne. They receive *xicollis* (garments), shields, and arrows. A sun disc marks this event as "holy." The Sun God figure is seated on a mat with an elaborate multicolored border with seven colored tassels and five unpainted supports. These supports give the impression that the mat is elevated, and the jaguar throne is elevated above the mat. The Sun God presents the two males with solar insignia. The men, unnamed but assumed to be the Lords Three Reed and Ten Vulture, receive arrows and shields, quivers, a red warband-decorated *xicolli* (Lord Ten Vulture receives this latter garment), and Sun God emblems. The ceremony continues below.

+36 years from the date on Page 9c

Tableau 2. Year 5 House Day 7 Snake. The year is number 31, and the days are number 55 in Tonalpohualli 43 and number 315 in Tonalpohualli 44.

Two males each stand atop the outstretched hands of a god seated on a jaguar throne. The male to the right and directly beneath the day name Seven Snake has a bow and arrow and also an atlatl thrower. He wears jaguar pants with a tail and claws, along with a jaguar helmet, and green-colored sound or smoke comes from his right leg. The male to the left has an atlatl thrower, darts, and a shield, but no bow. He wears a white breechcloth, an elaborate collar, and an eagle helmet. Yellow firelike sound or smoke issues from his left leg.

Tentative identification has it that these two males are the ones seated in the tableau above the Sun God. Caso's text (1984, 2:166) continues the confusion:

> The episode finishes this by relating that in Year 5 Reed on Day 7 Serpent, which is when they were nineteen years old, it seems that the Sun God inducts one brother into the brotherhood of Eagle Warriors (represented by Lord 3 Reed) and the other into the Tiger Warriors (represented by Lord 4 Tiger); the first [is] armed with [an] atlatl and the second with bow, arrow, and also atlatl . . .

However, Caso errs on the date, citing Year 5 Reed instead of the recorded Year 5 House. The distance from Year 8 House on Page 9c to Year 5 Reed would be ten years. The distance from Year 8 House to the recorded Year 5 House is thirty-six years. Also, though unnamed, the male Caso identifies as Lord Three Reed is actually Ten Vulture of the Eagle Warriors, and the male Caso identifies as Four Jaguar (Tiger) wears the unvarying face paint and ear ornament of Lord Three Reed of the Jaguar Warriors. This completes the ceremonial introduction, and the genealogies follow in the text.

Pages 9–10a span 134 years.

Page 10b: First Genealogy

Tableau 3. Date 1 Reed Day 1 Alligator. FIRST MARRIAGE: Lady Eight Lizard + Lord Five (Six) Flower. The toponym for this site is a green hill with a red and white temple inset into it. Water flows into the temple, there are green plumes or reeds within, and the number 7 surrounds it. Caso (1984, 2:106b) says that Lady Eight Lizard married Lord Five Flower and they ruled Seven Waters Hill. They founded their dynasty in Year 1 Reed. They are the dynasty founders, and one of them is likely the descendant of Lord Three Reed, whom we met in the introduction.

Tableau 4. SECOND MARRIAGE: Lord Two Lizard + Lady Nine Monkey. A skyband with an elaborate insect-wing star with skull and sacrificial knife-nose is directly beneath their feet. Her personal name is Bee-Bird Jeweled Skull Knife-Nose. Caso (1984, 2:106b) thinks the female is a daughter of Lord Eight Wind Eagle Flints of Suchixtlan, and I agree. This means that the Lord Eight Wind of the Suchixtlan dynasty married into this present one and explains why the first genealogy is foregrounded in Zouche-Nuttall Pages 1–2, and the Toltec history is simply added to it. Lord Two Lizard is presumed to be the son of the previous marriage of Lady Eight Lizard and Lord Five (Six) Flower.

Discussion

As is the case with codex Pages 1–2, which provide the premarital history of Lord Eight Wind of Suchixtlan by giving an elaborate founding or founder's story, this genealogical section of Codex Zouche-Nuttall Part IB follows exactly the same procedure. Pages 9a–10a constitute a series of founding stories centered on Lord Nine Rain (10a) and proceeding with the divinely born demigod Lord Three Reed.

The problem with Alfonso Caso's reading of the codex tableaux on Page 9a is this: he confuses the day names of the males. In Tableau 1, Lord Nine Rain is born from Olla River in Year 1 Reed on Day 1 Alligator and is husband of Lady Nine Rain. In Tableau 2, Lord Nine Rain emerges from a walled enclosure and marries Lady Four Water, his second wife, whom he marries in Year 5 House on Day 7 Snake, thirty-one years later.

Caso confuses the day names of males and females between these two tableaux. On Page 9b, Tableaux 1 and 2, the female (named Five Deer) shown to be the mother of Lord Three Reed is the daughter of Lord Nine Rain and Lady Four Water. Five Deer is worthy of being chosen by the Sun God himself to bear a son, Lord Three Reed. This event happens in Year 12 Rabbit (year number 12) Day 13 Vulture.

Subsequently, in Year 8 House (year number 47) on Day 4 Jaguar, thirty-five years later when he was sixty-seven years old, Lord Three Reed performs a dog sacrifice at Descending Quetzal Temple attended by (or Three Reed is assisted by) a male named Ten Vulture. After this ceremony, Three Reed's father, the Sun God, presents his son, Three Reed, and Lord Ten Vulture with royal accoutrements. Yet another deity establishes the two males in the castes of Eagle Warrior (Lord Ten Vulture) and Jaguar Warrior (Lord Three Reed). The year of this presentation is 5 House on Day 7 Snake, so Lord Three Reed would have been advanced in years to age seventy-eight. This paradigm of elderly accomplishment reinforces that established in the first story—the biography of Lord Eight Wind of Suchixtlan, who achieved his political goals in the first fifty-two years of his life and finally married at age seventy-two, engendering numerous offspring via three wives. One of those offspring, Lady Nine Monkey, is the wife presented in the second marriage of this genealogy.

The entire span of events from Year 1 Reed Day 1 Alligator to the second Year 5 House Day 7 Snake is 135 years. That is: Lord Nine Rain appears from Olla River in 1 Reed 1 Alligator (year number 1); thirty years later, he marries Lady Four Water in Year 5 House (year number 31) on Day 1 Alligator; thirty-three years later, in Year 12 Rabbit on Day 13 Vulture, the Sun God impregnates their daughter Lady Five Deer, who consequently bears Lord Three Reed; thirty-five years later, in Year 8 House on Day 4 Jaguar, Lord Three Reed and Lord Ten Vulture Jeweled Eagle conduct the dog-sacrifice ceremony; and, finally, thirty-six years later, in the second Year 5 House Day 7 Snake, the installation ceremony of the Eagle Warriors and Jaguar Warriors occurs.

However, neither Three Reed nor Ten Vulture is shown marrying and producing offspring. Thus the point of this foundation story (or stories) seems to be the founding of the warrior clans, Jaguar and Eagle, by two gods and a demigod. The founder of the Jaguar warrior clan is Lord Three Reed, known to be a demigod. The genealogy begins immediately after this event, on Page 10b. Tableau 1 lists the marriage of Lord Five (Six) Flower and Lady Eight Lizard. In the tableau following this, their child, Lord Two Lizard, marries Lord Eight Wind of Suchixtlan's daughter, Nine Monkey. Therefore, the descendants of one divinely inspired genealogy (Lord Eight Wind of Suchixtlan) marry the descendants of yet another (Lord Three Reed).

Caso identifies the place or locale of this genealogy as Culhuacan (1984, 2:166a). If he is correct in this identification, then geographical location is foregrounded here. Culhuacan is thought by some to be the first Toltec city and was located in the Valley of Mexico. Mixcoatl founded it, and it was not until approximately AD 1300 that the Aztecs became vassals to the ruling lord there (Pohl 1991:6a). Another source says that in AD 1299, Culhuacan's *tlatoani* (ruler), Cocoxtli, helped the Tepanecs of Azcapotzalco, the Xochimilca, and people from other cities expel the Mexica from Chapultepec. The expulsion was successful, and Cocoxtli gave the Mexica permission to occupy the hostile land of Tizapan, thus effectively making them vassals.

Some thought exists that the original Culhuacan was contemporaneous with later phases of Teotihuacan (N. Davies 1977:130–131). Given this, the Zouche-Nuttall foundation stories recorded on Pages 9a–10a precede the arrival of the Mexica in the Valley of Mexico and establish a Mixtec marriage presence with Toltecs whose founding story may have happened long before the birth of the Mixtec protagonist, Lord Eight Wind of Suchixtlan. Mixtec involvement with Toltecs is repeated in the biography of Lord Eight Deer Jaguar Claw that occupies the entirety of Codex Zouche-Nuttall Document 2 (reverse). Therefore this newer document (Zouche-Nuttall obverse) emphasizes Mixtec-Toltec alliances.

From the final date above, Year 5 House Day 7 Snake, to the beginning of the dynasty on Page 10b in Year 1 Reed Day 1 Alligator is an interval of 22 years, making the totality of events span 126 years—nearly the same amount of time that encompasses the birth of Lord Eight Wind of Suchixtlan to the meeting of his mummy with the boy-king, Lord Two Rain of Tilantongo. The episodes are not contemporaneous, but they do intersect.

Since the daughter of Lord Eight Wind of Suchixtlan, Lady Nine Monkey, marries the son of the first family recorded on Page 10b, and since Lord Eight Wind of Suchixtlan married his three wives in years AD 1008 (his first wife, Lady Ten Deer), AD 1010 (his second wife, Lady Five Grass, who is probably the mother of Lady Nine Monkey), and AD 1011, then it is possible to assume that the founding story for this dynastic sequence is roughly contemporaneous with or precedes that of Lord Eight Wind of Suchixtlan (b. AD 935–d. AD 1027), that is, from AD 935 to AD 1011.

If we assume for the sake of approximate dating that Lady Nine Monkey was born fourteen years after Lord Eight Wind's marriage to Lady Five Grass (she was the seventh child of that marriage, and an average of two years between children is estimated), then her marriage to Lord Two Lizard occurred in approximately AD 1038 (marriage of Eight Wind and Five Grass in AD 1010 + 14 years to birth of Lady Nine Monkey + 14 years, presumed age of Lady Nine Monkey at marriage). If we subtract the initial years of events on Pages 9a–10a from 1038, then the beginning date is AD 916, nineteen years before the birth of Lord Eight Wind of Suchixtlan in AD 935.

However, to be congruent with the Mixtec calendar, Year 1 Reed Day 1 Alligator is either AD 935 (the beginning date in the codex's Document 1 and the birth date of Lord Eight Wind) or the preceding cycle fifty-two years earlier, AD 883—which is entirely possible, since the Mixtecs did not employ the device of a Long Count to identify successive cycles of time.

As a result, a certain amount of ambiguity exists for this second founding story and results in Caso referring to it as "mythological." However, for the beginning of the actual genealogy on Codex Zouche-Nuttall Page 10b (Year 1 Reed Day 1 Alligator), ambiguity is reduced. If it is an actual date and not a metaphor implying "in the beginning" or "it happened long ago," then it can only be the cycle after Lord Eight Wind of Suchixtlan became a Tree-born noble, that is, AD 986 (Year 13 Rabbit). The subsequent cycle beginning with Year 1 Reed Day 1 Alligator is AD 987.

If the Page 10b genealogy begins the cycle after that, then it is AD 1039. This is possible, given the fact that Lady Nine Monkey, the daughter of Lord Eight Wind of Suchixtlan, marries the son of this first marriage, Lord Two Lizard. Beginning on Page 11a, their first son, Lord Six (?) Dog, is an Eagle warrior. Their second son, Lord One (?) Wind, marries Lady Eight Water, and their son, Lord One Water (name eroded), marries Lady Ten Dog. It should be noted that just below the number circles for Lady Ten Dog are one or two number circles that appear to have been erased. Lord One Water has three more wives, the ladies Three Reed, Five Wind, and Two Monkey. At this point, the first genealogy ends and the locale shifts to another site.

Although inaccuracy is assumed to some degree, the point of the founding story told on Pages 9–10a is that it is contemporaneous with and thus of equal prestige or antiquity to that of Lord Eight Wind of Suchixtlan, whose story begins Codex Zouche-Nuttall Document 1. The major thrust of the founding story is to demonstrate a connection with the Toltecs of Culhua-can. Given this, it is possible that the founding story initiated on Page 9 of Codex Zouche-Nuttall begins the cycle preceding the birth of Lord Eight Wind of Suchixtlan. As we will see, the next founding story, which begins on Page 14, is also precedent to the birth of Lord Eight Wind, recording the founding of the ruling dynasty and clans of Wasp Hill.

Pages 11–12

Page 11a: First Genealogy (continued)

Tableau 1. Lord Six (eroded) Dog, who is presumably the child of Lord Two Lizard and Lady Nine Monkey who are shown on the previous page. The toponym is a hill surmounted by an eagle head with four sacrificial knives atop its feather crest, and a Xipe-Totec white bib with red stripe descends from beneath the eagle beak.

Tableau 2. THIRD MARRIAGE: Lady Eight Water + Lord One Wind Grass Knot Rain. Caso (1984, 2:224b) says of Lady Eight Water: "(She is) spouse of male One Wind Naked with Quetzals, second son of male Two Lizard Quetzal Tiger and female Nine Monkey Malachite Skull, (they are the) second lords of Seven Waters with Quetzals."

Tableau 3. FOURTH MARRIAGE: Lady Ten Dog + Lord One (eroded) Water. His other wives are the Ladies Three Reed, Five Wind, and Two Monkey. Caso (1984, 2:246a) identifies Lord One Water as a son of male Two Lizard and female Nine Monkey, and this couple as the second lords of Seven Waters with Quetzals. However, Lord One (eroded) Water appears to be the son of Lord One Wind and Lady Eight Water, the THIRD MARRIAGE.

Page 11b: Second Genealogy

Tableau 1. FIRST MARRIAGE: Lady Eight Grass + Lord Ten Rabbit. Caso (1984, 2:282b) identifies this couple as "Masters of Malacatepec" (Spindle Hill in the modern state of Puebla), and indicates that Ten Rabbit's younger brother Seven Reed (see Tableau 3, below) continues the dynasty of the place. However, there are several Malacatepecs in Mexico, including one in the Mixe district of Oaxaca as well as another two, one in Puebla and another in Chiapas. To their right is . . .

Tableau 2. Year 12 Flint. SECOND MARRIAGE: Lady One Flower + Lord One Jaguar. Of Lord One Jaguar, Caso writes (1984, 2:317a) that he is prob-ably a lord of Malacatepec in Puebla, and his brother was Seven Reed who married Lady Seven Grass. It is important to note that the place sign — a valley between two snow-capped mountains — also appears on Page 14. In this toponym, however, a town named Spindle Town is shown at the foot of one of the mountains.

Tableau 3. THIRD MARRIAGE: It is shown directly beneath the twin peaks toponym, namely, Lord Seven Reed Incense Torch + Lady Seven Grass Smoking Star. Lord Seven Reed appears on Page 14 f. Their child is Lord Nine Wind Rabbit Knives.

Tableau 4. FOURTH MARRIAGE: Lord Ten Monkey + Lady One Water Twenty (eroded) Spindles. Their children are the Lords Seven Monkey, Three Flower, Eight Snake, and . . .

Page 12a

. . . the Ladies Ten Jaguar and (eroded) Flower.

Page 12b–c: Third Genealogy

Date 13 Flint Day 1 Rain. The toponym is a river from which rises a Fire Serpent emerging from a cave. A digging stick is stuck in the river.

Tableau 1. FIRST MARRIAGE: Lord Eight Snake + Lady Three Motion. Their children are the Lords Eight Rain, One Wind, and Seven Death.

Tableau 2. SECOND MARRIAGE: Lord Nine Motion + Lady Twelve Jaguar.

Tableau 3. THIRD MARRIAGE: Lord Eight Motion + Lady Two Vulture.

Tableau 4. FOURTH MARRIAGE. Date 2 Reed (number 41) 4 Eagle (number 15 and number 315). The toponym is a green hill with a temple at its peak and a skyband and ballcourt within. This is part of Tableau 3. From Year 13 Flint to Year 2 Reed is fifteen years.

Page 13: Fourth Genealogy

Year 13 Rabbit (number 352) Day 7 Lizard (number 229).

Tableau 1. FIRST MARRIAGE: Lord One Death Sun Hill + Lady Nine House Flower Jaguar. Their children are Lord Seven Death and the Ladies Eight Eagle and One Eagle.

Tableau 2. SECOND MARRIAGE: Lord Nine House + Lady Eleven Alligator. Their children are Lord Ten Rabbit, who is born in Year 6 Reed; Lord Flint, who is born in Year 12 House; and Lord Three Lizard, born in Year

Table 4.2. Approximate Chronology in Years for Pages 10b–13

1 Reed (#1) 1 Alligator, Page 10b
+25 years
13 Flint (#26) 1 Rain, Page 12b
+15 years
2 Reed (#41) 3 Eagle, Page 12b
+11 years
13 Rabbit (#52) 7 Lizard, Page 13
+45 years
6 Reed (#45) 10 Rabbit, Page 13
+6 years
12 House (#51) 4 Flint, Page 13
+3 years
2 Flint (#2) 3 Lizard, Page 13

2 Flint; also the Ladies One Water, Two Jaguar, Four Vulture Arrow Heart Jewel Garment, and Two Alligator Plume Fan.

Pages 10b to 13 record a span of 105 years. Pages 9–10a record a span of 134 years. Pages 1–8 record a span of 165 years. A total of 404 years are recorded from Pages 1–13, but only the dates on Pages 1–8 have a secure chronological context when related to the European calendar.

END OF PART IB

Figure 4.1. Codex Zouche-Nuttall, Page 1 erased figure. Photo by Johann Sawyer.

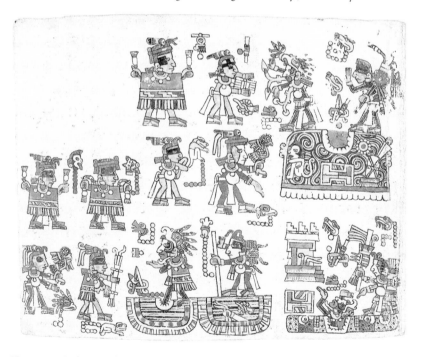

Figure 4.2. Codex Zouche-Nuttall (obverse), Page 1. © The Trustees of the British Museum.

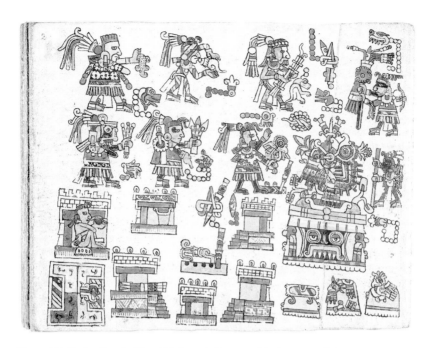

Figure 4.3. Codex Zouche-Nuttall (obverse), Page 2. © The Trustees of the British Museum.

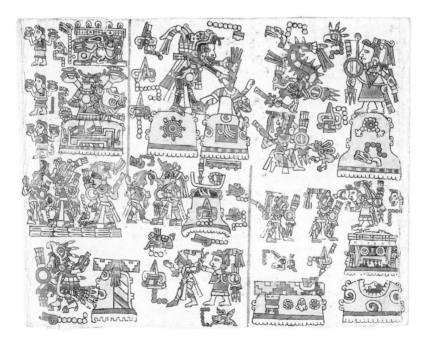

Figure 4.4. Codex Zouche-Nuttall (obverse), Page 3. © The Trustees of the British Museum.

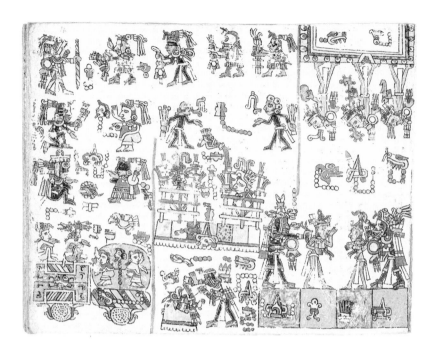

Figure 4.5. Codex Zouche-Nuttall (obverse), Page 4. © The Trustees of the British Museum.

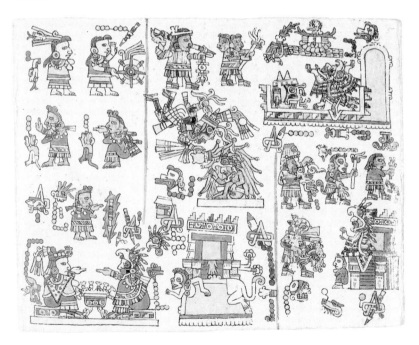

Figure 4.6. Codex Zouche-Nuttall (obverse), Page 5. © The Trustees of the British Museum.

Figure 4.7. Codex Zouche-Nuttall (obverse), Page 6. © The Trustees of the British Museum.

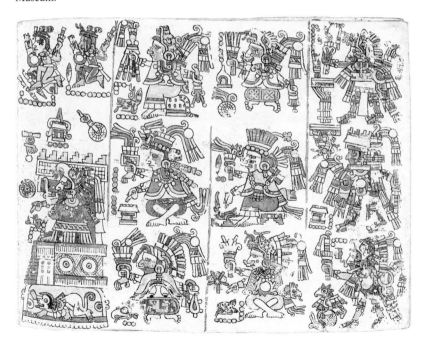

Figure 4.8. Codex Zouche-Nuttall (obverse), Page 7. © The Trustees of the British Museum.

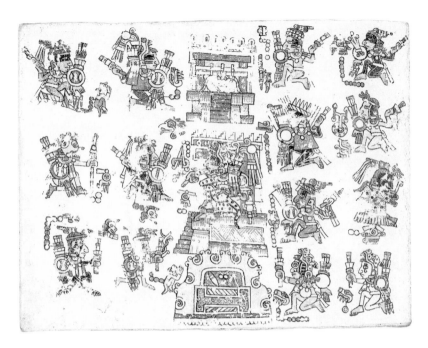

Figure 4.9. Codex Zouche-Nuttall (obverse), Page 8. © The Trustees of the British Museum.

Figure 4.10. Codex Zouche-Nuttall (obverse), Page 9. © The Trustees of the British Museum.

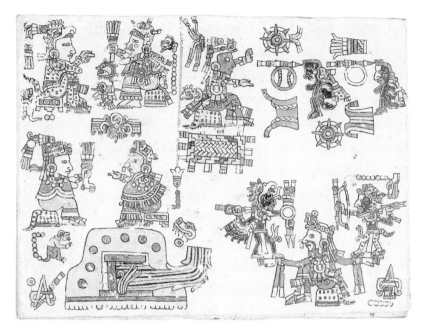

Figure 4.11. Codex Zouche-Nuttall (obverse), Page 10. © The Trustees of the British Museum.

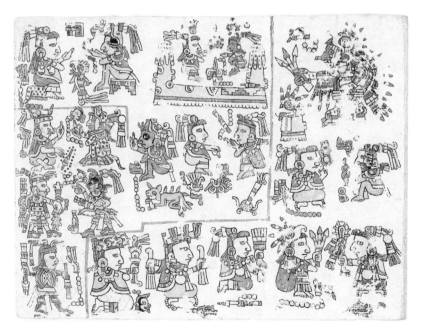

Figure 4.12. Codex Zouche-Nuttall (obverse), Page 11. © The Trustees of the British Museum.

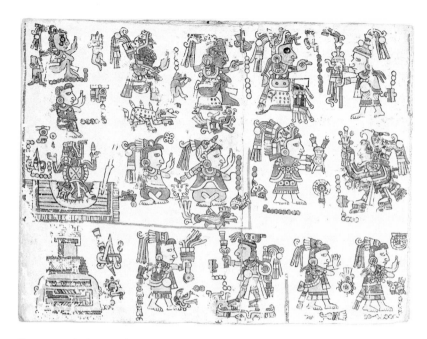

Figure 4.13. Codex Zouche-Nuttall (obverse), Page 12. © The Trustees of the British Museum.

Figure 4.14. Codex Zouche-Nuttall (obverse), Page 13. © The Trustees of the British Museum.

5 Document 1 (Obverse), Part IIA, Pages 14–19: The Ladies Three Flint

Pages 14–19: The Ladies Three Flint, the Great Temples, and the War from Heaven

The first section of Part II is written on Pages 14 through Double-page 19. The first page (14) is an introduction, and the reading order is ambiguous, though it reads from right to left. It is composed of six tableaux, paired in twos, one above the other, thus the format resembles that seen on Page 40. My numbering of the six tableaux found on Page 14 is arbitrary and calculated to end with Tableau 6 in the upper-left corner because the first tableau of the next page begins in the upper-right corner. This procedure is consonant with the previously mentioned "visual bridge" technique employed on the reverse, Document 2, Pages 42–84.

However, the one unambiguous tableau is obviously intended to be first. Of course that is Tableau 1, which introduces Lady Three Flint Elder and Lord Five Flower. It is located in the upper-right corner of Page 14. The text describing these pages includes reading order, tableau number, and any other devices illuminating the pictogram contents as may be necessary from time to time.

Beginning with the introductory Page 14, intention seems to be focused on establishing six locations within the purview of the royal leaders, Lady Three Flint Elder and Lord Five Flower. Subsequently, Pages 15–16 and 17–18 are paired by reading orders and interpreted as temple-founding/cult-bearing ceremonies and associated events as may appear on them. Page 19 is a double page containing a large map with multiple tableaux.

The two dominant female actors are Lady Three Flint Elder and her daughter, Three Flint Younger. The husband of the elder woman appears to be Lord Five Flower, and that of the younger, Lord Twelve Wind Smoke-Eye from the Sky (Pages 18b, 19a–b, 20a, 21a, 22). Nevertheless, these two women are delightfully ambiguous in the narratives, and this ambiguity will be discussed. In aid of resolving their ambiguous identities is the fact that, after Page 14, the narrative pages are paired: 15–16, 17–18, 19a–19b, and 20–21. Subsequently, Pages 22 through 24 provide a "set" of three pages relating the first dynasty of Tilantongo. The next "set" begins on Page 25, that is, beginning the second dynasty of Tilantongo. As mentioned previously, Pages 20–21 relating the War from Heaven in the southern Nochixtlan Valley can be omitted by connecting Double-page 19 directly to Page 22. The reason for this structure seems clear: if the War from Heaven pages (20–21) are omitted, then the last major figure on Page 19b—Lady One Death, the geneatrix of the first dynasty of Tilantongo—is directly connected to that dynasty, which begins on Page 22. Since Page 22 is ambiguous as to her role in the founding of Tilantongo's first dynasty, the reverse of Codex Vindobonensis Mexicanus I, Page 1, clarifies her prominent position in the founding of that important family. She is also a major figure on Codex Zouche-Nuttall Page 21b.

Page 14: Introduction (Figure 5.1)

The reading order for this page corresponds to that on Page 40, that is, beginning in the upper right. Thereafter it becomes unclear. Page 14 is not separated from Page 15 by a full-length red line. It displays six tableaux paired one above the other in three vertical columns or two horizontal bands—a device that also appears on Page 40. The two horizontal levels of reading per page also appear on Pages 36–41.

Tableau 1. Year 7 Reed Day 5 Flower (AD 916). This may simply be a year date, with the day name, 5 Flower, identifying the actor. At or from Stone Sky Cave, Lord Five Flower appears and travels to Lady Three Flint Elder. Lady Three Flint wears a distinctive nose ornament.

Tableau 2. Directly beneath Tableau 1, the Lords Ten Vulture and Ten Reed stand on their islands. These males appear on Page 15a in the procession and severally throughout this narrative section.

Tableau 3. Just to the left of Tableau 1, the Lords One and Seven Rain are on their respective hills. These males are prominently featured in the third story, on Pages 36–39.

Tableau 4. Year 4 Flint Day 8 Motion. Just beneath Tableau 3, the Lords Ten Grass and Ten Rain stand on their hills. These males also appear on Page 15a in the procession and severally throughout this section.

Tableau 5. Year 7 Flint Day 8 Motion. Just to the left of Tableau 4, the Lords Six/Seven Death and Seven Reed stand in a valley between two snow-capped mountains. Lord One Death, the Sun God, is seated in a yellow fringed circle above the right-hand mountain, and Lady Nine Snake is seated in a red fringed circle above the left-hand mountain. Caso (1984, 1, Plate 20) refers to this place as "Dos ceros nevados."

Tableau 6. It is located directly above Tableau 5 and displays the Lords Two Reed and Four Jaguar the Toltec. The implied reading order now proceeds to the top of Page 15 to column "a." Mary Elizabeth Smith (1973:253) tentatively identifies this place as San Pedro Jicayán.

Discussion of Page 14

The first tableau, dated Year 7 Reed Day 5 Flower, has the day and day name of the principal male shown simultaneously, implying this to be the year and day of his birth. However, since he travels from Stone Sky Cave to meet Lady Three Flint Elder, this is not his birth event. Either the date is the year and day of his birth or it is the year he traveled to meet Lady Three Flint, and that date of the travel event is paired with his day name, Five Flower. He appears by location and circumstance to be a god or demigod.

If so, then this tableau demonstrates a theme previously elucidated, namely, the marital union of a god or demigod with a mortal (Zouche-Nuttall Pages 1–6, 9–10a). As such, the present tableau initiates a founding story and presents territories related to the authority of these two rulers, Lord Five Flower and Lady Three Flint Elder.

Each district shown in the remaining five tableaux has rulers or gods that preside over it. Tableau 2 shows Lords Ten Vulture and Ten Reed each presiding over his individual island, and both face to the viewer's left. They are in procession here and reappear in procession on the next page, 15a. Each of the two lords shown here bears a distinctive staff, and on Page 15a they have switched staffs and have assumed different attire.

Tableau 3 displays the Lords One and Seven Rain facing each other. Each stands on his respective hill, and a valley separates them. Seven Rain carries a cloth-bound bundle torch in his left hand, and his right arm is tucked under his left arm. Lord One Rain points to Lord Seven Rain, which is a typical speaking gesture. One Rain also has his arm tucked. These males are the prime subjects in the last story told on Pages 36–39.

Tableau 4 is dated Year 4 Flint Day 8 Motion. Lords Ten Rain and Ten

Grass stand on their respective hills and process to the left, in the reading-order direction. They also appear last in the procession on Page 15a and hold the same bowls topped with codices and smoking incense bundles.

Tableau 5 is dated Year 7 Flint Day 8 Motion. The Lords Six Death and Seven Reed are in their valley, facing each other and in communication. Some numbers in Lord Six Death's name seem eroded, so his name may be "Seven" or "Eight." Caso (1984, 2:439a) focuses on the gods above them, Lady Nine Snake and Lord One Death "Tlaloc." The Lady Nine Snake is in a circular cloud cartouche just above a mountain, and Lord One Death is in another above a second mountain. For Caso, these mountains suggest the Central Mexican Valley volcanoes Popocatépetl and Iztaccíhuatl. The codex artist renders them as snowcapped.

Tableau 6 displays the Lords Two Reed and Four Jaguar standing within a masonry enclosure atop a low hill. They face each other. Lord Two Reed carries a sacrificial bird and has a back rack containing the white flag of human sacrifice. Lord Four Jaguar carries a red, blue-topped wand decorated with a jaguar pelt.

In the six tableaux on Page 14, the individuals in Tableaux 1, 3, 5, and 6 face one another. Individuals in Tableaux 2 and 4 do not. These latter individuals are in procession and bear ceremonial objects or offerings. Individuals shown in procession on Page 14—Lords Ten Reed, Ten Vulture, Ten Rain, and Ten Grass—also appear in the procession that begins Page 15a, led by Lord Five Flower and Lady Three Flint Elder. Their exchange of objects held has been noted above, as well as their change of attire from Page 14 to Page 15a. The conclusion is, then, that the four lords shown in procession on Page 14 continue that procession on Page 15, led by the two chief actors, Lord Five Flower and Lady Three Flint Elder. Therefore, this introductory Page 14 is an initiating part of the narrative flow of the story that follows.

Two of the non-processing lords shown here in Tableau 3—One Rain and Seven Rain—also are major actors in the last story of Codex Zouche-Nuttall Document 1 (obverse), appearing on Pages 36–39. However, they also reappear in this present story on Page 17a, where they conduct a bird-decapitation sacrifice before Lady Three Flint Elder. In fact, all of the males on Page 14 bearing the number "Ten" in their day names reappear at various times in subsequent narratives involving both Lady Three Flint Elder and her daughter, Three Flint Younger. Only Lords Four Jaguar, Two Reed, Eight Death, and Seven Reed do not.

The following narrative that begins on Page 15 introduces the device of "descent," which continues to be employed through Page 22. By this device, actors descend or peregrinate into scenes and tableaux in the upper portion of the right side of Pages 15, 19, 21b, and 22. The suggestion is that they descend from the sky, and this is graphically illustrated on Page 19a.

Pages 15–16

Page 15 (Figure 5.2)

Tableau 1. Page 15a. This tableau illustrates a processional descent: first, Lords Ten Grass and Ten Rain, then Lords Ten Vulture and Ten Reed, and finally, leading the procession, Lord Five Flower followed by Lady Three Flint Elder, wearing her distinctive nose ornament.

Tableau 2. Page 15b. Year 10 Reed Days 9 Wind and 7 Rain—both days occur once in Year 10 Reed, with 9 Wind preceding 7 Rain by thirty-six days. This scene is a series of three ascending, interrelated tableaux illustrating ceremonies over a thirty-six-day period.

The first part, on the bottom row, occurs at Fire Serpent Ballcourt facing a body of water with the goddess of rivers, lakes, and water in general, Lady One Eagle, in it. Lady Three Flint Elder appears from a serpent's mouth in the water before One Eagle; she holds a smoking *incensario* in her right hand and a trilobed vegetation branch in the other. She also wears her distinctive nose ornament.

A large temple—Serpent Temple—with a Nine Wind Quetzalcoatl bundle inside it, stands above a place sign, "The Mouth of the Earth." This temple extends upward into the next tableau on the top row. Before the temple, Lady Three Flint Elder—without her distinctive nose ornament—stands at the foot of Jaltepec Mountain and holds a perforator in her left hand and a smoking *incensario* in her right hand. Directly before her but on the other side of Jaltepec Mountain are two lords; one of them is Lord Ten Reed and the other is unnamed but presumed to be Ten Vulture. Both hold incense bags, but Ten Reed holds a trilobed vegetation wand and the presumed Ten Vulture holds a bird for sacrifice.

Above row two, Lord Five Flower lets blood by piercing his ear. He holds an incense bag and stands before two mountains. The one directly before him is a mountain emitting flames and named Motion or Earthquake. The mountain behind it is named Stone Throne Town.

Discussion of Pages 14–15

Pages 14–15 begin a series of important actions on the part of various personnel, chiefly Lady Three Flint Elder and Lord Five Flower. Page 14 displays them (Tableau 1) at Stone Sky Cave, from which Lord Five Flower emerges to meet Lady Three Flint. This tableau accompanies five others that represent specific geographical locations. Four of the twelve individuals shown on Page 14—Lords Ten Reed and Ten Vulture, and Lords Ten Grass and Ten Rain—are displayed in processional pose, thus the procession shown on Page 15a begins here on Page 14, and on Page 15a includes Lady Three Flint Elder and Lord Five Flower.

On Page 15a, the males named Ten Rain and Ten Grass, Ten Reed and Ten Vulture, and Lady Three Flint Elder and Lord Five Flower are in processional descent to the place of action on Page 15b. This place is a specific location in the Tilantongo Valley (Pohl 1994:33). Then a tripartite ceremony occurs.

The first ceremony is in water, where Lady Three Flint Elder transforms and emerges from the mouth of a supernatural serpent before the goddess of lakes and rivers, Lady One Eagle. This occurs at Fire Serpent Ballcourt Place. The second ceremonial event occurs before Serpent Temple. The temple itself is just above a place qualifier resembling that from which Lord Eight Wind Eagle Flints was born on Page 1, Tableau 1. The third part of the ceremony, conducted by Lord Five Flower, is described above. Regarding this page, Pohl (1994:33) says:

> Two elders and two priests accompany 5 Flower and Lady 3 Flint to establish the cult of 9 Wind Ehecatl-Quetzalcoatl at a location in the Tilantongo Valley. 5 Flower's first act as a priest is to make an offering of blood from his ear at the institution of the temple and its cult.

Synopsis: The procession of six individuals travels to Serpent Ballcourt Place, where Lady Three Flint Elder transforms and meets with the supernatural Lady One Eagle in the water. Then, at Mouth of the Earth, at the foot of Jaltepec Mountain, Lady Three Flint Elder conducts a ceremony assisted by Ten Reed and the presumed Ten Vulture. Subsequently, or at the same time, Lord Five Flower stands in the district of two mountains and lets blood.

The action now proceeds across to Page 16a. Whereas the previous page (15) had two columns of text, Page 16 has three.

Page 16 is the second page of a two-page set consisting of Pages 15–16. The reading order makes a smooth transition from the upper-left column of Page 15b to the upper-right column of Page 16a.

Tableau 1 (Page 16a). Year 3 Flint Day 3 Flint (AD 925). Lords Nine Motion and Ten Wind are each displayed atop a mountain in their respective districts, facing each other across a valley. Between them, seemingly floating in the air, is a white hill identified by two steambaths. On the valley floor between them are three bundles.

Tableau 2. Birth of Lady Three Flint Younger in Year 3 Flint on Day 3 Flint. A small red *quechquemitl* appears directly beneath her but touches her mother's foot, as the mother, Lady Three Flint Elder, enters a cave.

Tableau 3 (Page 16a–b). Lady Three Flint Elder, now wearing a red *quechquemitl*, enters a cave/temple and the underworld. Attending are Lords Ten Reed and Ten Grass. Both of these lords appeared in the procession on Page 15a and were displayed as processionalists on Page 14.

The cave Lady Three Flint Elder enters is one of seven displayed on that hill, but this particular cave is the entrance to a temple that has the water of the underworld flowing downward from it. The cave waters are identified by a snail, the same visual device formerly shown on Lady Three Flint Elder's *quechquemitl*. From this point forward in the narrative, Lady Three Flint Elder is identified as Three Flint Red Quechquemitl. In previous literature, this cognomen was thought to be reserved for her daughter, Lady Three Flint Younger. This will be discussed later in the text. However, the river flowing downward from the cave/temple leads us to the next tableau.

Tableau 4 (Page 16b). Year 7 Rabbit Day 3 Flower. Lords Nine Wind and Seven Flower wait atop the river that flows from the cave/temple shown in the preceding tableau.

Tableau 5 (Page 16b–c). Lady Three Flint Red Quechquemitl and Lord Five Flower, looking left, now face, in the top-left column, . . .

Tableau 5, continued (Page 16c). . . . Lords Five Wind and Five Eagle. Five Wind holds a bound torch, and Five Eagle holds a sacrificial bird. A fire-drilling bundle flanked by two ceremonial staffs is positioned behind the two lords.

Tableau 6. Year 7 Rabbit Day 3 Flower. This tableau is complex and represents the ceremonial conclusion of events begun on Page 15a, Tableau 1. A great tree grows from a river or lake. Lady One Eagle (who appeared with

Lady Three Flint Elder on Page 15a, Tableau 1) is seated on the water's surface before the tree, and she points downward. In the center of the river and mostly above it is the two-faced god, Lord Ten Alligator. He faces both Lady One Eagle, on the left, and, to the reader's right, Lord Four Death, who is also seated on the water's surface.

Below Lord Ten Alligator, Lady Three Flint is shown nude with a large conch shell on her back, but she holds on to two-faced Lord Ten Alligator's clawed feet that are in the water with her. Lady Three Flint faces—and converses with—Lady One Eagle's husband, Lord One Grass. One Grass is seated at the underwater roots of the great tree. Lord Four Deer is directly behind Lady Three Flint and directly beneath Lord Four Death. Therefore, the ceremonial complex that began on Page 15b with Lady Three Flint Elder in the water with Lady One Eagle ends on Page 16c with Lady Three Flint Elder again in the water before Lady One Eagle's husband, One Grass. For a continuation of this discussion regarding the Lords Four Death and Four Deer, see Chapter 8, the subsection about Pages 37b–38.

The conundrum concerned with the ceremonial complex displayed on Pages 15–16 is this: Alfonso Caso has it that Lady Three Flint Elder died in childbirth and entered the underworld, and this has persisted as dogma in the literature. As is obvious by the comments above (Page 16a, Tableau 3), I have proposed another interpretation and will supply more rationale for it in text below.

Pages 17–18

Page 17a (Figure 5.4)

Three ceremonies are displayed in this column of pictogram text, from top to bottom. The ceremonies in all three levels occur with different sets of male actors and Lady Three Flint Elder.

Ceremony 1. Lady Three Flint with Lords Seven Rain and One Rain conduct a bird-decapitation sacrifice. These lords are primary actors in the third story, Pages 36–39.

Ceremony 2. Lady Three Flint Elder and Lord Five Flower, along with Lords Ten Grass and Ten Rain, conduct a bird and dog sacrifice.

Ceremony 3. Lady Three Flint in the water with Lords Four Deer and Four Death. These two lords appear in the last story, on Pages 37b–38, and appeared previously in this story on Page 16c.

Three levels of ceremonial action ascend on Page 17b, and four gods attending in ascending order are displayed on Page 18a. The action occurs in a valley, flanked left and right by two mountains. Lords Four Motion (displayed on the viewer's left) and Seven Reed (on the viewer's right) rule these mountains.

At the lowermost level of action in these tableaux, in the valley presided over by Lords Four Motion and Seven Reed, the Lords Nine Flower and Ten Rain stand to either side of a temple platform. The first lord holds a torch bundle, and the second holds a bowl with a bundle atop it and a smoking incense ball atop that. He also holds a sacrificial bird in his other hand. A large pyre with an incense ball in a bowl is atop the burning pyre. Lady Nine Grass, the Oracle of the Dead, and Lord Seven Flower appear at this level of ceremonial action but on Page 18a. Lord Nine Alligator holds a perforator and incense pipe at or before Fire Serpent Ballcourt.

At the next level of action, midpage, Lords Ten Vulture, holding a trilobed wand and an incense bag, and Ten Reed, blowing a conch-shell trumpet, stand before Serpent Temple. The temple contains a fire-drilling bundle, and the two staffs, previously displayed on Page 16c with the fire-drilling bundle, are standing erect before the temple. The Lords Ten Vulture and Ten Reed face the staffs and the temple. At this level of ceremonial action, but on Page 18a, is Lord Nine Wind Quetzalcoatl with a bone perforator.

The uppermost level of action shows Lord Five Flower and Lady Three Flint Elder in their house, which is positioned just in front of the temple roof. Lord One Death stands just outside the house, and on Page 18a, Lord Two Dog, holding a bent staff and an incense bag, stands behind Lord One Death.

This series of tableaux on Pages 17b and 18a is generally taken as the marriage of Lord Five Flower and Lady Three Flint. However, considering the nature of the tableaux and the supernaturals in attendance, I propose that the complex displayed on these pages is the apotheosis of Five Flower and Three Flint Elder, in other words, their elevation to divine status. Hereafter, these two primary actors no longer appear in the narrative. Page 18b introduces a primary actor in the next section, Lord Twelve Wind Smoke-Eye from the Sky. Also, Page 18b is not separated in reading order from the following page, 19a. Page 18b ends at the upper left, and Page 19a begins at the upper right.

Page 18b (Figure 5.5)

The action on Page 18b begins at the top of the page in the sky of the ancestors Lord Four House and Lady Five Snake. Their heads appear on temple platforms in the sky, and a sun disk is between them. Directly below the starry skyband is a cave opening. A shining cloud rope descends from it, and several males descend along it in procession. From last to first, these males are Lord Three Flint Twenty Pearls, bearing an incense bag and the red Venus staff; an unnamed male bearing a red-and-white bundle staff; Lord Five Dog, bearing the implements of a warrior; and, finally, the primary actor, Lord Twelve Wind Smoke-Eye from the Sky, bearing a temple on his back via a serpent tumpline. He also carries an incense bag and points upward.

The date is Year 4 House Day 7 Wind. A fire-drilling paraphernalia complex rises from a cave in the water at Apoala directly in front of Lord Twelve Wind Smoke-Eye. In the water are Lord Five Vulture and Lady (One) Eagle, though this latter person is identified only by "Eagle." Five Vulture presents offerings to Lady One Eagle. From last to first, the Lords Six Water, holding a bone perforator and a sacrificial bird; Six Death, holding a bundle torch; and Seven Eagle, holding an incense bag and an *incensario*, stand on the bank overlooking the river in which are Lord Five Vulture and Lady One Eagle and from which rises the fire-drilling bundle. At the level of the fire-drilling bundle, Lord Twelve Wind holds an incense bag and presents a smoking *incensario* before Fire Serpent Ballcourt (see Page 15b). Directly above this, Lords Nine Motion, holding a bundle torch, and Seven Eagle, holding war instruments, stand at another Serpent Temple. This is the same temple borne from the sky by Lord Twelve Wind Smoke-Eye, and now the serpent tumpline he used to carry it has become the temple's name. Before the temple are the two staffs borne from the sky, and a red-and-white bundle is situated between them.

This temple, sans serpent, is the same temple displayed on Page 19a. It appears to be the royal temple of Wasp Hill. With this in mind, the action now proceeds to Double-page 19, specifically Page 19a.

The Identity of Lady Three Flint Elder

The first scene of ceremonial action involving Lady Three Flint Elder and Lord Five Flower occurs at Jaltepec Mountain on Page 15b. The first appear-

Table 5.1. Sequencing of Dates on Pages 14–18

Sequence/ Page	Date	Event
2. 14	7 Reed (#33) 5 Flower (AD 916)	Meeting of ♀ Three Flint & ♂ Five Flower
	−3 years	
1. 14	4 Flint (#30) 8 Motion (AD 913)	♂♂ Ten Rain & Ten Grass
	+16 years	
3. 14	7 Flint (#46) 8 Motion (AD 929)	♂♂ Seven Reed & Seven Death + ♀ Nine Snake & ♂ One Death
	+3 years	
5. 15b	10 Reed (#49) Days 9 Wind & 7 Rain (AD 932)	At Serpent Temple
	−7 years	
4. 16a	3 Flint (#42) 3 Flint (AD 925)	Birth of Three Flint Younger
	+30 years	
6. 16b	7 Rabbit (#20) 3 Flower (AD 955)	At the sacred tree
	+11 years	
7. 18b	4(5) House (#43) 7 Wind (AD 96)5	Fire-drilling bundle at Apoala
	Total = 50 years	

ance of Lady Three Flint Younger occurs on Page 16a when she is born. Immediately after giving birth, a female presumed to be Lady Three Flint Elder but wearing a red *quechquemitl* is shown going into a cave with water flowing downward from a temple inside it. Supporting the assumption that the female now wearing a red *quechquemitl* instead of the previous snail *quechquemitl* is Three Flint Elder is the fact that the flint identifier of the day name points directly at her (other examples of calendar identifiers as pointers are cited in this present work).

This is the tableau cited by Caso as Three Flint Elder's death (1984, 2:378). However, this is unlikely. More likely is the fact that at the birth of her daughter, Lady Three Flint Snail Quechquemitl (the Elder) changed her personal name to Lady Three Flint Red Quechquemitl. The same sort of name change involving the female *quechquemitl* garment is recorded in Codex Selden in a later generation for Lady Six Monkey of Jaltepec.[1] Part of the confusion concerning the identities of mother and daughter has to do with the positioning of the identifying red *quechquemitl* in the tableau showing the daughter's birth. The small red identifying *quechquemitl* is positioned directly below the baby's foot, but it actually touches the mother's foot as she enters the cave to the underworld. Also, the partial figure of the mother, Lady Three Flint Elder, is shown wearing the red *quechquemitl* as she enters the cave-temple-river complex.

Since this is so, and because the previous action for Three Flint Elder happened at Jaltepec, it is reasonable to interpret this tableau as a name change for the Elder heroine. This being the case, then the younger Lady Three Flint only appears on codex Pages 14 through 18 once—at her birth. Subsequently, the daughter only appears on Pages 19a–b and 20a.

The Three Flint Stories

Alfonso Caso (1984, 2:389a–399b) established the story of the Ladies Three Flint in its modern form as the stories of a mother and daughter both named Three Flint. Previously, Zelia Nuttall (1902) thought that Pages 14–19 of the manuscript that bears her name told the story of one woman named Three Flint who, in media res, changed her personal name from Quechquemitl with Snail (now considered the elder woman) to Red Quechquemitl (now considered the younger woman). It has been noted previously that a female name change represented by changing garments is also recorded in Codex Selden for one woman named Lady Six Monkey (of Jaltepec).

According to Caso, the elder female Three Flint gives birth to Three Flint Younger in Year 3 Flint on Day 3 Flint, then dies in childbirth. Thereafter, the father, Lord Five Flower, raises the child, and she subsequently marries Lord Twelve Wind Smoke-Eye from the Sky. They rule, or are the lineage founders, of a place now referred to in the literature as Wasp Hill, which was subsequently destroyed in the sixteen-year War from Heaven.

Birth of Lady Three Flint Younger in Year 3 Flint on Day 3 Flint

There are many problems with chronology concerning Lady or Ladies Three Flint. For example, there is a significant problem with the birth of Lady Three Flint Younger in Year 3 Flint on Day 3 Flint. One calendar cycle assigns the European calendar date of AD 976 to this event. When the War from Heaven ended in AD 979, the younger Three Flint would have been three years old and would also have had a husband. So we have to reject that interpretation and move back in time to the preceding cycle, which assigns the European calendar date of AD 924. This is a reasonable date for her birth. She would have been fifty-five years old when the War from Heaven ended and her lineage was exterminated. It is notable that no specific genealogy attaches to her and her husband, Lord Twelve Wind Smoke-Eye from the Sky.

Another problem — which began with Nuttall's commentary — is the generally accepted idea that there was only one woman named Three Flint. Nuttall writes that

> . . . the Lady Three Flint became the consort of two lords, and that her marriage, lying-in, and installation as Woman-Serpent were attended by the most solemn and elaborate ceremonials, in which priests and priestesses officiated. (1902:32a)

This idea is interesting because the birth of Lady Three Flint Younger on Zouche-Nuttall Page 16a shows the mother wearing a female garment adorned with a snail. Yet this garment appears with a female Three Flint only one other time in the sequence, namely, on Page 15b. However, in the birth scene (her "lying-in"), the mother is specifically named Three Flint, and during Caso's implied death of the mother, the figure seen going into the hill wears the red garment.

Another thorny problem is that if there is only one Lady Three Flint, she has two husbands. One is Five Flower, who appears in the first tableau of the sequence on Page 14. He disappears from the narrative after Page 17b, and the tableau supposedly showing them as a married couple is undated. The supposed second husband first appears on Page 18b. He then came from a sky cave on Page 19a and marries Lady Three Flint on Page 19b. It is he who is shown with her as the lineage rulers in the first tableau on Page 21, preceding the War from Heaven and the subsequent extermination of the Wasp Hill lineage clans.

However, genealogies are not written for either woman, and the only birth appearing in this complex series of tableaux is that of Three Flint Younger. Chronologies are proposed for Pages 14–18 and 19a–b. The dates are not chronologically sequential, that is, they do not progress necessarily according to Time's Arrow. Given that, however, AD 924 is a possible date for the birth of Lady Three Flint Younger.

The proposal for the existence of only one Lady Three Flint (by Zelia Nuttall) is interesting but not credible. I have proposed a resolution for the conflict of identity concerning these two women in previous text. Whereas Caso thinks the Elder, or mother, Three Flint died while birthing the younger Three Flint, I do not. Since the first major ceremony associated with the mother and her husband, Five Flower, occurs at a site that appears to be Jaltepec—a site that in a later generation had female rulers, one of whom changed names by change of garment—I propose that rather than dying in childbirth, the mother Three Flint changed her name to Red Quechquemitl and that the daughter does not appear again in the codex until her marriage to Lord Twelve Wind Smoke-Eye Twenty from the Sky on Double-page 19.

By this solution, the action of the elder woman and her husband as cult bearers is foregrounded, and they are the dominant actors in events shown on Pages 14–18. Subsequently, on Pages 19a–b and 20a, the statement is made that Lord Twelve Wind Smoke-Eye Twenty from the Sky and Lady Three Flint Red Quechquemitl (the Younger) are the lineage heads of the Wasp Hill clans, those same clans that were eradicated in the War from Heaven. Alfonso Caso did not correlate place, custom, event, and personnel when he assumed that Lady Three Flint Elder died in childbirth.

Therefore, in the narrative, the elder Lady Three Flint, and to some degree her husband, Five Flower, are displayed as dynamic and active in supernatural events important to the founding of the religion of their clans, although no descent is recorded other than their daughter. The elder Three Flint and her husband, Five Flower, are even given an elegant apotheosis. Against this backdrop of activity for the engaging parent couple—across a one-page introduction (Page 14) and two double-page sets (Pages 15–16 and 17–18)—they are seen as very dynamic in supernatural/political events.

The individual double-page map (Page 19) for the daughter Three Flint shows her as passive. She engaged in no supernatural activities and appears first merely as Lord Six Water from Wasp Hill Temple carries her via tumpline to her wedding to Lord Twelve Wind Smoke-Eye Twenty. They appear together only once more: on Page 20a, displayed as leaders of the destroyed clan of Wasp Hill nobles. Only three brief tableaux constitute the appearances of Lady Three Flint Younger since her birth on Page 16a. Otherwise, there are forty persons shown on Double-page 19 (Lord Twelve Wind Smoke-Eye is shown four times). Her marriage is the important event for display on these two pages.

Double-page 19: At Wasp Hill and Its Surrounds

Pages 19a–19b (Figures 5.6, 5.7)

Year 7 Rabbit Day 12 Wind (AD 954; Byland and Pohl 1994:236). This date is twenty-two days after Year 7 Rabbit Day 3 Flower on Page 16b. The upper-right tableau occurs in the sky. This tableau is in consistent reading order with the last tableau on Page 18b, although it is difficult to demonstrate a direct reading connection with it, except that it shares personnel, the protagonist Lord Twelve Wind Smoke-Eye from the Sky and his entourage: Lords Three Flint and Five Dog.

Tableau 1, in the sky. Lord Twelve Wind Smoke-Eye, plus a temple and a fire-drilling apparatus, is seated between Lord Four Alligator, appearing from a vision serpent, and Lord Eleven Alligator, appearing from a vision serpent.

Tableau 2. Three sky appendages extend downward from Tableau 1. First, to the viewer's left, there is the moon with a U-shaped bracket containing a snail, from which Lord Three Flint descends holding a Venus staff. The central appendage hangs from a cave in the sky, and Lord Twelve Wind Smoke-Eye descends from it. He bears the temple in a serpent tumpline. The third appendage appears on the viewer's right and contains the sun with a motion symbol inside it. An unnamed lord holds a red-and-white bundle staff and descends from it.

Tableau 3. A cloud rope descends from the cave through the second appendage, and a procession moves downward along it. The procession consists of (from last to first) Lords Five Dog and Twelve Wind Smoke-Eye, who bears the temple but without the serpent tumpline; instead it is a white-banded fabric tumpline. Beneath them are (from last to first) Lords Nine Motion, bearing a bundled torch, and Seven Eagle, bearing a trilobed wand and an incense bag.

Year 7 Rabbit Day 12 Wind. The cloud rope touches the earth, and there is a woven grass mat with a layered bundle inside.

Tableau 4. A delegation on the earth meets the descendants from Tableau 2 above. They are (from first to last) Lords Ten Death, bearing a sacrificial bird; Ten Rain with folded arms; Twelve Lizard, bearing a *xicolli* garment; and Twelve Vulture with folded arms.

Tableau 5. Year 10 House Day 2 Eagle (AD 957; Byland and Pohl 1994:236). There is a procession from Wasp Hill Temple. The processionalists are (from first to last) Lords Nine Alligator, bearing a bound torch; Nine Flower, blowing a conch-shell trumpet; Seven Flower, bearing an *incensario* and an unidentified object; Six Motion, bearing a flowering branch and an incense bag; Six Water, bearing a staff, an incense bag, and the presumed Lady Three Flint Younger in a tumpline; and Lord Six Death, bearing a wrapped maguey plant. Lord One Flower, who presents a red *xicolli*, and Lord Ten Reed, who

Table 5.2. Sequencing of Dates on Double-page 19a–b

Page/Tableau	Date	Event
19a, Tab. 1	Year 7 Rabbit (#20; AD 954)	Descent to the earth
	+3 years	
19b, Tab. 5	Year 10 House (#23; AD 957)	Nuptial bath
	+11 years	
19b, Tab. 7	Year 8 Flint (#34; AD 968)	Lord One Alligator flies through the earth
	+11 Years	
19b, Tab. 8	Year 5(6) Reed (#5; AD 979)	Marriage house events
	Total = 25 years	

presents an incense bag and a trilobed vegetation wand, greet this procession along the way.

Tableau 6. The procession with Lady Three Flint Younger ends at a bathhouse. Inside are Lady Three Flint Younger and Lord Twelve Wind Smoke-Eye, both nude. The Ladies Six Flint and Ten House pour water over them. Outside the house, Lady One Eagle White Flint Hill presents a curled, conical red-and-white-striped hat.

Tableau 7. Year 8 Flint Day 8 Motion (AD 968). A *yaha yahui* priest named One Alligator flies through the rock.

Tableau 8. Year 5(6) Reed Day 12 Alligator (AD 977). Lords Ten Vulture and Ten Reed—the former carrying the red-and-white bundle staff and the latter carrying the Venus staff—are outside the nuptial house. Within the house are Lady Three Flint Younger and Lord Twelve Wind Smoke-Eye from the Sky. Lord Ten Rain, bearing a sacrificial bird and a bowl, sits enthroned outside the house and faces three bound staff bundles. Opposite him sits Lord One Grass.

Tableau 9. There is a procession from left to right across the top of the page. The individuals are (from last to first): Lord Ten Alligator, Lord Twelve Alligator the Two-Faced, Lord One Alligator, Lady Thirteen Flower, Lord Six Water, Lord Six Death, Lord One Alligator, and Lord Thirteen Flower. They meet at Fire Serpent Ballcourt, where, between two plants, Lady One Death emerges from a cave in the earth. Wasp Hill Temple with a Venus staff before it is behind Lady One Death, and there is a bundle inside the temple topped by a sacrificial knife and fire-drilling apparatus.

Discussion: Lady One Death

This complex series of tableaux (on Double-page 19) displays chronologically progressive scenarios. The date of Lady One Death's birth is not given, and the only codex providing it (Bodley, 1-V) is eroded. The Page-19 statement is a general one, saying merely that she was born from the earth in the territory of Wasp Hill and near Fire Serpent Ballcourt. Therefore, she is a progenitor of the dynasty from that place. It is known that she and her husband Lord Four Alligator (Codex Zouche-Nuttall, Page 21b) married in AD 940 (Codex Bodley 1-III; Codex Vindobonensis Mexicanus I, reverse, Page I) and had a daughter named One Vulture who was born at Achiutla. Codex Zouche-Nuttall Page 21b shows her and her husband Four Alligator at Achiutla. One Vulture married Lord Four Rabbit of Wasp Hill, and they had two daughters, Ladies Five Reed and Five Jaguar. According to Caso (1984, 2:145b), Lady One Vulture also married Lord Ten Motion (Vindobonensis reverse, Page II-3).

Lady Five Reed married into the first dynasty of Tilantongo (Codex Zouche-Nuttall, Page 23a), and the other daughter, Five Jaguar, married into the dynasty of Tilantongo's rival, Hua Chino (Red-and-White Bundle) after the War from Heaven. In fact, Lady Five Reed married the founder of Tilantongo's first dynasty, Lord Nine Wind Stone Skull, in Year 4 Rabbit (AD 991; Vindobonensis Mexicanus I reverse, Page IV, and Bodley 4-V).

According to both Zouche-Nuttall and Bodley, Wasp Hill and its clans became extinct during the war. Therefore, these marriages represent a resolution of the conflict, even though both Tilantongo and Hua Chino became rivals because of it. That rivalry ended in the time of Lord Eight Deer Jaguar Claw of Tilantongo when he attacked Hua Chino in AD 1100 and destroyed its royal family in AD 1101.

The subject of Lady One Death will be revisited in a subsequent chapter.

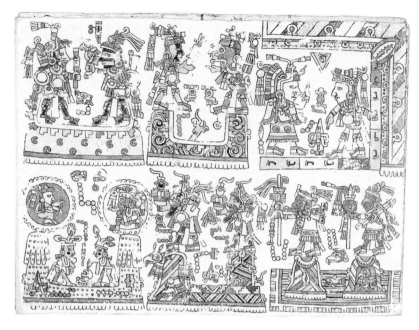

Figure 5.1. Codex Zouche-Nuttall (obverse), Page 14. © The Trustees of the British Museum.

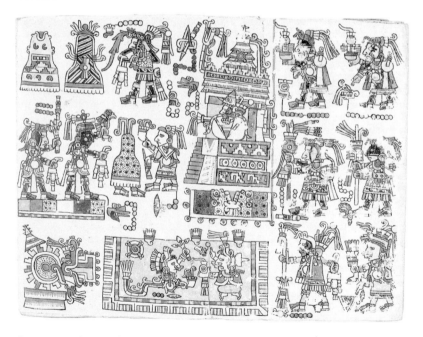

Figure 5.2. Codex Zouche-Nuttall (obverse), Page 15. © The Trustees of the British Museum.

Figure 5.3. Codex Zouche-Nuttall (obverse), Page 16. © The Trustees of the British Museum.

Figure 5.4. Codex Zouche-Nuttall (obverse), Page 17. © The Trustees of the British Museum.

Figure 5.5. Codex Zouche-Nuttall (obverse), Page 18. © The Trustees of the British Museum.

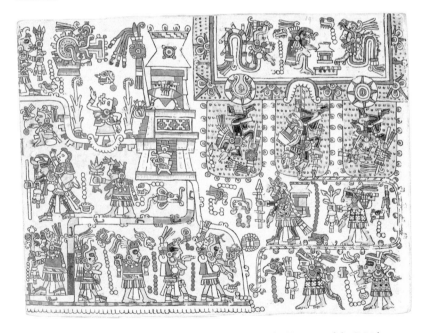

Figure 5.6. Codex Zouche-Nuttall (obverse), Page 19a. © The Trustees of the British Museum.

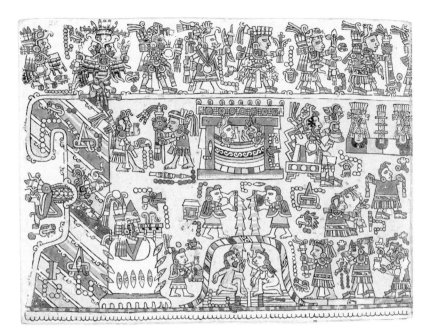

Figure 5.7. Codex Zouche-Nuttall (obverse), Page 19b. © The Trustees of the British Museum.

6 Document 1 (Obverse), Part IIA continued, Pages 20–21: The War from Heaven and Lady One Death

Pages 20–21: The War from Heaven

Page 20a–b

Lord Twelve Wind Smoke-Eye and Lady Three Flint Younger represent the Wasp Hill royalty. They are displayed as such, and the lower part of their tableau is a full-column stop. It occupies the entire lower portion of the column and makes a visual "stop" between the seated nobles above and the vegetation toponyms that follow below.

Eleven such toponyms follow Lord Twelve Wind Smoke-Eye and Lady Three Flint Younger. The corpses of Thirteen Jaguar and Thirteen Grass bound to plant bundles begin the War from Heaven sequences. They are presumably nobles of Wasp Hill.

Karl Taube (1986) notes another interpretation of plant bundles associated with people in his essay on Teotihuacan writing. Describing a group of murals from Tlacuilapaxco and citing Rene Millon (1988:85, 88), he writes:

> Richly dressed figures stand below an elaborate textile featuring a bicephalic serpent and other motifs. In front of each figure there is a long bound element with five, or more rarely four, vertically placed maguey leaves, or *pencas*, similar to examples known in other glyphic contexts at Teotihuacan. The repeating element in front of the figures constitutes the group as a whole. This sign is almost surely an early form of the Aztec *zacatlpayolli*, a bound grass bundle used to hold the maguey spines administered during penitential bloodletting. This sign in the Tlacuilapaxco murals may denote the priestly office of the individuals, the verbal action of bloodletting, or perhaps the place of bloodletting.

More pertinent to the immediate purpose of this codex scene, however, each plant bleeds at the bottom, and maguey is present as well as a sacrificial knife. Spines are present on at least two of the non-maguey plants, and two plants (second and third from bottom right) are combinations of sacred plants (Codex Zouche-Nuttall, Page 2). In addition, including the two bound and sacrificed nobles—Thirteen Jaguar and Thirteen Grass—on Page 20b, there are exactly thirteen figures of plants or combinations of people and plants following the seated figures of Lord Twelve Wind Smoke-Eye and Lady Three Flint Younger. The Lords Thirteen Jaguar and Thirteen Grass are bound to plant bundles. Codex Bodley reverse (Page 35-I) shows exactly thirteen Wasp Hill nobles either sacrificed by or fleeing from the Oracle of the Dead, Lady Nine Grass. On Zouche-Nuttall Page 20b and Bodley Page 34-I, she prosecutes the war.

Page 20b–c: The War from Heaven in the Southern Nochixtlan Valley (Figures 6.1.a, 6.1.b, 6.1.c, 6.2)

Lady Nine Grass of Chalcatongo fights against a priest named Lord Nine Wind (Byland and Pohl 1994:14). This battle is shown directly above the two deceased rulers, Lord Twelve Lizard and Lady Twelve Vulture.

Year 3 Reed Days 1 Lizard, 6 Dog, and 8 Motion (AD 963). Lord Nine Wind Quetzalcoatl battles against Stone Men. One Stone Man is named Eight Motion, and another stands behind this violence and wields a copper axe. Directly below this scene, an unnamed Stone Man captures and kills Lord Four House, whose funeral is coupled with that of Lord Three Monkey. These latter two males are children of the Wasp Hill rulers, Lord Twelve Lizard and Lady Twelve Grass, as are the deceased males Twelve Vulture and Twelve Lizard (Byland and Pohl 1994:237). In each case, a priest presides over the obsequies: Lord One Lizard for Twelve Vulture and Twelve Lizard, and Ten Rain (who sings of Seven Flower) for Four House and Three Monkey.

This latter ceremony provides an interesting visual device. The year sign—3 Reed—has two reed arrows used as pointers: one points to the Day 6 Dog for Lord Three Monkey, and the other points to the Day 8 Motion for Lord Four House. This tells us that the funerals for the two dead lords did not happen on the same day; rather, the one for Lord Three Monkey happened first, on Day 6 Dog. The mummy ceremony for Lord Four House was conducted second, on Day 8 Motion. Both days—6 Dog and 8 Motion—occur twice in vague solar year 3 Reed, with Day 6 Dog preceding Day 8 Motion always by forty-seven days. The first occurrence of Days 6 Dog/8 Motion are in Tonalpohualli 40, the second in Tonalpohualli 41 of the 52-year cycle.

To avoid confusion of sequence, the original scribe or scribes writing this scene used the unique combination of two reeds/arrows in one A-O year sign as pointers. The use of individual year signs as pointers is not unique, however: it occurs on Zouche-Nuttall Page 5c to connote the death of Lord Eight Wind of Suchixtlan (in Year 2 Reed) and also on Zouche-Nuttall Page 9c to point out the actor Lord Three Reed and distinguish him for the day of a ceremonial event. That day—4 Jaguar—is connected to his foot by a black line. This is an excellent example of a subtle technique employed in narrative structure to assure that the original recitation of events remains specific on certain points.

Page 21a: The War with the Striped Men from the Sky (Figure 6.3)

Tableau 1. Year 12 Flint Day 12 Flint (AD 972). This complex tableau occupies Page 21a. The Zouche-Nuttall cognate for the northern Nochixtlan Valley is Page 4a. The display from top to bottom begins with the sky of the gods Eleven Alligator and Four Alligator. On Page 4a, it was the sky of Two Alligator and Seven Flower and the same year date. The solar disk is between Eleven Alligator and Four Alligator, and directly beneath it is an upturned bowl-shaped cave opening. A Striped Man-warrior with a device possibly representing a thundercloud emerging from his head descends from the cave. To the viewer's left, a warrior making a loud sound and holding what appears to be a heavy object descends from two stars. To the viewer's right, another warrior descends from two stars. He holds an indistinct object in one hand, and water issues from his head. All three descending warriors are in watery, oblong cartouches. Page 4 has a similar correspondence of elements with these descending warriors: the left-hand warrior makes a loud sound and holds a rocklike object, the central warrior holds a starry cloudlike object, and the right-hand warrior holds a gout of water. However, the Page 4 striped warriors are not displayed in watery cartouches. The association of these figures on both pages with meteorological elements is inescapable.

The days for Page 4 are 8 Wind and 8 Alligator in Year 12 Flint. On Page 21a, the event occurs on Day 12 Flint. Twelve Flint is the 38th year of the 52-year cycle. Day 8 Wind occurs once in Year 12 Flint, as day number 257, or eighteen days before the end of Tonalpohualli 53, day 242 of that *tonalpo-hualli*. Day 8 Alligator occurs twice in Year 12 Flint, as days 36 and 296, or days 21 of Tonalpohuallis 53 and 54. Day 12 Flint occurs twice in Year 12 Flint, as days 53 and 313—the 38th day of Tonalpohualli 53 and the 38th day of Tonalpohualli 54.

Tableau 2. The date, Year 12 Flint Day 12 Flint, occurs beneath the sky tableau. To either side of the date are two lords. To the viewer's left, Lord Ten Rain securely grips the long hair of a bleeding head with both his hands. To the viewer's right, Lord Ten Reed holds a grass knot and an incense bag.

Tableau 3. The bottom tableau in this column gives the location of this complex series of events as White Flint Hill, last seen on Page 19b. The central figure of three male figures at White Flint Hill is Lord Nine Wind Quetzalcoatl, last seen on Page 20c killing Stone Men. Lord Nine Wind is armed for war and sacrifice and shouts while looking upward. To the viewer's left is Lord Four Alligator, also armed for war. To the viewer's right is Lord One Alligator, holding the ropes of a bound Striped Man.

Page 21b: Lady One Death Events at Achiutla

The White Flint Hill toponym from Page 21a extends slightly into this tableau, indicating, therefore, that the events shown on Page 21a to 21b are not entirely separate. A significant ceremonial object composed of a round grass mat with a bound bundle emitting flames and two leaves of a sacred plant (last seen on Page 2 at Yucuñudahui) is positioned between columns "a" and "b" of Page 21. The action on Page 21b ascends in three levels.

Tableau 1. The lower level is located as Sun Curtain Hill, which I take to be Achiutla. Lady One Death (last seen on Page 19a) is there, directing her husband, Lord Four Alligator, who moves forward as he holds a bound torch. An eagle ingesting blood walks before him.

Tableau 2. Year 1 Reed Day 1 Alligator (AD 987): This is the beginning of the third Mixtec year cycle, AD 987–AD 1038. The War from Heaven is ended. The middle tableau of Page 21b shows Lord Four Alligator—now attired in a Rain God mask—directing the eagle to enter the temple of Lord Nine Wind Quetzalcoatl. The temple contains a fire-drilling apparatus atop a bound set of staffs and a partly opened bundle. Lord Twelve Wind Smoke-Eye from the Sky stands directly behind Lord Four Alligator. He displays a Venus staff and carries a temple via a tumpline.

Tableau 3. Directly above Lord Twelve Wind is his companion, Lord Three

Flint, carrying a different staff. Directly before Lord Three Flint and above the middle temple tableau is the sky of Four Snake and Four House, who are presumed to be ancestors and the parents of Lady One Death. A solar disk is situated in the middle of the sky display, and a "sun curtain" descends from it. The same solar disk and sun curtain is displayed in the lowest tableau as a toponymic identifier for the hill where the Lady One Death–Lord Four Alligator–blood-ingesting eagle event occurs.

Pages 20–21: Lady One Death

This royal female Lady One Death is a complex figure at best, but an extremely important one. She married the first lord of Tilantongo, Four Alligator, and their daughter (One Vulture) married one of the first lords of Wasp Hill, a prominent site in the Tilantongo Valley and, thus, the southern Nochixtlan Valley. Wasp Hill was founded in the Classic Period (Byland and Pohl 1994:111). The Tilantongo Valley was home to several powerful polities in the Late Classic to early Postclassic Periods: Achiutla (Hill of the Sun), seemingly the location of a Birth Tree apart from the one at Apoala; Tilantongo; Tilantongo's rival, Jaltepec; Hua Chino (Red-and-White Bundle); and Wasp Hill.

Lady One Death and Lord Four Alligator's daughter, One Vulture, and her husband, Four Rabbit, produced daughters who married prominent rulers: Five Reed and Ten Alligator both married the Lord of Hua Chino, while the third daughter, Four Jaguar, married the first ruler of Tilantongo, Lord Nine Wind Stone Skull. The Wasp Hill alliances, and offspring, were destroyed by Lady Nine Grass, the Oracle of the Dead at Chalcatongo, in the War from Heaven (Byland and Pohl 1994:111; Codex Bodley, Pages 3–4-II). Zouche-Nuttall Page 20b–c shows the destruction of the Wasp Hill scions by Lady Nine Grass and the defeat of the indigenous Stone Men by Lord Nine Wind Quetzalcoatl.

However, Achiutla was also the source of a Birth Tree that produced royalty, namely, Lady One Death, who ruled the precinct (Zouche-Nuttall, Page 21b). It is likely also the very Birth Tree that produced the first lords of Jaltepec's first, and failed, dynasty. One Death and her husband, Four Alligator, are displayed as the cult bearers for Achiutla. They act in cooperation with Lord Twelve Wind Smoke-Eye from the Sky and Lord Three Flint to found the fire-drilling bundle cult of Lord Nine Wind Quetzalcoatl there.

How does the figure of Lady One Death relate to the preceding narrative(s) of the Ladies Three Flint? Regarding the story of Lady Three Flint Elder—Zouche-Nuttall, Pages 14–16 and 17–18—the first page (14) introduces her and her husband, Lord Five Flower, then the first two-page set (15–16) provides rituals leading up to the birth of her daughter (Three Flint Younger), after which, on Page 15b, the renamed Lady Three Flint Elder displays her magical abilities by entering the world of the gods and consulting with four prominent figures, among them the Lords Four Deer and Four Death; Lady One Eagle; and her husband, One Grass.

The second two-page set (17–18) shows the apotheosis of Three Flint Elder and her husband, Five Flower, then displays rituals conducted by the supernatural male who will be husband to Lady Three Flint Younger: Lord Twelve Wind Smoke-Eye from the Sky. The last two-page set of panel pages (19a–b) is essentially a dynamic map providing geographical and ritual context for the marriage of Three Flint Younger and her husband, Lord Twelve Wind. This sets up narrative context for Lady One Death, whose birth near Wasp Hill is shown on Page 19a and whose story continues on Page 21b after the War from Heaven. She and her husband, Four Alligator, are identified as the religious/political rulers of Achiutla and its districts.

Figure 6.1.a. Codex Zouche-Nuttall
(obverse), Page 5c. The Pointing Arrows.
© The Trustees of the British Museum.

Figure 6.1.b. Codex Zouche-Nuttall
(obverse), Page 9c. The Pointing Arrow.
© The Trustees of the British Museum.

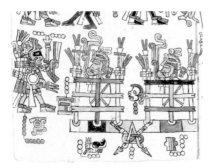

Figure 6.1.c. Codex Zouche-Nuttall
(obverse), Page 20c. The Pointing Arrows.
© The Trustees of the British Museum.

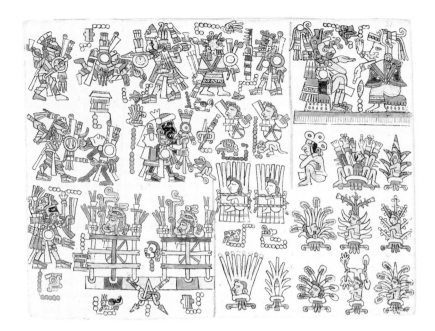

Figure 6.2. Codex Zouche-Nuttall (obverse), Page 20. © The Trustees of the British Museum.

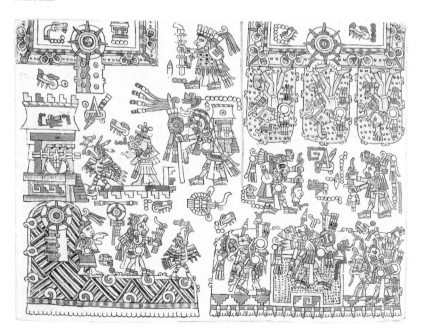

Figure 6.3. Codex Zouche-Nuttall (obverse), Page 21. © The Trustees of the British Museum.

7 Document 1 (Obverse), Part IIB, Pages 22–35: Genealogies

Page 22: A Map Page Corresponding to Double-page 19: The Introduction to the First Dynasty of Tilantongo (Figure 7.1)

This complex panel-page map generally follows the layout established for Double-page 19. The reasoning here is that since the preceding two pages concerning the War from Heaven can be folded out by connecting Double-page 19 to this one, a similarity between them can be drawn as well as deeper inferences regarding content. That is to say, the later founding of the first dynasty of Tilantongo (Page 22) is corresponded in importance to the founding of the previous and now defunct dynasty of Wasp Hill (Double-page 19). The scribes who composed this section of Codex Zouche-Nuttall were writing retrospectively; consequently, they knew that—as was the case with the Wasp Hill dynasties—the first dynasty of Tilantongo also ended. For this reason, the similarity of their portrayals of both dynasties and the ability to connect them for side-by-side comparison is a statement that adds to the story.

The reading order for Page 22 is essentially the same as that for Double-page 19. From the upper right, one follows the descent of individuals from the sky, then the reading order proceeds within the map from right to left, then up the left side and across to the right, to the central event showing Lord Seven Death and Lady One Snake seated at Monte Negro. The dates appearing on Page 22 are shown in Table 7.1.

Lady One Snake begins the narrative on this page. She was the daughter of Lord Four Alligator and Lady One Death, founders of the first reigning house in Tilantongo. She married Lord Seven Death Jaguar, who was perhaps son of the two individuals seated behind him: Lord Four Lizard and Lady Eight House. Alfonso Caso (1984, 2:120a) interprets this relationship as a Teozacoalco tradition and assigns male parentage of Lord Seven Death to

Table 7.1. Dates on Page 22

Date	Event
Year 7 Flint (#46) Day 7 Flint	Lady One Snake in the river
Year 1 Reed	With no day from the *tonalpohualli* attached, this year probably means "beginning."
Year 1 Reed (#1) Day 1 Alligator	The seating of ♂ Seven Death and ♀ One Snake before the ♂ Nine Wind Temple at Monte Negro
	Total = 6 years

a Lord Nine Wind Quetzalcoatl-Flint. A rational for this is that Lord Seven Death is not mentioned elsewhere.

The Day 7 Flint in Year 7 Flint is associated here with Lady One Snake. The Codex Vindobonensis Mexicanus I (Page 1-I) and Codex Bodley assign that date as the beginning of royalty in Tilantongo. This panel-page map displays other married couples representing various districts around Monte Negro, and these individuals may be the offspring of the founding couple, Lord Seven Death and Lady One Snake—at least according to the traditions written here.

Pages 22–35: Genealogies—The First and Second Dynasties of the Lords of Tilantongo

The First Dynasty of Tilantongo

The devastating sixteen-year War from Heaven did not completely eradicate the ruling dynasty at Wasp Hill, only its authority to preside. Lady One Vulture and Lord Four Rabbit married at Wasp Hill (Codex Bodley 3-I). Of their three daughters, two married into the ruling family at Hua Chino (Red-and-White Bundle) and one married the first named lord of Tilantongo (Bodley 4-I, 4-V), Lord Nine Wind Stone Skull. He married Lady Five Reed of Wasp Hill (Codex Vindobonensis Mexicanus I reverse, Page IV; Codex Bodley, 4-V). Thus the lineage survived in the female princesses of Wasp Hill and began two dynasties that would, in time, become rivals—Hua Chino and Tilantongo.

It is possible that this migration of three royal females from Wasp Hill accounts for the similarity in format between Double-page 19 of Codex

Zouche-Nuttall (Wasp Hill) and Page 22, the introduction of the first dynasty at Tilantongo.

Although the reading order for Page 22 is obvious, the events displayed thereon are not. The presence of and descent of Lord Twelve Wind Smoke-Eye from the Sky (associated with Wasp Hill and married to its last female queen, Lady Three Flint Younger) indicates the genealogical affinity between his family at Wasp Hill and the new first dynasty of Tilantongo. The water ceremony—a conflated tableau of Lady One Snake in Year 7 Flint on Day 7 Flint—may be similar in importance to the water journey undertaken by Lady Three Flint Elder immediately after the birth of her daughter. If so, it would represent a local tradition for prime ruling families. Also, Lady Three Flint Younger and Lord Twelve Wind Smoke-Eye from the Sky underwent a water ceremony at their betrothal. The rulers of Red-and-White Bundle (Hua Chino), Lady Seven Flower and Lord Four Rain, are displayed with the date Year 1 Reed, but the expected Day 1 Alligator is absent. The last tableau at the lower left of Page 22 shows Lord Six Motion and his wife, Lady Nine House, in their district but without a date.

Moving up the left side of the page, in the valley between Rabbit Hill and Monte Negro, we see the rulers Lord One Motion and his wife, Lady Ten House. Above them, the dominant tableau appears at the top of the page. The lords of Monte Negro—Lord Seven Death and Lady One Snake—are enthroned there. Lady Eight House and Lord Four Lizard—who are either their children or the parents of Lord Seven Death—appear behind them.

Behind Lady One Snake is a sky temple featuring an animated open bundle inside it. A full-figure Lord Nine Wind Quetzalcoatl emerges from the bundle and faces the married couple seated on Monte Negro. The date, Year 1 Reed Day 1 Alligator, appears between the temple and Monte Negro, and the implied meaning of "it happened long ago" or "beginning" is assumed. It is also a specific date recording the beginning of a calendar cycle. In a previous tableau containing this Nine Wind Quetzalcoatl bundle—Page 15b in the district of Jaltepec—no full figure of Lord Nine Wind emerges.

The other temple bundles displayed in preceding tableaux (Pages 17b, 18b, 19a) have both fire-drilling and Quetzalcoatl associations. This fire-drilling association is emphasized in the temple tableau shown at Achiutla on Page 21b. The husband of Lady One Death (Lord Four Alligator) proceeds at her direction from Sun Curtain Hill to the Nine Wind Temple, where he presents an eagle consuming blood. The eagle descends into or emerges from a cave directly before the temple with its contained bundle displayed before the eagle–Lord Four Alligator complex. The date for this tableau on Page 21b is Year 1 Reed Day 1 Alligator. The Page 21b scene at Achiutla is also emphasized by a descent of Lord Twelve Wind Smoke-Eye from the Sky and his companion, Lord Three Flint. On Page 21b at Achiutla, Lord Twelve Wind Smoke-Eye bears the temple in a tumpline. On Page 22, Lord Three Flint, not Twelve Wind Smoke-Eye, carries the temple via tumpline.

These symbolic representations imply both similarities and dissimilarities between the scenes in which they appear. On Pages 18b, 19a, 21b, and 22, the descent from the sky tableaux always features these two males in association: Twelve Wind Smoke-Eye and Three Flint. On Pages 18b, 19a, and 21b, Lord Twelve Wind Smoke-Eye is always the temple bearer and appears first in the processional descent. Although he appears in the sky descent on Page 22 and is first in line, Lord Three Flint is the temple bearer. In fact, in the descent tableau on Page 22, Lord Three Flint, bearing the temple, actually appears directly behind the temple; this juxtaposition of static images reinforces Three Flint's association with the founding of Nine Wind Temple in the district of Monte Negro.

It is difficult to avoid the conclusion that Lord Twelve Wind Smoke-Eye from the Sky has retained prominence by appearing first in procession, but is demoted in rank and no longer bears the temple from sky to earth. Codex Bodley (reverse) indicates that a Lord Three Flint was instrumental in or at least present at the destruction of the Wasp Hill dynasties. His figure is shown venerating the mummy bundles of the Wasp Hill lineage leaders on Bodley 35-I.

Pages 23–24: The Linear Genealogy of the First Dynasty of Tilantongo (Figures 7.2, 7.3)

1. Page 23a. Year 11 House Day 10 House (AD 944).

a. At Conquered Stone Man River, Lord Ten House + Lady One Grass. She is the daughter of the Tree-born Apoala lineage founders, Lord Five Wind and Lady Nine Alligator (Caso 1960:20b).

b. Their son is Lord Three Eagle.

c. Lord Three Eagle + Lady Four Rabbit. They have two sons, named Thirteen Eagle and Six Deer.

+45 years

d. At Maguey Hill, the son of Lord Three Eagle and Lady Four Rabbit is Lord Nine Wind Stone Skull. He marries Lady Five Reed. Codex Zouche-

Nuttall does not record the year for this marriage, but Codices Vindobonensis Mexicanus I and Bodley do. It is in the third Mixtec year cycle (AD 987–AD 1038): Year 4 Rabbit (AD 989).

+2 years

2. Page 23b. Their children, Lord Ten Flower, born in Year 6 Flint (AD 991), and Lord Five Motion.

+21 years

a. Lord Ten Flower + Lady Two Snake in Year 1 House (AD 1013). The date is from Codex Bodley 5-V.

+30 years

b. Their children are Lady Twelve Jaguar and Lord Twelve Lizard Arrow Legs.

3. Page 23c. Lord Twelve Lizard Arrow Legs + Ladies Four Alligator and Four Flint in Year 5 Reed (AD 1043). These two sisters are his nieces (Caso 1960:31a).

a. Their children are:

+4 years

1) Lord Two Grass + Lady Thirteen Grass in Year 9 Reed Day 4 Jaguar (AD 1047);

2) at Teozacoalco, Lord Ten Reed + Lady Twelve Jaguar.

3) The other children are: Lords Nine Monkey, Ten Grass, and Nine Lizard; Ladies One Vulture and One Rain; and Lords Ten Flower and Eight Eagle. Note: Lady One Vulture will marry Lord Thirteen Dog of Tilantongo's second dynasty. They are the parents of Lord Five Alligator, the father of Lord Eight Deer Jaguar Claw.

b. On Page 24a, there are more offspring: Lords Twelve Water and Five Motion, and Ladies Three Motion and One Flint.

+28 years

4. Page 24a–b. Lords Twelve Water and Five Motion, and Ladies Three Motion and One Flint.

a. Lord Five Motion + Lady Two Death. Their child is the controversial Lord Two Rain Twenty Jaguars, born in Year 11 Reed on Day 9 Reed (AD 1075) but named on Day 2 Rain.

Lord Two Rain Twenty Jaguars is the last king of Tilantongo's first dynasty. Both Codices Nuttall and Vindobonensis give two days for his birth: 9 Reed and 2 Rain. According to Caso (1960:31b), the Day 9 Reed is unlucky and falls only six days before Day 2 Rain, so it seems that this prince was named on the better day. He died unmarried and childless in AD 1096 and was, therefore, the last king of Tilantongo's first dynasty. However, there was an interregnum listed for other places, and it dates to AD 1091.

+16 years

b. Year 1 Reed Day 1 Alligator (AD 1091). Lord Six Death + Lady Six Water. The toponym indicates that they are not lords of Tilantongo.

5. Page 24c. Lord Nine Flint + Lady Seven Deer. Their children are the Ladies Two Monkey, Twelve Grass, and Eleven Water.

a. Lord Nine Lizard + Lady Ten Vulture.

b. Lord Five Reed + Lady Two Motion.

From AD 944 to AD 1075 is 131 years, plus 16 years = 146 years recorded for the first dynasty of Tilantongo.

The Second Dynasty of Tilantongo

The third marriage of this dynasty records that Lord Thirteen Dog wed Lady One Vulture (see Page 23c, above), who was originally from Wasp Hill antecedents. She was the aunt of Lord Five Motion (Codex Zouche-Nuttall, Page 23b) of Tilantongo's first dynasty. He was the father of the ill-fated Lord Two Rain Twenty Jaguars. Lord Thirteen Dog and Lady One Vulture were parents to Lord Five Alligator, father of Lord Eight Deer Jaguar Claw of Tilantongo, who is the subject of the entire Zouche-Nuttall reverse (Document 2). He appears in every major surviving Mixtec codex as well as on the Mapa de Teozacoalco. This observation has been extant since the beginning of the twentieth century (Clark 1912; Caso 1960:37b).

The schematic of the second Tilantongo dynasty listed below is offered without elaboration. The same dynasty recorded on the reverse of Codex Vindobonensis Mexicanus I (V-3) begins with Lord Thirteen Dog and Lady One Vulture, as is also the case with Codex Bodley (6-I). However, in the Zouche-Nuttall text, the dynastic recording begins earlier than in either Vindobonensis or Bodley, with Lord Two Water and Lady Four Jaguar, then proceeds with Two Water's second marriage, to Lady Ten Snake, who were parents of Lord Thirteen Dog. Therefore, noting here the extra generation in Zouche-Nuttall and its omission in Vindobonensis and Bodley, further elaboration is omitted below.

Pages 25–26: The Linear Genealogy of the Second Dynasty of Tilantongo (Figures 7.4, 7.5)

1. Page 25a, beginning at the bottom right. Year 8 Reed Day 10 Alligator (AD 1005).

2. Toponym—place of origin of the dynastic family, identified by Pohl (1994:35) as Ayuta/Atoyaquillo in the Achiutla Valley—with Lord Two Water + Lady Four Jaguar.

3. Lord Two Water + Lady Ten Alligator.

4. Page 25b. Their children, Lords Thirteen Dog and Three Snake.

5. Lord Thirteen Dog + Lady One Vulture. As remarked before, she was the aunt of Lord Five Motion (Page 24b), who was the father of Lord Two Rain, the last king of Tilantongo's first dynasty (Caso 1960:33a).

6. Page 25b–c. Their son, Five Alligator, was chief of the Council of Four at Tilantongo.

+24 years (from Year 8 Reed, Page 25a, to Year 5(6) Reed, below)

7. Page 25c. Year 5(6) Reed Day 1 Alligator (AD 1030). Lord Five Alligator auto-sacrifices before the fire-drilling bundle temple.

+6 years

8. Year 12 House Day 7 Motion (AD 1036). Lord Five Alligator and another male engaged in a ceremony.

9. Page 26a. Beginning at top right, Year 6 Flint Day 7 Eagle (AD 1043). Lord Five[1] Alligator + Lady Nine Eagle.

10. Their children:

   a. Year 7 House Day 12 Motion (AD 1045): Lord Twelve Motion,

   b. Lord Three Water,

   c. Lady Six Lizard.

11. Page 26a–b. Year 10 House Day 6 Deer (AD 1061): Lord Five Alligator + Lady Eleven Water.

12. Their children:

   a. Year 12 Reed Day 8 Deer (AD 1063): Lord Eight Deer Jaguar Claw;

   b. Year 3 Reed Day 9 Flower (AD 1067): Lord Nine Flower;

   c. Year 13(12) Flint Day 9 Monkey (AD 1076): Lady Nine Monkey.

13. Page 26c. Year 13 Reed Day 12 Snake (AD 1103). Lord Eight Deer Jaguar Claw + Lady Thirteen Snake of Hua Chino (Red-and-White Bundle). She is sister to the executed scions of Hua Chino (Ten Dog and Six House) and also Eight Deer's niece (Byland and Pohl 1994:243).

14. Their children are:
    a. Year 7 Rabbit (AD 1110): Lord Four Dog Peccary;
    b. Year 9 Flint (AD 1112): Lord Four Alligator.

Discussion

This section relates the brief biography of Lord Five Alligator and provides the parentage statements of his children. It departs from a linear genealogy form and tells of Five Alligator's status as a member of the Council of Four and displays two important ceremonies he undertook. Codex Vindobonensis Mexicanus I reverse provides a similar discourse for this remarkable man.

Vindobonensis begins Five Alligator's story on Page V-3 immediately after the death of Lord Two Rain Twenty Jaguars of Tilantongo. It lists Five Alligator's parents, Lord Thirteen Dog and Lady One Vulture. Subsequently, Five Alligator is displayed as chief of the Council of Four, and they are before a temple. A Zapotec-style date is shown: Year 13 Owl. Then Five Alligator meets with two priests (one of whom is named Ten Reed). After the meeting, before a temple in Year 6 Reed Day 5 Arrow (AD 1030), there is a procession of individuals: a male in Year 10 Reed Day 9 Reed (AD 1034) and another male in Year 1 Reed on Day 1 Alligator (AD 1038). Subsequently, in Year 5 Reed on Day 7 Eagle (AD 1042), another male is displayed. Then Lord Five Alligator marries Lady Seven (Nine) Eagle. Their first child is born in Year 7 House on Day 11(12) Motion (AD 1045). Subsequently, Lady Six Lizard is born in Year 8(9) Reed on that day (AD 1047). The last child of Five Alligator's first marriage is Lord Three Water, who was born on that day in Year 9(10) Flint (AD 1048). Then Five Alligator marries Lady Eleven Water in Year 11(10) House on Day 6 Deer (AD 1061; Vindobonensis VII-1). The last note of Lord Five Alligator in Codex Vindobonensis Mexicanus I displays his death in Year 5 Rabbit on Day 7 Dog (AD 1092).

The Codex Bodley biography of Lord Five Alligator is even more fulsome. In that codex, Five Alligator's parentage statement begins on Page 6-I with the toponymic identifier for his parents, followed by Lord Thirteen Dog facing his wife, One Vulture. A natal cord issues from Lady One Vulture and connects to Lord Five Alligator, who faces away from them and toward the events on the next page. No birth year is provided. Five Alligator's biography occupies the entirety of Bodley Pages 7–8.

According to the Bodley pictography, Five Alligator pursues a dedicated and ambitious life. On Pages 7-I–8-I, in Year 13 House on Day 10 Flower (AD 1025), three priests visit Five Alligator, who is, presumably, a very young boy. Gifts are presented (to Five Alligator), and he travels to a district ruled by Lord Seven Motion, where Five Alligator either presents gifts to Seven Motion or receives gifts from him. Subsequently, Five Alligator travels to Snake River, the ancestral home of the rulers of Tilantongo, and offers gifts there. On Pages 7-II–8-II, two priests—Ten Flower, who bears a torch, and Seven Reed, blowing a conch trumpet—greet Five Alligator.

Still in Year 13 House but on Day 7 Motion—237 days after Day 10 Flower—Lord Five Alligator offered incense at the Temple of Heaven in Tilantongo. In Year 6 Reed on Day 1 Alligator (AD 1031), Five Alligator received symbols of rank (flint knives, *xicolli*, and a fan); in Year 10 Reed (AD 1035) and in Year 1 Reed (AD 1039), his rank advanced. In that year on Day 1 Alligator, Lord Five Alligator (Pages 7-III–8-III) received status gifts from two priests. Maarten Jansen and G. A. Pérez Jiménez (2005:60b) interpret this final status presentation as Five Alligator having completed twelve years of service in the Temple of Heaven at Tilantongo and now having the status to marry. This is logical because his marriage to Lady Eleven Water is displayed next, for Year 5 Reed on Day 7 Eagle (AD 1043). However, the scribes for Bodley are in error, listing as they do Five Alligator's second marriage (to Lady Eleven Water) as his first. Next is presented a lengthy description of Lady Eleven Water's parentage and previous marriage and offspring by that previous marriage. Subsequently, the children of her marriage with Five Alligator are listed: in Year 7 House, Lord Twelve Motion Jaguar Head (Pages 8-IV–7-IV); in Year 9 Reed (AD 1047), Lady Six Lizard Jeweled Fan; in Year 10 Flint (AD 1048), Lord Nine Motion the Hummingbird; in Year 10 House (AD 1061), Lord Three Water Cormorant. The sons Three Water and Nine Motion were killed in battle in Year 9 Rabbit on Day 8 Death (AD 1086) at Quetzal Town. In Year 10 House on Day 6 Deer (AD 1061), Lord Five Alligator married his second wife, Lady Nine Eagle. Her parentage statement follows.

The children of the second marriage (actually the children of Lady Eleven Water and Five Alligator) were: Lord Eight Deer Jaguar Claw, born in Year 12 Reed (AD 1063); Lord Nine Flower, born in Year 3 Reed (AD 1067), and a daughter, Lady Nine Monkey, born in Year 13 Flint (AD 1064).

After a lengthy, interesting, and distinguished career, Lord Five Alligator died in Year 5 Rabbit on Day 9 Dog (AD 1082). His biography is elaborated and all his distinguished accomplishments noted in Codex Bodley because the prestige of the father attaches to the son—in this case Lord Eight Deer Jaguar Claw, who is mentioned in every major codex and who, during the course of his career, accomplished close relationships with the Toltecs and, ultimately, the unification of the Mixteca.

Bodley does not seem to mention (or else I do not recognize it in the pictography) the event mentioned in both Codices Zouche-Nuttall obverse and Vindobonensis reverse, namely, that he was president of a governing entity I call "the Council of Four" at Tilantongo. No date is provided for it in Codex Zouche-Nuttall, Page 25b–c, or in Vindobonensis Pages V-III-6-3, and therefore it cannot be corresponded with the Bodley pictography by date. The Council of Four is, however, mentioned in two preconquest codices as an important function of Lord Five Alligator and is a part of his prestige. On Vindobonensis Mexicanus I Pages 14–15, important priests grouped as a procession of four individuals appear bearing gifts to the Oracle of the Dead, Lady Nine Grass of Chalcatongo. Four such individuals are displayed again on Vindobonensis Page 36, but in different ceremonial attire. Pohl (1994:35) considers these four individuals to be stakeholders who, though not in the direct line of royal succession, nevertheless exercised significant religious, political, and economic functions within the structure of Mixtec society.

Five Alligator is presented in Codex Bodley as a religious functionary (priest), political entity, and important progenitor of his famous son, the warlord, politician, and usurper of Tilantongo, Lord Eight Deer Jaguar Claw.

Pages 27–28: From Tilantongo to Teozacoalco (Figures 7.6 and 7.7)

1. Page 27a presents the other wives of Lord Eight Deer Jaguar Claw.
    a. Ladies Ten Vulture, Six Wind, Eleven Snake, and Ten Flower.
    b. In Year 2 House Day 3 Deer (AD 1105), Eight Deer married Lady Five Eagle.
2. Page 27b. The children of Eight Deer and Five Eagle are:
    a. born in Year 9 Flint (AD 1112), Lord Six House (Page 27a),
    b. Lord Ten Motion,
    c. Lady Two Grass, and,
    d. on Page 27c, Lord Five Dog. This son of Lord Eight Deer Jaguar Claw of Tilantongo and Lady Five Eagle marries into the dynasty of Teozacoalco. At this point in the pictography, Page 27c and 28a ascend together

as one column, with the first four ascending figures in both columns facing one another.

    3. Pages 27c and 28a.

        a. In Year 9 House on Day 6 Eagle (AD 1025), Lord Five Dog married Lady Six Wind of Teozacoalco.

        b. Lord Four Dog (born in Year 7 Rabbit [AD 1110], son of Eight Deer and Lady Thirteen Snake) + Lady Four Death of Teozacoalco.

The child of Four Dog and Lady Four Death is Lord Thirteen Dog, who, in Year 8 House on Day 4 Dog (AD 1137) marries Lady Eight Vulture at Teozacoalco. He also marries Lady Four Rabbit. Their children are:

        1) born in Year 7 House (AD 1149), Lord Seven Water, and

        2) Lord Three Wind.

    3. Lord Seven Water + Lady Eleven Water at Teozacoalco.

        a. Their sons are Thirteen Eagle and . . .

Pages 29–31 (Figures 7.8, 7.9, 7.10)

        b. . . . . on Page 29a, Lord Nine Wind.

    4. In Year 5(6) Reed (AD 1187), Lord Thirteen Eagle + Lady Thirteen Death at Teozacoalco. Their children are:

        a. on Page 29b, Lord Two Wind Death Jaguar;

        b. Lord One Eagle;

        c. on Page 29c, Lady Ten Deer Jaguar Pelt Quechquemitl;

        d. the Lords Eight Snake and Two Flower; and

        e. Lady Seven House.

    5. On Page 30a, Lord Thirteen Eagle married for the second time. His wife is shown as Lady Eight Reed Little Child at Teozacoalco. The children of Lord Thirteen Eagle's second marriage are:

        a. born in Year 8 House (AD 1189), Lord Eight Rabbit Moving Fire Temple;

        b. an unnamed female who may be Lord Eight Rabbit's fraternal twin;

        c. Lady Eleven Motion; and on Page 30b, the Ladies Ten Deer, Thirteen Rabbit, and Nine Monkey, and their brother, Lord Six Water.

    6. Lord Eight Rabbit (see 5a, above) + Lady 6 Grass at Teozacoalco. Their children are:

        a. on Page 31a, Lord Twelve House;

        b. another male named House, but without a number, whose personal name is something like Jaguar Blood Sky;

c. the Lords Three Rabbit; and, on Page 31b, Eight Dog; and

d. Lady Eleven Alligator.

7. On Page 31b–c, Lady Eleven Alligator + Lord Twelve House at Teoza-coalco. Their children are:

a. Lord Twelve Dog and

b. Lord Nine Motion + Lady Two Jaguar at Teozacoalco. Their children are:

1) the Ladies Four Death,

2) One Eagle,

3) Four Rabbit, and,

4) on Page 32a, Lady Six Reed.

Page 32 (Figure 7.11)

1. On Page 32a, Lady Six Reed + Lord Two Dog at Teozacoalco. Their children are:

a. the Ladies Six Flint and Six Water and

b. Lord Nine House.

2. Lord Nine House + Lady Three Rabbit. Their children are:

a. the Lords Two Water and Eight Flint and

b. the Ladies Five Eagle Flints and Four Deer.

3. Lord Two Water + Lady Two Vulture at Teozacoalco. Their children are:

a. the Ladies Twelve Flower and Three Alligator,

b. Lord Five Reed Twenty Jaguars Twenty Pearls, and, . . .

Page 33a (Figure 7.12)

. . . on Page 33a, Lady Twelve Reed, Lord Five Rain Hummingbird, Lady Eight Wind, and Lord Ten Vulture Fire Serpent Hummingbird.

The families of Tilantongo and Teozacoalco end on Page 33a.

Page 33b: The Families of Zaachila and Teozacoalco

1. Year 1 Flint Day 1 Flint (AD 1312 or AD 1260). At Mitla, Lord Seven Rain Xipe-Totec is in the temple. Lord Five Flower of Zaachila + Lady Four Rabbit. Lady Four Rabbit appears on Page 31c as the daughter of Lord Nine Motion and Lady Two Jaguar of Teozacoalco. Lord Five Flower also marries Lady Ten Monkey, and their royal descent of Zaachila is shown on Pages

34–35 of Codex Zouche-Nuttall and also on the Lienzo de Guevea (Byland and Pohl 1994:251).

2. Their son Nine Snake + Lady Eleven Rabbit. Their children are: . . .

Pages 34–35: The Families of Teozacoalco and Zaachila (Figures 7.13, 7.14)

    a. . . . Lord Two Dog Flint Belt;

    b. Lady Eleven Flint; and

    c. the Ladies Two Reed, Ten Monkey, and Two Vulture.

    d. Lord Three Alligator.

1. Lord Three Alligator + Ladies Twelve Flint and Ten House at Teozacoalco. Their children are:

    a. Lords One Grass and Eleven Water;

    b. Lady Two Vulture and an unnamed female; and,

    c. on Page 35a, Lord Twelve Alligator Flints Little Man.

2. On Page 35b, Lord Eleven Water + Ladies Eight Motion and Thirteen Snake. His children by Lady Eight Motion are:

    a. Ladies Three Alligator and Two Jaguar;

    b. Lord Eleven Motion; and,

    c. on Page 35c, the Ladies Seven Alligator and Nine Alligator; and

    d. Lord Six Water Three Staffs.

Discussion

The first section of Codex Zouche-Nuttall obverse (Document 1) ends with five pages of genealogy (Pages 9–13). The second section ends with thirteen pages of genealogy (Pages 22–35), and the third or last section ends with two genealogical pages (Pages 40–41). By observing the rule of space showing importance, the second section's concluding genealogies occupy the most page space in Codex Zouche-Nuttall Document 1.

The genealogies of the second section record the first and second dynasties of Tilantongo, and the majority of the pagination is devoted to the dynasties of Teozacoalco (Pages 27–35), including the statement on Page 33 regarding the marriage of the Zapotec Lord Five Flower of Zaachila and the Mixtec Lady Four Rabbit at Mitla—eight pages in all. Therefore nearly 61 percent of the genealogy pages related to the second dynasty of Tilantongo are devoted to the lords of Teozacoalco. The Map of Teozacoalco (Figure 1.1) has this inscription in Spanish:

> These are the principals and lords and ladies that in ancient times went from the town of Tilanton to this one of Teozacoalco, and their successors, who are alive today, Don Felipe de Santiago and Don Francisco de Mendoza, his son. (Caso 1998)

Alfonso Caso (1949:9) notes that the map, painted on European paper, was made as part of the Relación by Hernando de Cervantes and the priest, Juan Ruiz Zuazo. He goes on to say that from the artistic perspective of the map, one sees an example of how much the "precious indigenous drawing of the pre-Columbian manuscripts had degenerated when it was exposed to European technique; but the map is interesting also because we can see that even by 1580, only sixty years after the Conquest, a rapid process of the mingling of the two cultures (*mestizaje*) had begun."

The establishment of Tilantongo as the royal genealogical source for Teozacoalco by the Colonial Period Map of Teozacoalco explains the large amount of pagination devoted to the dynasties in Codex Zouche-Nuttall obverse. This emphasis is also evidentiary of the nobles who commissioned this section of the manuscript text in pre-Hispanic times.

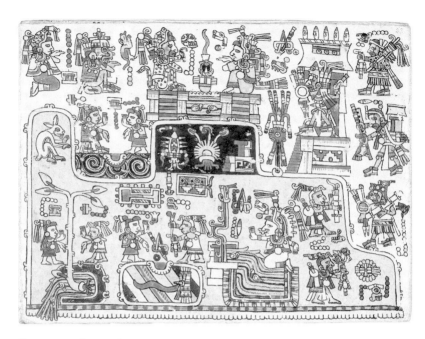

Figure 7.1. Codex Zouche-Nuttall (obverse), Page 22. © The Trustees of the British Museum.

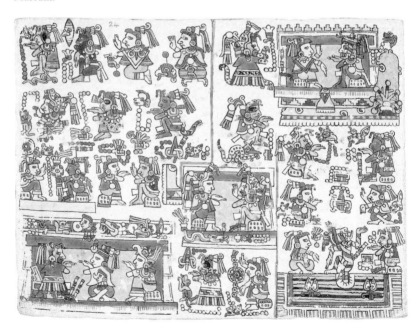

Figure 7.2. Codex Zouche-Nuttall (obverse), Page 23. © The Trustees of the British Museum.

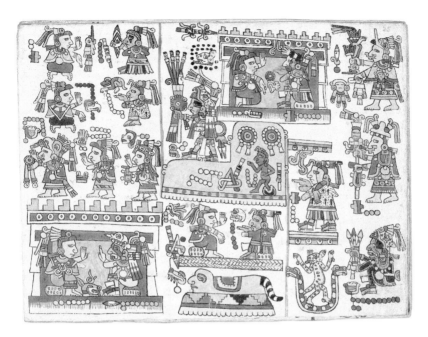

Figure 7.3. Codex Zouche-Nuttall (obverse), Page 24. © The Trustees of the British Museum.

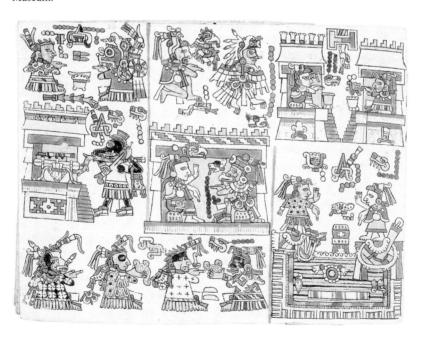

Figure 7.4. Codex Zouche-Nuttall (obverse), Page 25. © The Trustees of the British Museum.

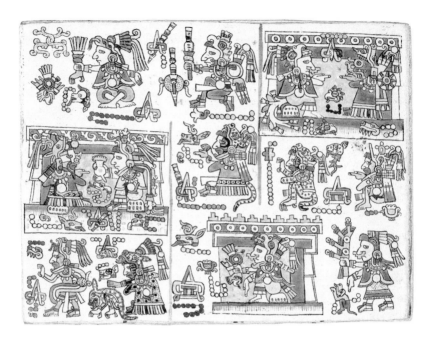

Figure 7.5. Codex Zouche-Nuttall (obverse), Page 26. © The Trustees of the British Museum.

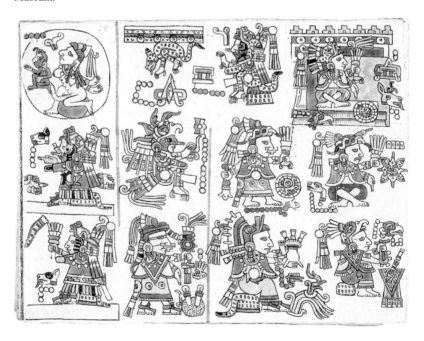

Figure 7.6. Codex Zouche-Nuttall (obverse), Page 27. © The Trustees of the British Museum.

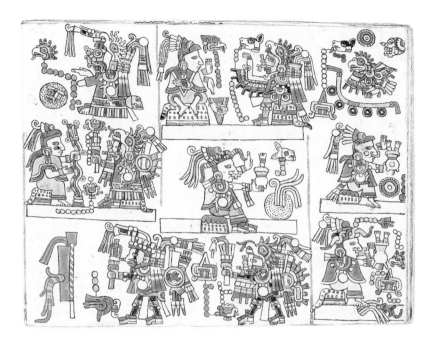

Figure 7.7. Codex Zouche-Nuttall (obverse), Page 28. © The Trustees of the British Museum.

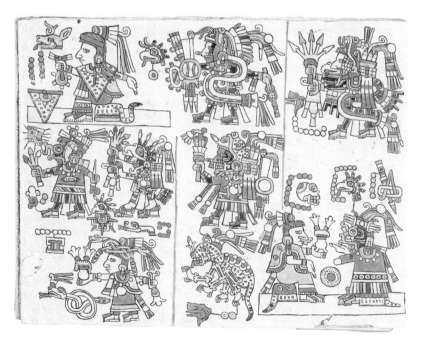

Figure 7.8. Codex Zouche-Nuttall (obverse), Page 29. © The Trustees of the British Museum.

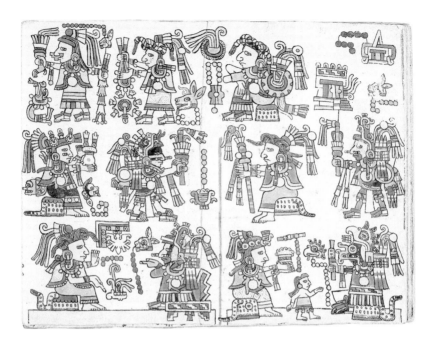

Figure 7.9. Codex Zouche-Nuttall (obverse), Page 30. © The Trustees of the British Museum.

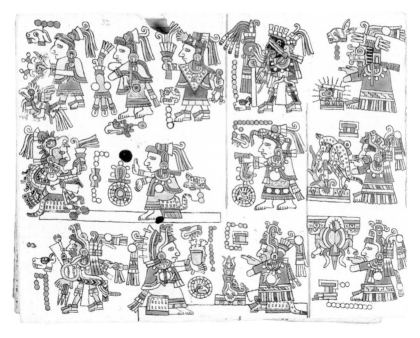

Figure 7.10. Codex Zouche-Nuttall (obverse), Page 31. © The Trustees of the British Museum.

Figure 7.11. Codex Zouche-Nuttall (obverse), Page 32. © The Trustees of the British Museum.

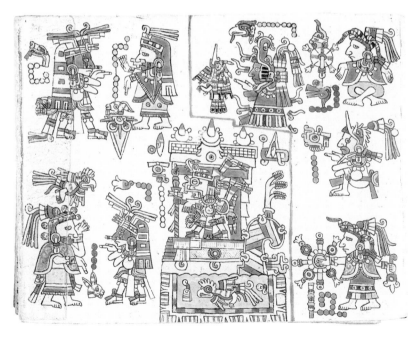

Figure 7.12. Codex Zouche-Nuttall (obverse), Page 33. © The Trustees of the British Museum.

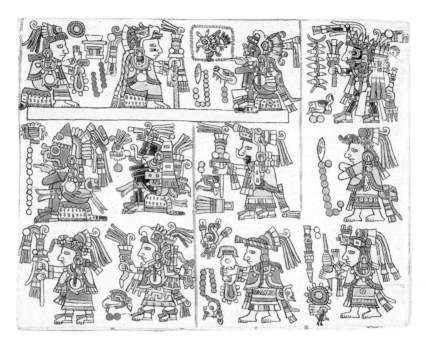

Figure 7.13. Codex Zouche-Nuttall (obverse), Page 34. © The Trustees of the British Museum.

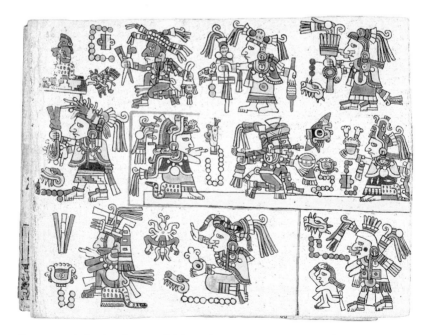

Figure 7.14. Codex Zouche-Nuttall (obverse), Page 35. © The Trustees of the British Museum.

8   Document 1 (Obverse), Part IIIA–B, Pages 36–41: The Four Lords from Apoala

As is the case with Codex Zouche-Nuttall Document 1, Parts I and II, Part III presents an introductory story and a final genealogy. This final episode and genealogy differ, however, from the preceding two in that whereas Parts I and II were amazingly complex, obscure, and busy, this Part III is amazingly simple, straightforward, and obscure. The most obvious difference between Part III and the others is that it employs a different narrative structure. It has no boustrophedon to determine reading order. Instead it progresses by a right-to-left footpath that moves the reader's attention from Page 36 to Page 39 (see Figure 8.7). While footpaths and footprints are not unknown in Mixtec codices, they seldom appear as replacements for boustrophedon determination by red lines. Even where no red lines are used to determine reading order—for example, Zouche-Nuttall Pages 1–2, 14, and 40—footpaths seldom replace them. An exception in the preceding Zouche-Nuttall narrative occurs on Double-page 19, where a footpath directs us from Wasp Hill to the site of Lady Three Flint Younger and Lord Twelve Wind Smoke-Eye from the Sky's nuptial bath.

As mentioned above, Pages 1 and 2 of Zouche-Nuttall Part I have no boustrophedon to determine reading order. But if one reads them by a similarity of dates, they progress in a roughly linear fashion, and the final date connects with the first date on Page 3, Year 3 Reed in both cases. If, however, one reads Pages 1 and 2 by a chronological progression of dates, then it reads in a roughly circular fashion from lower right to upper right, Pages 3 and 4 depicting the War from Heaven can be omitted by folding out, and then Page 2 can be connected directly to Page 5 to create a biography of Lord Eight Wind Eagle Flints of Suchixtlan as lineage founder. Pages 14, 19, and 22 have no boustrophedon. Pages 19 and 22 have a similarity to Pages 1 and 2, however. For reasons explained previously in the text, Page 19 can connect directly to Page 22, and the second telling of the War from Heaven on Pages 20 and 21 can be omitted. This indicates that in the instances cited, there are two ways to read these sections just mentioned: one is a more or less obvious manner of reading, and the other is less obvious, or occulted. The third story, "The Four Lords from Apoala," also contains occulted data. It can be read in the obvious fashion, according to the footpath from its beginning on Page 36 to its conclusion on Page 39; or a second, occulted manner of reading can be utilized to produce an alternate version of the story.

This third story has other distinguishing characteristics of narrative structure, namely, as is the case with Pages 14 and 40–41, there are generally two levels of text, upper and lower, but this is not necessarily unvarying because the scribes produced their literature to be visually creative. This practice of visual creativity is displayed throughout Codex Zouche-Nuttall Document 1 for the same reasons that authors using closed (alphabetic or symbolic) writing systems strive for linguistic variety and creativity. The lower registers of Pages 36–39 are generally toponymic and associated with static, identifying personnel. This is especially obvious on Pages 36, 37b–38, and 39.

As is the case with the usual forms of boustrophedon texts, Pages 36–39 do have red lines. Page 37 has a red line extending from the top to approximately three-quarters of the distance down the page; it creates 37a and 37b. A second red line is more difficult to distinguish because it is found in the worn page fold separating Pages 38 and 39 and extends from the bottom of the fold approximately one-half the distance up the page, terminating just below the beginning of the guiding footpath. This means that in the final story of Codex Zouche-Nuttall, red lines are used as page dividers to distinguish topics on those pages and not used to enforce a boustrophedon reading sequence.

This narrative story occurs in three parts or episodes. The first of them is an introduction on Page 36. The second episode occurs on Pages 37–38 and consists of the journey to Sayutepec (Page 37a) and then the ceremony conducted at Sayutepec (Pages 37b–38b). Because this ceremony occupies the most pagination of any one episode in this four-page story, it is the focus of narrative attention. The third episode is the conclusion on Page 39 at Yanhuitlán (Pohl, personal communication, 2011). As is the case in both Parts I and II, and as mentioned previously, this story (Part III) contains occulted data and, consequently, there are two ways to read it.

The first or obvious reading is to proceed along the footpath from Page 36 to Page 39. The second or occulted reading is the less obvious procedure and will be demonstrated in the text. Also, the second episode can be distinguished from the third or final episode by the use of two visual devices: first, the red line in the eroded page fold extending approximately one-half of the way up the page, beginning at the bottom; and second, the actors in the Sayutepec ceremony (the major subject of the second episode) face against the right-to-left reading order, indicating a visual stop. The visual stop has been demonstrated for the pictographic structures in Part II. This latter device—the visual stop—provides the hint of occulted data; subsequently that hint is reinforced by the recorded chronology of events.

It must also be noted that on Page 38 the scribes appear to have switched the day names of Lords One and Seven Rain. Virtually all of the visual identifiers for Seven Rain now have the day name One Rain attached, and vice versa. Even the placement of the footpath behind the supposedly misidentified One Rain (who should be Seven Rain) suggests a mistake. Seven Rain—on Page 39—leads the procession away from Sayutepec, yet on Page 38 the footpath appears behind the male identified as One Rain but who appears to be Seven Rain in every aspect.

Page 36: First Episode: Introduction at Apoala (Figure 8.1)

This introductory page has upper and lower levels of text. The toponym for Apoala is static and occupies the majority of the page. It consists of a U-shaped bracket defining stone valley walls that extend upward approximately three-quarters of the page on the right and left. The upper-right valley wall displays a waterfall topped by a tree. The waterfall flows over the lower part of a human body and is an Aztec pictogram word, *tzin*, a suffix derived from *tzintli* (buttocks) and meaning "little." Directly beneath the waterfall and next to the valley wall is a white-fringed circle with a mouthlike cave opening from which a red-colored sound emerges. The circle has a red and green interior. Directly beneath this circular device is a white-fringed square with a red border, a green interior, and a central red spot.

An open-mouthed serpent's head facing right tops the left-hand valley wall. This is an Apoala Valley feature, similar to the waterfall, and in this case represents Serpent's Mouth Cave, named in Colonial Period times as the Archbishop's Cave. Directly above the Serpent's Mouth Cave is a round grass mat, horizontally divided by a red-and-white bound bundle.

The bottom of the U-shaped bracket represents the stone valley floor, and two rivers are shown there. The river to the viewer's left displays Lord One

Flower and Lady Thirteen Flower. They are the lineage founders for the Tree-born Lords at Apoala. The river contains a conch, an eel-like fish, two snails, and a grass knot. Lady Nine Alligator and Lord Five Wind are seated on a river shown at the viewer's right. She is the daughter of the Lord One Flower and Lady Thirteen Flower; he is the grandson of Lord Nine Wind Quetzal-coatl. Their river has the toponymic identifier for Apoala: a hand holding a green feather plume. It also displays a fish and an open bivalve shell. This toponym stands in contrast to the usually conflated Apoala sign.

The upper part of this page is not static. Four males are displayed facing the direction of motion (right to left). They are, from last to first, the Lords Seven Rain, One Rain, Four Snake, and Seven Snake. All are ceremonially attired and appear to move so as to enter Serpent's Mouth Cave. The lord last in the procession—Seven Rain—stands just before the waterfall and tree. A date, Year 5 Flint Day 4 Motion, occurs between the tree/waterfall and Lord Seven Rain. This date is number 18 in the 52-year vague solar calendar, and Day 4 Motion occurs twice within it: first, as day number 52 in the year, or day number 17 in Tonalpohualli 25; second, as day number 312 in the year, or also the 17th day of Tonalpohualli 26. Year 5 Flint corresponds to AD 1056.

This introductory page establishes that the origin of a journey under-taken by four lords was the sacred lineage site of Apoala. From this we con-clude that Codex Zouche-Nuttall Document 1, Part IIIA concerns lineage descent—as do the previous two stories. Part IA is the story of Lord Eight Wind Twenty of Suchixtlan, who derived his lineage authority from the Tree Birth event at Apoala. This is mentioned obliquely in the Zouche-Nuttall events on Page 1; it is mentioned directly in Codex Vindobonensis Mexi-canus I obverse. Apoala also appears in Part II. One of the two Apoala rivers produces an important fire-drilling bundle used by the cult bearer Lord Twelve Wind Smoke-Eye from the Sky to empower a temple in the southern Nochixtlan Valley district of Fire Serpent Ballcourt.

We can see that the lower part of Codex Zouche-Nuttall's Page 36 is the complete identifier for Apoala. It is also shown in Codex Vindobonensis Mexicanus I on Page 35-I–II. Virtually all relevant data on the Vindobo-nensis page, excepting those regarding the Serpent's Mouth Cave geological feature, the waterfall, and the Zouche-Nuttall date, appear here on Zouche-Nuttall Page 36.

The Codex Vindobonensis Mexicanus I Data

The Vindobonensis pages display the Tree-born lineage founders, Lord One Flower and his wife, Lady Thirteen Flower, facing each other on a woven marriage mat. Their daughter, Lady Nine Alligator, was born on that day in Year 8 Flint, thirty-four years after Year 13 Rabbit (the date of the Vindobonensis Page 35 text). Then, spanning columns I–II of Vindobonensis Page 35, the god Lord Nine Wind Quetzalcoatl is shown speaking to Lord One Flower. Subsequently, in Sky Town, Lord Nine Wind Quetzalcoatl speaks to his grandson, Lord Five Wind. Their familial relationship is defined in Codex Bodley, on Pages 40-V–39-V.

In Year 9 Rabbit, Lady Nine Alligator married Lord Five Wind when she was fourteen years old. Their woven marriage mat stretches across the river that identifies the Apoala toponym. Therefore this powerful icon of Lord One Flower and Lady Thirteen Flower and Lord Five Wind and Lady Nine Alligator, all of whom are associated with Apoala lineage, becomes a de facto identifier of the place Apoala.

The first date on Zouche-Nuttall Page 36 is Year 5 Flint (AD 1056), thus the events that transpire there occur seventy years after the Apoala Tree Birth event in Year 13 Rabbit (AD 986) and twenty-two years after Lady Nine Alligator marries Lord Five Wind of Sky Town. This implies that at least Lord Five Wind and Lady Nine Alligator were alive when the Zouche-Nuttall event begins—they are not symbolic. It is not possible that the founding lords, ♂ One and ♀ Thirteen Flower, were also living because both Zouche-Nuttall Page 36 and Vindobonensis Mexicanus I Page 35 show them as being very old, that is, they have the prestige status of "elders."

The argument that Zouche-Nuttall Part IIIA begins in AD 1056 gives this episode the latest starting date for a biographical/historical event in the codex. From this it is possible to assume that the genealogy (Part IIIB) following this episode is also of late initiation, although one cannot be absolutely certain. The reasons for this uncertainty will appear as this presentation of Part IIIA progresses.

Although Lord Seven Rain is last in the procession of males that begins this episode, he is first, or the last mentioned male, at the end of it on Page 39. In other words, he begins and ends this story. He is prominent in Codex Vindobonensis Mexicanus I obverse, so it is there that we must seek data for his identification.

On Page 50c of that manuscript, the eight children of First Father (♂ One

Table 8.1. Chronology of Vindobonensis Mexicanus Page 35 and Zouche-Nuttall Page 36

Codex and Page Number	Date	Event
VM 35	Year 13 Rabbit (AD 986)	Tree Birth marriage of ♂ One Flower and ♀ Thirteen Flower
	+34 years	
VM 35	Year 8 Flint (AD 1020)	Birth of ♀ Nine Alligator
	+14 years	
VM 35	Year 9 Rabbit (AD 1034)	Marriage of ♀ Nine Alligator and ♂ Five Wind
	+22 years	
Z-N 36	Year 5 Flint (AD 1056)	Beginning of "The Four Lords from Apoala" story
	Total = 70 years	

Deer) and First Mother (♀ One Deer) are shown descending to, or otherwise associated with, the prototypal Birth Tree. One of these offspring of the progenitor couple is Lord Seven Rain (Vindobonensis Page 50a). The date for this Tree Birth event is the first date in Vindobonensis obverse, namely, Year 5 Flint Day 5 Flint. The first date on Zouche-Nuttall Page 36 is Year 5 Flint Day 8 Motion. Although 8 Motion is 159 days after 5 Flint, the two recordings of the Year 5 Flint are not in the same cycle. The Vindobonensis Year 5 Flint occurs prior to the Tree Birth event, and the Zouche-Nuttall Year 5 Flint occurs after it, therefore the two of them must be separated by at least 52 years.

Lord Seven Rain has several important functions in the Vindobonensis stories, one of which is the carving of male symbols on the Birth Tree (Page 37b), thus defining or empowering the tree's ability to give birth to human beings of that sex. He is also a consultant in the conference with Lord Nine Wind Quetzalcoatl that sets up the Apoala Tree Birth event (Vindobonensis Page 37a). For this reason, Lord Seven Rain is as much an identifier of Apoala Tree Birth nobility enfranchisement as the two married couples shown seated on the Apoala lineage rivers on Codex Zouche-Nuttall Page 36. In fact, while the seated figures are passive, Seven Rain is active throughout this narrative.

The two males who lead this procession on Page 36, Lords Four and Seven

Snake, are Seven Rain's brothers, having been born also of First Father and First Mother, the Lords One Deer (Vindobonensis Page 51b–c). They also appear in Vindobonensis Pages 33a and 5, where they are identified as the primary deities of the sanctified territories—five mountains, four valleys, four towns, and four temples—that conclude the sacred ordering rites of places in that codex.

Only Lord One Rain is not of divine birth, and thus not related to the gods Seven Rain, Four Snake, and Seven Snake. He is therefore a "stand-out" in this procession. He appears only once in Codex Vindobonensis, on Page 1a (the last page), where he is shown as co-ruler of a town with a Lord One Reed. We must assume, therefore, that this episode in Codex Zouche-Nuttall Part IIIA concerns the seemingly mortal Lord One Rain. He appears more frequently in Codex Zouche-Nuttall Document 1—and in association with Lord Seven Rain.

In the introduction page to Zouche-Nuttall Part IIA (Page 14), Lords One and Seven Rain are displayed in Tableau 3, each atop his respective hill and facing each other across a valley. Seven Rain holds a torch. They appear next on Page 17a, Tableau 1, where Lord Seven Rain performs a bird-decapitation ceremony for Lady Three Flint Elder. One Rain assists him by holding a torch. This exchange of ceremonial items as well as costume between them is frequent on Pages 36–39. Also, Lord One Rain appears without Seven Rain on Zouche-Nuttall Page 1, Tableau 4, at Suchixtlan/Monkey Hill.

The procession of the four lords entering Serpent's Mouth Cave at Apoala is led by Lords Seven and Four Snake, followed by One Rain and Seven Rain.

Pages 37–38 (Figures 8.2, 8.3)

Page 37a: After Leaving the Cave

The four lords follow a footpath from the cave across a territory represented by two mountains and a valley. On the valley floor are four objects: (1) a cradleboard containing (2) a Rain God effigy head and (3) a round grass mat with yellow center and topped by (4) a grass knot. Among these four objects, the first two—cradleboard and effigy head—are associated, and the second two—yellow-centered grass mat and grass knot—are associated. Presumably, this is a conflated tableau suggesting to us that the four lords performed certain ceremonies at this place. The four processing males have mostly reversed order. Lord Seven Rain, who is followed by One Rain, Seven Snake, and Four Snake, now leads them as they approach Sayutepec.

Pages 37b–38: At Sayutepec

These two pages present the dominant tableaux for this story. They display a complex ceremony that is, essentially, a Lord Nine Wind Quetzalcoatl sacrifice. It occurs in Year 7 Reed on Day 7 Reed (AD 1071), or fifteen years after the journey began at Apoala. The Sayutepec toponym displayed in the lower register of Pages 37b–38 is complex and therefore loaded with information.

The lords of Sayutepec, Four Death and Four Deer, sit facing each other in the valley between two mountains. A temple is shown at the foot of the mountain directly behind Lord Four Death. A mountain marked by a parrot at its base, a blue and white frilled band with a knot midway up it, and a skyband with cave opening at its top is directly behind Lord Four Deer. Two shieldlike objects, one with two dangles and one with three dangles, are above the skyband. These two gods—Four Death and Four Deer—were seen previously on Zouche-Nuttall Page 16b. In that tableau, Four Death sits on the water facing the god Ten Alligator the Two-faced One and Lady One Eagle. Four Deer is directly beneath Four Death, thus sitting underwater and facing the submerged Lady Three Flint Elder, who, in turn, faces Lord One Grass, seated directly opposite Lord Four Deer. In the very next tableau (Page 17a), Lady Three Flint Elder interacts ceremonially with Lords One and Seven Rain—the chief actors in the story presently discussed. Afterward, Lady Three Flint Elder is again underwater, but this time both Four Deer and Four Death are with her. She offers incense to Four Deer and, by inference, to both gods.

This has interesting implications affecting the reading order for Zouche-Nuttall Pages 16b–17a. The underwater tableau on Page 16b in which lords Four Death and Four Deer appear with Lady Three Flint Elder is followed visually, directly opposite on Page 17a, by another underwater tableau with them. It is likely that they are intended to be sequential events. This is reinforced by the fact that the reading order between Pages 16 and 17 is discontinuous. That is, Page 16b reads from the top downward, ending at the bottom; and Page 17a also begins at the top, which means that one does not read across the pages from 16b top to 17a top. One reads from 16b at the bottom left to 17a bottom right. Therefore the ceremonies displayed on 17a are stacked on top of the underwater ceremonies and occur in three ascending levels. The implication is not so much to direct us in a sequence moving either up or down, but rather to provide us with three moments from a complex ceremony that ultimately culminates with the apotheosis of Lady Three Flint Elder and Lord Five Flower on Pages 17b and 18a.

Continuing with Part IIIA, the city of Sayutepec is between the two lords. It is supported by a foundation of six maguey plants. A yellow U-shaped bracket fringed by masonry L-shaped stones defines the city precincts. A half-stone hill topped by the figure of an insect is within the city wall and directly before Lord Four Death. The central element that occurs after the insect hill is a temple surmounted by human hearts. The temple faces the insect hill and Lord Four Death. The hearts are on the temple roof and extend down the back of it to touch the temple platform. Between temple and insect hill is a spider web enclosed by a yellow (or gold) circle.

An ornamented bowl with short legs floats above the central temple. It contains white flags signifying sacrifice. Above the bowl and flags is a decapitated bird whose blood flows onto a round grass mat topped by a white-and-red striped bundle, which is itself surmounted by a smoking incense ball. The grass mat is directly above the spider web and floats in the air between Insect Hill and the Hearts Temple. All of the above imagery gives the impression of being static and is the lower register of the tableau.

Above the Sayutepec toponym with its complex imagery are the actors. To the viewer's right, on Page 37b, are the Lords Four and Seven Snake. To the viewer's left, on Page 38, is Lord Nine Wind Quetzalcoatl, holding the white sacrificial flag of human sacrifice. Directly behind him are the Lords Seven Alligator, wearing a monkey mask, and Seven Monkey, also wearing a monkey mask. Standing directly behind Lord Seven Monkey is Lord One Rain, and beneath him, down toward the page baseline, is Lord Seven Rain. One and Seven Rain's names have been exchanged—One Rain appears as Seven Rain and vice versa. Of the nine males displayed on Pages 37b–38, seven are actors, and two—Lords Four Death and Four Deer—are part of the toponymic identifier for Sayutepec.

The ceremony displayed here seems to be a human sacrifice led by or in honor of Lord Nine Wind Quetzalcoatl. A similar sacrifice is pictured on Codex Zouche-Nuttall reverse (Document 2) Pages 45d–46a and occurs as part of the ceremonial complex undertaken when Lord Eight Deer Jaguar Claw becomes ruler of Tututepec. The idea that the sacrificial victims are the god-brothers Four and Seven Snake is suggested because they are separated from and facing the other five males (Nine Wind Quetzalcoatl, Seven

Alligator, Seven Monkey, and One and Seven Rain). Because two of the five males—Seven and One Rain—continue the action on Page 39, they are not the ones sacrificed. The conclusion is, therefore, that they are part of the sacrificing ceremonialists. Furthermore, the reason for this story (Pages 36–39) is stated in the present tableau, namely, to perform a ritual rulership sacrifice in behalf of Lords One and Seven Rain at Sayutepec.

The layout of the reading order previously discussed suggests that the dominant action is now completed. Page 39 is a kind of epilogue. The date for the sacrifice event at Sayutepec is Year 7 Reed Day 7 Reed.

Page 39: Conclusion of the Journey (Figure 8.4)

The date for the journey continues with Year 7 Reed Day 7 Reed. We know this because the date is situated directly on the guiding footpath. Only Lords Seven and One Rain appear walking on it, and Seven Rain leads, followed by One Rain, who carries the Venus staff. The footpath terminates at a location consisting of three mountains—two smaller ones on the left and right and a larger central mountain emitting flames. Both flanking mountains have cave openings at their apexes. The central mountain is identified by a yellow circle within which is a curving device that looks like a white-and-black-banded animal's tail. A masonry substrate underlies all three mountains. Lord One Rain stands approximately over the first or right-hand valley. The date Year 6 Rabbit Day 7 Snake is beneath him. Lord Seven Rain—still in the lead position—stands over the second or left-hand valley, with the date Year 9 Flint Day 7 Wind between himself and the valley. The A-O year sign is ornamented with eyes and feathers so as to resemble an owl. This brief, ambiguous event concludes Part IIIA.

In summation, the episode portrayed in tableaux on Pages 36–39 consists of events occurring in continuous forward progression through the years (see Table 8.2).

A second way of reading the data in Pages 36–39 is to consider the events as occurring in one 52-year cycle (see Table 8.3).

We have a conundrum of dates. If reading proceeds always in a forward progression, then from Year 5 Flint (the first date) to Year 9 Flint (the last date) 107 years elapse. If we read years within one 52-year cycle, meaning that Year 6 Rabbit and Year 9 Flint are not forwardly progressive but negatively regressive, then these events occur in three years. The assumption is, then,

Table 8.2. Pages 36–39: Chronology One

Page	Date	Event
36	Year 5 Flint Day 8 Motion	Journey begins at Apoala
	+15 years	
37b	Year 7 Reed Day 7 Reed	At Sayutepec
	+51 years	
39	Year 6 Rabbit Day 7 Snake	♂ One Rain at his valley
	+42 years	
39	Year 9 Flint Day 7 Wind	♂ Seven Rain at his valley
	Total = 108 years	

Table 8.3. Pages 36–39: Chronology Two

Page	Date	Event
36	Year 5 Flint Day 8 Motion	Journey begins through Serpent's Mouth Cave at Apoala
37a	No date	Journey continues through Cradleboard & Rain God Effigy Head Valley
	+15 years	
37b	Year 7 Reed Day 7 Reed	Ceremony at Sayutepec
	−1 year	
38	Year 6 Rabbit Day 7 Snake	♂ One Rain at his valley
	+10 years	
39	Year 9 Flint Day 7 Wind	♂ Seven Rain at his valley
	Total = 4 years	

that the Page 39 dates—6 Rabbit and 9 Flint—occurred before Year 7 Reed, the apex ceremony at Sayutepec. So the reading is this: The journey begins at Apoala in Year 5 Flint; three years later, the Year 9 Flint event occurs; then nine years later, the Year 6 Rabbit event occurs; and, finally, one year after Year 6 Rabbit, the Year 7 Reed event occurs. The sequence of events according to this chronology is shown in Table 8.4.

Table 8.4. Pages 36–39: Chronology Three

Page	Date	Event
36	Year 5 Flint	Journey begins at Apoala
	+4 years	
39	Year 9 Flint	♂ Seven Rain at his valley
	+10 years	
39	Year 6 Rabbit	♂ One Rain at his valley
	+1 year	
38–39	Year 7 Reed Year 7 Reed	At Sayutepec. The footpath date. Lords One and Seven Rain return to their valleys.
	Total = 13 years	

These data indicate that the journey began at Apoala through the Serpent's Mouth Cave; four years later, Seven Rain was in his valley; ten years later, One Rain was in his valley; one year later, the Sayutepec ceremony transpired. Then the two dominant actors, One and Seven Rain, returned to their valley via a second journey from Serpent's Mouth Cave. The reason for this return to Serpent's Mouth Cave and the two Rain-named lords returning to their respective valleys is this: the footpath for the second journey begins on Page 38 directly behind Lord One Rain (who should actually be Seven Rain—see above). It is at exactly the same height as the footpath leading from Serpent's Mouth Cave on Page 37a. It is marked with the same date (Year and Day) as the Sayutepec ceremony. Therefore there were two supernatural journeys through Serpent's Mouth Cave: The first led to Seven Rain's valley, then to One Rain's valley, then to Sayutepec; the second journey placed the two lords back at their respective locations. The first progression in continuous progressive chronology is the obvious reading order and moves seamlessly from Page 36 to Page 39. The occulted reading order does not; instead, it creates greater variety within the narrative and offers two possibilities for interpreting the story displayed on Pages 36–39. I do not believe that the original authors of this narrative section of Codex Zouche-Nuttall (Part IIIA) were intentionally vague, nor do I believe they had dyslexia. They may have been recording two variations on the same story using as little page space as possible, they may have intentionally given themselves and later performers as much variation as possible for story recitation, or, considering the use of the calendar, they may have been recording information in the second version reserved to a few elite. These are not the only possibilities; they are only the ones that come to mind.

The Four Lords Contextualized

The primary actors in the final story of Codex Zouche-Nuttall Document 1 (obverse) are four males. They are Lords Four and Seven Snake and Lords Seven and One Rain. Three of them—Four Snake, Seven Snake, and Seven Rain—are shown in Codex Vindobonensis Mexicanus I obverse as brothers born from First Father and First Mother (the Lords One Deer). Four and Seven Snake are shown paired on Vindobonensis Page 51-III. Seven Rain is shown paired with Seven Eagle on Vindobonensis Page 50-I, one page after the brothers Snake.

One Rain only appears on the last page of Vindobonensis (Page 1-I) and is never displayed in that document as an associate of Lord Seven Rain. In Zouche-Nuttall Document 1, however, it is a different story (so to speak). One Rain is shown as one of four lords greeting Lord Eight Wind Twenty of Suchixtlan at Suchixtlan on Page 1, Tableau 4. Seven Rain does not appear in the first story (Pages 1–8) at all. In the second story (Pages 14–19), One and Seven Rain are paired at a specific territory on the introductory Page 14, then again on Page 17a. Seven Rain appears attired as the god Xipe-Totec (wearing a human skin) at the town of Mitla during the marriage of the Zapotec Lord Five Flower and the Mixtec princess Lady Six Rabbit (Zouche-Nuttall Page 33b). After that, the two next appear as primary actors in the final story, Pages 36–39. Seven Snake appears once before the final story in Zouche-Nuttall Document 1. On Page 3a, he is a combatant in the War from Heaven, fighting against the Stone Men.

"Primary" thus applies only to One and Seven Rain rather than to all four of the processing lords—Seven and Four Snake, One and Seven Rain—because the brothers Snake disappear from the narrative after the ultimate scene on Pages 37b–38, and the story concludes with Lords Seven and One Rain on Page 39. The roles of all four males in the final story are, however, complex.

On the first, introductory Page 36, the procession into Serpent's Mouth Cave at Apoala is led by Seven Snake, followed by Four Snake, followed by One Rain, who is followed by Seven Rain. On Page 37a—after exiting Serpent's Mouth Cave—Seven Rain leads the procession. One Rain follows him, and he is followed by Seven Snake, who is in turn followed by Four Snake. During the ultimate tableau on Pages 37b–38, the Lords Four and Seven Snake are displayed at the top level with Lord Nine Wind Quetzalcoatl and his entourage, consisting of Lords Seven Monkey and Seven Alligator and One Rain and Seven Rain (the names of the Lords One and Seven Rain appear to have been switched). Four Snake, followed by Seven Snake, appears on Page 37b facing left toward Lord Nine Wind Quetzalcoatl and his entourage. Lord One Rain followed by Seven Rain are last in the Nine Wind Quetzalcoatl entourage, face toward Four and Seven Snake, and also form a "frame" to the viewer's left from top to bottom, ending the scene. In other words, the Nine Wind Quetzalcoatl entourage is roughly L-shaped with the base of the L formed from top to bottom on the left side of Page 38.

Subsequently, in the same year and on the same day as the Nine Wind Quetzalcoatl ceremony, Lord Seven Rain leads Lord One Rain as they emerge from Serpent's Mouth Cave a second time. Page 39 shows them following the footpath, and then they are displayed finally in their respective valleys. Each has an associated date in their respective valleys: Lord Seven Rain (who is first) has the date Year 9 Flint Day 7 Wind. The A-O year sign is ornamented with eyes and feather topknots.[1] One Rain has the date Year 6 Rabbit Day 7 Snake. Of interest here is that the Lords Four and Seven Snake are often identified only by their day names. This ends the superficial description of the Four Lords from Apoala story.

Four Snake and Seven Snake in Codex Vindobonensis

The Lord Four Snake is found—frequently along with his brother, Seven Snake—in Vindobonensis obverse and Zouche-Nuttall obverse, but not in the later codices, Selden and Bodley. The Vindobonensis pagination for them is 51, 33, 30, 26, 5, and 2. Zouche-Nuttall displays them on Pages 4, 6, 36, and 37. According to Caso (1984, 2:122a), they also appear in Codex Yanhuitlán on Page 40. Caso notes their importance in his remarks on Four Snake:

> Es uno de los más importantes dioses mixtecos. Hijo de ♂ 1 Venado y ♀ 1 Venado; y uno de los 14 dioses serpientes, cuya enumeración puede verse en la biografía de ♂ 4 Lagarto, "Serpiente de Lagarto"; pero con el que tiene la más íntima conexión es con ♂ 7 Serpiente "Serpientes entrelazadas-Pedernales-Aguila negra". . .

Indeed, these two deities are among the most important in the Mixtec pantheon. The pantheon includes Lords Nine Wind Quetzalcoatl, Four Motion, Seven Wind, Seven Motion, and, of course, Four and Seven Snake. All of them are often displayed with black body paint (Furst 1978a:16). Four and Seven Snake are the ninth pair of offspring born of the One Deer couple (Vindobonensis, Page 51). Actually, the preceding eighteen children are shown as pairs; the brothers Four and Seven Snake are the only ones to appear as a triplet—the third is Lord Four Alligator.

On Vindobonensis Page 33c, Year 10 House Day 4 Snake, the two brothers, Four Snake (whose name is not repeated because it is given in the date) and Seven Snake, preside at a conference initiated in Year 13 Rabbit Day 7 Snake—the latter's day name is repeated. Attending the conference are the gods Lady Nine Reed (the lineage goddess of the Tree), Lord Two Dog, Lord Four Motion born in Year 7 Reed, Lord Seven Flower born in Year 13 Rabbit, Lady One Eagle (goddess of rivers, lakes, and water), Lady Nine Grass (the Oracle of the Dead at Chalcatongo), Lord Seven Rain, Lady Twelve Vulture, Lord Seven Wind Two Faces, Lord Seven Motion, Lord Seven Motion Jaguar, Lady Twelve Vulture, Lord Ten Lizard, Lady Eleven Snake, Lord Seven Wind, Lady Eight Deer, Lady Five Death, Lord One Alligator, Lady Thirteen Flower (who marries Lord One Flower on Vindobonensis Page 35), Lady Two Flower, Lady Three Alligator, and Lady Six Eagle.

The conference ends in Year 13 Rabbit on Day 2 Deer. This conference leads directly to the ordering ritual for Steambaths Town by Lord Nine Wind Quetzalcoatl on Vindobonensis Pages 32d–33. This event occurs in Year 6 Rabbit on Day 3 Alligator. The only named actor is Lord Nine Wind Quetzalcoatl. Subsequently, on Pages 30–29, Lord Nine Wind Quetzalcoatl presides at another conference, presenting a trilobed vegetation wand to Four Snake. Seven Snake sits directly behind his brother and is followed by forty-two individuals on Pages 29a–27a. Page 27b is the beginning of the "agricultural rituals."

Page 27b shows a complex scene that seems to involve favorable weather for cultivation. Pages 26–25 illustrate the pulque ritual preceded by a maize ritual—the maturation of the maize plant (Furst 1978a:161). Four and Seven Snake participate in the maize ritual on Page 26a. Vindobonensis Page 5 actually shows the territory dedicated to Four and Seven Snake. In Year 5 House on Day 7 Snake, they begin the fire-drilling ordering ritual there, and it is completed in Year 5 House on Day 9 Snake, eighty days later (Williams 2009:136).

These important deities are often identified by their day names and are occasionally interchangeable as to costume. They appear—though without day names—as escorts accompanying Lord Nine Wind Quetzalcoatl as he descends from the sky on Vindobonensis Page 48c. Insignias name them: Four Snake is "Fire Serpent" and Seven Snake is "Descending Eagle."

Lord Seven Rain

The deity Lord Seven Rain appears in Codex Vindobonensis Mexicanus I on Pages 33c, 29b, 26a, and 25b. He appears in Codex Zouche-Nuttall in the second story (Pages 14–19) and, to our interest, on Pages 36–39. Caso (1984, 2:423a) identifies him this way:

> Creo que es el nombre de Xipe-Totec, dios principal de Culhuacán-Río de quetzal [Cuilapan ?].

Furst (1978a:351) calls him "the Mixtec equivalent of Xipe-Totec." This deity has ceramic miniatures extending back into the Middle Formative Era and he is transcultural. According to one source (Nicholson 1985:48), Xipe-Totec is

> . . . an aspect of the shabby and despised god Nanautzin who sacrificed himself in the fire to enable the sun to continue lighting the world. He is also the flayed god and is said to make the seeds germinate the earth.

Among the Aztecs, Xipe appears in Codex Magiabecchiano (Page 90) associated with the gods Chicomecoatl (Maize Goddess) and Mictlantecuhtli (God of Death) as an Aztec male who consumes hallucinogenic mushrooms. In Codex Fejérváry-Mayer, Xipe-Totec appears in the maize sequence in the last panel and is associated with sprouting corn. He is displayed literally pulling the sprouting Maize God from the earth.

Among the Aztecs, the god Totec had two manifestations: first, as Xipe and, second, as Yohuallahuan. The precise translation of Xipe is vague, but Burr Cartwright Brundage (1979:72) thinks it may mean "he with the phallus." For the Aztecs, Xipe-Totec was the virile young god who could represent flowers of the new blooming season and who then passed away in the bloom of life. Human victims were sacrificed to him by being splayed on a scaffold and then shot to death with arrows, their blood dripping down upon a special round stone. The stone itself was later deified, being transfigured and called Itztapaltotec, "the Lord, the Flat Stone."

In short, our perspective of Xipe-Totec is vague because he transforms as he is utilized from culture to culture over time. Probably the best representation of Xipe-Totec, despite his gruesome ceremonial associations, is as the god of springtime who offered to humans the bountiful goodness produced by the earth. For Fray Diego Durán, Xipe-Totec was "a universal god" (1977:174). I interpret the word "universal" to mean "found everywhere." Durán provides us with the precise meanings of the two-word name, Xipe-Totec: "Totec," he says, "means Awesome and Terrible Lord Who Fills One With Dread," while Xipe means "One Who Has Been Flayed and Ill-Treated." Durán remarks that on the feasts of Xipe-Totec, more men were sacrificed than on any other, owing to the popularity of the celebration.

Who was Seven Rain to the Mixtecs? The Xipe-Totec associations did survive among them because we see him displayed at Mitla wearing a human skin (Zouche-Nuttall, Page 33b). Otherwise, Codex Vindobonensis obverse shows him directly associated with the great tree that gives birth to the new Mixtec nobles who assumed land ownership and authority after the collapse of Monte Albán. In fact, Seven Rain is one of two gods who carves male and female symbols into the tree's bark so it can produce both sexes (Vindobonensis, Page 37b). Seven Rain carves the male-symbolic atlatl darts. He is even present at the first Tree Birth ceremony (before it bore nobles) on Vindobonensis Page 50d. The ceremony even ended on his name day in Year 3 House (it began three years earlier in Year 13 Rabbit on Day 9 Reed). The conclusion is, then, that Lord Seven Rain is intimately associated with the Apoala Birth Tree and lineage validation.

Part IIIB, Pages 40–41: The Final Genealogy

Page 40: Four Couples (Figure 8.5)

1. Lord Five Lizard + Lady Ten Snake.
2. Lord Six Reed + Lady Twelve Jaguar.
3. Lord Ten Lizard + Lady Five Death.
4. Lord Five Alligator + Lady Seven Death.

Page 41: The Last Family (Figure 8.6)

1. Lord Two Grass + Lady Six Reed. Their children are:
   a. Lords Six Reed, Ten Snake, Fifteen (?) Grass, and Three Wind.
2. Lord (name eroded) + Lady Twelve Eagle.

The reading order indicates that Codex Zouche-Nuttall Document 1 (Pages 1–41) is complete.

Commentary on the Final Genealogy

Page 40 continues the upper and lower parallel format by displaying four males in the upper register. Four females paired with them are drawn in the lower register. Although these individuals are named, their identities remain obscure except to say that they are the predecessors of the two marriages that compose the final page of the codex (41). Caso (1984, 2:301b) merely says that Page 40 is composed of eight persons, four males and four females; then he names them. He dismisses the idea that the final male, a priest named Five Alligator, is the Five Alligator who fathered Lord Eight Deer Jaguar Claw. The paternity of this male in relation to Eight Deer Jaguar Claw is, he says, "very doubtful." Caso's comments on this particular Five Alligator conclude with "We do not know anything more of these persons since they are not mentioned in another codex. None have personal names and so their identification is very difficult and insecure" (1984, 2:25a). He also mentions that among the offspring of the first married couple on Page 41, the male name "Fifteen Grass" is a mistake (1984, 2:275a).

It is possible that Caso is mistaken about the identity of male Five Alligator: he may indeed be the father of Lord Eight Deer Jaguar Claw of Tilantongo, but listed with a previously unidentified wife. Such genealogical lacunae as this are not unnoticed in the codices. The female who founds the second dynasty of Jaltepec (Lady Nine Wind; Codex Selden, Page 5c) is a previously unmentioned child of Lord Eight Wind of Suchixtlan and his first wife, Lady Ten Deer. Therefore, we may assume that in the interest of genealogical prominence, the author of this present genealogy was working for the final family recorded on Page 41. In exercise of that job, he provided them with the distinction of being related—though distantly—to the famous Eight Deer Jaguar Claw and his equally prominent father, Five Alligator. If this is true, then this particular text (Zouche-Nuttall, Page 40) is the only record of Five Alligator's marriage to female Seven Rain. It is interesting that the circular format of Page 41 has the scions of the second marriage facing Lord Five Alligator. It is as though they make the pictographic statement: "We are your grandchildren." Therefore the possibility of a relationship to Lord Eight Deer Jaguar Claw's illustrious parent cannot be dismissed.

The circular format of Page 41—beginning in the lower right and ending at the upper right with a distinct red line—tells us that the document is complete and not, as is the codex reverse (Document 2), unfinished. Given that observation, it is also noted that the parallel upper and lower format of Page 40 is followed on Page 41, and that three, possibly four unpainted pages remain on the obverse. Three of those pages are the last strip of deerskin completing the entire fanfold, and they are also unpainted on the codex reverse.

The final genealogy is undated. All dates occur within the story on Pages 36–39, and this sets the final genealogy in Codex Zouche-Nuttall obverse (Document 1) apart from all the rest. As is the case with many of the inscribed pages of this codex, the blank page after Page 41 with its inscribed genealogy gives no indication that it once bore figures that were subsequently scraped and erased. Although it is difficult to ascertain from photographic reproductions, the remaining four blank pages have no remaining evidence—however slight—of previous text subsequently removed.

Figure 8.1. Codex Zouche-Nuttall (obverse), Page 36. © The Trustees of the British Museum.

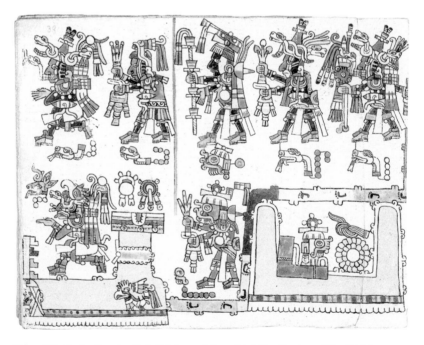

Figure 8.2. Codex Zouche-Nuttall (obverse), Page 37. © The Trustees of the British Museum.

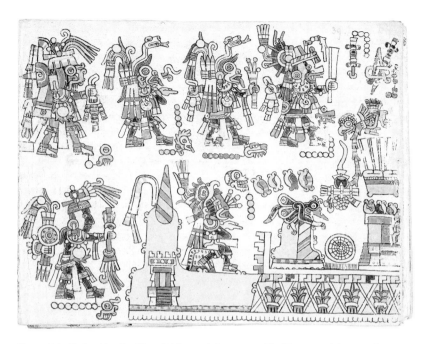

Figure 8.3. Codex Zouche-Nuttall (obverse), Page 38. © The Trustees of the British Museum.

Figure 8.4. Codex Zouche-Nuttall (obverse), Page 39. © The Trustees of the British Museum.

Figure 8.5. Codex Zouche-Nuttall (obverse), Page 40. © The Trustees of the British Museum.

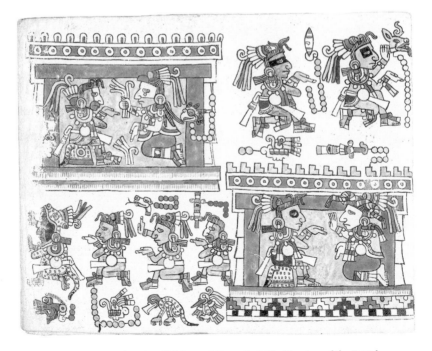

Figure 8.6. Codex Zouche-Nuttall (obverse), Page 41. © The Trustees of the British Museum.

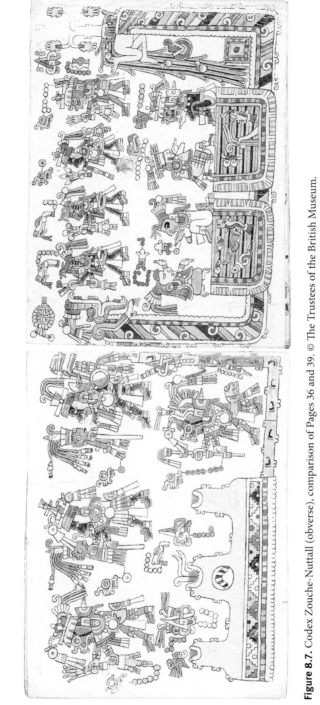

Figure 8.7. Codex Zouche-Nuttall (obverse), comparison of Pages 36 and 39. © The Trustees of the British Museum.

9   Document 1 (Obverse):
Discussion and Interpretation

The Mixteca/Puebla Art Style

The pictography of the Mixtec codices is the distinctive Mixteca/Puebla (or "international") style. Once thought to be an Epiclassic Period phenomenon, examples of it can be found in the Tepantitla complex at Teotihuacan, including the use of footpaths to suggest direction of motion. Beginning with the Epiclassic Period, however, the use of this particular style diversified and became almost universal or international in southern Mexico and in Mesoamerica in general. Examples of it can be demonstrated in cultures from Panama, to Belize, to Oaxaca, to Puebla, as well as in Aztec Tenochtitlán, in Cholula, and also in parts of the North American Southwest.

The Mixteca/Puebla style was used in diverse media: ceramics, architecture decoration, jewelry, and, of course, native books. In short, it is a communication technique manifesting as art rather than as a language encoded in spoken words. Elizabeth Brumfiel (1989) suggests that the broad cultural diversification of Mixteca/Puebla-style art could represent cultural attempts to stabilize competitive factional, interacting political networks as well as political/economic networks. H. B. Nicholson (1966:260) provides perhaps the best definition of Mixteca/Puebla-style art. According to him, the style is

> characterized by an almost geometric precision in delineation. Symbols are standardized and rarely so highly conventionalized that their original models cannot be ascertained. Colors are numerous, vivid, and play an important symbolic role in themselves. In general, there is much that is akin to modern caricature and cartooning of the Disney type with bold exaggeration of prominent features.

Codex Zouche-Nuttall Contents

Codex Zouche-Nuttall Document 1 consists of three complex stories, each followed by genealogical statements. Remembering that codex historical data are essentially a combination of history and religion, we can say that each initial story is biographical and concerns founders of lineages and religion. Each story has an introduction.

The first story is the biography of Lord Eight Wind Eagle Flints of Suchixtlan. The introduction occurs on Pages 1–2, wherein the first fifty-two years of his long and very eventful life are highlighted. The second story (Pages 14–19) is the fascinating and sometimes vague detailing of the cult-bearing Ladies Three Flint (Elder and Younger) of Wasp Hill and their husbands, the Lords Five Flower and Twelve Wind Smoke-Eye from the Sky. Page 14 is their introduction, displaying the meeting of Three Flint Elder with her husband, Lord Five Flower. It is then followed by five tableaux detailing five districts and their rulers. The elder Three Flint and her husband, Five Flower, are associated with the institution of religious cults rather than the founding of genealogies. The third story tells about the Four Lords from Apoala, and Page 36 introduces it. As is the case with the preceding two stories, this third story concludes with a genealogical statement.

The formatting of each story differs from the others to some extent. All tableaux—no matter the story—are conflated, presenting highlights of much longer episodes that could, no doubt, be detailed from memory during performance. Each section, whether biography or genealogy, has interpretable dates. At times those dates can be corresponded to the modern calendar and therefore become history we can fix in time. Pages 3–7, 9–10, 16–18, 20–21, and 23–35 are all composed in vertical ascending and descending boustrophedon. Pages 1–2, 8, 14, 19a–b, 20, 40, and 41 have no red-line boustrophedon format at all. Pages 11b–13 have a roughly comma-shaped reading order determined by red lines. Pages 36–39 have no boustrophedon but determine progress through the narrative by using a footpath. Also, Pages 36–42 are generally divided into upper and lower registers.

The three biographical stories have thematic elements in common as well as curiously dissimilar elements shared by two but not by another. First, neither Lord Eight Wind of Suchixtlan, nor the Ladies Three Flint, nor the four lords from Apoala have precedent ancestry. This statement might be modified in regard to the four lords from Apoala because Codex Vindobonensis Mexicanus I tells us three of them were gods descendant from First

Father and First Mother, the Lords One Deer. Second, all three stories record the sacrifice of two males. In the first story, they are Four Motion and Seven Flower; in the second, they are Three Monkey and Four House; and in the last story, they are the god-brothers Four and Seven Snake. Third, all three stories have connections to the lineage site, Apoala. The recovered or implied chronologies place the first two stories at the beginning of (or in the case of the second story, slightly before) the tenth century of the Common Era. The final story appears to initiate at the end of that century.

The three stories connect in some way to the life of the culture hero and founder of the second dynasty of Tilantongo, Lord Eight Deer Jaguar Claw. The first story takes Lord Eight Wind (in the form of his mummy) into the era of Eight Deer. The second story begins before the time of Eight Deer Jaguar Claw but connects to it by the presence of the female founder of Tilantongo's first dynasty, namely, Lady One Death. The third story, in its genealogy, seems to imply a connection with Eight Deer's father, Lord Five Alligator. The first two stories imply connections with the Toltecs, but this connection cannot be demonstrated for the final story. Themes relating to the god Nine Wind Quetzalcoatl appear in the second and third stories but seem curiously absent in the first. And finally, the first two stories detail the War from Heaven (in different parts of the Nochixtlan Valley), but the third story does not—presumably because it occurs after the war ended in AD 979.

Each post-story genealogy has an introduction, some elaborated, as in the genealogy/genealogies shown on Pages 9–13. Only one actor in the subsequent genealogy has been identified as a child of lineage founder Lord Eight Wind of Suchixtlan. Alfonso Caso suspects that the family or families displayed in that genealogy are located in a territory in the modern state of Puebla and not in the Nochixtlan Valley of Oaxaca. In yet another commentary (1984, 2:265a–266b), he assigns the marriage site to a Toltec town in the Valley of Mexico.

The second set of genealogies—and the longest of them—occurs on Pages 22–35. An elaborate mural map (Page 22) introduces it. Displayed thereon is a documentation of rulers of areas in the district of Monte Negro. It is formatted so as to reflect the layout of the Page 19 map-mural terminations of the Ladies Three Flint episodes. It is keyed to the first dynasty of Tilantongo that it introduces. The third story is introduced on Page 36 with an elaborate toponym of the source of the sacred lineage of the Lords of the Tree from Apoala. The story itself tells of two peregrinations involving ceremonies and precedes the shortest lineage in the entire Codex Zouche-Nuttall obverse, namely, that on Pages 40–41. The reading order of this final genealogy indicates that Zouche-Nuttall Document 1 is complete, although four blank pages remain unwritten.

Regarding the lineage-verifying site of Apoala, the first story about Lord Eight Wind of Suchixtlan has inferences tying him to the Tree Birth event there. He is even shown going to Apoala one year after the War from Heaven ends and remaining until the Tree Birth ceremony several years later. The second story has one such Apoala reference for the Wasp Hill cult-bearing ceremonies, and it does relate the birth of Lady One Death from a place near Wasp Hill.

Her biography begins Codex Bodley (1-V) and tells us that Lady One Death was Tree born, although no reference to Apoala survives in that greatly eroded page and band. The third story begins at Apoala, and therefore all subsequent events in it—and in the final genealogy—are associated with the sacred lineages from it. Thus we see that all three stories have, in one way or another, Apoala as their lineage enfranchisement source. In the first story, Lord Eight Wind of Suchixtlan was enfranchised there during the actual tree ceremony itself—although Page 1 of Codex Zouche-Nuttall tells us that he was born from (came from within) the earth. The earth is also the source for Lady One Death. The final story has one chief actor, Lord Seven Rain, who is born from the first progenitors, and his companion, Lord One Rain, has no precedent origin statement. The husbands of Ladies Three Flint Elder and Three Flint Younger seem to come from the sky, appearing as they do from caves there.

In the first story, Lord Eight Wind Eagle Flints of Suchixtlan travels through the earth and appears from caves in the earth and in temple buildings eight times on Pages 1–6. After his Rain God water ceremony on Page 6a–b, he no longer does so, but instead marries three women and founds large families. In the second story, the elder Lady Three Flint has four underwater events on Pages 15–17. On Page 19b, the younger Lady Three Flint has a nuptial bath with her husband, Twelve Wind Smoke-Eye. In the final story, the four lords pass through a valley displaying a distinctive Rain God effigy head sitting within a cradleboard.

On Page 22—the ideological source for the first dynasty of Tilantongo—the female, Lady One Snake, kneels upon a river flowing from Serpent Temple. Thereafter she and her husband, Six Death, are shown atop their respective temple platforms displayed on opposite sides of a river. Subsequently, rivers are toponymic identifiers for the progenitors of both first and second dynasties of Tilantongo, with iconic human figures emerging from caves in those rivers. Of course, in the final story, the Apoala toponym shows the two lineage couples—Lord One Flower and Lady Thirteen Flower and their daughter, Lady Nine Alligator, and her husband, Five Wind—sitting atop two rivers.

Codex Zouche-Nuttall obverse is, then, a retrospective foundational document dealing with individuals who were surely founders of both lineage and religion during a complex time in Mixtec history when they were establishing themselves in the Nochixtlan Valley (and elsewhere) as rulers sine qua non. The lengthiest genealogy in the codex displays the second dynasty of Tilantongo in all its diversity. Among the various towns and districts enfranchised by the second dynasty of Tilantongo, the most entries occur for the town of Teozacoalco.

The First Story: Summary and Interpretation

Pages 1–8 provide the first lineage-founding biography in Codex Zouche-Nuttall Document 1. The unique and sometimes puzzling layout is employed because the scribes took great pains to move forward in time from the death of Lord Eight Wind of Suchixtlan (the lineage founder) to the time of his great- (or great-great-) grandson, Lord Two Rain Twenty Jaguars of Tilantongo. The scribes also undertook a clarification of an event told on Codex Zouche-Nuttall Document 2, Page 82, where Lord Eight Deer Jaguar Claw consults with Two Rain's mummy.

In effect, the terminus of the Lord Eight Wind of Suchixtlan story provides a rationale whereby Lord Eight Wind's mummy (shown as alive and sitting in a temple illustrated on Page 7) consults with his boy-king great- (or great-great-) grandson. Codex Selden tells us that this consultation started a marriage-alliance war between Tilantongo, Jaltepec, and Hua Chino (Red-and-White Bundle Town) that was only resolved in the regency of Lord Eight Deer Jaguar Claw. The codex scribes both provide us with explanation of the marriage-alliance war and give ample testimony of the powerful authority of the mummy bundles of lineage lords. The mummy of Eight Wind of Suchixtlan is shown as alive and, subsequently on Page 8b, so is the mummy bundle of his now adult great- (or great-great-) grandson Two Rain. The pictography displaying these two living mummies implies that such important kings and queens were displayed in miniature temple structures—a device that undoubtedly reinforced postmortem authority.

The religious event for which Eight Wind is given the most prestige occurs on Page 2. Three introductory tableaux occur on Page 1, but the entirety of Page 2 is the dominant tableau to which the other three tableaux are auxiliary. It is an "ordering" event, that is, the sanctification of a place or area that occurs over a period of time and is initiated and conducted by a single powerful individual, perhaps with assistants. The Page 2 tableaux tell us that Lord Eight Wind ordered Yucuñudahui, otherwise known as Rain God Hill. The Zouche-Nuttall Page 2 is geographically relevant, displaying as it does the Classic Period apex of the hill (where the action occurs) and the Postclassic Period settlement below it.

Codex Vindobonensis Page 47b lists Yucuñudahui as one of at least three places (one of which is Apoala) in an important district in the northern Mixteca known as "the place where the sky was." The sky was lifted above this district by the god Nine Wind Quetzalcoatl. When it came time to order or sanctify the Mixtec places under the sky, Nine Wind Quetzalcoatl sanctified his hometown, Steambaths, as displayed on Vindobonensis Pages 32d–31, then empowered (Vindobonensis Page 30a) one of the gods named Lord Two Dog to do the same for other districts, as depicted on Vindobonensis Pages 22–21. Codex Zouche-Nuttall Page 6a displays Lord Eight Wind as ruler of Suchixtlan; Lord Two Dog is one of four (in the Council of Four) priests who pay homage to him.

The lifting up of and display of a wand constructed of three sacred plants is paramount in most of the ordering rituals in Vindobonensis. On Zouche-Nuttall Page 2, Lord Eight Wind is displayed at Yucuñudahui with the sacred plants as an inherent part of his person and attire. For these reasons, it can be assumed that the Zouche-Nuttall scribes for Document 1, Pages 1–8, intended to convey that Eight Wind was of higher status than Two Dog and akin to Nine Wind Quetzalcoatl in importance.

Furthermore, after his political career and after the War from Heaven, an elderly Eight Wind of Suchixtlan was married to three women and produced an exceptionally large number of offspring. Not all of them are actually listed in Codex Zouche-Nuttall Document 1, Pages 1–13. One such is the female ruler of Jaltepec, Lady Nine Wind, who founded the second dynasty of that town. She appears only in Codex Selden, the royal document of Jaltepec. Selden itself, though a palimpsest painted in the preconquest format, was produced in the Colonial Period, ca. 1556. The obvious conclusion is that Colonial Period descendants of Eight Wind had vested interest in demonstrating their right to rule as testimony before Spanish colonial courts. That right came from the distinctive prestige of Lord Eight Wind Twenty of Suchixtlan.

The Second Story: Summary and Interpretation

The second story begins slightly before the first story. It coincides with the first story in that it presents the second telling of the War from Heaven—instead of the war in the northern Nochixtlan Valley, it relates the war in the southern Nochixtlan Valley.

However, the intention of the second story is to present the importance of the lineage founders of Wasp Hill prior to its destruction in the War from Heaven. The importance of these founders—Lady Three Flint Elder and her husband, Lord Five Flower—is chiefly religious, namely, the founding of religious cults centered on bundles of power. Those bundles are the Nine Wind Quetzalcoatl Bundle and the Fire-Drilling Bundle. The latter is obtained from Apoala.

Initially, on the introductory Page 14, Lord Five Flower travels from Stone Sky Cave to Lady Three Flint Elder. Four important district rulers or gods are displayed as paired—Lords Ten Rain and Ten Grass, and Lords Ten Reed and Ten Vulture. They accompany the couple to the district of Jaltepec in the southern Mixteca near Serpent Ballcourt (Page 15). There a Nine Wind Quetzalcoatl bundle is installed in Snake Temple. Subsequently, Lady Three Flint Elder births Lady Three Flint Younger; changes her name because of the prestige of this event; and goes to the underworld, where she is presented with two staffs of power and a fire-drilling bundle (Page 16). After the apotheosis of Three Flint Elder and Lord Five Flower (Pages 17b–18a), Lord Twelve Wind Smoke-Eye from the Sky, who will found temples and marry Lady Three Flint Younger, then receives this same bundle at Apoala (Page 18b).

The important Double-page 19 displays the marriage of Lord Twelve Wind Smoke-Eye from the Sky and Lady Three Flint Younger. However, this has been detailed previously in text. The apex event appears to concern the birth of Lady One Death from the earth near Wasp Hill. After the War from Heaven (Pages 20–21a), she and her husband, Four Alligator, are prominent in the fire-drilling-bundle cult at Achiutla (Page 21b). Codex Vindobonensis

Mexicanus I reverse, Page I, Band 1, tells us that Lady One Death and Lord Four Alligator founded the first dynasty of Tilantongo. Although princesses from Wasp Hill descent married into the first dynasty of Tilantongo, it was Lady One Death—born near the temple at Wasp Hill—and her husband who founded it. Zouche-Nuttall Document 1 makes no clear statement to this effect but, rather, implies it. Vindobonensis reverse says it explicitly and without the possibility of intrusive ambiguity.

The subsequent genealogies first detail the marriages and offspring of the first dynasty of Tilantongo. They end with the statement that the ill-fated last king—named Two Rain Twenty Jaguars—left no offspring (Page 24b). Thereafter two marriages and offspring are shown, but not at Tilantongo (Page 24b–c).

The genealogies of the second dynasty of Tilantongo begin on Page 25 and present the largest number of succeeding generations listed in Codex Zouche-Nuttall Document 1. This dynasty occupies Pages 25–35, and of the families presented there, those on Pages 27c–33a are lords of Teozacoalco. Therefore five and one-half pages out of ten pages are devoted to Teozacoalco royalty, or slightly more than 50 percent of the pagination. After the marriage of the Mixtec princess Four Rabbit to Five Flower, the Zapotec lord of Zaachila (Page 33b), the genealogy ends with Pages 34 and 35 displaying more Teozacoalco descendants. This final listing makes a clear statement: although the Mixtecs married into the Zapotec royalty at Zaachila, the descendants of that union were Mixtec lords of Teozacoalco.

The Third Story: Summary and Interpretation

The third story is distinctive because of its markedly different format. It abandons boustrophedon and utilizes a footpath to direct the motion of action. Generally it is divided into upper and lower registers, although upper descends to lower on Pages 37 and 39. In each case, the descent indicates the actors have arrived at specific destinations. On Page 37a, the actors pass over or through a valley without stopping. Subsequently, they stop at Sayutepec for the main event of the sequence (Pages 37a–38). Then, after the Sayutepec ceremony, they journey again through Serpent's Mouth Cave at Apoala, and the footpath descends on Page 39 to indicate that Lords Seven and One Rain have arrived at their destination.

The chronological placement of the story is important. Since it begins at

Table 9.1. The War from Heaven and Postwar Chronology

Codex/Page	Date	Event
Z-N 2	3 Reed (AD 963)	♂ Eight Wind arrives at Yucuñudahui
Z-N 3a	3 Reed (AD 963)	War begins at Yucuñudahui
	+16 years	
Z-N 3b	5(6) Reed (AD 979)	End of War from Heaven
	+1 year	
Z-N 1	7 Flint (AD 980)	♂ Eight Wind goes to Apoala
	+6 years	
Z-N 4 VM 37–35	13 Rabbit (AD 986)	Tree Birth at Apoala and marriage of ♂ One Flower and ♀ Thirteen Flower
	+34 years	
VM 35	8 Flint (AD 1020)	Birth of ♀ Nine Alligator
	+14 years	
VM 35	9 Rabbit (AD 1034)	Marriage of ♀ Nine Alligator and ♂ Five Wind
	+22 years	
Z-N 36	5 Flint (AD 1056)	Beginning of Four Lords from Apoala story
	+4 years	
Z-N 39	9 Flint (AD 1060)	♂ Seven Rain at his valley
	+10 years	
Z-N 39	6 Rabbit (AD 1070)	♂ One Rain at his valley
	+1 year	
Z-N 37b	7 Reed (AD 1071)	Sayutepec ceremony and return to valleys

Apoala with the two lineage families there, the time of the events on Pages 36–39 is placed after the War from Heaven and, therefore, after the Tree Birth lineage-validation events at Apoala.

The entire chronology from the beginning of the war to the Sayutepec ceremony spans 108 years. Lord Eight Deer Jaguar Claw of Tilantongo was born in AD 1063 and died in AD 1115. The Four Lords from Apoala story begins in AD 1056, seven years before Eight Deer's birth, and the remainder of the Four Lords event occurs entirely within Eight Deer's lifetime. Eight Deer became lord of Tututepec in AD 1083, twelve years after the Four Lords story ends (according to Zouche-Nuttall reverse, Pages 44d–48). Because of the switching of Lord Seven Rain's and One Rain's names on Page 38—during the important ceremony at Sayutepec—the apparent vagueness of the story is reduced. In the Sayutepec ceremony, Lord One Rain was empowered because Lord Seven Rain acted in his name. Associate that with the lineage-enfranchisement implications written on Page 36, and we can see that One Rain becomes a fully empowered lord with extraordinary abilities, and his prestige as a lineage founder, possibly for the last genealogy on Pages 40–41, is enhanced.

The Chronological Perspective of Mixtec History

So far as is known, virtually all Mesoamerican pre-European cultures used the two Mesoamerican calendars integrated in some form or another. Alfonso Caso (1971:333–348) details the use of northern Mesoamerican calendar systems as it varied from culture to culture. If we look at inscriptions from two pre-Hispanic Mesoamerican cultures, namely, Isthmian and Classic Period Maya, we note that they tended to initiate them with elaborate recordings of dates. The assumption is, therefore, that these cultures employed a precise Long Count system that allowed them to fix dates specifically within long calendar cycles. They tended to use dates as markers for historical events, that is, they used dates to find events.

For those without the efficient Long Count, such as the Mixtecs, the tendency seems to have been to use events to find dates. For those who study Mixtec written pictography, this creates a certain ambiguity, which is often frustrating. As a result, there are those who justify not dealing with the calendar at all, except in the sense of dates as written metaphor instead of as specific dated events. Examples of dates as metaphor only do exist in Mixtec codices. All dates can have metaphorical content and thereby add to historical data. However, they are also dates and as such imply and record sequences that can be understood as moving along Time's Arrow—from past to present to future. For Mixtecs, each 52-year cycle was distinct, and the connection between them along Time's Arrow was maintained by memory and used for recitation of the stories or the progression of genealogy. This is obvious in the recording of genealogies themselves. Each genealogical section is in forward progression. The one following it may be precedent or successive.

I use the "Time's Arrow" concept when using Mixtec dates to recover their pictographic histories. Generally, this works well, but sometimes it does not suffice to resolve chronological ambiguities.

The first story begins in AD 935, the second story (Page 14b, Year 4 Flint), in perhaps AD 914. Thereafter the second-story events are possibly dated as follows: Page 14a, meeting of Three Flint Elder and Lord Five Flower, Year 7 Reed (AD 916); birth of Three Flint Younger, Page 16b, Year 3 Flint (AD 925); Lord Twelve Wind descends from the sky, Page 19a, Year 7 Rabbit (AD 954). In Year 10 House (AD 957), Lady Three Flint Younger would have been thirty-two years old when she married/bathed with Lord Twelve Wind Smoke-Eye from the Sky in that year. The War from Heaven began in Year 3 Reed (AD 963). The Four Lords from Apoala story begins (on Page 36) in Year 5 Flint (AD 1056)—seventy-seven years after the War from Heaven ended and seventy years after the Tree Birth event in Apoala.

This chronological perspective—even given its ambiguities—tells us something important about the three stories and their genealogies recorded in Codex Zouche-Nuttall Document 1. They all cluster in an era commonly referred to as the Epiclassic Period—a transitional period between the collapse of Classic Period civilizations and the establishment of Postclassic Period civilizations. Previously, in the Classic Period, Zapotec- and Teotihuacan-controlled dynasties at Wasp Hill dominated the Mixtecs. In fact, there is a tendency among some contemporary scholars to identify Wasp Hill so closely with the Zapotecs that it appears they refer to it not as Wasp Hill, but as Monte Albán (Jansen and Pérez Jiménez 2005).

Codex Zouche-Nuttall Document 1 details the overthrow of these Wasp Hill clans twice: once in the first story of Lord Eight Wind of Suchixtlan (Pages 1–8, in the northern Nochixtlan Valley) and again immediately following the Ladies Three Flint story (Pages 14–19, in the southern Nochixtlan Valley). The specific geographies of these two theaters of war make the explicit statement that the overthrow of foreign influence was complete. They also relate that the War from Heaven began with the original inhabitants of the Mixteca—the Stone Men—and that, subsequently, an alliance was made with them.

Interpretative chronology from these first two stories tells us that the third and final story occurs after the resolution of the War from Heaven. While all three stories associate in some way with Apoala—the site where new lineages were enfranchised to rule and control territory after the War from Heaven—only story three (the Four Lords from Apoala) initiates with a full-page explicit statement of the lineage-enfranchisement authority of the Apoala Tree Birth lords. This does not imply that the same author composed each story, but it does imply that each author was aware of an overall message that defined Mixtec royal histories and the oral traditions concerning them for successive generations.

10 Document 2 (Reverse), Pages 42–84:
Introduction to the Political Biography of Lord Eight Deer Jaguar Claw of Tilantongo

The reverse of Codex Zouche-Nuttall is thought to be the older of the two sides of the fanfold manuscript. There are various reasons for this, but the main one is that paint from the newer obverse document (Pages 1–41) seeped through cracks in the leather pagination and overlaid the previously painted reverse (Pages 42–84). The stylistic reason for this assumption is that the final story on the obverse abandons the traditional boustrophedon format in favor of the footpath technique seen in later codices. Also, the codex obverse consists of three stories each followed by genealogies, and they display a variety of reading orders or techniques, not merely horizontal or vertical boustrophedon techniques defined by red lines.

The codex reverse, on the other hand, is a continuous vertical ascending and descending boustrophedon and reads from right to left (as does the obverse). The single exception to the boustrophedon format is Page 75, which reads from right to left but abandons the boustrophedon style for a single-page panel/mural type of tableau. Page 75 does follow a reading structure similar to Pages 14, 40, and 41 of Zouche-Nuttall obverse, namely, the action occurs in the upper register, and the lower register (reading from right to left) contains auxiliary material augmenting the upper-register storyline.

Also unlike the obverse manuscript(s), the reverse is incomplete. This has led to speculation that the reverse manuscript is unfinished and perhaps was snatched out of the hands of scribes by invaders before they could complete it. However, examination of high-resolution photographs of the last page (84) shows traces of figures in the "unfinished" portion (84b–c) that are now erased. This is not unexpected. Virtually all Mixtec manuscripts surviving today display evidence of alteration in various sections of text. For some examples, the rationale for alteration is evident, but sometimes it is obscure.

The reverse manuscript, although a biography of one subject (Eight Deer), nevertheless occurs in several sections by topic as it presents his life.

Section divisions in the obverse manuscript(s) are distinct, but here subject determines them. These sections are:

1. Parentage statement: Pages 42a–43b.
2. Childhood military career: Pages 43b–44a.
3. The Chalcatongo event: Page 44a–b.
4. Transition from Chalcatongo to Tututepec: Pages 44c–45b.
5. Eight Deer as lord of Tututepec: Pages 45b–46a.
6. Territorial expansions of Tututepec hegemony: Pages 46a–50d.
7. Eight Deer's Toltec Alliance and a conference with Lady Nine Reed: Pages 50d–52d.
8. Conquests with the Tolteca/Chichimeca: Pages 53a–d.
9. Eight Deer Jaguar Claw, Lord of Tilantongo: Page 53d.
10. Conference of Eight Deer and his half brother Twelve Motion with 112 lords (unification of the Mixteca): Pages 54–68a.
11. Peregrinations from Tilantongo and ceremonies and conquests with the Toltecs: Pages 68b–70.
12. Conquests: Pages 71–74c.
13. The Battle in the Sky and Eight Deer becomes a Sun God lord: Pages 75–80b.
14. The assassination of Lord Twelve Motion and the Siege of Hua Chino: Pages 81–84.

This is a political biography because Eight Deer's marriages and offspring are omitted, and the substance of the reverse codex narrative emphasizes Lord Eight Deer's political activities: his rise to power through the town of Tututepec, his many conquests, his unification of the Mixteca, and his alliance with the Toltecs. The newer obverse document details Eight Deer's wives and children following the second story, where it details the second dynasty of Tilantongo and Teozacoalco. Although written as a continuous vertical ascending and descending boustrophedon (with one exception noted above), the reverse narrative does have certain helpful reading techniques that will be noted and discussed as they occur in the text.

The reverse narrative varies in detail according to the data presented. For example, the conquests of Tututepec hegemony (number 6 above) are detailed by place and explanatory day dates. Explanatory day dates in the sacred calendar (or, in Nahuatl, the *tonalpohualli*) are not necessarily chronologically progressive, although in other narrative sections of the document they are and thus advance the narrative according to Time's Arrow. Some res gestae tableaux demonstrate conflation, or the compression of a complex series of events into a single tableau. For example, the Chalcatongo event (number 3 above) is highly conflated into a single tableau showing the Oracle of the Dead at Chalcatongo with the deceased Lord Three Lizard and the living Lady Six Monkey (of Jaltepec, although we are not told the name of her polity) and Lord Eight Deer (not yet lord of Tututepec or Tilantongo).

If this document were the only one surviving, we would have no idea of Lady Six Monkey's identity and age, nor would we know that the deceased Lord Three Lizard was one of her grandfather's twin sons. Those who recited and performed this story knew omitted data and presented it here in conflation, but we have to rely on the complex and interesting information presented in Codex Selden to "fill in the blanks," as it were. On the other hand, if Codex Selden were the only surviving Mixtec codex, we would know much about Lady Six Monkey, but of Eight Deer we would only know that he was the father of two Tilantongo princesses that married Lady Six Monkey's sons, the princes One Alligator and Four Wind, long after Eight Deer killed Lady Six Monkey in AD 1101 and after his own assassination in AD 1115.

Hence conflation is a device of pictogram texts used to function as "memory triggers" assisting those who had memorized the oral histories, narratives, and stories and were obligated upon occasion to perform them. While these seemingly occulted data present obscurities to us, they enriched the narrative performance possibilities for the original storytellers. The conflations are also political. For example, Tilantongo and Jaltepec were bitter enemies, so Jaltepec-oriented Codex Selden refers only rarely to Tilantongo and Lord Eight Deer Jaguar Claw, and Tilantongo-oriented documents minimize references to Lady Six Monkey.

11 Document 2 (Reverse), Sections 1–6, Pages 42–50: Parentage Statement, Childhood Military Career, Chalcatongo Event, Transition from Chalcatongo to Tututepec, Eight Deer as Lord of Tututepec

Sections 1 and 2, Pages 42–43: Parentage Statement and Childhood Military Career

Pages 42 and 43 establish a two-page reading format generally employed in this reverse document. The same two-page format is also employed to establish the narrative structure of the obverse document (Pages 1–41). A parentage statement is presented from the beginning of Page 42a until the lower portion of Page 43b. Then, beginning in the upper part of column 43b, we see the boyhood military career of Lord Eight Deer Jaguar Claw at the age of eight years. This continues until the last toponym (place sign) conquered by boy Eight Deer at the bottom of Page 43c.

Since the rule for intact codices that read from right to left is to begin in the lower right corner of the first page, reading begins there. The succeeding columns of pictogram text are signified by the lowercase letters "a," "b," and "c," and events in them are described below and numbered sequentially in Tables 11.1 and 11.2 with Arabic numerals—1, 2, 3, etc.—that ascend or descend according to the boustrophedon narrative structure.

The text begins telling the first story of Lord Eight Deer's parentage in the lower-right corner of the first column (a) of Page 42. It is in effect "the families of Lord Five Alligator." In Year 6 Flint on Day 7 Eagle (AD 1043), Lord Five Alligator married the Lady Nine Eagle. This event happened in the Temple of Heaven at Tilantongo. Their first child, a son, was born in Year 7 House on Day 12 Motion (AD 1045), thus his formal name was Twelve Motion and his personal name was Bleeding Jaguar Head. Their second child was the prince Three Water, and their third child the princess Six Lizard. This codex does not provide dates for their nativities. All three offspring (Twelve Motion, Three Water, and Six Lizard) face against the reading order and, by

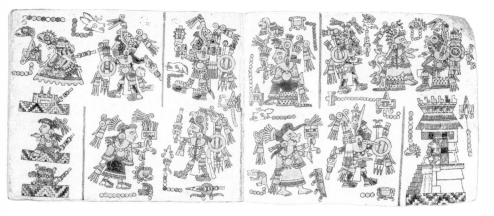

Figure 11.1. Codex Zouche-Nuttall (reverse), Pages 42—43. © The Trustees of the British Museum.

Figure 11.2. Codex Zouche-Nuttall (reverse), Page 42. © The Trustees of the British Museum.

Table 11.1. Events on Page 42a–c from Year 6 Flint (AD 1043) to Year 10 House (AD 1061) = 18 years

Column "c"	Column "b"	Column "a"
11. Lord Five Alligator marries Lady Eleven Water.	6. First child, Lord Twelve Motion, born in . . .	5. Marries Lady Nine Eagle.
		4. Lord Five Alligator
10. Year 10 House Day 6 Deer (AD 1061)	7. . . . Year 7 House (AD 1045).	3. Year 6 Flint Day 7 Eagle (AD 1043)
9. Third child is Lady Six Lizard.	8. Second child is Lord Three Water.	2. Temple of Heaven
		1. at Tilantongo

Figure 11.3. Codex Zouche-Nuttall (reverse), Page 43. © The Trustees of the British Museum.

doing so, determine this first family narrative to be distinct from the one that follows it.

The father of these children, Lord Five Alligator, is emphasized on this first page of the reverse manuscript but is unmentioned hereafter. Codex Bodley provides a more complete biography for him. Specifically, he was the son of Lord Thirteen Dog and the Lady One Vulture (Bodley 6-I; Zouche-Nuttall 25). His birth is undated, but Bodley tells us that he has a prominent career and even reforms the Mixtec calendar, purging Zapotec elements from it (Caso 1960:34). The ceremony commemorating this accomplishment is shown in Bodley but also, to our interest, on Zouche-Nuttall obverse Page 25c in Year 5 Reed on Day 1 Alligator (AD 1044). Bodley (8-V) gives Five Alligator's death as occurring in Year 5 Rabbit on Day 9 Dog (AD 1082).

The sequence of events displayed on Codex Zouche-Nuttall reverse Pages 42–43 is shown in the tables below. It begins in the lower-right of the first column of Page 42, as does the obverse codex, and proceeds according to the codex reading order to the top of column "a," then from the top of column "b" to the bottom, then from the bottom of column "c" to the top. The reading transitions to Page 43, where column "a" reads from top to bottom, column "b" from bottom to top, then column "c" from top to bottom. Each tableau sequence or its components on Page 42 is numbered from 1 to 11 in Table 11.1.

Page 43 begins with the most important child of Lord Five Alligator's marriage to Lady Eleven Water, Lord Eight Deer Jaguar Claw, born in AD 1063. It also displays the second and third children of this marriage, namely, the Lord Nine Flower and the Lady Nine Monkey. Lady Nine Monkey faces against the reading order and determines thereby that the narrative of this second family of Lord Five Alligator has ended. Then, moving to the next narrative pictogram display, the boy Lord Eight Deer conquers four places in AD 1071 when he was eight years old. This page ends at the bottom left of the third, or "c," column. The next page, 44, begins at the top right of the first, or "a," column, indicating a chronological narrative disjunction of eight years to a time when Lord Eight Deer was sixteen years old. Table 11.2 follows the codex progression of events for Page 43.

Summary of Pages 42 and 43

Beginning in column "a" at the lower right, the black-and-white frieze identifies the town of Tilantongo. Sitting atop it is the Temple of the Sky. Both

Table 11.2. Events on Page 43a–c from Year 12 Reed (AD 1063) to Year 7 Reed (AD 1071) = 8 years

Column "c"	Column "b"	Column "a"
17. . . . conquers Stone Eagle Hill in	16. Lord Eight Deer at age eight . . .	12. First child, Lord Eight Deer, is born in
18. Year 7 Reed on Day 10 Vulture (AD 1071)		13. Year 12 Reed (AD 1063).
19. and Two Spindles Town,	15. Third child, Lady Nine Monkey.	14. Second child, Lord Nine Flower.
20. Lady Town,		
21. and Turtle Town.		

are the location of the succeeding actions. The date Year 6 Flint Day 7 Eagle (AD 1043) begins the chronology of events. The male, Lord Five Alligator (42a, top), marries the female, Lady Nine Eagle (42b, top), and their first and most important offspring is a son, Lord Twelve Motion, who is born on that day in Year 7 House (AD 1045). In the Zouche-Nuttall reverse narrative, Lord Twelve Motion is a frequent companion of his half brother Eight Deer Jaguar Claw. The second child is also a son, Lord Three Water, and the third child is the female Lady Six Lizard (Page 42c, bottom). The dates of their births are unrecorded, but all three offspring face against the reading order, thereby indicating that this initial section dealing with Lord Five Alligator's first family is a statement to itself and has ended.

The next series of tableaux deal with Lord Five Alligator's second marriage and family. In Year 10 House on Day 6 Deer (AD 1061, sixteen years after the first marriage), Five Alligator marries Lady Eleven Water (42c, top), presumably at Tilantongo. Moving to Page 43a, their first and most important child is the subject of this political biography, Lord Eight Deer Jaguar Claw. He was born on Day 8 Deer in Year 12 Reed (AD 1063). The second child of this union is Lord Nine Flower, and the third is Lady Nine Lizard (Page 43b, bottom). She faces against the reading order and signifies that this section of the parentage statement—and indeed all the parentage statements—has ended.

The remainder of Page 43b and the entirety of 43c are devoted to Lord Eight Deer's childhood military career, undertaken when he was eight years old. The year is 7 Reed (AD 1071), and during that year he conquers four places on Day 10 Vulture: Stone Eagle Hill, Two Spindles Town, Lady Town, and Turtle Town.

Sections 3–4, Pages 44–45: The Chalcatongo Event and Transition to Tututepec

Page 44a (top). Conquest of Digging Stick Town (continuation of conquest series from previous page).

Page 44a (middle). Year 2 Reed Day 10 Flower (AD 1079). Conquest of Two Plumes Town.

Page 44a events in Year 2 Reed end Eight Deer's childhood military career at age sixteen.

Page 44b (bottom to top). At Chalcatongo, Year 6 Reed Day 6 Snake (AD 1083), dead Lord Three Lizard and Lady Six Monkey.

Page 44c (top to bottom). Lord Eight Deer Jaguar Claw, in Year 6 Reed on Day 6 Snake, the Holy Tree Ceremony at Eleven Caves Hill.

Page 44d (bottom to top). Year 1 Reed Day 6 Water (AD 1091), conquest of Blue Parrot Town and Lake Town. In Year 5 Reed on Day 2 Water (AD 1095), Eight Deer and his half brother Twelve Motion conduct an animal sacrifice.

The events on Page 44 occur from AD 1079 to AD 1095, or over sixteen years. Eight Deer is now thirty-two years old. A total of forty years have elapsed since the reverse manuscript began on Page 42.

Page 45a (top to bottom). Continuing in Year 5 Reed (AD 1095), on Day 2 Flower, conquest of Lake Temple; on Day 13 Motion, conquest of Cradleboard and Incense Hill.

Page 45b (bottom to top). On Day 7 Lizard, conquest of Rain God Town Temple Hill; on Day 7 Vulture, Lord Eight Deer in a cave at a deer-hoof ceremony.

Page 45c (bottom). On Day 6(7) Snake, a ballcourt ceremony.

Page 45d (bottom to top). At Tututepec, a Nine Wind Quetzalcoatl ceremony (continued on Page 46a).

The sequence of events that start on Page 44a and end on 46a, top right, establishes Lord Eight Deer Jaguar Claw as lord of Tututepec. Note: After the top of Page 45d, which shows Lord One Deer, Lord Nine Wind Quetzalcoatl is displayed as the first figure on Page 46a, so he is part of this procession whose participants are Lord Nine Wind, Lord One Deer, and Lord Seven Snake. This visual bridge between pages is a frequent technique employed on

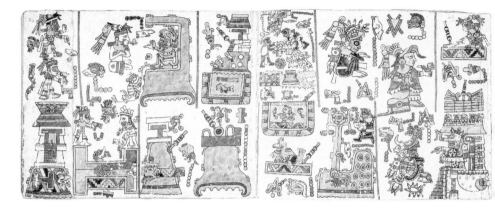

Figure 11.4. Codex Zouche-Nuttall (reverse), Pages 44—45. © The Trustees of the British Museum.

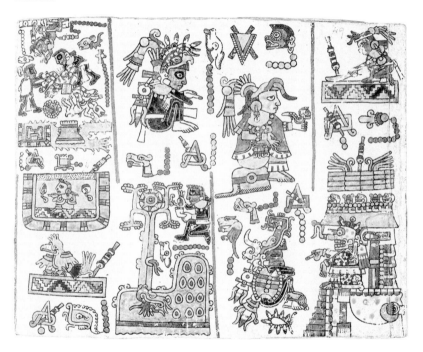

Figure 11.5. Codex Zouche-Nuttall (reverse), Page 44. © The Trustees of the British Museum.

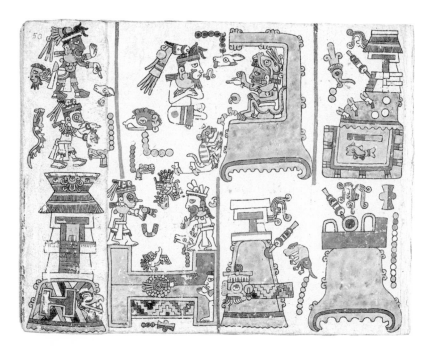

Figure 11.6. Codex Zouche-Nuttall (reverse), Page 45. © The Trustees of the British Museum.

the reverse of Codex Zouche-Nuttall. The vague solar year day numbers are: 156 days in Year 5 Reed; 2 Flower = day 180, 13 Motion = day 217, 6 Lizard = day 184, 7 Vulture = day 276, 3 Motion = day 336. On the previous page, Day 2 Water = day 89. Except for Day 13 Motion, these events are presented in two chronological sequences: 2 Water (89), 2 Flower (180), 6 Lizard (184); then, 13 Motion (217), 7 Vulture (276), 3 Motion (336).

Summary of Pages 44 and 45

For this section of text, the boustrophedon shifts from three columns per page to four, indicated here as "a," "b," "c," and "d." Page 44a continues Eight Deer's youthful military career in Year 2 Reed (AD 1079), when he was sixteen years old. It is also important to note that the boustrophedon reading sequence for Page 43 ended at the bottom of column 43c. The next boustrophedon reading sequence begins at the top of Page 44a, indicating a disjunction in reading order that begins a new section separating Eight Deer's military conquests at age eight years from those at age sixteen years, when he conquers two places: Digging Stick Town and Two Plumes Town.

The Chalcatongo event begins next and extends from Pages 44a to 44c. The place is identified by a prominent skull-shaped temple within which is seated the Oracle of the Dead (unidentified by name here but known to be Lady Nine Grass), who is speaking to a deceased *yaha yahui* priest named Three Lizard. The year is 6 Reed (AD 1083). Lord Eight Deer is twenty years old. First shown in this mortuary conference is Lady Six Monkey of Jaltepec (prior to her name change to Six Monkey War Quechquemitl). Second is Eight Deer wearing the accoutrements of a *yaha yahui* priest. The day is 6 Snake.

In the same year and on the same day, Eight Deer is shown after the Chalcatongo conference conducting a ceremony at the holy tree at Eleven Caves Hill. Then in Year 1 Reed (AD 1091) on Day 6 Water, he conquers two places (Page 44c), Blue Parrot Town and Lake Town. In Year 5 Reed (AD 1095) on Day 2 Water, Eight Deer and Lord Twelve Motion (his half brother) conduct an animal sacrifice ceremony with the god Lord Thirteen Reed.

The action continues to Page 45a, where the conquest of two places is listed: one is a lake and temple on Deer Hoof Hill on Day 2 Flower, and the other is Cradleboard and Incense Hill on Day 13 Motion. A third conquest begins Page 45b, that of Rain God Town and its hilltop temple, conquered on Day 7 Lizard. The top half of Page 45b, though not at Tututepec, shows Eight Deer's cave empowerment ceremony as lord of Tututepec. The individual speaking to Eight Deer is unnamed but is not a Mixtec. He appears at the top of Page 45c facing Eight Deer, who is seated in the cave. The day is 7 Vulture.

The bottom half of Page 45c is a bird-decapitation ceremony in a ballcourt. The day is 3 Motion. The participants are Eight Deer (identified by his personal name, Jaguar Claw) and a male named Six (or Seven) Snake. Page 45d is a Lord Nine Wind Quetzalcoatl ceremony conducted at Tututepec's Star Temple. The temple is located on the hill, and the previously mentioned ballcourt is halfway up it. Two priests stand above the temple; one is named Seven Snake and the other is One Deer. The god Nine Wind Quetzalcoatl is the first figure on Page 46a and forms a visual bridge connecting Pages 45 and 46.

Section 5, Pages 45b–46a: The Lord of Tututepec

All is not as it seems. The first dynasty of Tilantongo had been in power for several generations. The last king of it, Lord Two Rain Twenty Jaguars, was ill fated. When the Oracle of the Dead at Chalcatongo—Lady Nine Grass—reassigned the marriage alliance of Jaltepec (Lady Six Monkey) contra Tilantongo and pro Hua Chino, Lord Two Rain Twenty Jaguars (six years old at the time) was, in effect, royally spurned. At the time of the alliance reassignment, Jaltepec and Hua Chino were larger and more prosperous than Tilantongo. The effect of the Chalcatongo event (AD 1083) described in Codex Zouche-Nuttall's Page 44 was to establish a political instability of such magnitude that the last scion of Tilantongo's first dynasty committed suicide in AD 1096. The oracle at Chalcatongo had vacated Tilantongo's marriage alliance, so he was unmarried and childless but left behind a valuable commodity: a vacant throne. Lord Eight Deer was not in the line of succession at Tilantongo. The Tututepec events unfold against this background of political instability at Tilantongo as Eight Deer moves to establish himself as a military and political power. After Tututepec, he usurped power at Tilantongo, and Tututepec disappears from the codiacal record in Codex Zouche-Nuttall.

The town did not disappear, however. Tututepec is situated in the lower Rio Verde region of the western coast of Oaxaca. It had existed as a non-Mixtec polity from antiquity, with settlements documented from the Late Formative Period (400 BC–150 BC), but had experienced times of varying prosperity, growing and shrinking over the ages. Its ethnic identity was neither Mixtec nor Zapotec but probably Chatino. After AD 1100—roughly corresponding to Eight Deer Jaguar Claw's occupancy of the area—it was Mixtec and persisted in prosperity to be conquered by Pedro de Alvarado in 1522. It remains today (see Joyce et al. 2004).

The sequence of events related to Lord Eight Deer becoming lord of Tututepec is also written in Codex Bodley in more detail. The narrative occurs after the death of Eight Deer's father, Lord Five Alligator, in Year 5 Rabbit on Day 9 Dog (AD 1082). The Eight Deer–Tututepec sequence on Bodley begins on Page 9-V and is continued on 10-V, 10-IV–9-IV, and 9-III. In these sequential tableaux, there are nine preceding events that culminate with Eight Deer's enthronement as Tututepec's lord. Here, paraphrased, is Caso's (1960:38–38) description of these events: (1) Year 3 Flint Day 4 Rain, Eight Deer leaves one cave and goes to another with the shrine of Lord Three Reed;

(2) on a following day, 5 Flower, he visits the elders Lord Ten Flower and Lady Four Rabbit, lords of Mouth Mountain (Lady Four Rabbit was sister of Lord Twelve Lizard Arrow Legs, third king of Tilantongo's first dynasty, and she was great-aunt of Tilantongo's last king, Two Rain)—it may be that Eight Deer visits their shrine rather than visiting them in person; (3) next, Eight Deer visits a cave that contains 4 Flower Temple; (4) thereafter he visits a town called Bound Bundles with its Temple of the Sky—Lord One Death (of the sun) presides there; (5) in Year 4 House on Day 6 Serpent, Eight Deer goes to a town called Mask and River Hill; (6) then, he plays ball with Lord One Motion (Venus); (7) subsequently they conquer a town called Jewel River; (8) in Year 6 Reed on Day 13 Flower, Eight Deer conquers Sky Tiger Hill, and on Day 6 Snake of that year (forty-five days later), Eight Deer offers a heart to Lady Nine Grass of Chalcatongo; (9) then, in Year 6 Reed, Eight Deer visits Lord One Death and Lady Nine Grass. Thereafter, in the next tableau, he is shown seated as lord of Tututepec (Page 9-III). Number 8 above is the only mention of the Chalcatongo event in this Bodley sequence; neither Lady Six Monkey nor the deceased Lord Three Lizard appears in it. Rather, the focus is placed entirely on Lord Eight Deer and the Oracle of Chalcatongo, Lady Nine Grass. Caso overlooks or misnames this later event but mentions that subsequently Eight Deer receives four ambassadors representing Lord Four Jaguar the Toltec (Bodley, 10-III). He does this while lord of Tututepec. The chronology—including a flashback—is:

5 Rabbit 10 Dog (AD 1082), Death of Five Alligator

  -2 years

3 Flint (AD 1080), Eight Deer leaves a cave

  +1 year

4 House (AD 1081), Eight Deer plays ball

  +2 years

6 Reed (AD 1083), conference of Eight Deer and Six Monkey with Lady Nine Grass at Chalcatongo, and, finally, Eight Deer at Tututepec.

By this chronological reckoning, we can see that Eight Deer began his career to be lord of Tututepec two years before the death of his father, Five Alligator. He succeeded one year after his father's death. Of interest is that Codex Zouche-Nuttall lists the ball game in Year 4 House as happening on Day 3 Motion, and Codex Bodley lists it as Day 6 Snake. From Day 3 Motion to Day 6 Snake in that year is forty-eight days.

Table 11.3

Zouche-Nuttall	Year	Bodley
	(AD 1080)	3 Flint, leaves a cave
	(AD 1081)	4 House, plays ball
	(AD 1082)	5 Rabbit, Five Alligator dies
6 Reed, Chalcatongo	(AD 1083)	6 Reed, Chalcatongo
1 Reed, two conquests	(AD 1091)	
5 Reed ceremony and Tututepec	(AD 1095)	

Codex Zouche-Nuttall lists the Chalcatongo event as occurring in Year 6 Reed (AD 1083), after which Eight Deer does a sun-in-tree ceremony. Then in Year 1 Reed on Day 6 Water (AD 1091), he conquers another two places. In Year 5 Reed on Day 2 Water (AD 1095), he and his half brother Twelve Motion do an animal sacrifice and Eight Deer becomes lord of Tututepec. Between Bodley and Zouche-Nuttall, we have two complementary narrative traditions regarding the chronology of events.

In this progression, Eight Deer was seventeen years old in Year 3 Flint, eighteen years old in Year 4 House, twenty years old in Year 6 Reed, twenty-eight years old in Year 1 Reed, and thirty-two years old in Year 5 Reed. Citing Mary Elizabeth Smith (1963), Byland and Pohl (1994:242) opt for Year 6 Reed for both Chalcatongo and the subsequent Tututepec events.

The Chalcatongo event is also written in Codex Selden, Page 6-III, IV. In this Selden event, the date 5 Reed is listed, but to be congruent with the subsequent events following in both Zouche-Nuttall and Bodley, it must be Year 6 Reed. If Year 5 Reed is intended in Codex Selden, then it is the time of the animal sacrifice by Eight Deer and Twelve Motion shown on Zouche-Nuttall Page 44d and prior to Eight Deer's assumption as lord of Tututepec. In the case of Selden displaying Year 5 Reed, I have proposed augural purposes to explain it because in the same scene a prominent male named Eleven Wind is named Ten Wind instead. Subsequently in Codex Selden, his name is correctly written as Eleven Wind, as though no mistake had occurred. If the Selden Year 5 Reed is accurate, then the following dated events in that text are from a variant tradition regarding these episodes. Therefore, the recording of Year 5 Reed in Codices Selden and Zouche-Nuttall are variances in memorized traditions.

The Zouche-Nuttall account of the Tututepec conquests of Eight Deer changes the year to 6 Flint, the year following 5 Reed, on Page 48b, so they stick with the Year 5 Reed narrative. Year 6 Flint (AD 1096) is also the year of the death of Lord Two Rain, the last king of Tilantongo's first dynasty. In the year following—7 House (AD 1097)—Eight Deer receives his Toltec nose ornament.

In the Zouche-Nuttall tradition regarding Lord Eight Deer, we have:

Year 12 Reed (AD 1063): Eight Deer is born.

Year 7 Reed (AD 1071): Eight Deer is eight years old and conducts three military conquests.

Year 2 Reed (AD 1079): Eight Deer is sixteen years old and conducts two military conquests.

Year 6 Reed (AD 1083): Eight Deer at Chalcatongo; he is twenty years old.

Year 1 Reed (AD 1091): Eight Deer is twenty-eight years old and has two military conquests.

Year 5 Reed (AD 1095): Eight Deer is thirty-two years old and does the dog sacrifice ceremony, then goes to Tututepec and becomes lord of the place.

Year 6 Flint (AD 1096): Eight Deer conquests for Tututepec; he is thirty-four years old. This is also the year Lord Two Rain Twenty Jaguars commits suicide.

Year 7 House (AD 1097). Eight Deer is received by Toltec Lord Four Jaguar. Eight Deer is thirty-five years old. Codex Bodley (10-II/9-II) agrees here with date and event. It is noteworthy that the Year 7 House and Day 1 Wind in Codex Bodley follow an erasure and, although the A-O year sign is colored, the "house" qualifier and entire Day 1 Wind are uncolored, giving the impression that they were erased and changed from a previous date.

Section 6, Pages 46a–50d: Territorial Expansions of Tututepec Hegemony

The *tonalpohualli* chronology for this section is not sequential. The first figure in column "a" on Page 46, top, is Lord Nine Wind Quetzalcoatl. He is part of the Tututepec Star Temple scene concluding on Page 45d. Page 46 shows seven conquered places and six days in Year 5 Reed (AD 1095). The fourth day, shown on 46c, is 1 Alligator and indicates the beginning of Tonalpohualli 7.

On Page 47a–b, four towns submit to Eight Deer without conquest. They may represent towns in the preceding unconquered district of Smoking

Figure 11.7. Codex Zouche-Nuttall (reverse), Pages 46—47. © The Trustees of the British Museum.

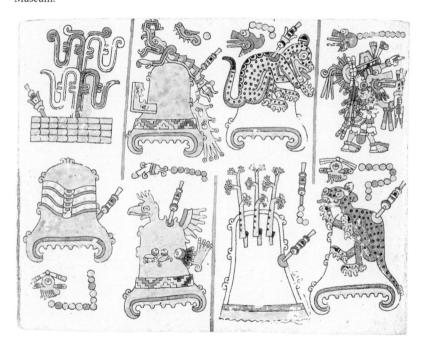

Figure 11.8. Codex Zouche-Nuttall (reverse), Page 46. © The Trustees of the British Museum.

Table 11.4. Conquests Shown on Page 46

Places Conquered	Day
Red Jaguar Hill	13 Rain
Three Flute Tree Hill	4 Reed
Jaguar Hill	5 Wind
Fire Serpent Hill and Waterfall	1 Alligator
Blue Cormorant Hill	7 Flower
Spine and Ribs Hill, Smoking Plain*	12 Rain

*Smoking Plain is shown without a conquest arrow.

Plain. A mask and a male named Five Wind offering a jaguar cub represent the first town. A flowering maguey and the male Five Eagle offering a bird for sacrifice represent the second town. A split façade and the male Nine Motion offering a gold pectoral represent the third town. The fourth town is represented by a gray bird and the male Nine Deer offering a plumed fan, as well as the males on Page 47c, Six Flower offering cacao and Seven Alligator offering a corn god or goddess effigy.

The toponyms with males named Five Eagle and Nine Motion are replacements for a preceding scene that has been erased.

On Page 47d, two places are conquered: Venus Staff Hill on Day 13 House and Star Torch River on Day 7 Flower.

Column "a" of Page 48 displays two conquered places: Stone Hill with Cave Temple on Day 7 Motion, and Stone Serpent Hill and Town on Day 10 Grass.

Column "b" has a temporal change to Year 6 Flint (AD 1096), Tonalpohualli 8; and thereafter six conquered places are listed: Sacrificed Cormorant Hill and Town on Day 11 Death, White Olla Hill on Day 3 Deer, Jade Mask Hill and town on Day 10 Rabbit, Two Stalks Hill (the original toponym has been erased) on Day 12 Dog, Strange Place on Day 3 Jaguar, and Smoke Town and Hill on Day 4 Flower. An emblem atop the hill of this last place has been partly erased.

In column "a" of Page 49 are two conquered places: White Hill and town and Temple Hill and town. In column "b" are two conquered places, each with a day assigned: Water Top Hill and town on Day 9 Flower; a lake and river on Day 6 Lizard. In column "c," the first three places are either erased with new places left uncolored, or the original places were left uncolored (as are two days). Faint traces remain of previous images. They are Ñuu in Hill

Figure 11.9. Codex Zouche-Nuttall (reverse), Page 47. © The Trustees of the British Museum.

Figure 11.10. Codex Zouche-Nuttall (reverse), Pages 48—49. © The Trustees of the British Museum.

Figure 11.11. Codex Zouche-Nuttall (reverse), Page 48. © The Trustees of the British Museum.

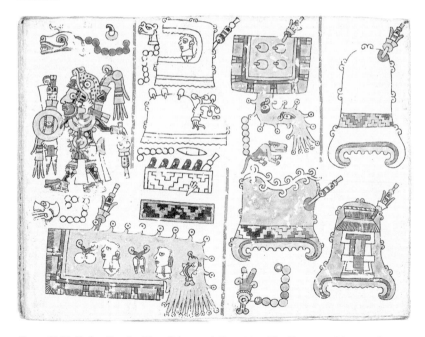

Figure 11.12. Codex Zouche-Nuttall (reverse), Page 49. © The Trustees of the British Museum.

Figure 11.13. Codex Zouche-Nuttall (reverse), Pages 50–51. © The Trustees of the British Museum.

Cave on Day 10 Snake, Bent Tree Hill on Day 7 Flint, and Five Beans Town. The next place is colored and appears to represent the black frieze characteristic of Tilantongo. Then there is a river and waterfall with the uncolored Day 11 Wind. The last figure in column "d" (top) is Lord Eight Deer Jaguar Claw attired as conqueror. He faces across the page divide, and the scene continues on Page 50. This position with Eight Deer as the dominant figure and as the last in a column "d" is repeated on Pages 50d–51a leading to a tableau with Lady Nine Reed on Page 51.

However, on Page 49d, Eight Deer as conqueror faces two males from Chalcatongo submitting without conquest on Day 1 Alligator, which is likely the beginning of Tonalpohualli 9 in Year 6 Flint (AD 1096).

On Page 50a–b two unnamed males representing Chalcatongo offer gifts to Eight Deer the Conqueror (on Page 49d). The first offers a sacrificial bird and a round woven grass mat with grass knot, and the second offers a torch. The day is 1 Alligator and begins Tonalpohualli 9. The goddess Lady Nine Grass is absent from the temple at Chalcatongo. Directly above the Chalcatongo toponym (Page 50b, bottom) is Tututepec's Star Temple. The day is 4 Flint, and Eight Deer offers an animal sacrifice before the temple (Page 50c, top). Day 4 Flint is forty-two days before Day 1 Alligator, thus is in Tonalpohualli 8. Following Eight Deer on Page 50c is an unconquered hill identified by a *techutli* lord sitting on a red-and-gold stone throne. On Page 50d is unconquered Jaguar Hill. This completes sections 5 and 6: Eight Deer as Lord of Tututepec and the Territorial Expansion of Tututepec. The beginning of Eight Deer as a *techutli* lord of the Tolteca/Chichimeca now begins.

12 Document 2 (Reverse), Sections 7–12, Pages 51–74: Eight Deer's Toltec Alliance through the Conquests with the Toltecs

The Lady Nine Reed Events

The last figure on Page 50d (top) is Lord Eight Deer facing Lady Nine Reed, who is the first figure on Page 51a. Eight Deer is preceded by the date Year 7 House (AD 1097) Day 9 Snake (the numeral circles cross the page fold). Lady Nine Reed is the lineage goddess and in Codex Vindobonensis Mexicanus I is identified as the holy tree that gives birth to Mixtec nobles (Furst 1978a:137). In her 1979 dissertation on Codex Vindobonensis Mexicanus I, Furst mistakenly reads the name Ten Reed for this goddess, when in actuality there is a rubbed-out streak at the end of the "reed" figure that causes it to be mistaken for an extra numeral circle. Since her dissertation is dated 1979 and the facsimile publication of Codex Zouche-Nuttall was not issued until 1987, it may be that she examined the Dover publication of Zelia Nuttall's Peabody Museum artists' copy of the codex that does give the name as Ten Reed. Alfonso Caso (1966:127a) makes the same mistake because he seems to have assumed that the Zelia Nuttall artists' rendering of the codex bearing her name was accurate in all respects. In any event, the female figure shown on Page 51a is Lady Nine Reed without doubt.

This encounter between Lord Eight Deer and Lady Nine Reed is more elaborated in the Colombino fragment. In fact, this Zouche-Nuttall conflation becomes quite suggestive in Colombino, specifically on Colombino Pages 9–10-I, 11-I, and 11–12-I. Codex Zouche-Nuttall gives the superficial impression that Eight Deer and his entourage (Page 52a–d) simply march up to the Toltec Lord Four Jaguar, who presents Eight Deer with a lineage bundle and a nose-piercing. Colombino tells a different story entirely. After two rejections of Eight Deer by Four Jaguar, Lady Nine Reed seems to intercede with him on Eight Deer's behalf. The ♀ Nine Reed events in Colombino are complex and detailed but remain elusive because the manuscript has suffered extensive damage. However, since Lady Nine Reed is strongly identified with lineage validation, we may assume that the Zouche-Nuttall meeting between her and Lord Eight Deer (who is not accoutered as a conqueror but as a *yaha yahui* priest) is a conflation representing her intercession on Eight Deer's behalf with Lord Four Jaguar of the Tolteca/Chichimeca.

The Codex Alfonso Caso (Colombino-Becker I) tableaux, although severely defaced, are an important traditional narrative concerning Lady Nine Reed, Lord Eight Deer, and Lord Four Jaguar the Toltec. Paraphrasing from Alfonso Caso's 1966 commentary on Codex Colombino, the tableaux are:

1) A person (probably female) seated in a river faces and converses with Lady Nine Reed;

2) Eight Deer attired as a *yaha yahui* priest meets with and makes an offering to Lady Nine Reed—and this is the subject of the conflated tableau on Codex Zouche-Nuttall Pages 50d–51a;

3) Codex Alfonso Caso (Colombino) Page IX shows a female (probably Lady Nine Reed) being borne by tumpline in a procession. All this precedes complex events that culminate in Eight Deer's meeting with Lord Four Jaguar the Toltec.

After the meeting between Eight Deer and Nine Reed (Pages 50d–51a), Eight Deer and his half brother Twelve Motion peregrinate through five places. The final place occurs as the last figure in the upper left of Page 51d, and as we have become accustomed to seeing, Eight Deer is seated there and forms a visual bridge to the first scene on Page 52a, Earthquake Hill. After this tableau, Eight Deer and his companions go to see Four Jaguar.

Codex Bodley presents yet another tradition regarding the events between Eight Deer and Four Jaguar. According to Bodley Pages 9-III–10-III and 10-II–9-II, after Lord Eight Deer is seated as ruler of Tututepec, Lord Four Jaguar sends four emissaries to visit Lord Eight Deer. Subsequently, Eight Deer (seemingly acting on a request from Four Jaguar) attacks a town and captures its ruler, Lord Three Alligator. Then Eight Deer marches the captured lord to Lord Four Jaguar and presents him as a sacrificial present. This results in Eight Deer receiving the Toltec dignity title of *techutli*, "lord" or "lineage founder."

Section 7, Pages 50d–52d: Eight Deer's Toltec Alliance and a Conference with Lady Nine Reed

On Page 50a–b, two males appear with gifts for Eight Deer, followed by the Chalcatongo Temple of Death. On Page 50b–c (top), Eight Deer is shown before Tututepec Star Temple. Page 50c–d (bottom) has images of two hills. Page 50d shows Eight Deer seated facing Lady Nine Reed, who is on Page 51a. The date Year 7 House has been erased and moved up in the pictogram tableau.

On Page 51a (top), Lady Nine Reed faces Eight Deer (on Page 50d). After this conference, Eight Deer and Twelve Motion peregrinate through four places (Page 51a–d), and Eight Deer is shown seated on the fifth (Page 51d, top).

On Page 52a at the top right, coming after Day 12 Flower, is the sixth place in the peregrination of Lord Eight Deer and his half brother Twelve Motion. Subsequently, also on Page 52a, Lord Eight Deer is seen seated on a motion/stone sign, the same sign shown as the identifier for the sixth place. Below him is a seventh place, a hill with an effigy of a Rain God head. From this

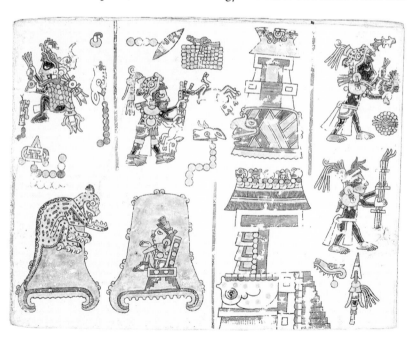

Figure 12.1. Codex Zouche-Nuttall (reverse), Page 50. © The Trustees of the British Museum.

Figure 12.2. Codex Zouche-Nuttall (reverse), Page 51. © The Trustees of the British Museum.

Figure 12.3. Codex Zouche-Nuttall (reverse), Pages 52—53. © The Trustees of the British Museum.

location and on Page 52b (bottom), Eight Deer's brother Nine Flower carries a red-and-white bound staff; ahead of him, on Page 52b–c (top), Lord Eight Deer stands before a kneeling Lord Four Jaguar the Toltec. Between them is a great ceremonial bundle topped by the very staff previously borne by Lord Nine Flower. The Year is 7 House Day 13 Alligator (AD 1097). After this bundle-presentation ceremony, a priest named Eight Death pierces Eight Deer's nose on Day 1 Wind, the day after Day 13 Alligator. This ceremonial nose-piercing is the official bestowal of the *techutli*, or "lord," dignity on Eight Deer. Directly above Lord Eight Death (Page 52d) are the Lords One Snake and Eight Snake.

Section 8, Page 53a–d: Conquests with the Tolteca/Chichimeca

This section of biographical topic 8 (see Chapter 10) begins Eight Deer's conquests with the Toltecs, Page 53a–d. Page 53a (top) shows the Lords Four Jaguar the Toltec and Eight Deer the Mixtec (now adorned with his turquoise nose ornament of a lineage founder lord) performing a bird-decapitation sacrifice on Day 4 Snake, three days after the nose-piercing. Unlike the mystifying use of days in Eight Deer's Tututepec conquests, days are used here to elaborate a progressive chronological sequence.

Page 53a–c displays Eight Deer's conquests as a Toltec/Mixtec *techutli* lord. Five places are conquered on the following days: 7 Rabbit (three days after the bird-decapitation ceremony on Day 4 Snake), one day later on 8 Water, fifty-one days later on 7 Flower, forty-one days later on 9 Alligator, and 4 Flint. Only the last day, 4 Flint, is out of sequence for Year 7 House (see below).

On Page 53d (bottom), Eight Deer is shown as a warrior-lord approaching Tilantongo on Day 1 Alligator, and a Venus staff is placed before the temple there on Day 9 Wind (Page 53d, top).

Although the transition from Year 7 House to Year 8 Rabbit is unmarked by a year sign—it only appears on Page 68b with Day 4 Wind—the suggested day count here is by *tonalpohualli*, not vague solar years. Day 4 Wind is Tonalpohualli 127 of Year 8 Rabbit.

Section 9, Page 53d: Eight Deer Jaguar Claw, Lord of Tilantongo

Page 53d shows Eight Deer arriving at the Temple of Heaven at Tilantongo and the establishment of the Nine Wind cult in the temple there. This activity took place in Year 8 Rabbit and took twenty-two days (from Day 1 Alligator to Day 9 Wind). The narrative action continues to Page 54a.

Figure 12.4. Codex Zouche-Nuttall (reverse), Page 52. © The Trustees of the British Museum.

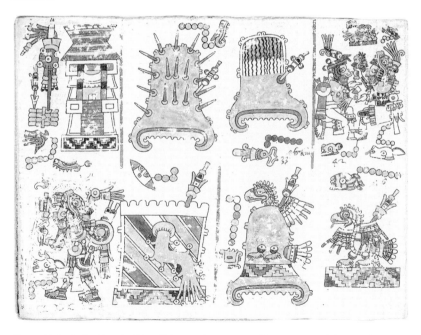

Figure 12.5. Codex Zouche-Nuttall (reverse), Page 53. © The Trustees of the British Museum.

Table 12.1. Chronology of Page 53

Days on Page 53, Year 7 House (AD 1097)		
Page	*Day*	*Event*
53a, top	4 Snake, day 115 of Year 7 House	Eight Deer and Four Wind bird sacrifice
53a, bottom	7 Rabbit, day 118 of Year 7 House	Conquest of Eagle Town
53b, bottom	8 Water, day 119 of Year 7 House	Conquest of dismembered Eagle Town and hill
53b, top	7 Flower, day 150 of Year 7 House	Conquest of Smoking Hill
53c, top	9 Alligator, day 211 of Year 7 House	Conquest of Cactus Spines Hill
Days on Page 53, Year 8 Rabbit (AD 1098)		
Page	*Day*	*Event*
53c, bottom	4 Flint, day 23 of Year 8 Rabbit	Conquest of Stone Hill and River Town
53d, bottom	1 Alligator, day 26 of Year 8 Rabbit	Eight Deer at Tilantongo. Begins Tonalpohualli 11.
53d, top	9 Wind, day 37 of Year 8 Rabbit	Venus Staff at Tilantongo

Section 10, Pages 54–68a: The Conference of Eight Deer and His Half Brother Twelve Motion with 112 Lords (Unification of the Mixteca)

Lord Twelve Motion is shown first at the top of Page 54a, followed by Eight Deer. Page 54b begins the list of the 112 lords they met with. Not all are Mixtec. Each lord is accompanied by his day name. They are listed sequentially as they occur in text.

Figure 12.6. Codex Zouche-Nuttall (reverse), Pages 54—55. © The Trustees of the British Museum.

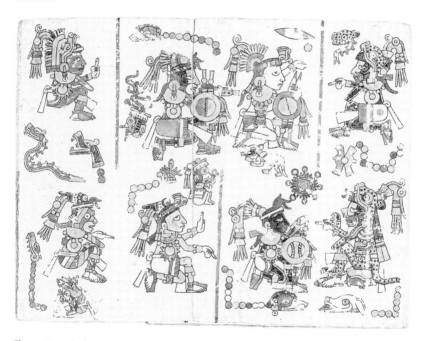

Figure 12.7. Codex Zouche-Nuttall (reverse), Page 54. © The Trustees of the British Museum.

Table 12.2. Lords on Page 54

Page	Lord No.	Day Name
Pg. 54b (bottom)	#1	12 Vulture
Pg. 54b (top)	#2	1 Flint
Pg. 54c (top)	#3	9 Vulture
Pg. 54c (bottom)	#4	7 Grass
Pg. 54d (bottom)	#5	10 Alligator
	(Lord Ten Alligator is a Stone Man, and a small figure beneath him (his personal name) sits on an erased place sign.)	
Pg. 54d (top)	#6	2 Snake

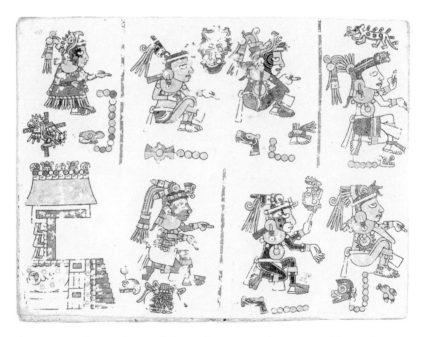

Figure 12.8. Codex Zouche-Nuttall (reverse), Page 55. © The Trustees of the British Museum.

Table 12.3. Lords on Page 55

Page	Lord No.	Day Name
Pg. 55a (top)	#7	5 Death
Pg. 55a (bottom)	#8	9 Monkey
Pg. 55b (bottom)	#9	6 Snake
Pg. 55b (top)	#10	6 Snake
Pg. 55c (top)	#11	4 Motion
Pg. 55c (bottom)	#12	1 Death
Pg. 55d (bottom)	Lord 1 Death sits before an empty Chalcatongo Temple.	
Pg. 55d (top)	#13	13 Dog

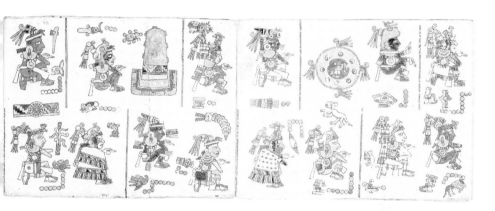

Figure 12.9. Codex Zouche-Nuttall (reverse), Pages 56—57. © The Trustees of the British Museum.

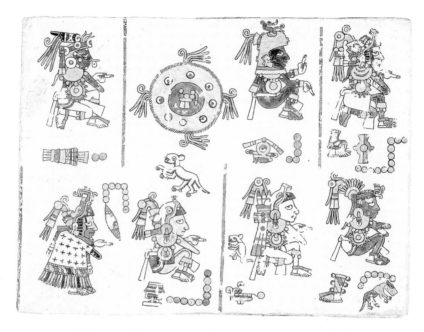

Figure 12.10. Codex Zouche-Nuttall (reverse), Page 56. © The Trustees of the British Museum.

Table 12.4. Lords on Page 56

Page	Lord No.	Day Name
Pg. 56a (top)	#14	12 Motion
Pg. 56a (bottom)	#15	7 Lizard
Pg. 56b (bottom)	#16	1 Death
Pg. 56b (top)	#17	5 Rain
Pg. 56c (top)	A circular toponym	
Pg. 56c (bottom)	#18	10 House
Pg. 56d (bottom)	#19	10 Flint
Pg. 56d (top)	#20	2 Reed

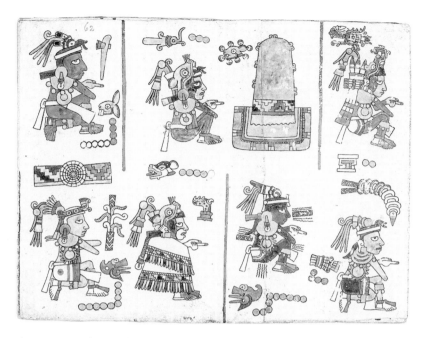

Figure 12.11. Codex Zouche-Nuttall (reverse), Page 57. © The Trustees of the British Museum.

Table 12.5. Lords on Page 57

Page	Lord No.	Day Name
Pg. 57a (top)	#21	2 House
Pg. 57a (bottom)	#22	4 Reed
Pg. 57b (bottom)	#23	10 Wind
Pg. 57b (top)	A toponym: hill in a lake	
Pg. 57c (top)	#24 Lord of Hill in Lake	3 Flower
Pg. 57c (bottom)	#25	4(5) Dog
Pg. 57d (bottom)	#26	9 Wind War Smoke
Pg. 57d (top)	#27	9 Rabbit

Figure 12.12. Codex Zouche-Nuttall (reverse), Pages 58—59. © The Trustees of the British Museum.

Figure 12.13. Codex Zouche-Nuttall (reverse), Page 58. © The Trustees of the British Museum.

Table 12.6. Lords on Page 58

Page	Lord No.	Day Name
Pg. 58a (top)	#28	1 Alligator
Pg. 58a (bottom)	#29	10 Grass
Pg. 58b (bottom)	#30	5 Water
Pg. 58b (top)	Hill toponym	
Pg. 58c (top)	#31, Lord of the Hill toponym	7 Monkey
Pg. 58c (bottom)	#32	1 Alligator
Pg. 58d (bottom)	Hill toponym	
Pg. 58d (top)	#33	13 Jaguar

Figure 12.14. Codex Zouche-Nuttall (reverse), Page 59. © The Trustees of the British Museum.

Table 12.7. Lords on Page 59

Page	Lord No.	Day Name
Pg. 59a (top)	#34	13 Lizard
Pg. 59a (bottom)	#35	10 Vulture
Pg. 59b (bottom)	#36	10 Death
Pg. 59b (top)	#37	2 Lizard
Pg. 59c (top)	#38	10 Eagle
Pg. 59c (bottom)	#39	10 Vulture
Pg. 59d (bottom)	#40	1 Vulture
Pg. 59d (top)	#41	8 Flower

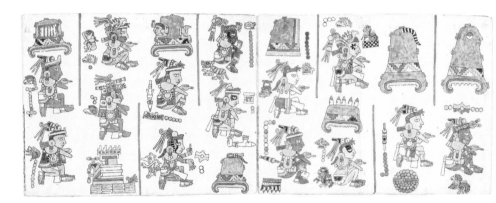

Figure 12.15. Codex Zouche-Nuttall (reverse), Pages 60—61. © The Trustees of the British Museum.

Figure 12.16. Codex Zouche-Nuttall (reverse), Page 60. © The Trustees of the British Museum.

Table 12.8. Lords on Page 60

Page	Lord No.	Day Name
Pg. 60a (top)	Town and hill toponym	
Pg. 60a (bottom)	#42	5 Motion
Pg. 60b (bottom)	#43	7 Reed
Pg. 60b (top)	Town and hill toponym	
Pg. 60c (top)	#44	4 Eagle
Pg. 60c (middle)	Town and hill toponym	
Pg. 60c (bottom)	#45	4 Rain
Pg. 60d (bottom)	#46	10 Reed
Pg. 60d (middle)	#47	7 Grass
Pg. 60d (top)	Town and hill toponym	

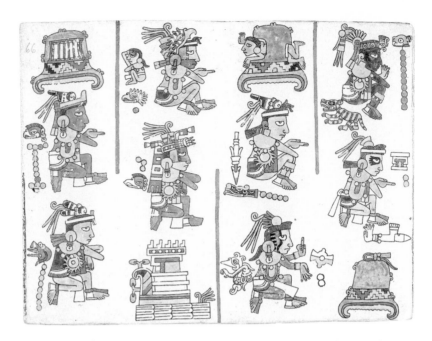

Figure 12.17. Codex Zouche-Nuttall (reverse), Page 61. © The Trustees of the British Museum.

Table 12.9. Lords on Page 61

Page	Lord No.	Day Name
Pg. 61a (top)	#48	10 Jaguar
Pg. 61a (middle)	#49	2 House
Pg. 61a (bottom)	Town and hill toponym	
Pg. 61b (bottom)	#50	2 Motion
Pg. 61b (middle)	#51	5 Snake
Pg. 61b (top)	town and hill toponym	
Pg. 61c (top)	#52	1 Eagle
Pg. 61c (middle)	#53	3 Vulture
Pg. 61c (bottom)	Plain, hill, temple toponym	
Pg. 61d (bottom)	#54	8 Wind
Pg. 61d (middle)	#55	13 Vulture
Pg. 61d (top)	Town and hill toponym	

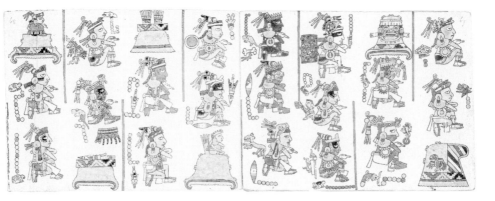

Figure 12.18. Codex Zouche-Nuttall (reverse), Pages 62—63. © The Trustees of the British Museum.

Figure 12.19. Codex Zouche-Nuttall (reverse), Page 62. © The Trustees of the British Museum.

Table 12.10. Lords on Page 62

Page	Lord No.	Day Name
Pg. 62a (top)	#56	2 Rain
Pg. 62a (middle)	#57	3 Wind
Pg. 62a (bottom)	Town and hill toponym	
Pg. 62b (bottom)	#58	7 Flower
Pg. 62b (middle)	#59	8 Alligator
Pg. 62b (top)	Rain God Hill	
Pg. 62c (top)	#60	5 Reed
Pg. 62c (middle)	#61	12 Alligator
Pg. 62c (bottom)	#62	9 Dog
Pg. 62d (bottom)	#63	5 Flint
Pg. 62d (middle)	#64	8 Flint
Pg. 62d (top)	#65	8 Lizard

Figure 12.20. Codex Zouche-Nuttall (reverse), Page 63. © The Trustees of the British Museum.

Table 12.11. Lords on Page 63

Page	Lord No.	Day Name
Pg. 63a (top)	#66	2 Flower
Pg. 63a (middle)	#67	6 Flint
Pg. 63a (bottom)	Hill toponym	
Pg. 63b (bottom)	#68	10 Reed
Pg. 63b (middle)	#69	11 Reed
Pg. 63b (top)	Town atop hill toponym	
Pg. 63c (top)	#70	10 Dog
Pg. 63c (middle)	#71	7 Lizard
Pg. 63c (bottom)	Arrow Town atop hill	
Pg. 63d (bottom)	#72	10 Jaguar
Pg. 63d (middle)	#73	11 Jaguar
Pg. 63d (top)	Town and hill toponym	

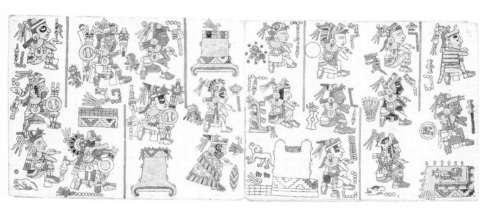

Figure 12.21. Codex Zouche-Nuttall (reverse), Pages 64—65. © The Trustees of the British Museum.

Figure 12.22. Codex Zouche-Nuttall (reverse), Page 64. © The Trustees of the British Museum.

Table 12.12. Lords on Page 64

Page	Lord No.	Day Name
Pg. 64a (top)	#74	10 Motion
Pg. 64a (middle)	#75	7 Motion
Pg. 64a (bottom)	Town and lake toponym	
Pg. 64b (bottom)	#76	3 Dog
Pg. 64b (middle)	#77	3 Alligator
Pg. 64b (top)	#78	12 Rain
Pg. 64c (top)	#79	7 Snake
Pg. 64c (middle)	#80	10 Reed
Pg. 64c (bottom)	#81	13 Monkey
Pg. 64c–d (bottom)	Partly colored hill and town toponym	
Pg. 64d (middle)	#82	10 Reed
Pg. 64d (top)	#83	12 Reed

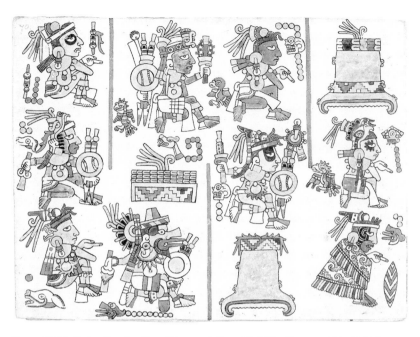

Figure 12.23. Codex Zouche-Nuttall (reverse), Page 65. © The Trustees of the British Museum.

Table 12.13. Lords on Page 65

Page	Lord No.	Day Name
Pg. 65a (top)	Town and hill toponym	
Pg. 65a (middle)	#84	5 Rain
Pg. 65a (bottom)	#85	3 Wind
Pg. 65b (bottom)	Town atop hill toponym	
Pg. 65b (middle)	#86	3 Death
Pg. 65b (top)	#87	10 Death
Pg. 65c (top)	#88	9 Snake
Pg. 65c (middle)	Plains and town toponym	
Pg. 65c (bottom)	#89	9 Wind Quetzalcoatl
Pg. 65d (bottom)	#90	1 Rabbit
Pg. 65d (middle)	#91	3 Rabbit
Pg. 65d (top)	#92	7 Reed

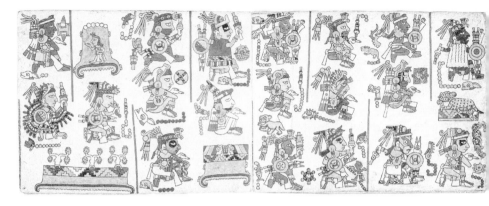

Figure 12.24. Codex Zouche-Nuttall (reverse), Pages 66—67. © The Trustees of the British Museum.

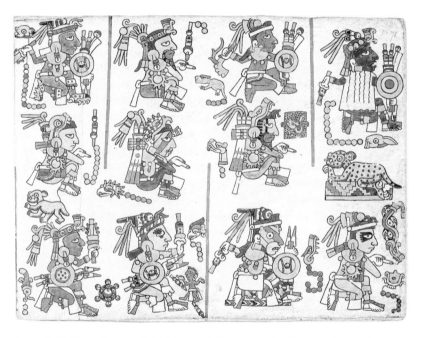

Figure 12.25. Codex Zouche-Nuttall (reverse), Page 66. © The Trustees of the British Museum.

Table 12.14. Lords on Page 66

Page	Lord No.	Day Name
Pg. 66a (top)	#93	13 Rabbit
Pg. 66a (middle)	Jaguar Town toponym	
Pg. 66a (bottom)	#94	8 Water Warsnake
Pg. 66b (bottom)	#95	10 Alligator
Pg. 66b (middle)	#96	2 Snake
Pg. 66b (top)	#97	4 Lizard
Pg. 66c (top)	#98	3 Reed
Pg. 66c (middle)	#99	5 Eagle
Pg. 66c (bottom)	#100	5 Vulture
Pg. 66d (bottom)	#101	2 Flower
Pg. 66d (middle)	#102	10 Reed
Pg. 66d (top)	#103	13 Jaguar

Figure 12.26. Codex Zouche-Nuttall (reverse), Page 67. © The Trustees of the British Museum.

Table 12.15. Lords on Page 67

Page	Lord No.	Day Name
Pg. 67a (top)	#104	9 Rabbit
Pg. 67a (middle)	#105	8 Flower
Pg. 67a (bottom)	Town and hill toponym	
Pg. 67b (bottom)	#106	4 Rabbit
Pg. 67b (middle)	#107	10 Deer
Pg. 67b (top)	#108	7 Flower
Pg. 67c (top)	Hill toponym	
Pg. 67c (middle)	#109	10 Reed
Pg. 67c–d (bottom)	Three Trees Town	
Pg. 67d (middle)	#110	8 Monkey
Pg. 67d (top)	#111	2 Dog

Figure 12.27. Codex Zouche-Nuttall (reverse), Pages 68—69. © The Trustees of the British Museum.

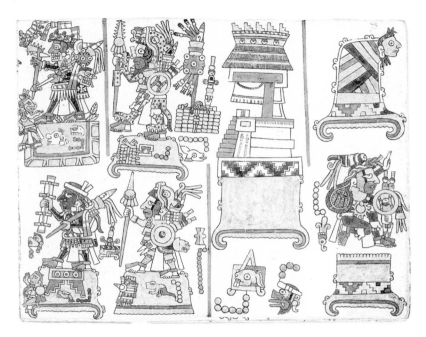

Figure 12.28. Codex Zouche-Nuttall (reverse), Page 68. © The Trustees of the British Museum.

Table 12.16. Lords on Page 68

Page	Lord No.	Day Name
Pg. 68a (top)	Rock Hill Mask Town toponym	
Pg. 68a (middle)	#112	7 Flower
Pg. 68a (bottom)	Flattop Hill Town toponym	

This ends the conference with the 112 lords.

Sections 11–12, Pages 68b–74: Peregrinations from Tilantongo and Ceremonies and Conquests with the Toltecs

Page 68b (bottom). Year 8 Rabbit (AD 1098) Day 4 Wind. From Day 4 Flint of Year 8 Rabbit (Page 53) to Year 8 Rabbit Day 4 Wind (Page 68b), a total of 123 days have elapsed.

Figure 12.29. Codex Zouche-Nuttall (reverse), Page 69. © The Trustees of the British Museum.

Page 68b (middle to top). At Tilantongo Temple of Heaven.

Page 68c (top and bottom). Lord Eight Deer journeys to a place and arrives on Day 5 House, one day after Day 4 Wind. He then travels to another place (Red-and-White Bundle) and arrives on Day 6 Lizard, one day after Day 5 House.

Page 68d (bottom). Lord Two Monkey arrives at Stone Throne Hill on Day 7 Snake, one day after Day 6 Lizard.

Page 68d (top). Eight Deer arrives at a lake on Day 8 Death, one day after Day 7 Snake.

Page 69a (top). Eight Deer atop Temple Platform Hill.

Page 69a–b (bottom). Year 8 Rabbit Day 10 Rabbit, two days after Day 8 Death. Eight Deer in his animal spirit form battles an eagle, a dog is sacrificed, and Lord Nine Flower (Eight Deer's brother) sacrifices a man.

Page 69b (middle to top). Two toponyms, the second with Day 11 Water, one day after Day 10 Rabbit.

Page 69c (top to bottom). The peregrination continues through three places.

Page 69d (bottom to top). Two more toponyms, and then a third with Day 2 Reed, the fourth day after Day 11 Water. This event took eleven days.

Page 70a–b (top to bottom). Lord Eight Deer arrives at three places and is greeted by two males—one named Nine Alligator—bearing the torch, bird, and round woven grass mat for a sacrifice.

Page 70b–c (top). On Day 9 Snake, at Tilantongo, Lord Four Jaguar the Toltec and Lord Eight Deer are shown in combat poses facing each other. The Day 9 Snake is seventy-two days after Day 2 Reed, seen on Page 69d.

Page 70c–d (bottom). On Day 2 Motion, at a temple platform, Lord Four Jaguar the Toltec and Lord Eight Deer perform a bird-decapitation sacrifice. Day 2 Motion is thirty-two days after Day 9 Snake.

Page 70d (top). A male named Twelve Vulture, attired as a *yaha yahui* priest, leads a peregrination to two places shown on the next page, 71a. The male Twelve Vulture forms a visual link to the next scene and takes the reader across pages, beginning Lord Four Wind and Lord Eight Deer's Mixtec/Toltec military campaigns.

Page 71a (top and middle). Two conquered hills.

Page 71a (bottom). A town and hill conquered on Day 8 Eagle. This day is fifty-eight days after Day 2 Motion, day 15 of Tonalpohualli 12, and day 300 of Year 8 Flint.

Page 71b (bottom). Bird's Beak Town and hill conquered on Day 12 Eagle, 140 days after Day 8 Eagle and day 95 in Year 9 Reed (AD 1099).

Page 71b (middle and top). Two conquered towns and hills, the last on Day 11 Snake, day 185 of Year 9 Reed.

Page 71c (top to bottom). Three conquered hill towns, the second of them on Day 13 Rain, day 239 of Year 9 Reed.

Page 71d (bottom to top). Two conquered hills and one conquered town on Days 7 Grass, 5 Monkey, and 1 Jaguar, respectively. 7 Grass is day 272 of Year 9 Reed, 5 Monkey is day 231 of Year 9 Reed, and 1 Jaguar is day 214 of Year 9 Reed.

Page 72a (top). Conquered hill town.

Page 72a (middle). Conquered town on Day 2 Eagle, day 215 of Year 9 Reed.

Page 72a (bottom). Conquered hill on Day 7 Jaguar, day 194 of Year 9 Reed.

Page 72b (bottom). Conquered hill town on Day 12 Grass, day 212 of Year 9 Reed.

Page 72b (middle). Conquered hill on Day 4 Monkey, day 191 of Year 9 Reed.

Figure 12.30. Codex Zouche-Nuttall (reverse), Pages 70—71. © The Trustees of the British Museum.

Figure 12.31. Codex Zouche-Nuttall (reverse), Page 70. © The Trustees of the British Museum.

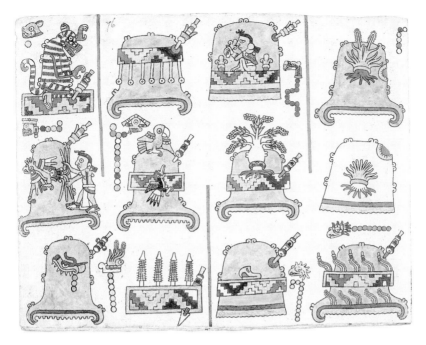

Figure 12.32. Codex Zouche-Nuttall (reverse), Page 71. © The Trustees of the British Museum.

Figure 12.33. Codex Zouche-Nuttall (reverse), Pages 72—73. © The Trustees of the British Museum.

Figure 12.34. Codex Zouche-Nuttall (reverse), Page 72. © The Trustees of the British Museum.

Page 72b (top). Conquered hill on Day 11 Dog, day 250 of Year 9 Reed.

Page 72c (top). Conquered town on Day 13 Deer, day 187 of Year 9 Reed.

Page 72c (middle). Conquered hill town with river temple, on Day 1 Rabbit, day 188 of Year 9 Reed.

Page 72c (bottom). Conquered hill on Day 2 Water, day 189 of Year 9 Reed.

Page 72d (bottom). Conquered hill on Day 3 Dog, day 190 of Year 9 Reed.

Page 72d (middle). Conquered hill town on Day 4 Monkey, day 191 of Year 9 Reed.

Page 72d (top). Conquered hill on Day 6 Reed, day 193 of Year 9 Reed.

Page 73a (top). Conquered hill town on Day 8 Eagle, day 195 of Year 9 Reed.

Page 73a (middle). Conquered town on Day 9 Vulture, day 196 of Year 9 Reed.

Page 73a (bottom). Conquered hill town on Day 10 Motion, day 197 of Year 9 Reed.

Page 73b (bottom). Conquered town on Day 11 Flint, day 198 of Year 9 Reed.

Page 73b (middle). Conquered town on Day 12 Rain, day 199 of Year 9 Reed.

Page 73b (top). Conquered hill town on Day 5 Lizard, day 244 of Year 9 Reed.

Page 73c (top). Conquered hill on Day 4 Monkey, day 191 of Year 9 Reed.

Page 73c (middle). Conquered forest on Day 10 Flower, day 80 or 340 of Year 9 Reed.

Page 73c (bottom). Conquered town on Day 10 Deer, day 67 or 327 of Year 9 Reed.

Page 73d (bottom). Conquered hill town on Day 3 Vulture, day 216 of Year 9 Reed.

Page 73d (middle). Conquered town on Day 4 Motion, day 217 of Year 9 Reed.

Page 73d (top). Conquered hill town, apparently also on Day 4 Motion.

A format change occurs on Page 75. Although Page 74 retains the four-column continuous vertical boustrophedon of the preceding pages, Page 75 is a right-to-left linear mural panel with five parts. The two-page format

Figure 12.35. Codex Zouche-Nuttall (reverse), Page 73. © The Trustees of the British Museum.

Figure 12.36. Codex Zouche-Nuttall (reverse), Pages 74—75. © The Trustees of the British Museum.

Figure 12.37. Codex Zouche-Nuttall (reverse), Page 74. © The Trustees of the British Museum.

is retained, however, because Lord Nine Water (top of Page 74d) forms the visual bridge to Page 75. Note that he is the "guide" for the expedition across the water.

Although Page 75 begins Section 13, "The Battle in the Sky," it actually continues Sections 11 and 12 and their Mixtec/Toltec conquests. The locale merely moves from the world of men to the world of the Sun God.

Page 74a (top). Hill conquest on Day 7 Flower, day 220 of Year 9 Reed.

Page 74a (middle). Town conquest on Day 2 Dog, day 150 of Year 9 Reed.

Page 74a (bottom). Lake and temple conquest on Day 12 Grass, day 212 of Year 9 Reed.

Page 74b (bottom). Conquest of town and hill on Day 11 Monkey, day 211 of Year 9 Reed.

Page 74b (middle). Conquest of Weeping Man Town.

Page 74b (top). Conquest of Ballcourt Town on Day 2 Monkey, day 111 of Year 9 Reed.

Page 74c (top). Conquest of a lake on Day 9 Jaguar, day 14 or 274 of Year 9 Reed.

Page 74c (middle). Conquest of a town.

Page 74c (bottom). Conquest of a lake town on Day 4 Deer, day 87 or 347 of Year 9 Reed.

Page 74d (bottom). A town.

Page 74d (middle to top). Lord Nine Water of Woodpecker Town.

13 Document 2 (Reverse), Sections 13–14, Pages 75–84: The Battle in the Sky through the Siege of Hua Chino

Section 13, Pages 75–80b: The Battle in the Sky and Eight Deer Becomes a Sun God Lord

Page 75a (far right). Lord Four Jaguar in a Toltec-style canoe. Day 10 Snake, day 105 of Year 9 Reed.

Page 75b. Lord Eight Deer in a Toltec-style canoe. Day 11 Death, day 106 of Year 9 Reed. Four Jaguar and Eight Deer share the same canoe.

Page 75c. Lord Nine Water in a different Toltec-style canoe.

Page 75d. Conquest of Five Caves Island Town on Day 12 Deer, day 107 of Year 9 Reed.

Page 75e (far left). The Place Where the Sky Is Held Up.

The water creatures below each of the heroes, Eight Deer and Four Jaguar, are potentially formidable. The final creature, the large supernatural alligator, appears just below Five Caves Island. The Colombino fragments (Pages 22–23; see Figure 13.2) show another tradition that tells us that before conquering the island, the heroes had to do battle with this monster. Eight Deer is the one who overcomes it as well as the tremendous waves and two maelstroms it generates.

These effaced pages of the Colombino fragments show the conquest of the alligator-like monster. One hero is struggling in the water on Page 22 (left), Eight Deer remains in his canoe and conquers it on Page 23 (right), while still another man (presumably Lord Nine Water) swims to the waterfront town on the island. The monster's jaws are open, face upward, and span the bottom of both pages.

Having conquered the entrance to The Place Where the Sky Is Held Up, Eight Deer and company conquer several places. At one of these places—Fire Serpent Hill—Eight Deer's brother Nine Flower is sacrificed. Subsequently, Eight Deer defeats the fourteen sacrificed warriors of the sun, thir-

Figure 13.1. Codex Zouche-Nuttall (reverse), Page 75. © The Trustees of the British Museum.

teen of whom hold the white flag of sacrifice. In the Colombino fragment, some of these warriors are shown with their chests cut open for heart excision but still fighting. After this battle, Eight Deer banishes the Lord of Death and conquers four more places. Then he, Twelve Motion, and Four Jaguar defeat the two monster warriors of the sun, after which they have an audience with the Sun God, Lord One Death.

Page 76a (top). Dibble Stick Town conquered on Day 11 Motion, day 237 of Year 9 Reed.

Page 76a (middle). Incense and Plumes Plains conquered on Day 13 Eagle, day 135 of Year 9 Reed.

Page 76a (bottom). Ñuu Forest conquered from Days 8 Death to 12 Water, day 306 to 69 or 329, respectively, of Year 9 Reed.

Page 76b (bottom). Conquest of a place identified by a Rain God effigy with tree and a bleeding tree.

Page 76b (middle). Conquest of a waterfall on Day 7 Flower, day 220 of Year 9 Reed.

Figure 13.2. Codex Colombino, Pages 22–23. © The Trustees of the British Museum.

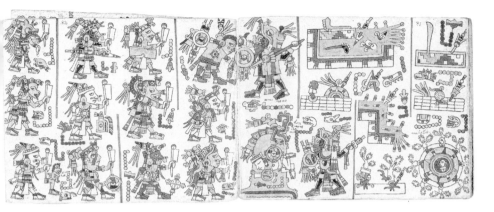

Figure 13.3. Codex Zouche-Nuttall (reverse), Pages 76a—76b. © The Trustees of the British Museum.

Page 76b-c (top). Year 9 Reed Day 4 Alligator, day 61 or 341 of Year 9 Reed. Conquest of a lakeside town.

Page 76c (middle). Conquest of Rising Ñuu and Plume Sun Plain.

Page 76c-d (bottom). Lord Eight Deer and the sacrifice of Lord Nine Flower at Fire Serpent Hill on Day 12 Death, day 186 of Year 9 Reed.

Page 76d (top). Lord Eight Deer facing across the page on Day 9 Death, day 66 or 226 of Year 9 Reed.

This is part one of the Battle in the Sky: the Battle with the Sacrificed Warriors of the Sun.

Page 76a (top). Weeping Lord Two Flower is defeated.

Page 76a (middle). Sacrificed Lord Thirteen Rain is defeated.

Page 76a (bottom). Sacrificed Lord Ten Jaguar is defeated.

Page 76b (bottom). Sacrificed Lord Thirteen Motion is defeated.

Page 76b (middle). Sacrificed Lord Seven Flower is defeated.

Page 76b (top). Sacrificed Lord Seven Flower is defeated.

Page 76c (top). Sacrificed Lord Four Motion is defeated.

Page 76c (middle). Sacrificed Lord Nine Wind is defeated.

Page 76c (bottom). Sacrificed Lord Thirteen Rabbit is defeated (his name is attached to his garment).

Page 76d (bottom). Sacrificed Lord Twelve Death.

Page 76d (middle). Sacrificed Lord Thirteen Death.

Page 76d (top). Sacrificed Lord Twelve Water.

This is the final part of the Battle in the Sky (Pages 77a–78a), then Eight Deer and Four Jaguar are shown meeting with the Sun God, Lord One Death.

Figure 13.4. Codex Zouche-Nuttall (reverse), Page 76a. © The Trustees of the British Museum.

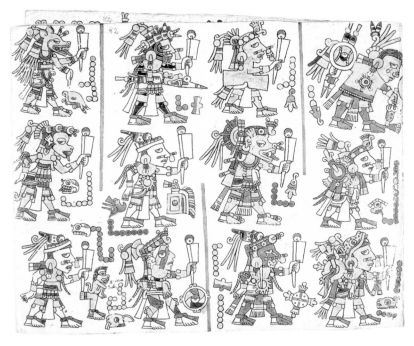

Figure 13.5. Codex Zouche-Nuttall (reverse), Page 76b. © The Trustees of the British Museum.

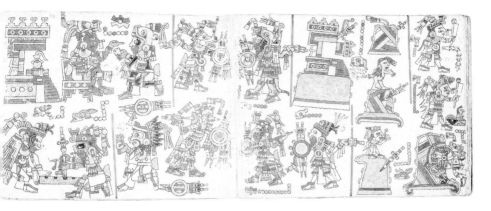

Figure 13.6. Codex Zouche-Nuttall (reverse), Pages 77—78. © The Trustees of the British Museum.

In the tableau on Page 78b–c (top), the Sun God points directly to Lord Eight Deer's nose. Then in the tableau following (the fire-drilling tableau) on Page 78c, Lord Eight Deer wears the Sun God nose ornament in conjunction with his Toltec nose ornament (Victoria Ingalls, personal communication, 2009). Eight Deer also wears this additional nose ornament in tableaux on Pages 79c, 80a, 82a, and 83a. From this point in the narrative, Lord Eight Deer is not only a Toltec *techutli* but also a Sun God lord. Each of the sacrificed warriors of the sun wears similar nose adornments. Eight Deer's companion—his half brother Twelve Motion—wears the ornament, but the Toltec benefactor, Four Jaguar, does not.

Page 77a (top). Sacrificed Lord Three Snake is defeated.

Page 77a (middle). Sacrificed Lord Eleven Snake is defeated.

Page 77a (bottom). The Lord of Death flees into a cave at Stone Hill on Day 9 Snake, day 105 or 365 of Year 9 Reed.

Page 77b (bottom). Conquest of Singing Man Hill on Day 11 Deer, day 107 of Year 9 Reed.

Page 77b (middle). Conquest of Naked Woman with Wrinkled Abdomen Hill.

Page 77b (top). Conquest of Stone and Loincloth Hill.

Page 77c (top). Conquest of Blue Temple on Day 11 Rabbit, day 68 or 308 of Year 9 Reed. A partially obliterated gloss in European writing (presumably Spanish) appears beneath the day name.

Page 77c (bottom). Lord Four Jaguar the warrior.

Page 77d (bottom). Lord Twelve Motion the warrior.

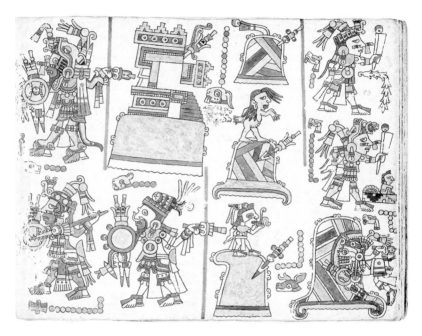

Figure 13.7. Codex Zouche-Nuttall (reverse), Page 77. © The Trustees of the British Museum.

Page 77d (top). Lord Eight Deer the warrior.

Page 78 uses the three-column format rather than the four-column format. The rationale for this is that the final two tableaux are larger, thus more emphasized than the preceding ones.

Page 78a (top). An animal-headed warrior (monster warrior of the Sun God).

Page 78a (bottom). A death (skeletal) warrior.

Page 78b (bottom). Lord Four Jaguar with a gift. He is part of the following tableau.

Page 78b–c (top). Day 7 Motion, day 77 or 337 of Year 9 Reed. The Sun God sits before a temple. He faces Eight Deer and points at Eight Deer's nose. Eight Deer is without his vertical turquoise nose ornament. The Sun God wears a horizontal nose ornament with a turquoise bangle.

Page 78c (bottom). Four Jaguar and Eight Deer drill for fire. Eight Deer wears his vertical turquoise nose ornament and a horizontal nose ornament similar to the Sun God's.

Page 79 is in the usual four-column format (a, b, c, d), but Page 80 has two

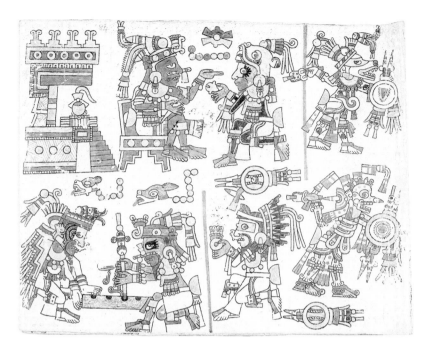

Figure 13.8. Codex Zouche-Nuttall (reverse), Page 78. © The Trustees of the British Museum.

Figure 13.9. Codex Zouche-Nuttall (reverse), Pages 79—80. © The Trustees of the British Museum.

enlarged tableaux appearing in a three-column format with two place signs following them.

Page 79a (top). Day 9 Death, day 66 or 326 of Year 9 Reed. Conquest of Fire Serpent Hill. This is where Eight Deer's brother Nine Flower was sacrificed on Page 76d. The hill was unconquered at that time.

Page 79a–b (bottom). The Sun God, with his name, One Death, is seated on a jaguar throne. The day is 11 Death, day 146 of Year 9 Reed. The Sun God points upward to the next tableau.

Page 79b–c (top). Lord Eight Deer and Lord Four Jaguar appear on a temple platform. The temple platform sits on the sky and the two lords point to a cave opening in the middle of it. Eight Deer is without the Sun God nose ornament for this tableau.

Page 79c–d (bottom to top). The Sun God presents Eight Deer with a gift on Day 3 Monkey, day 151 of Year 9 Reed. Lord Four Jaguar is present at this ceremony.

Page 80a–b (top). Lords Four Jaguar, Eight Deer (with his two nose ornaments), and Twelve Motion, each in separate Toltec-style canoes, journey across a body of water on Day 9 Motion, day 157 of Year 9 Reed.

Page 80b (bottom). Lord Eight Deer with his two nose ornaments and Lord Four Jaguar in a ballcourt on Day 6 Jaguar, day 29 or 309 of Year 10 Flint (AD 1100).

Page 80b–c (bottom). A hill town on Day 8 Eagle, day 190 or 350 of Year 10 Flint.

Page 80c (top). A smoking hill on Day 8 Rabbit, day 103 or 363 of Year 10 Flint.

Section 14, Pages 81–84: The Assassination of Lord Twelve Motion and the Siege of Hua Chino

Page 81a (bottom). In Year 10 Flint on day 41 or 281, 11 Death, Lord Twelve Motion is assassinated in a sweat bath.

Page 81a (top). His mummy is prepared, on Days 9 Motion (day 52 or 312) to 12 Motion (day 172), an interval of 120 days (day 52–172).

Page 81b (top). A bundle ceremony on Day 7 Flower, day 115 of Year 10 Flint.

Page 81b–c (bottom to top). Five unnamed males bearing ceremonial objects.

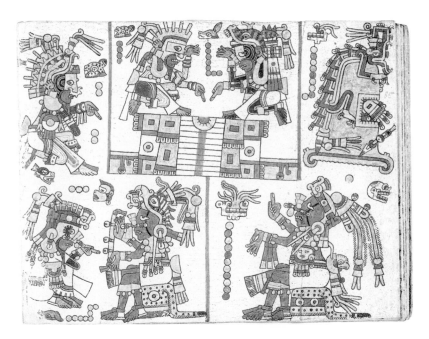

Figure 13.10. Codex Zouche-Nuttall (reverse), Page 79. © The Trustees of the British Museum.

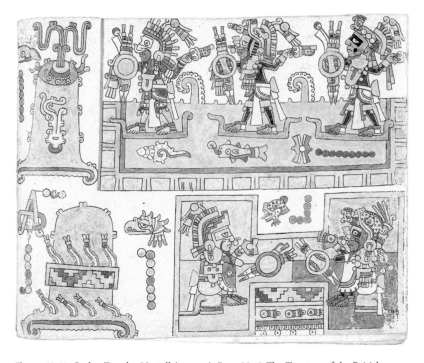

Figure 13.11. Codex Zouche-Nuttall (reverse), Page 80. © The Trustees of the British Museum.

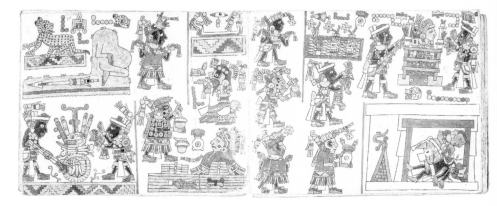

Figure 13.12. Codex Zouche-Nuttall, Pages 81—82. © The Trustees of the British Museum.

Figure 13.13. Codex Zouche-Nuttall (reverse), Page 81. © The Trustees of the British Museum.

Page 82a (top to bottom). (Year 10 Flint) Day 2 Flint (day 253). Eight Deer consults with the mummy of the last king of Tilantongo's first dynasty. For identification of this mummy, see Codex Zouche-Nuttall Page 8.

Page 82b (bottom to top). Two unnamed males participate.

Page 82c (top to bottom). In Year 10(11) House (AD 1101), on Day 6 Jaguar (day 204) at Jaguar Town at Pregnant Hill, war plans are made. Lord Two Rain's mummy is burned.

Page 83a (bottom). Year 11 House (AD 1100), Day 12 Monkey (day 1 or 261). Conquest of Red-and-White Bundle Town (Hua Chino).

Page 83a–b (top). Capture of Lord Four Wind.

Page 83b–c (bottom). Year 12 Rabbit (AD 1101), Day 7 Snake, day 190 of Year 12 Rabbit.

Page 83c–d (top). Lord Eight Deer, attired as his spirit animal (Jaguar), sacrifices Lord Ten Dog. He is assisted by another male, who is unnamed.

Page 83d (bottom). A male attired as the god of death sacrifices . . .

Page 84a (bottom). . . . Lord Six House/Water.

Page 84a–b (top). Ritual bird decapitation on Day 9 Wind (day 167).

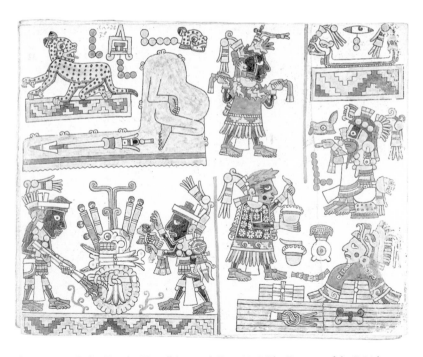

Figure 13.14. Codex Zouche-Nuttall (reverse), Page 82. © The Trustees of the British Museum.

Figure 13.15. Codex Zouche-Nuttall (reverse), Pages 83—84. © The Trustees of the British Museum.

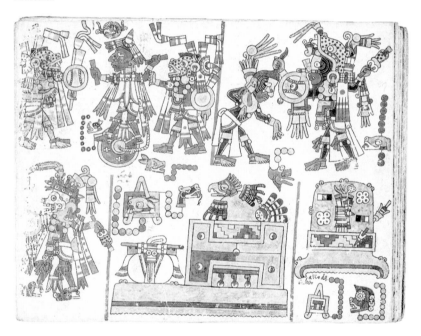

Figure 13.16. Codex Zouche-Nuttall (reverse), Page 83. © The Trustees of the British Museum.

Figure 13.17. Codex Zouche-Nuttall (reverse), Page 84. © The Trustees of the British Museum.

Page 84b–c (bottom). A mummy burning on Day 2 Vulture (day 121).

The remaining text after 84c has been erased. A previous boustrophedon line that defines column "c" is barely visible to the left of the unnamed male holding a sacrificial bird at the mummy burning. Faint traces of images are visible just above him. In what was column "c" are the words "1 acatl, 2 tochtli, 3 tecpatl, 4 calli," written by a later hand. Thus this document of Codex Zouche-Nuttall has long been considered "unfinished."

14 The Four Voices of Mixtec History

As mentioned previously, Codex Selden documents the history and genealogy of the royal families of the town of Jaltepec or, in Mixtec, Añute. The founding of royal families there was problematical, and subsequent history was wracked with turmoil. The first dynasty (Selden, Pages 1 through 5-III) failed when the last king, Three Rain, and his wife, Seven Death, did not produce offspring. The codex does not tell us why they died childless, or if there was a catastrophe after their wedding. The tableau narrative simply breaks off, and—rather than a male king—a royal woman descended from the great lineage founder Eight Wind Twenty (of Suchixtlan) and his wife, Ten Deer (Codex Zouche-Nuttall, Pages 1–5a), ruled. This ruler, Lady Nine Wind, established the sacred bundle in the Jaltepec temple, as a male priest would do, and wed a royal male from nearby Tilantongo named Ten Eagle (also descended from Lord Eight Wind Twenty and Lady Ten Deer). Ultimately, their daughter, Lady Six Monkey, ruled Jaltepec and became a fulcrum upon which turbulent Mixtec history turned.

Because the bards who knew these stories by memory are no more, we have now four codex informers or voices to tell this story to us because no single codex tradition tells it all. First, as mentioned, is Codex Selden—a colonial palimpsest manuscript written in the pre-Hispanic style and dating to AD 1556. The second voice is the scribe/reciter of Codex Bodley, which dates from approximately AD 1520. The third and fourth of our informers are the scriveners/reciters of Codex Zouche-Nuttall, the two manuscripts (obverse and reverse) of which date from approximately AD 1450/1350, and Codex Alfonso Caso, ca. AD 1275.

The historical events date sequentially but appear here in chronological tables as the stories sung by each political voice. The first table is events in Codex Selden. The second table (voice) adds story from Codex Zouche-

Nuttall, and the third and fourth voices complete the native narrative with data from Codices Bodley and Alfonso Caso.

First Voice, Codex Selden: The Royal Women of Jaltepec

Table 14.1

Selden Page	Date	Event
5-IV	Year 3 House (AD 1041)	♀ Nine Wind + ♂ Ten Eagle
	+32 years	
5-IV, 6-I	Year 9 House (AD 1073)	Their three male children—One Reed, Twelve Water, Three Water—are sacrificed at Chalcatongo, and their daughter, Six Monkey, is born there. This is the first mention of Jaltepec's political alliance with the powerful female Oracle of the Dead at Chalcatongo.
	+8 years	
6-II	Year 4 House (AD 1081)	Tilantongo attacks Jaltepec and is defeated.
	+2 years	
6-III	Year 5(6) Reed (AD 1083)	♀ Six Monkey consults with two priests; travels underground; then travels to Chalcatongo; consults with the Oracle of the Dead, Lady 9 Grass; and is betrothed to ♂ Eleven Wind, king of Hua Chino, Tilantongo's rival.
	+4 years	
7-I	Year 10 Reed (AD 1087)	Nuptial ceremonies
	+2 years	
7-I	Year 12 House (AD 1089)	Nuptial bath of ♂ Eleven Wind and ♀ Six Monkey
	+1 year	
7-II, III	Year 13 Rabbit (AD 1090)	♀ Six Monkey journeys to Hua Chino. She and her caravan are attacked and insulted by Lords Six Lizard and Two Alligator.
7-IV	Same	♀ Six Monkey, unable to continue her journey, consults with ♀ Nine Grass, the Oracle of the Dead at Chalcatongo. The oracle delivers instruments of war and an army to ♀ Six Monkey.

Table 14.1 Continued

Selden Page	Date	Event
8-I	Same	In the heat of battle, warrior-queen ♀ Six Monkey defeats and captures ♂ Six Lizard and ♂ Two Alligator. ♂ Two Alligator dies by heart excision in the temple at Jaltepec.
8-II	Same	♀ Six Monkey takes her second captive, ♂ Six Lizard, to her new home, Hua Chino. He is sacrificed in the temple there.
8-III	Same	An emissary of the Oracle of the Dead conducts a name-change ceremony for ♀ Six Monkey, the new queen of Hua Chino. She is now ♀ Six Monkey Warpath Garment, or The Warrior.
8-III	Same	♀ Six Monkey and ♂ Eleven Wind are the ruling lords of the ancient city of Hua Chino.
	+2 years	
8-IV	Year 2 Flint (AD 1092)	Their first son, Four Wind, is born.
	+3 years	
8-IV	Year 5 Reed (AD 1095)	Their second son, One Alligator, is born.
	+12 years	
8-IV, 9-I	Year 12 Rabbit (AD 1102)	♂ Four Wind + ♀ Ten Flower of Tilantongo, daughter of Lord Eight Deer Jaguar Claw.
	+20 years	
9-I, II	Year 12 Rabbit (AD 1122)	♂ One Alligator becomes priest-king of Jaltepec and marries ♀ Six Wind of Tilantongo, daughter of Lord Eight Deer Jaguar Claw.
End of the First-Voice Narrative.		

Codex Selden has given us eighty-one years of history of the royal women of Jaltepec. It is an intensely political document for many reasons but is of interest in this chapter for one particular reason, namely, Lord Eight Deer Jaguar Claw of Tilantongo. He appears only as the father of two princesses of Tilantongo who married the sons of ♀ Six Monkey Warpath Garment and ♂ Eleven Wind of Hua Chino. Lord Eight Deer of Tilantongo figures prominently in virtually every major surviving Mixtec codex, yet here he appears in brief mention only as the progenitor of two royal women who wed the scions of Jaltepec/Hua Chino.

Rightly, we expect occultation of data about Eight Deer. The reverse of Codex Zouche-Nuttall (museum-numbered Pages 42–84) in its entirety is the political biography of Lord Eight Deer; the codex obverse (museum-numbered Pages 1–41) gives supplemental personal data about him, including his genealogy and marriages. The first half of the hideously mutilated and fragmentary Codex Alfonso Caso relates Eight Deer's political biography, and sections of Codex Bodley tell his expanded biography, including his death in AD 1115.

Therefore, we have before us a mystery of omission. To solve it and satisfy our curiosity, we must turn now to the other Mixtec voices. As before, these new data are presented here as a schematic table of events and complement the first voice/table. Beginning with the narrative tableaux in Codex Zouche-Nuttall, called our "second voice," the new data provided by the second voice appear within brackets in Table 14.2.

Second Voice, Codex Zouche-Nuttall

Table 14.2

Selden Page Z-N Page	Date	Event
5-IV	Year 3 House (AD 1041)	♀ Nine Wind + ♂ Ten Eagle
	+32 years	
5-IV, 6-I	Year 9 House (AD 1073)	Their three male children—One Reed, Twelve Water, Three Water—are sacrificed at Chalcatongo, and their daughter, Six Monkey, is born there. This is the first mention of Jaltepec's political alliance with the powerful female Oracle of the Dead at Chalcatongo.
	+8 years	
[Z-N 7b–8a	Year 4 House (AD 1081)	♂ Two Rain, the six-year-old king of Tilantongo, consults with the mummy bundle of his great-grandfather, Eight Wind Twenty, on Day 1 Rain. Three days later, on Day 4 Wind, Two Rain's great-uncle ♂ Three Lizard (son of Eight Wind Twenty) attacks

Table 14.2 Continued

Selden Page Z-N Page	Date	Event
[Z-N 7b–8a (*continued*)	Year 4 House (AD 1081) (*continued*)	Jaltepec on behalf of the young king of Tilantongo and loses the war, i.e., he is killed in battle, according to Selden.]
6-II	Year 4 House (AD 1081)	Tilantongo attacks Jaltepec and is defeated.
	+2 years	
6-III	Year 5(6) Reed (AD 1083)	♀ Six Monkey consults with two priests; travels underground; then to Chalcatongo; consults with the Oracle of the Dead, Lady Nine Grass; and is betrothed to ♂ Eleven Wind, king of Hua Chino, Tilantongo's rival.
[Z-N 44a	Year 6 Reed (AD 1083)	♂ Eight Deer Jaguar Claw of Tilantongo and ♀ Six Monkey of Jaltepec are at Chalcatongo while the Oracle, ♀ Nine Grass, consults with the mummy bundle of ♂ Three Lizard, who died in the battle of Tilantongo against Jaltepec. This meeting is the oracle's transference of marriage alliance from Jaltepec/Tilantongo to Jaltepec/Hua Chino. Subsequently, Eight Deer Jaguar Claw travels south and becomes ruler of the prosperous coastal town of Tututepec.]
	+4 years	
7-I	Year 10 Reed (AD 1087)	Nuptial ceremonies
	+2 years	
7-I	Year 12 House (AD 1089)	Nuptial bath of ♂ Eleven Wind and ♀ Six Monkey
	+1 year	
7-II, III	Year 13 Rabbit (AD 1090)	♀ Six Monkey journeys to Hua Chino. She and her caravan are attacked and insulted by Lords Six Lizard and Two Alligator.
7-IV	Same	♀ Six Monkey, unable to continue her journey, consults with ♀ Nine Grass, the Oracle of the Dead at Chalcatongo. The oracle delivers instruments of war and an army to ♀ Six Monkey.

Table 14.2 Continued

Selden Page Z-N Page	Date	Event
8-I	Same	♀ In the heat of battle, warrior-queen ♀ Six Monkey defeats and captures ♂ Six Lizard and ♂ Two Alligator. ♂ Two Alligator dies by heart excision in the temple at Jaltepec.
8-II	Same	♀ Six Monkey takes her second captive, ♂ Six Lizard, to her new home, Hua Chino, and sacrifices him in the temple there.
8-III	Same	An emissary of the Oracle of the Dead conducts a name-change ceremony for ♀ Six Monkey, the new queen of Hua Chino. She is now ♀ Six Monkey Warpath Garment.
8-III	Same	♀ Six Monkey and ♂ Eleven Wind are the ruling lords of the ancient city of Hua Chino.
	+2 years	
8-IV	Year 2 Flint (AD 1092)	Their first son, Four Wind, is born.
	+3 years	
8-IV	Year 5 Reed (AD 1095)	Their second son, One Alligator, is born.
	+2 years	
[Z-N 50c–d	Year 7 House (AD 1097)	Eight Deer consults with the lineage goddess ♀ Nine Reed.
Z-N 52	Year 7 House (AD 1097)	Having become prosperous and powerful as lord of Tututepec, Eight Deer forms an alliance with ♂ Four Jaguar of the Tolteca/Chichimeca and becomes a Toltec king and lineage founder and rules at Tilantongo. Eight Deer and his half brother Twelve Motion conference with 112 lords (both Mixtec and non-Mixtec) and unify the Mixteca. (What happened to the king Two Rain? Zouche-Nuttall reverse is elusive about his fate.)
	+1 year	
Z-N 68–74	Year 7 Rabbit (AD 1098)	Those polities that do not submit to Eight Deer and the Toltec Four Jaguar are conquered, forty places in all. Then, as supreme lord, Eight Deer,

Table 14.2 Continued

Selden Page Z-N Page	Date	Event
Z-N 68–74 (*continued*)	Year 7 Rabbit (AD 1098) (*continued*)	along with his companions, begins the Battle in the Sky. They conquer The Place Where the Sky Is Held Up; defeat the warriors of the Sun God, One Death; form an alliance with the Sun God; and return to earth. During this episode, Eight Deer wears a Sun God nose ornament along with his Toltec nose ornament.
Z-N 8, 80–84	Year 10 Flint (AD 1100)	♂ Eight Deer conferences with the mummy bundle of the deceased king of Tilantongo, Lord Two Rain (Z-N Page 8) and collects an army. This is the first mention of Two Rain's death in Codex Zouche-Nuttall obverse. After this conference, ♂ Eight Deer burns ♂ Two Rain's mummy (Pages 80–84).
Z-N 82–84	Year 11 House (AD 1101)	The Siege of Hua Chino. Eight Deer conquers Hua Chino and captures the boy Four Rain, son of ♀ Six Monkey and ♂ Eleven Wind. Then Eight Deer sacrifices ♂ Eleven Wind's sons by a previous marriage, the Lords Ten Dog and Six Rain. Subsequently, he burns their bodies. At this point, Codex Zouche-Nuttall is unfinished.]
Sel. 9-I	Year 12 Rabbit (AD 1102)	♂ One Alligator rules Jaltepec.
	+20 years	
Sel. 9-II	Year 6 Rabbit (AD 1122)	♂ One Alligator marries ♂ Eight Deer's daughter, Six Wind.
	+3 years	
Bod. 29-IV	Year 9 House (AD 1125)	♂ Four Wind + ♀ Ten Flower of Tilantongo, daughter of Lord Eight Deer Jaguar Claw.
End of the First- and Second-Voice Narratives.		

Our suspicions that Codex Selden omitted history selectively are well founded. In this second-voice narrative, we read the entirety of ♂ Eight Deer's astonishing exploits as warlord, Toltec king, destroyer of Hua Chino, and unifier of the Mixtec territories. They do not appear in Codex Selden. Our third- and fourth-voice narratives (Codices Bodley and Alfonso Caso, respectively) reveal some few details that serve to complete our picture of this Mixtec historical schematic. The first-voice narrative from Codex Selden appears in plain text, as is shown here. The second-voice narrative from Codex Zouche-Nuttall is bracketed. The third-voice narrative (Bodley) is italicized, and the fourth-voice narrative (Alfonso Caso) is in bold text. Whereas Codex Zouche-Nuttall was abbreviated as "Z-N," Bodley appears below as "Bod." and Alfonso Caso as "AC."

Third (Bodley) and Fourth (Alfonso Caso) Voices

Table 14.3

Selden Page Z-N Page Bod. Page AC Page	Date	Event
5-IV	Year 3 House (AD 1041)	♀ Nine Wind + ♂ Ten Eagle
	+32 years	
5-IV, 6-I	Year 9 House (AD 1073)	Their three male children—One Reed, Twelve Water, Three Water—are sacrificed at Chalcatongo, and their daughter, Six Monkey, is born there. This is the first mention of Jaltepec's political alliance with the powerful female Oracle of the Dead at Chalcatongo.
	+8 years	
[Z-N 7b–8a	Year 4 House (AD 1081)	♂ Two Rain, the six-year-old king of Tilantongo, consults with the mummy bundle of his great-grandfather, Eight Wind Twenty, on Day 1 Rain. Three days later, on Day 4 Wind, Two Rain's great-uncle ♂ Three Lizard (son of Eight Wind Twenty) attacks Jaltepec on behalf of the young king of Tilantongo and loses the war, i.e., he is killed in battle, according to Selden.]
6-II	Year 4 House (AD 1081)	Tilantongo attacks Jaltepec and is defeated.
	+2 years	
6-III	Year 5(6) Reed (AD 1083)	♀ Six Monkey consults with two priests; travels underground; then to Chalcatongo; consults with the Oracle of the Dead, Lady Nine Grass; and is

Table 14.3 Continued

Selden Page Z-N Page Bod. Page AC Page	Date	Event
6-III (continued)	Year 5(6) Reed (AD 1083) (continued)	betrothed to ♂ Eleven Wind, king of Hua Chino, Tilantongo's rival.
[Z-N 44a	Year 6 Reed (AD 1083)	♂ Eight Deer Jaguar Claw of Tilantongo and ♀ Six Monkey of Jaltepec are at Chalcatongo while the Oracle, ♀ Nine Grass, consults with the mummy bundle of ♂ Three Lizard, who died in the battle of Tilantongo against Jaltepec. This meeting is the oracle's transference of marriage alliance from Jaltepec/Tilantongo to Jaltepec/Hua Chino. Subsequently, Eight Deer Jaguar Claw travels south and becomes ruler of the prosperous coastal town of Tututepec.]
	+4 years	
7-I	Year 10 Reed (AD 1087)	Nuptial ceremonies
	+2 years	
7-I	Year 12 House (AD 1089)	Nuptial bath of ♂ Eleven Wind and ♀ Six Monkey
	+1 year	
7-II, III	Year 13 Rabbit (AD 1090)	♀ Six Monkey journeys to Hua Chino. She and her caravan are attacked and insulted by Lords Six Lizard and Two Alligator.
7-IV	Same	♀ Six Monkey, unable to continue her journey, consults with ♀ Nine Grass, the Oracle of the Dead at Chalcatongo. The oracle delivers instruments of war and an army to ♀ Six Monkey.
8-I	Same	♀ In the heat of battle, warrior-queen ♂ Six Monkey defeats and captures ♂ Six Lizard and ♂ Two Alligator. ♂ Two Alligator dies by heart excision in the temple at Jaltepec.
8-II	Same	♀ Six Monkey takes her second captive, ♂ Six Lizard, to her new home, Hua Chino. She sacrifices him in the temple there.
8-III	Same	An emissary of the Oracle of the Dead conducts a name-change ceremony

Table 14.3   Continued

Selden Page Z-N Page Bod. Page AC Page	Date	Event
8-III (continued)	Same (continued)	for ♀ Six Monkey, the new queen of Hua Chino. She is now ♀ Six Monkey Warpath Garment, or The Warrior.
8-III	Same	♀ Six Monkey and ♂ Eleven Wind are the ruling lords of the ancient city of Hua Chino.
	+2 years	
8-IV	Year 2 Flint (AD 1092)	Their first son, Four Wind, is born.
	+3 years	
8-IV	Year 5 Reed (AD 1095)	Their second son, One Alligator, is born.
	+1 year	
Bod. 5-I	Year 6 Flint (AD 1096)	♂ Two Rain of Tilantongo commits suicide. His mummy is interred at Serpent Lake.
	+1 year	
[Z-N 50c–d	Year 7 House (AD 1097)	Eight Deer consults with the lineage goddess Lady Nine Reed.
Z-N 52	Year 7 House (AD 1097)	Eight Deer consults with the lineage goddess Lady Nine Reed.
Z-N 52	Year 7 House (AD 1097)	Having become prosperous and powerful as lord of Tututepec, Eight Deer forms an alliance with ♂ Four Jaguar of the Tolteca/Chichimeca and becomes a Toltec king and lineage founder and rules at Tilantongo. Eight Deer and his half brother Twelve Motion conference with 112 lords (both Mixtec and non-Mixtec) and unify the Mixteca. (What happened to the king Two Rain? Zouche-Nuttall reverse is elusive about his fate. Yet we note above that Codex Bodley is not. The failed king of Tilantongo killed himself. See Bodley 5-I above.)
	+1 year	
Z-N 68–74	Year 7 Rabbit (AD 1098)	Those polities that do not submit to Eight Deer and the Toltec Four Jaguar are conquered, forty places in all. Then, as supreme lord, Eight Deer, along with his companions, begins

Table 14.3 Continued

Selden Page Z-N Page Bod. Page AC Page	Date	Event
Z-N 68–74 (*continued*)	Year 7 Rabbit (AD 1098) (*continued*)	the Battle in the Sky. They conquer The Place Where the Sky Is Held Up; defeat the warriors of the Sun God, One Death; form an alliance with the Sun God; and return to earth.
Z-N 8, 80–84	Year 10 Flint (AD 1100)	♂ Eight Deer conferences with the mummy bundle of the deceased king of Tilantongo, Lord Two Rain (Z-N Page 8) at Serpent Lake and then collects an army. This is the first mention of Two Rain's death in Codex Zouche-Nuttall. After this conference, ♂ Eight Deer burns ♂ Two Rain's mummy.
Z-N 82–84	Year 11 House (AD 1101)	The Siege of Hua Chino. Eight Deer conquers Hua Chino and captures the boy Four Rain, son of ♀ Six Monkey and ♂ Eleven Wind. Then Eight Deer sacrifices ♂ Eleven Wind's sons by a previous marriage, the Lords Ten Dog and Six Rain. Subsequently, he burns their bodies. At this point Codex Zouche-Nuttall is unfinished.]
AC 11	**Same**	**Eight Deer sacrifices ♀ Six Monkey and ♂ Eleven Wind.**
Bod. 34-I, 33-I	Same (AD 1101)	*♂ Eight Deer of Tilantongo presents ♂ Four Wind's half brothers Ten Dog and Six Rain before Four Wind, who is seated in a cave. This is a cave-empowerment ceremony, similar to that which Eight Deer himself enjoyed when he became lord of Tututepec. Subsequently, the two half brothers become sacrificial victims.*
	+1 year	
8-IV, 9-I	Year 12 Rabbit (AD 1102)	♂ One Alligator rules Jaltepec.
8-IV		♂ Four Wind + ♀ Ten Flower of Tilantongo, daughter of ♂ Eight Deer Jaguar Claw of Tilantongo.
Bod. 14-V	Year 12 Reed (AD 1115)	*During a battle, Eight Deer is captured and sacrificed.*
	+4 years	

Table 14.3 Continued

Selden Page Z-N Page Bod. Page AC Page	Date	Event
Bod. 34-I	Year 3 Reed (AD 1119)	♂ Four Jaguar the Toltec makes ♂ Four Wind a Toltec lord/lineage founder. Lord Four Wind has replaced Eight Deer.
	+3 years	
9-I, II	Year 12 Rabbit (AD 1122)	♂ One Alligator marries ♀ Six Wind of Tilantongo, daughter of Lord Eight Deer Jaguar Claw.
Bod. 29-IV	Year 8 Flint (AD 1124)	♂ Four Wind marries Eight Deer's daughter Ten Flower.
End of the Third- and Fourth-Voice Narratives.		

Conclusion

The first occultation in Codex Selden hides in plain sight, like Edgar Allen Poe's "purloined letter." In all other Mixtec codices, men are the dominant actors. However, Codex Selden states in the history of Jaltepec's second dynasty that males are secondary to females. When Tilantongo's prince Ten Eagle weds Jaltepec's queen Nine Wind, she is fully enthroned on the marriage mat; he merely touches it with one edge of his jaguar cushion. One receives the impression that Prince Ten Eagle "married up." As the text proceeds and their daughter ♀ Six Monkey captures the two insulting lords, one of them is sacrificed in Jaltepec's temple and the other in the temple situated at Hua Chino. The actual person sacrificing them does not appear, but the implication in this suddenly ambiguous text is that ♀ Six Monkey does it. Finally, when ♀ Six Monkey and ♂ Eleven Wind die at the hand of ♂ Eight Deer Jaguar Claw of Tilantongo, her body, chest ripped open, is shown before her husband's (reading from bottom to top) in the Codex Alfonso Caso tableau.

Our first voice, Codex Selden, only refers to ♂ Eight Deer Jaguar Claw of Tilantongo as the father of two princesses who marry the scions of Jaltepec/ Hua Chino, the Lords Four Wind and One Alligator. It declines to narrate ♂ Eight Deer's extensive career as warlord, political innovator, and the executioner of ♀ Six Monkey Warpath Garment of Jaltepec and her husband,

♂ Eleven Wind of Hua Chino. Perhaps this information was considered too well known to merit repetition—a distinct possibility, since the Selden Manuscript was composed well into the Spanish Colonial Period and probably was intended to establish property rights of indigenous Mixtec elites descended from both ♂ Eight Deer and ♀ Six Monkey. Yet it also omits to note that ♀ Six Monkey and ♂ Eleven Wind's son, ♂ Four Wind—who had every genealogical right to rule as a Mixtec king—became a Toltec king and therefore the replacement for ♂ Eight Deer Jaguar Claw.

The focus is on ♀ Six Monkey and ♂ Eleven Wind and their children entirely. Had only Codex Selden and the obverse of Vindobonensis Mexicanus I survived the vicissitudes of history, we would only know of Eight Deer Jaguar Claw as the father of two princesses who married into the Jaltepec/Hua Chino family of royals.

Conversely, our second voice, Codex Zouche-Nuttall in the reverse document, returns the favor and mentions ♀ Six Monkey only once (Page 44a–b). This extremely conflated tableau concerns itself with the meeting of ♀ Six Monkey and ♂ Eleven Wind with the Oracle of the Dead, ♀ Nine Grass, at Chalcatongo (Selden, 6-IV). The Zouche-Nuttall Page 44a–b tableau, however, entirely omits ♂ Eleven Wind of Hua Chino and replaces him with ♂ Eight Deer Jaguar Claw of Tilantongo. The thrust of this Tilantongo-oriented document is not that the oracle betrothed ♀ Six Monkey and ♂ Eight Deer. Rather, we understand that the events provoked ♂ Eight Deer to embark on a course of action that would ultimately rectify the failure of the Tilantongo king, ♂ Two Rain Twenty Jaguars, to conquer Jaltepec and its queen, ♀ Six Monkey, and Hua Chino and its king, ♂ Eleven Wind. Without doubt, the bards who recited, sang, and danced this story understood all these events in their day, but we must reconstruct them piecemeal as best we can.

The real mystery, the most occulted actor in the panoply of Mixtec history, is, however, the failed king of Tilantongo, ♂ Two Rain Twenty Jaguars. We know his boyhood attack on Jaltepec occurred when ♀ Six Monkey—aided and abetted by her confederate, ♀ Nine Grass, the Oracle of the Dead at Chalcatongo—transferred the marriage alliance from Jaltepec/Tilantongo to Jaltepec/Hua Chino. We know of the disastrous outcome of this war. Further, the text says that ♂ Two Rain Twenty Jaguars never married, thus never had offspring, and that the first dynasty of Tilantongo ended with him. He committed suicide at age twenty-six; some interpret the Bodley text as death in a shamanic journey (Jansen and Pérez Jiménez 2005:59b), and indeed the depiction of it in Codex Bodley has shamanic overtones.

This king seems ill fated from the first in the codex narratives. Why? Only Codex Zouche-Nuttall (Page 24a–b) gives us a hint. He was actually born in Year 11 Reed (AD 1075) on Day 9 Reed; therefore, his name should have been Nine Reed, not Two Rain. Day 2 Rain occurs six days after Day 9 Reed. Apparently, according to the auguries of Day 9 Reed, the birth was unfavorable, so his naming occurred six days later on the more auspicious day, 2 Rain. The codex seems to say that one cannot escape one's fate.

Mixtec manuscripts occult historical information for several reasons. One is conflation of narrative tableaux to conserve space. In this particular instance, considering the codices are intended to stimulate memories of reciting and performing bards, one conflated tableau would serve as a mnemonic device and call forth the entire story from a bard's stock of remembered narratives. A second reason for historical occultation is political. Jaltepec and Tilantongo were bitter rivals. At first, the polity of Jaltepec defeated Tilantongo (in fact, disgraced it); but, later, Lord Eight Deer Jaguar Claw of Tilantongo turned the tables on his rival polity. Therefore, Codex Selden, the histories of Jaltepec, only mentions Eight Deer as a progenitor of two princesses of Tilantongo who married scions from Jaltepec/Hua Chino. A third reason may reside in sociocultural fact or convention, namely, that although of royal patriline via Lord Eight Wind Twenty of Suchixtlan, women of the second dynasty of Jaltepec ruled the polity and served in the usually male function of priest.

This chapter does not cover elided information concerning Eight Deer's suppression of Jaltepec's ally, the Chalcatongo Oracle of the Dead, and his replacing of it with the Oracle of the Sun at Achiutla. The relevant narrative in Zouche-Nuttall tells us Eight Deer performs a sun ceremony, becomes king of prosperous Tututepec, expands its territory by conquest a hundredfold, and defeats Chalcatongo, whose oracle has mysteriously vanished. The oracle, ♀ Nine Grass, who was a close confederate of Jaltepec's ♀ Six Monkey, does not reappear until after ♀ Six Monkey's son, ♂ Four Wind, begins his rise to power (Bodley, Page 33-V).

Schematic of the Aztec/Mixtec 52-Year 365-Day Calendar

1. 1 Reed (Acatl)
2. 2 Flint (Tecpatl)
3. 3 House (Calli)
4. 4 Rabbit (Tochtli)

5. 5 Reed
6. 6 Flint
7. 7 House
8. 8 Rabbit

9. 9 Reed
10. 10 Flint
11. 11 House
12. 12 Rabbit

13. 13 Reed
14. 1 Flint
15. 2 House
16. 3 Rabbit

17. 4 Reed
18. 5 Flint
19. 6 House
20. 7 Rabbit

21. 8 Reed
22. 9 Flint
23. 10 House
24. 11 Rabbit

25. 12 Reed
26. 13 Flint
27. 1 House
28. 2 Rabbit

29. 3 Reed
30. 4 Flint
31. 5 House
32. 6 Rabbit

33. 7 Reed
34. 8 Flint
35. 9 House
36. 10 Rabbit

37. 11 Reed
38. 12 Flint
39. 13 House
40. 1 Rabbit

41. 2 Reed
42. 3 Flint
43. 4 House
44. 5 Rabbit

45. 6 Reed
46. 7 Flint
47. 8 House
48. 9 Rabbit

49. 10 Reed
50. 11 Flint
51. 12 House
52. 13 Rabbit

The year cycle begins again with 1 Reed, etc.

APPENDIX 2 Occurrence of 260-Day Sacred Calendars in the 365-Day Mixtec Solar Calendar

The 365-day solar calendar (vague solar year) runs for 52 consecutive years and during that span contains 73 260-day sacred (Augural, Divinatory, Tonalpohualli) cycles for a total of 18,980 days per complete cycle. While each 365-day cycle is named by year bearer (Reed, Flint, House, Rabbit) and numbered repeatedly from one through thirteen, the 260-day cycles are not named. However, throughout the 365-day vague solar year, each Day 1 Alligator begins a new 260-day cycle. The combined cycles begin in Year 1 Reed on Day 1 Alligator, and at the completion of 18,980 days, the 52-year cycle begins anew in Year 1 Reed on Day 1 Alligator (see Codex Zouche-Nuttall Pages 1–2). This initial year-day combination not only is a specific date in the 52-year calendar but also has the metaphorical meanings of "in the beginning," "beginning," or "it happened long ago." However, because the 260-day sacred calendars running concurrently with the 365-day solar years are unnamed and are unequal to the 356-day solar years, they are listed below with the 365-day years in which they occur.

Solar Year Number and Name	Sacred Calendar Number
1. 1 Reed	1, 2
2. 2 Flint	2, 3
3. 3 House	3, 4, 5
4. 4 Rabbit	5, 6
5. 5 Reed	6, 7, 8
6. 6 Flint	8, 9
7. 7 House	9, 10
8. 8 Rabbit	10, 11, 12
9. 9 Reed	12, 13
10. 10 Flint	13, 14, 15
11. 11 House	15, 16
12. 12 Rabbit	16, 17
13. 13 Reed	17, 18, 19
14. 1 Flint	19, 20
15. 2 House	20, 21, 22
16. 3 Rabbit	22, 23

17. 4 Reed	23, 24
18. 5 Flint	24, 25, 26
19. 6 House	26, 27
20. 7 Rabbit	27, 28, 29
21. 8 Reed	29, 30
22. 9 Flint	30, 31
23. 10 House	31, 32, 33
24. 11 Rabbit	33, 34
25. 12 Reed	34, 35, 36
26. 13 Flint	36, 37
27. 1 House	37, 38
28. 2 Rabbit	38, 39, 40
29. 3 Reed	40, 41
30. 4 Flint	41, 42, 43
31. 5 House	43, 44
32. 6 Rabbit	44, 45
33. 7 Reed	45, 46, 47
34. 8 Flint	47, 48
35. 9 House	48, 49, 50
36. 10 Rabbit	50, 51
37. 11 Reed	51, 52
38. 12 Flint	52, 53, 54
39. 13 House	54, 55
40. 1 Rabbit	55, 56, 57
41. 2 Reed	57, 58
42. 3 Flint	58, 59
43. 4 House	59, 60, 61
44. 5 Rabbit	61, 62
45. 6 Reed	62, 63, 64
46. 7 Flint	64, 65
47. 8 House	65, 66
48. 9 Rabbit	66, 67, 68
49. 10 Reed	68, 69
50. 11 Flint	69, 70, 71
51. 12 House	71, 72
52. 13 Rabbit	72, 73

1. 1 Alligator	41. 2 Alligator	81. 3 Alligator	121. 4 Alligator
2. 2 Wind	42. 3 Wind	82. 4 Wind	122. 5 Wind
3. 3 House	43. 4 House	83. 5 House	123. 6 House
4. 4 Lizard	44. 5 Lizard	84. 6 Lizard	124. 7 Lizard
5. 5 Snake	45. 6 Snake	85. 7 Snake	125. 8 Snake
6. 6 Death	46. 7 Death	86. 8 Death	126. 9 Death
7. 7 Deer	47. 8 Deer	87. 9 Deer	127. 10 Deer
8. 8 Rabbit	48. 9 Rabbit	88. 10 Rabbit	128. 11 Rabbit
9. 9 Water	49. 10 Water	89. 11 Water	129. 12 Water
10. 10 Dog	50. 11 Dog	90. 12 Dog	130. 13 Dog
11. 11 Monkey	51. 12 Monkey	91. 13 Monkey	131. 1 Monkey
12. 12 Grass	52. 13 Grass	92. 1 Grass	132. 2 Grass
13. 13 Reed	53. 1 Reed	93. 2 Reed	133. 3 Reed
14. 1 Jaguar	54. 2 Jaguar	94. 3 Jaguar	134. 4 Jaguar
15. 2 Eagle	55. 3 Eagle	95. 4 Eagle	135. 5 Eagle
16. 3 Vulture	56. 4 Vulture	96. 5 Vulture	136. 6 Vulture
17. 4 Motion	57. 5 Motion	97. 6 Motion	137. 7 Motion
18. 5 Flint	58. 6 Flint	98. 7 Flint	138. 8 Flint
19. 6 Rain	59. 7 Rain	99. 8 Rain	139. 9 Rain
20. 7 Flower	60. 8 Flower	100. 9 Flower	140. 10 Flower
21. 8 Alligator	61. 9 Alligator	101. 10 Alligator	141. 11 Alligator
22. 9 Wind	62. 10 Wind	102. 11 Wind	142. 12 Wind
23. 10 House	63. 11 House	103. 12 House	143. 13 House
24. 11 Lizard	64. 12 Lizard	104. 13 Lizard	144. 1 Lizard
25. 12 Snake	65. 13 Snake	105. 1 Snake	145. 2 Snake
26. 13 Death	66. 1 Death	106. 2 Death	146. 3 Death
27. 1 Deer	67. 2 Deer	107. 3 Deer	147. 4 Deer
28. 2 Rabbit	68. 3 Rabbit	108. 4 Rabbit	148. 5 Rabbit
29. 3 Water	69. 4 Water	109. 5 Water	149. 6 Water
30. 4 Dog	70. 5 Dog	110. 6 Dog	150. 7 Dog
31. 5 Monkey	71. 6 Monkey	111. 7 Monkey	151. 8 Monkey
32. 6 Grass	72. 7 Grass	112. 8 Grass	152. 9 Grass

33. 7 Reed	73. 8 Reed	113. 9 Reed	153. 10 Reed
34. 8 Jaguar	74. 9 Jaguar	114. 10 Jaguar	154. 11 Jaguar
35. 9 Eagle	75. 10 Eagle	115. 11 Eagle	155. 12 Eagle
36. 10 Vulture	76. 11 Vulture	116. 12 Vulture	156. 13 Vulture
37. 11 Motion	77. 12 Motion	117. 13 Motion	157. 1 Motion
38. 12 Flint	78. 13 Flint	118. 1 Flint	158. 2 Flint
39. 13 Rain	79. 1 Rain	119. 2 Rain	159. 3 Rain
40. 1 Flower	80. 2 Flower	120. 3 Flower	160. 4 Flower

161. 5 Alligato	201. 6 Alligator	241. 7 Alligator
162. 6 Wind	202. 7 Wind	242. 8 Wind
163. 7 House	203. 8 House	243. 9 House
164. 8 Lizard	204. 9 Lizard	244. 10 Lizard
165. 9 Snake	205. 10 Snake	245. 11 Snake
166. 10 Death	206. 11 Death	246. 12 Death
167. 11 Deer	207. 12 Deer	247. 13 Deer
168. 12 Rabbit	208. 13 Rabbit	248. 1 Rabbit
169. 13 Water	209. 1 Water	249. 2 Water
170. 1 Dog	210. 2 Dog	250. 3 Dog
171. 2 Monkey	211. 3 Monkey	251. 4 Monkey
172. 3 Grass	212. 4 Grass	252. 5 Grass
173. 4 Reed	213. 5 Reed	253. 6 Reed
174. 5 Jaguar	214. 6 Jaguar	254. 7 Jaguar
175. 6 Eagle	215. 7 Eagle	255. 8 Eagle
176. 7 Vulture	216. 8 Vulture	256. 9 Vulture
177. 8 Motion	217. 9 Motion	257. 10 Motion
178. 9 Flint	218. 10 Flint	258. 11 Flint
179. 10 Rain	219. 11 Rain	259. 12 Rain
180. 11 Flower	220. 12 Flower	260. 13 Flower

181. 12 Alligator	221. 13 Alligator
182. 13 Wind	222. 1 Wind
183. 1 House	223. 2 House
184. 2 Lizard	224. 3 Lizard
185. 3 Snake	225. 4 Snake
186. 4 Death	226. 5 Death
187. 5 Deer	227. 6 Deer
188. 6 Rabbit	228. 7 Rabbit
189. 7 Water	229. 8 Water
190. 8 Dog	230. 9 Dog
191. 9 Monkey	231. 10 Monkey
192. 10 Grass	232. 11 Grass
193. 11 Reed	233. 12 Reed
194. 12 Jaguar	234. 13 Jaguar
195. 13 Eagle	235. 1 Eagle

APPENDIX 4 The Calendrics of Codex Zouche-Nuttall Pages 42–84

The Vague Solar Years in Codex Zouche-Nuttall Pages 42–84

Page	Year	AD Year	Tally
42a	6 Flint	1045	+ 1
42b	7 House	1045	+ 17
42c	10 House	1062	+ 1
43a	12 Reed's,		
	8 Deer's births	1063	+ 8
43c	7 Reed	1071	
		Total = 27 years	

The Parentage Statement + early military career, Pages 42–43, covers a total of twenty-seven years.

Page	Year	AD Year	Tally
44a	2 Reed	1079	+ 4
44b	6 Reed	1083	+ 8
44c	1 Reed	1091	+ 4
44c	5 Reed	1095	+ 1
48b	6 Flint	1096	+ 1
50d, 52c	7 House	1097	+ 1
68b, 69a	8 Rabbit	1098	+ 1
76b	9 Reed	1099	+ 1
60b	10 Flint	1100	+ 1
82c, 83a	10(11) House	1101	
		Total = 22 years	

Eight Deer's mature career covers twenty-two years.
Codex Zouche-Nuttall Pages 42–84 cover a span of forty-nine years.

Tonalpohualli in Codex Zouche-Nuttall Pages 42–84

Page 42
Year 6 Flint, Tonalpohualli 8, 9
Day 7 Eagle, Tonalpohualli 8, day 215; day 190 of Year 6 Flint

Year 7 House, Tonalpohualli 9, 10
Day 12 Motion, Tonalpohualli 10, day 77; day 227 of Year 7 House

Year 10 House, Tonalpohualli 31, 32, 33
Day 6 Deer, Tonalpohualli 32, day 227; day 257 of Year 10 House

Page 43
Year 12 Reed, Tonalpohualli 34, 35, 36
Day 8 Deer, Tonalpohualli 35, day 47; day 127 of Year 12 Reed

Year 7 Reed, Tonalpohualli 45, 46, 47
Day 10 Vulture, Tonalpohualli 46, day 36 or Tonalpohualli 47, day 36; day 56 and 316
　of Year 7 Reed

Pages 44–48
Year 2 Reed, Tonalpohualli 57, 58
Day 10 Flower, Tonalpohualli 58, day 140; days 100 and 360 of Year 2 Reed

Year 6 Reed, Tonalpohualli 62, 63, 64
Day 6 Snake, Tonalpohualli 63, day 45 or Tonalpohualli 64, day 45; day 105 of Year
　6 Reed

Year 1 Reed, Tonalpohualli 1, 2
Day 6 Water, Tonalpohualli 1, day 149; day 149 of Year 1 Reed

Year 5 Reed, Tonalpohualli 6, 7, 8
Day 2 Water, Tonalpohualli 6, day 249 or Tonalpohualli 7, day 249; days 89 and 349 of
　Year 5 Reed
Day 2 Flower, Tonalpohualli 7, day 80; day 180 of Year 5 Reed
Day 13 Motion, Tonalpohualli 7, day 117; day 217 of Year 5 Reed
Day 7 Lizard, Tonalpohualli 7, day 124; day 204 of Year 5 Reed
Day 7 Vulture, Tonalpohualli 6, day 176 or Tonalpohualli 7, day 176; day 276 of Year
　5 Reed
Day 3 Motion, Tonalpohualli 6, day 237 or Tonalpohualli 7, day 237; days 76 and 337
　of Year 5 Reed
Day 13 Rain, Tonalpohualli 7, day 39; day 139 of Year 5 Reed
Day 4 Reed, Tonalpohualli 6, day 173 or Tonalpohualli 7, day 173; days 13 and 253 of
　Year 5 Reed
Day 5 Wind, Tonalpohualli 7, day 122; day 222 of Year 5 Reed
Day 1 Alligator, Tonalpohualli 7, day 1 or Tonalpohualli 8, day 1; days 101 and 361 of
　Year 5 Reed
Day 7 Flower, Tonalpohualli 7, day 20; day 120 of Year 5 Reed
Day 12 Rain, Tonalpohualli 7, day 259; days 99 and 359 of Year 5 Reed
Day 4 Wind, Tonalpohualli 7, day 82; day 182 of Year 5 Reed
Day 5 Eagle, Tonalpohualli 7, day 135; day 235 of Year 5 Reed
Day 9 Motion, Tonalpohualli 6, day 217 or Tonalpohualli 7, day 217; days 276 and 337
　of Year 5 Reed

Day 9 Rabbit, Tonalpohualli 7, day 48; day 148 of Year 5 Reed

Day 6 Flower, Tonalpohualli 6 and 7, day 240; days 80 and 340 of Year 5 Reed

Day 7 Alligator, Tonalpohualli 6 and 7, day 241; days 101 and 341 of Year 5 Reed

Day 13 House, Tonalpohualli 7, day 143; day 243 of Year 5 Reed

Day 7 Motion, Tonalpohualli 7, day 137; day 237 of Year 5 Reed

Day 10 Grass, Tonalpohualli 6 and 7, day 192; days 32 and 392 of Year 5 Reed

Pages 48–50

Year 6 Flint, Tonalpohualli 8, 9. Tonalpohualli 8 is first of the last five days of Year
5 Reed.

Day 11 Death, Tonalpohualli 8, day 206; day 201 of Year 6 Flint

Day 3 Deer, Tonalpohualli 8, day 107 or Tonalpohualli 9, day 107; days 102 and 362 of
Year 6 Flint

Day 10 Deer, Tonalpohualli 8, day 127; day 161 of Year 6 Flint

Day 12 Dog, Tonalpohualli 8, day 90 or Tonalpohualli 9, day 90; days 85 and 345 of
Year 6 Flint

Day 3 Jaguar, Tonalpohualli 8, day 94 or Tonalpohualli 9, day 94; days 89 and 349 of
Year 6 Flint

Day 4 Flower, Tonalpohualli 8, day 160; day 155 of Year 6 Flint

Day 9 Flower, Tonalpohualli 8, day 100 or Tonalpohualli 9, day 100; days 95 and 355
of Year 6 Flint

Day 6 Lizard, Tonalpohualli 8, day 84 or Tonalpohualli 9, day 84; days 79 and 239 of
Year 6 Flint

Day 10 Snake, Tonalpohualli 8, day 205; day 200 of Year 6 Flint

Day 7 Flint, Tonalpohualli 8, day 98 or Tonalpohualli 9, day 98; days 93 and 353 of
Year 6 Flint

Day 10 Wind, Tonalpohualli 8, day 62 or Tonalpohualli 9, day 62; days 57 and 317 of
Year 6 Flint

Day 1 Alligator, Tonalpohualli 9, day 1; day 256 of Year 6 Flint

Day 4 Flint, Tonalpohualli 8, day 238; day 233 of Year 6 Flint

Day 9 Deer, Tonalpohualli 8, day 87 or Tonalpohualli 9, day 87; days 82 and 342 of
Year 6 Flint

Day 9 Snake, Tonalpohualli 8, day 165; day 160 of Year 6 Flint

Day 11 Deer, Tonalpohualli 8, day 167; day 162 of Year 6 Flint

Day 11 Rain, Tonalpohualli 8, day 219; day 214 of Year 6 Flint

Day 12 Flower, Tonalpohualli 8, day 220; day 215 of Year 6 Flint

Pages 50–68

Year 7 House, Tonalpohualli 9, 10

Day 13 Alligator, Tonalpohualli 9, day 221; day 111 of Year 7 House

Day 1 Wind, Tonalpohualli 9, day 222; day 112 of Year 7 House

Day 8 Death, Tonalpohualli 10, day 86 (This day occurs in Tonalpohualli 9 but in
Year 6 Flint, not Year 7 House. Also, it is probably the name of the priest who
punctures Eight Deer's nose, not a sequential day name.); day 236 of Year 7 House

Day 7 Rabbit, Tonalpohualli 9, day 228; day 118 of Year 7 House

Day 8 Water, Tonalpohualli 9, day 229; day 119 of Year 7 House

Day 7 Flower, Tonalpohualli 10, day 20 (Day 7 Flower also occurs in Tonalpohualli 9 but in Year 6 Flint.); day 170 of Year 7 House

Day 9 Alligator, Tonalpohualli 10, day 61; day 211 of Year 7 House

Day 4 Flint, Tonalpohualli 9, day 238; day 128 of Year 7 House

Day 1 Alligator, Tonalpohualli 10, day 1; day 151 of Year 7 House

Day 9 Wind, Tonalpohualli 10, day 22 (This is the meeting with 112 lords. The Days listed there on Pages 54 to 68a are taken as day names of individuals, not as days of events, and so are not listed here. The next chronological listing occurs on Page 68b. Day 9 Wind is also the last day recorded in the codex, Page 84.); day 172 of Year 7 House

Pages 68–75

Year 8 Rabbit, Tonalpohualli 10, 11, 12. Only twenty days of Tonalpohualli 10 occur in Year 8 Rabbit.

Day 4 Wind, Tonalpohualli 11, day 82; day 127 of Year 8 Rabbit

Day 5 House, Tonalpohualli 11, day 83; day 128 of Year 8 Rabbit

Day 6 Lizard, Tonalpohualli 11, day 84; day 129 of Year 8 Rabbit

Day 7 Snake, Tonalpohualli 11, day 85; day 130 of Year 8 Rabbit

Day 8 Death, Tonalpohualli 11, day 86; day 131 of Year 8 Rabbit

*Day 10 Rabbit, Tonalpohualli 11, day 88; day 133 of Year 8 Rabbit

Day 11 Water, Tonalpohualli 11, day 89; day 134 of Year 8 Rabbit

Day 2 Reed, Tonalpohualli 11, day 93; day 138 of Year 8 Rabbit

Day 9(10) Alligator, Tonalpohualli 11, day 9 Alligator is day 61, and 10 Alligator is day 101. The text day 9 Alligator appears to have been added over an erasure. Day 10 Alligator is day 146 of Year 8 Rabbit, and day 9 Alligator is day 106 of Year 8 Rabbit, so I opt for 10 Alligator because it is in sequence with the preceding days.

Day 9 Snake, Tonalpohualli 11, day 145; day 210 of Year 8 Rabbit

Day 2 Motion, Tonalpohualli 11, day 197; day 242 of Year 8 Rabbit

Day 12 Vulture, Tonalpohualli 11, day 116. This could be a day name for an actor in text.

*Day 8 Eagle, Tonalpohualli 11, day 255. It is also day 255 in Tonalpohualli 10, appearing as days 40 and 300 in Year 8 Rabbit.

Day 12 Eagle, Tonalpohualli 11, day 155; day 200 in Year 8 Rabbit

Day 11 Snake, Tonalpohualli 11, day 245. It is also day 245 in Tonalpohualli 10, appearing as days 30 and 230 of Year 8 Rabbit.

Day 13 Rain, Tonalpohualli 11, day 39 or Tonalpohualli 12, day 39; days 84 and 344 of Year 8 Rabbit

Day 7 Grass, Tonalpohualli 11, day 72; day 117 of Year 8 Rabbit

Day 3 Alligator, Tonalpohualli 11, day 81; day 126 of Year 8 Rabbit

Day 5 Rain, Tonalpohualli 11, day 239; also Tonalpohualli 10 but day 24 of Year 8 Rabbit

Day 1 Jaguar, Tonalpohualli 11, day 14. Also Tonalpohualli 12; days 59 and 319 of Year
    8 Rabbit.
Day 2 Eagle, Tonalpohualli 11, day 15. Also Tonalpohualli 12; days 60 and 320 of Year
    8 Rabbit.
Day 7 Jaguar, Tonalpohualli 11, day 254. Also Tonalpohualli 10, day 254; days 39 and
    299 of Year 8 Rabbit.
*Day 12 Grass, Tonalpohualli 11, day 12. Also Tonalpohualli 10, day 12; days 57 and 317
    of Year 8 Rabbit.
*Day 4 Monkey, Tonalpohualli 11, day 251. Also Tonalpohualli 10, day 251; days 36 and
    296 of Year 8 Rabbit.
Day 11 Dog, Tonalpohualli 11, day 50. Also Tonalpohualli 12, day 50; days 95 and 355
    of Year 8 Rabbit.
Day 13 Deer, Tonalpohualli 11, day 247. Also Tonalpohualli 10, day 247; days 32 and
    292 of Year 8 Rabbit.
Day 1 Rabbit, Tonalpohualli 11, day 248; days 33 and 293 of Year 8 Rabbit
Day 2 Water, Tonalpohualli 11, day 249. Also Tonalpohualli 10, days 34 and 294 of
    Year 8 Rabbit.
*Day 4 Monkey, day 51: see * above.
Day 6 Reed, Tonalpohualli 11, day 253. Also Tonalpohualli 10, days 38 and 298 of Year
    8 Rabbit.
*Day 8 Eagle, Tonalpohualli 11, day 255: see * above.
Day 9 Vulture, Tonalpohualli 11, day 256. Also Tonalpohualli 10, days 41 and 301 of
    Year 8 Rabbit.
Day 10 Motion, Tonalpohualli 11, day 257. Also Tonalpohualli 10, days 42 and 302 of
    Year 8 Rabbit.
Day 12 Rain, Tonalpohualli 1, day 259. Also Tonalpohualli 10, days 44 and 304 of Year
    8 Rabbit.
Day 5 Lizard, Tonalpohualli 11, day 44; days 89 and 349 of Year 8 Rabbit
*Day 4 Monkey, Tonalpohualli 11, day 251: see * above.
Day 10 Flower, Tonalpohualli 11, day 140; day 185 of Year 8 Rabbit
*Day 10 Rabbi, Tonalpohualli 11: see * above.
Day 3 Vulture, Tonalpohualli 11, day 16; days 61 and 321 of Year 8 Rabbit.
Day 7 Flower Tonalpohualli 11 day 20; days 65 and 325 of Year 8 Rabbit.
Day 2 Dog, Tonalpohualli 11, day 210; day 259 of Year 8 Rabbit
Day 12 Grass: see day 12 * above.
Day 11 Monkey, Tonalpohualli 11, day 11; days 56 and 316 of Year 11 Rabbit
Day 2 Monkey, Tonalpohualli 11, day 171; day 216 of Year 8 Rabbit
Day 9 Jaguar, Tonalpohualli 11, day 74; day 119 of Year 8 Rabbit
Day 4 Deer, Tonalpohualli 11, day 147; day 192 of Year 8 Rabbit

Pages 75–76
Day 10 Snake, Tonalpohualli 11, day 205; day 250 of Year 8 Rabbit
Day 11 Death, Tonalpohualli 11, day 206; day 251 of Year 8 Rabbit
Day 12 Deer, Tonalpohualli 11, day 207; day 252 of Year 8 Rabbit

Day 11 Motion, Tonalpohualli 11, day 37 or Tonalpohualli 12, day 37; days 53 and 313 of Year 8 Rabbit

Day 13 Eagle, Tonalpohualli 11, day 195; day 240 of Year 8 Rabbit

Day 8 Death, Tonalpohualli 11, day 86; day 111 of Year 8 Rabbit

Day 12 Water, Tonalpohualli 11, day 129, the 174th day of Year 8 Rabbit

Day 7 Flower, Tonalpohualli 11, day 20 or Tonalpohualli 12, day 20; days 65 and 325 of Year 8 Rabbit

Page 76a

Year 9 Reed, Tonalpohualli 12 and 13

Day 4 Alligator, Tonalpohualli 12, day 121 or Tonalpohualli 13, day 121; days 61 and 321 of Year 9 Reed

Day 12 Death, Tonalpohualli 12, day 246; day 186 of Year 9 Reed

Day 9 Death (Eight Deer's battle with the warriors of the sun), Tonalpohualli 12, day 126 or Tonalpohualli 13, day 126; days 66 and 326 of Year 9 Reed

Page 76b

The twelve day names of the sacrificed warriors of the sun appear here.

Page 77

The day names of two warriors of the sun are in column "a." Then:

Day 9 Snake, Tonalpohualli 12, day 165; day 105 of Year 9 Reed

Day 11 Deer, Tonalpohualli 12, day 167; day 107 of Year 9 Reed

Day 11 Rabbit, Tonalpohualli 12, day 128 or Tonalpohualli 13, day 128; days 68 and 328 of Year 9 Reed

Page 78

Day 7 Motion (Eight Deer meets with the Sun God), Tonalpohualli 12, day 137 or Tonalpohualli 13, day 137; days 87 and 337 of Year 9 Reed

Day 8 Dog (Eight Deer and Four Jaguar drill for fire), Tonalpohualli 12, day 190; day 130 of Year 9 Reed

Page 79

Day 9 Grass, Tonalpohualli 12, day 152 or Tonalpohualli 13, day 152; days 92 and 352 in Year 9 Reed

Day 11 Grass, Tonalpohualli 12, day 232; day 172 in Year 9 Reed

Day 3 Monkey, Tonalpohualli 12, day 211; day 151 in Year 9 Reed

Page 80

Day 9 Motion, Tonalpohualli 12, day 217; day 197 in Year 9 Reed

Day 6 Jaguar, Tonalpohualli 12, day 214; day 154 in Year 9 Reed

Year 10 Flint, Tonalpohuallis 13 and 14

Day 8 Eagle, Tonalpohualli 13, day 255 or Tonalpohualli 14, day 255; days 90 and 350 in Year 10 Flint

Day 8 Rabbit, Tonalpohualli 14, day 8; days 103 and 363 in Year 10 Flint

Day 11 Death (assassination of Lord Twelve Motion), Tonalpohualli 13, day 206 or
   Tonalpohualli 14, day 206; days 41 and 301 in Year 10 Flint

Day 9 Motion, Tonalpohualli 13, day 217 or Tonalpohualli 14, day 217; days 52 and 312
   in Year 10 Flint

Day 12 Motion, Tonalpohualli 14, day 77; day 172 in Year 10 Flint

Day 2 Flint (consultation with Lord Two Rain's mummy; see Z-N Page 8),
   Tonalpohualli 14, day 158; day 253 in Year 10 Flint

Year 10(11) House, Tonalpohuallis 15 and 16

Day 6 Jaguar, Tonalpohualli 15, day 214; day 204 in Year 11 House

Year 11 House, Tonalpohuallis 15 and 16

Day 12 Monkey, Tonalpohualli 15, day 51 or Tonalpohualli 16, day 51; days 41 and 301
   in Year 11 House

Year 12 Rabbit, Tonalpohuallis 16 and 17

Day 6 Snake, Tonalpohualli 17, day 45; day 190 in Year 12 Rabbit

Day 9 Wind (The day name appears on Page 84 separated from the numeral. This is
   clearly indicative of the nature of the sacrifice of the two scions of Hua Chino,
   the princes Ten Dog and Six House; namely, a Lord Nine Wind Quetzalcoatl
   sacrifice.), Tonalpohualli 17, day 22; day 167 in Year 12 Rabbit

APPENDIX 5 The Mixtec Calendar Cycle Correspondences from Byland and Pohl (1994)

Cycle 1: AD 883–934   Cycle 8: AD 1247–1298
Cycle 2: AD 935–986   Cycle 9: AD 1299–1350
Cycle 3: AD 987–1038   Cycle 10: AD 1351–1402
Cycle 4: AD 1039–1090   Cycle 11: AD 1403–1454
Cycle 5: AD 1091–1142   Cycle 12: AD 1455–1506
Cycle 6: AD 1143–1194   Cycle 13: AD 1507–1558
Cycle 7: AD 1195–1246   Cycle 14: AD 1559–1610

These cycles of 52 years each are inclusive for all known recorded dates in the five major Mixtec manuscripts: Codices Selden, Bodley, Zouche-Nuttall, Vindobonensis Mexicanus I, and Alfonso Caso.

The Complete Mixtec/Aztec Calendar

With Aztec Nomenclature for *Tonalpohuallis* and *Trecenas*

In the complete, comprehensive calendar below, the beginnings of the *tonalpohuallis* (Days 1 Alligator) are shown in bold. The beginnings of the 13-day intervals called *trecenas* (any day beginning with the number 1) are italicized.

1. Year 1 Acatl

Days:

Cipactli (Alligator)
1 8 2 9 3 10 4 11 5 12 6 13 7 *1* 8 2 9 3

Ehecatl (Wind)
2 9 3 10 4 11 5 12 6 13 7 *1* 8 2 9 3 10 4

Calli (House)
3 10 4 11 5 12 6 13 7 *1* 8 2 9 3 10 4 1 5

Cuetzpalin (Lizard)
4 11 5 12 6 13 7 *1* 8 2 9 3 10 4 11 5 12 6

Coatl (Snake)
5 12 6 13 7 *1* 8 2 9 3 10 4 11 5 12 6 13 7

Miquiztli (Death)
6 13 7 *1* 8 2 9 3 10 4 11 5 12 6 13 7 *1* 8

Mazatl (Deer)
7 *1* 8 2 9 3 10 4 11 5 12 6 13 7 *1* 8 2 9

Tochtli (Rabbit)
8 2 9 3 10 4 11 5 12 6 13 7 *1* 8 2 9 3 10

Atl (Water)
9 3 10 4 11 5 12 6 13 7 *1* 8 2 9 3 10 4 11

Itzcuintli (Dog)
10 4 11 5 12 6 13 7 *1* 8 2 9 3 10 4 11 5 12

Ozomatli (Monkey)
11 5 12 6 13 7 *1* 8 2 9 3 10 4 11 5 12 6 13

Malinalli (Grass)
12 6 13 7 *1* 8 2 9 3 10 4 11 5 12 6 13 7 *1*

Acatl (Reed)
13 7 *1* 8 2 9 3 10 4 11 5 12 6 13 7 *1* 8 2
Ocelotl (Jaguar)
1 8 2 9 3 10 4 11 5 12 6 13 7 *1* 8 2 9 3
Quauhtli (Eagle)
2 9 3 10 4 11 5 12 6 13 7 *1* 8 2 9 3 10 4
Cozcaquauhtli (Vulture)
3 10 4 11 5 12 6 13 7 *1* 8 2 9 3 10 4 11 5

Ollin (Motion)
4 11 5 12 6 13 7 *1* 8 2 9 3 10 4 11 5 12 6
Tecpatl (Flint)
5 12 6 13 7 *1* 8 2 9 3 10 4 11 5 12 6 13 7
Quiahuitl (Rain)
6 13 7 *1* 8 2 9 3 10 4 11 5 12 6 13 7 *1* 8
Xochitl (Flower)
7 *1* 8 2 9 3 10 4 11 5 12 6 13 7 *1* 8 2 9

Five Remaining Days of Year 1 Acatl: Cipactli   10
                                       Ehecatl   11
                                       Calli   12
                                       Cuetzpalin   13
                                       Coatl   *1*

Tonalpohuallis 1 and 2 occur in Year 1 Reed; they are also *trecenas*. *Trecenas* in Year 1 Reed are:

1. 1 Alligator	9. 1 Snake	17. 1 Water	25. 1 Reed
2. 1 Jaguar	10. 1 Flint	18. 1 Wind	26. 1 Death
3. 1 Deer	11. 1 Monkey	19. 1 Eagle	27. 1 Rain
4. 1 Flower	12. 1 Lizard	20. 1 Rabbi	28. 1 Grass
5. 1 Reed	13. 1 Motion	21. 1 Alligator	29. 1 Snake
6. 1 Death	14. 1 Dog	22. 1 Jaguar	
7. 1 Rain	15. 1 House	23. 1 Deer	
8. 1 Grass	16. 1 Vulture	24. 1 Flower	

The next year (2 Tecpatl) occurs with Day 2 Miquiztli.

2. Year 2 Tecpatl

Days:
Miquiztli (Death)
2 9 3 10 4 11 5 12 6 13 7 *1* 8 2 9 3 10 4

Mazatl (Deer)
3 10 4 11 5 12 6 13 7 *1* 8 2 9 3 10 4 11 5
Tochtli (Rabbit)
4 11 5 12 6 13 7 *1* 8 2 9 3 10 4 11 5 12 6

Atl (Water)
5   12   6   13   7   *1*   8   2   9   3   10   4   11   5   12   6   13   7
Itzcuintli (Dog)
6   13   7   *1*   8   2   9   3   10   4   11   5   12   6   13   7   *1*   8
Ozomatli (Monkey)
7   *1*   8   2   9   3   10   4   11   5   12   6   13   7   *1*   8   2   9

Malinalli (Grass)
8   2   9   3   10   4   11   5   12   6   13   7   *1*   8   2   9   3   10
Acatl (Reed)
9   3   10   4   11   5   12   6   13   7   *1*   8   2   9   3   10   4   11
Ocelotl (Jaguar)
10   4   11   5   12   6   13   7   *1*   8   2   9   3   10   4   11   5   12
Quauhtli (Eagle)
11   5   12   6   13   7   *1*   8   2   9   3   10   4   11   5   12   6   13
Cozcaquauhtli (Vulture)
12   6   13   7   *1*   8   2   9   3   10   4   11   5   12   6   13   7   *1*

Ollin (Motion)
13   7   *1*   8   2   9   3   10   4   11   5   12   6   13   7   *1*   8   2
Tecpatl (Flint)
1   8   2   9   3   10   4   11   5   12   6   13   7   *1*   8   2   9   3
Quiahuitl (Rain)
2   9   3   10   4   11   5   12   6   13   7   *1*   8   2   9   3   10   4
Xochitl (Flower)
3   10   4   11   5   12   6   13   7   *1*   8   2   9   3   10   4   11   5
Cipactli (Alligator)
4   11   5   12   6   13   7   **1**   8   2   9   3   10   4   11   5   12   6

Ehecatl (Wind)
5   12   6   13   7   *1*   8   2   9   3   10   4   11   5   12   6   13   7
Calli (House)
6   13   7   *1*   8   2   9   3   10   4   11   5   12   6   13   7   *1*   8
Cuetzpalin (Lizard)
7   *1*   8   2   9   3   10   4   11   5   12   6   13   7   *1*   8   2   9
Coatl (Snake)
8   2   9   3   10   4   11   5   12   6   13   7   *1*   8   2   9   3   10

Five Remaining Days of Year 2 Tecpatl:

Miquiztli	11
Mazatl	2
Tochtli	13
Atl	*1*
Itzcuintli	2

Tonalpohualli 3 (Day 1 Alligator) occurs in Year 2 Flint. The *trecenas* are:

1. 1 Flint	8. 1 Water	16. 1 Reed	23. 1 Lizard
2. 1 Monkey	9. 1 Wind	17. 1 Death	24. 1 Motion
3. 1 Lizard	10. 1 Eagle	18. 1 Rain	25. 1 Dog
4. 1 Motion	11. 1 Rabbit	19. 1 Grass	26. 1 House
5. 1 Dog	12. 1 Alligator	20. 1 Snake	27. 1 Vulture
6. 1 House	13. 1 Jaguar	21. 1 Flint	28. 1 Water
7. 1 Vulture	14. 1 Deer	22. 1 Monkey	

The next year (3 Calli) begins with Day 3 Ozomatli.

3. Year 3 Calli

Days:

Ozomatli (Monkey)
3   10   4   11   5   12   6   13   7   *1*   8   2   9   3   10   4   11   5

Malinalli (Grass)
4   11   5   12   6   13   7   *1*   8   2   9   3   10   4   11   5   12   6

Acatl (Reed)
5   12   6   13   7   *1*   8   2   9   3   10   4   11   5   12   6   13   7

Ocelotl (Jaguar)
6   13   7   *1*   8   2   9   3   10   4   11   5   12   6   13   7   *1*   8

Quauhtli (Eagle)
7   *1*   8   2   9   3   10   4   11   5   12   6   13   7   *1*   8   2   9

Cozcaquauhtli (Vulture)
8   2   9   3   10   4   11   5   12   6   13   7   *1*   8   2   9   3   10

Ollin (Motion)
9   3   10   4   11   5   12   6   13   7   *1*   8   2   9   3   10   4   11

Tecpatl (Flint)
10   4   11   5   12   6   13   7   *1*   8   2   9   3   10   4   11   5   12

Quiahuitl (Rain)
11   5   12   6   13   7   *1*   8   2   9   3   10   4   11   5   12   6   13

Xochitl (Flower)
12   6   13   7   *1*   8   2   9   3   10   4   11   5   12   6   13   7   *1*

Cipactli (Alligator)
13   7   (4)**1**   8   2   9   3   10   4   11   5   12   6   13   7   (5)**1**   8   2

Ehecatl (Wind)
1   8   2   9   3   10   4   11   5   12   6   13   7   *1*   8   2   9   3

Calli (House)
2   9   3   10   4   11   5   12   6   13   7   *1*   8   2   9   3   10   4

Cuetzpalin (Lizard)
3   10   4   11   5   12   6   13   7   *1*   8   2   9   3   10   4   11   5

Coatl (Snake)
4   11   5   12   6   13   7   *1*   8   2   9   3   10   4   11   5   12   6

Miquiztli (Death)

5 12 6 13 7 *1* 8 2 9 3 10 4 11 5 12 6 13 7

Mazatl (Deer)

6 13 7 *1* 8 2 9 3 10 4 11 5 12 6 13 7 *1* 8

Tochtli (Rabbit)

7 *1* 8 2 9 3 10 4 11 5 12 6 13 7 *1* 8 2 9

Atl (Water)

8 2 9 3 10 4 11 5 12 6 13 7 *1* 8 2 9 3 10

Itzcuintli (Dog)

9 3 10 4 11 5 12 6 13 7 *1* 8 2 9 3 10 4 11

Five Remaining Days of Year 3 Calli: Ozomatli 12
Malinalli 13
Acatl *1*
Ocelotl 2
Quauhtli 3

Tonalpohuallis 4 and 5 (1 Alligator) occur in Year 3 House. The *trecenas* are:

1. 1 Wind	8. 1 Reed	16. 1 Motion	23. 1 Rabbit
2. 1 Eagle	9. 1 Death	17. 1 Dog	24. 1 Alligator
3. 1 Rabbit	10. 1 Rain	18. 1 House	25. 1 Reed
4. 1 Alligator	11. 1 Grass	19. 1 Vulture	26. 1 Deer
5. 1 Jaguar	12. 1 Snake	20. 1 Water	27. 1 Flower
6. 1 Deer	13. 1 Flint	21. 1 Wind	28. 1 Reed
7. 1 Flower	14. 1 Monkey	22. 1 Eagle	

The next year (4 Tochtli) begins with Day 4 Cozcaquauhtli.

4. Year 4 Tochtli

Days:

Cozcaquauhtli (Vulture)

4 11 5 12 6 13 7 *1* 8 2 9 3 10 4 11 5 12 6

Ollin (Motion)

5 12 6 13 7 *1* 8 2 9 3 10 4 11 5 12 6 13 7

Tecpatl (Flint)

6 13 7 *1* 8 2 9 3 10 4 11 5 12 6 13 7 *1* 8

Quiahuitl (Rain)

7 *1* 8 2 9 3 10 4 11 5 12 6 13 7 *1* 8 2 9

Xochitl (Flower)

8 2 9 3 10 4 11 5 12 6 13 7 *1* 8 2 9 3 10

Cipactli (Alligator)

9 3 10 4 11 5 12 6 13 7 (6)1 8 2 9 3 10 4 11

Ehecatl (Wind)

10 4 11 5 12 6 13 7 *1* 8 2 9 3 10 4 11 5 12

Calli (House)

11 5 12 6 13 7 *1* 8 2 9 3 10 4 11 5 12 6 13

Cuetzpalin (Lizard)

12 6 13 7 *1* 8 2 9 3 10 4 11 5 12 6 13 7 *1*

Coatl (Snake)

13 7 *1* 8 2 9 3 10 4 11 5 12 6 13 7 *1* 8 2

Miquiztli (Death)

1 8 2 9 3 10 4 11 5 12 6 13 7 *1* 8 2 9 3

Mazatl (Deer)

2 9 3 10 4 11 5 12 6 13 7 *1* 8 2 9 3 10 4

Tochtli (Rabbit)

3 10 4 11 5 12 6 13 7 *1* 8 2 9 3 10 4 11 5

Atl (Water)

4 11 5 12 6 13 7 *1* 8 2 9 3 10 4 11 5 12 6

Itzcuintli (Dog)

5 12 6 13 7 *1* 8 2 9 3 10 4 11 5 12 6 13 7

Ozomatli (Monkey)

6 13 7 *1* 8 2 9 3 10 4 11 5 12 6 13 7 *1* 8

Malinalli (Grass)

7 *1* 8 2 9 3 10 4 11 5 12 6 13 7 *1* 8 2 9

Acatl (Reed)

8 2 9 3 10 4 11 5 12 6 13 7 *1* 8 2 9 3 10

Ocelotl (Jaguar)

9 3 10 4 11 5 12 6 13 7 *1* 8 2 9 3 10 4 11

Quauhtli (Eagle)

10 4 11 5 12 6 13 7 *1* 8 2 9 3 10 4 11 5 12

Five Remaining Days of Year 4 Tochtli:	Cozcaquauhtli	13
	Ollin	*1*
	Tecpatl	2
	Quiahuitl	3
	Xochitl	4

Tonalpohualli 6 (Day 1 Alligator) occurs in Year 4 Rabbit. The *trecenas* are:

1. 1 Death	8. 1 Motion	15. 1 Rabbit	22. 1 Rain
2. 1 Rain	9. 1 Dog	16. 1 Alligator	23. 1 Grass
3. 1 Grass	10. 1 House	17. 1 Jaguar	24. 1 Snake
4. 1 Snake	11. 1 Vulture	18. 1 Deer	25. 1 Flint
5. 1 Flint	12. 1 Water	19. 1 Flower	26. 1 Monkey
6. 1 Monkey	13. 1 Wind	20. 1 Reed	27. 1 Lizard
7. 1 Lizard	14. 1 Eagle	21. 1 Death	28. 1 Motion

The next year (5 Acatl) begins with Day 5 Cipactli.

Days:
Cipactli (Alligator)
5 12 6 13 7 (7)1 8 2 9 3 10 4 11 5 12 6 13 7

Ehecatl (Wind)
6 13 7 *1* 8 2 9 3 10 2 11 5 10 6 13 5 *1* 8

Calli (House)
7 *1* 8 2 9 3 10 4 11 5 12 6 13 7 *1* 8 2 9

Cuetzpalin (Lizard)
8 2 9 3 10 4 11 5 12 6 13 7 *1* 8 2 9 3 10

Coatl (Snake)
9 3 10 4 11 5 12 6 13 7 *1* 8 2 9 3 10 4 11

Miquiztli (Death)
10 4 11 5 12 6 13 7 *1* 8 2 9 3 10 4 11 5 12

Mazatl (Deer)
11 5 12 6 13 7 *1* 8 2 9 3 10 4 11 5 12 6 13

Tochtli (Rabbit)
12 6 13 7 *1* 8 2 9 3 10 4 11 5 12 6 13 7 *1*

Atl (Water)
13 7 *1* 8 2 9 3 10 4 11 5 12 6 13 7 *1* 8 2

Itzcuintli (Dog)
1 8 2 9 3 10 4 11 5 12 6 13 7 *1* 8 2 9 3

Ozomatli (Monkey)
2 9 3 10 4 11 5 12 6 13 7 *1* 8 2 9 3 10 4

Malinalli (Grass)
3 10 4 11 5 12 6 13 7 *1* 8 2 9 3 10 4 11 5

Acatl (Reed)
4 11 5 12 6 13 7 *1* 8 2 9 3 10 4 11 5 12 6

Ocelotl (Jaguar)
5 12 6 13 7 *1* 8 2 9 3 10 4 11 5 12 6 13 7

Quauhtli (Eagle)
6 13 7 *1* 8 2 9 3 10 4 11 5 12 6 13 7 *1* 8

Cozcaquauhtli (Vulture)
7 *1* 8 2 9 3 10 4 11 5 12 6 13 7 *1* 8 2 9

Ollin (Motion)
8 2 9 3 10 4 11 5 12 6 13 7 *1* 8 2 9 3 10

Tecpatl (Flint)
9 3 10 4 11 5 12 6 13 7 *1* 8 2 9 3 10 4 11

Quiahuitl (Rain)
10 4 11 5 12 6 13 7 *1* 8 2 9 3 10 4 11 5 12

Xochitl (Flower)
11 5 12 6 13 7 *1* 8 2 9 3 10 4 11 5 12 6 13

Five Remaining Days of Year 5 Acatl: Cipactli   (8)**1**

                                           Ehecatl   2

                                           Calli   3

                                           Cuetzpalin   4

                                           Coatl   5

Tonalpohuallis 7 and 8 (Days 1 Alligator) occur in Year 5 Reed. The *trecenas* are:

1. 1 Dog	8. 1 Alligator	15. 1 Grass	22. 1 House
2. 1 House	9. 1 Jaguar	16. 1 Snake	23. 1 Vulture
3. 1 Vulture	10. 1 Deer	17. 1 Flint	24. 1 Water
4. 1 Water	11. 1 Flower	18. 1 Monkey	25. 1 Wind
5. 1 Wind	12. 1 Reed	19. 1 Lizard	26. 1 Eagle
6. 1 Eagle	13. 1 Death	20. 1 Motion	27. 1 Rabbit
7. 1 Rabbit	14. 1 Rain	21. 1 Dog	28. 1 Alligator

The next year (6 Tecpatl) begins with Day 6 Miquiztli.

6. Year 6 Tecpatl

Days:

Miquiztli (Death)

6 13 7 *1* 8 2 9 3 10 4 11 5 12 6 13 7 *1* 8

Mazatl (Deer)

7 *1* 8 2 9 3 10 4 11 5 12 6 13 7 *1* 8 2 9

Tochtli (Rabbit)

8 2 9 3 10 4 11 5 12 6 13 7 *1* 8 2 9 3 10

Atl (Water)

9 3 10 4 11 5 12 6 13 7 *1* 8 2 9 3 10 4 11

Itzcuintli (Dog)

10 4 11 5 12 6 13 7 *1* 8 2 9 3 10 4 11 5 12

Ozomatli (Monkey)

11 5 12 6 13 7 *1* 8 2 9 3 10 4 11 5 12 6 13

Malinalli (Grass)

12 6 13 7 *1* 8 2 9 3 10 4 11 5 12 6 13 7 *1*

Acatl (Reed)

13 7 *1* 8 2 9 3 10 4 11 5 12 6 13 7 *1* 8 2

Ocelotl (Jaguar)

1 8 2 9 3 10 4 11 5 12 6 13 7 *1* 8 2 9 3

Quauhtli (Eagle)

2 9 3 10 4 11 5 12 6 13 7 *1* 8 2 9 3 10 4

Cozcaquauhtli (Vulture)

3 10 4 11 5 12 6 13 7 *1* 8 2 9 3 10 4 11 5

Ollin (Motion)

4 11 5 12 6 13 7 *1* 8 2 9 3 10 4 11 5 12 6

Tecpatl (Flint)
5   12   6   13   7   *1*   8   2   9   3   10   4   11   5   12   6   13   7
Quiahuitl (Rain)
6   13   7   *1*   8   2   9   3   10   4   11   5   12   6   13   7   *1*   8
Xochitl (Flower)
7   *1*   8   2   9   3   10   4   11   5   12   6   13   7   *1*   8   2   9
Cipactli (Alligator)
8   2   9   3   10   4   11   5   12   6   13   7   (9)1   8   2   9   3   10

Ehecatl (Wind)
9   3   10   4   11   5   12   6   13   7   1   8   2   9   3   10   4   11
Calli (House)
10   4   11   5   12   6   13   7   *1*   8   2   9   3   10   4   11   5   12
Cuetzpalin (Lizard)
11   5   12   6   13   7   *1*   8   2   9   3   10   4   11   5   12   6   13
Coatl (Snake)
12   6   13   7   *1*   8   2   9   3   10   4   11   5   12   6   13   7   *1*

Five Remaining Days of Year 6 Tecpatl:

Miquiztli	2
Mazatl	3
Tochtli	4
Atl	5
Itzcuintli	6

Tonalpohualli 9 (Day 1 Alligator) occurs in Year 6 Flint. The *trecenas* are:

1. 1 Jaguar	8. 1 Snake	15. 1 Vulture	22. 1 Deer
2. 1 Deer	9. 1 Flint	16. 1 Water	23. 1 Flower
3. 1 Flower	10. 1 Monkey	17. 1 Wind	24. 1 Reed
4. 1 Reed	11. 1 Lizard	18. 1 Eagle	25. 1 Death
5. 1 Death	12. 1 Motion	19. 1 Rabbit	26. 1 Rain
6. 1 Rain	13. 1 Dog	20. 1 Alligator	27. 1 Grass
7. 1 Grass	14. 1 House	21. 1 Jaguar	28. 1 Snake

The next year (7 Calli) begins with Day 7 Ozomatli.

7. Year 7 Calli

Days:
Ozomatli (Monkey)
7   *1*   8   2   9   3   10   4   11   5   12   6   13   7   *1*   8   2   9

Malinalli (Grass)
8   2   9   3   10   4   11   5   12   6   13   7   *1*   8   2   9   3   10
Acatl (Reed)
9   3   10   4   11   5   12   6   13   7   *1*   8   2   9   3   10   4   11
Ocelotl (Octlot)
10   4   11   5   12   6   13   7   *1*   8   2   9   3   10   4   11   5   12

Quauhtli (Eagle)
11 5 12 6 13 7 *1* 8 2 9 3 10 4 11 5 12 6 13
Cozcaquauhtli (Vulture)
12 6 13 7 *1* 8 2 9 3 10 4 11 5 12 6 13 7 *1*

Ollin (Motion)
13 7 *1* 8 2 9 3 10 4 11 5 12 6 13 7 *1* 8 2
Tecpatl (Flint)
1 8 2 9 3 10 4 11 5 12 6 13 7 *1* 8 2 9 3
Quiahuitl (Rain)
2 9 3 10 4 11 5 12 6 13 7 *1* 8 2 9 3 10 4
Xochitl (Flower)
3 10 4 11 5 12 6 13 7 *1* 8 2 9 3 10 4 11 5
Cipactli (Alligator)
4 11 5 12 6 13 7 (10)**1** 8 2 9 3 10 4 11 5 12 6

Ehecatl (Wind)
5 12 6 13 7 *1* 8 2 9 3 10 4 11 5 12 6 13 7
Calli (House)
6 13 7 *1* 8 2 9 3 10 4 11 5 12 6 13 7 *1* 8
Cuetzpalin (Lizard)
7 *1* 8 2 9 3 10 4 11 5 12 6 13 7 *1* 8 2 9
Coatl (Snake)
8 2 9 3 10 4 11 5 12 6 13 7 *1* 8 2 9 3 10
Miquiztli (Death)
9 3 10 4 11 5 12 6 13 7 *1* 8 2 9 3 10 4 11

Mazatl (Deer)
10 4 11 5 12 6 13 7 *1* 8 2 9 3 10 4 11 5 12
Tochtli (Rabbit)
11 5 12 6 13 7 *1* 8 2 9 3 10 4 11 5 12 6 13
Atl (Water)
12 6 13 7 *1* 8 2 9 3 10 4 11 5 12 6 13 7 *1*
Itzcuintli (Dog)
13 7 *1* 8 2 9 3 10 4 11 5 12 6 13 7 *1* 8 2

Five Remaining Days of Year 7 Calli: | Ozomatli | 3
| Malinalli | 4
| Acatl | 5
| Ocelotl | 6
| Quauhtli | 7

Tonalpohualli 10 occurs in Year 7 House (Day 1 Alligator). The *trecenas* are:

1. 1 Flint	8. 1 Water	15. 1 Flower	22. 1 Monkey
2. 1 Monkey	9. 1 Wind	16. 1 Reed	23. 1 Lizard
3. 1 Lizard	10. 1 Eagle	17. 1 Death	24. 1 Motion

4. 1 Motion	11. 1 Rabbit	18. 1 Rain	25. 1 Dog
5. 1 Dog	12. 1 Alligator	19. 1 Grass	26. 1 House
6. 1 House	13. 1 Jaguar	20. 1 Snake	27. 1 Vulture
7. 1 Vulture	14. 1 Deer	21. 1 Flint	28. 1 Water

The next year (8 Tochtli) begins with Day 8 Cozcaquauhtli.

8. Year 8 Tochtli.

Days:

Cozcaquauhtli (Vulture)

8 2 9 3 10 4 11 5 12 6 13 7 *1* 8 2 9 3 10

Ollin (Motion)

9 3 10 4 11 5 12 6 13 7 *1* 8 2 9 3 10 4 11

Tecpatl (Flint)

10 4 11 5 12 6 13 7 *1* 8 2 9 3 10 4 11 5 12

Quiahuitl (Rain)

11 5 12 6 13 7 *1* 8 2 9 3 10 4 11 5 12 6 13

Xochitl (Flower)

12 6 13 7 *1* 8 2 9 3 10 4 11 5 12 6 13 7 *1*

Cipactli (Alligator)

13 7 (11)**1** 8 2 9 3 10 4 11 5 12 6 13 7 (12)**1** 8 2

Ehecatl (Wind)

1 8 2 9 3 10 4 11 5 12 6 13 7 *1* 8 2 9 3

Calli (House)

2 9 3 10 4 11 5 12 6 13 7 *1* 8 2 9 3 10 4

Cuetzpalin (Lizard)

3 10 4 11 5 12 6 13 7 *1* 8 2 9 3 10 4 11 5

Coatl (Snake)

4 11 5 12 6 13 7 *1* 8 2 9 3 10 4 11 5 12 6

Miquiztli (Death)

5 12 6 13 7 *1* 8 2 9 3 10 4 11 5 12 6 13 7

Mazatl (Deer)

6 13 7 *1* 8 2 9 3 10 4 11 5 12 6 13 7 *1* 8

Tochtli (Rabbit)

7 *1* 8 2 9 3 10 4 11 5 12 6 13 7 *1* 8 2 9

Atl (Water)

8 2 9 3 10 4 11 5 12 6 13 7 *1* 8 2 9 3 10

Itzcuintli (Dog)

9 3 10 4 11 5 12 6 13 7 *1* 8 2 9 3 10 4 11

Ozomatli (Monkey)

10 4 11 5 12 6 13 7 *1* 8 2 9 3 10 4 11 5 12

Malinalli (Grass)

11 5 12 6 13 7 *1* 8 2 9 3 10 4 11 5 12 6 13

Acatl (Reed)

12 6 13 7 *1* 8 2 9 3 10 4 11 5 12 6 13 7 *1*

Ocelotl (Jaguar)

13 7 *1* 8 2 9 3 10 4 11 5 12 6 13 7 *1* 8 2

Quauhtli (Eagle)

1 8 2 9 3 10 4 11 5 12 6 13 7 *1* 8 2 9 3

Five Remaining Days of Year 8 Tochtli: Cozcaquauhtli   4
                                          Ollin   5
                                          Tecpatl   6
                                          Quiahuitl   7
                                          Xochitl   8

Tonalpohuallis 11 and 12 (Days 1 Alligator) occur in Year 8 Rabbit. The *trecenas* are:

1. 1 Wind	8. 1 Reed.	15. 1 Lizard	22. 1 Eagle
2. 1 Eagle	9. 1 Death	16. 1 Motion	23. 1 Rabbit
3. 1 Rabbit	10. 1 Rain	17. 1 Dog	24. 1 Alligator
4. 1 Alligator	11. 1 Grass	18. 1 House	25. 1 Jaguar
5. 1 Jaguar	12. 1 Snake	19. 1 Vulture	26. 1 Deer
6. 1 Deer	13. 1 Flint	20. 1 Water	27. 1 Flower
7. 1 Flower	14. 1 Monkey	21. 1 Wind	28. 1 Rain

The next year (9 Acatl) begins with Day 9 Cipactli.

9. Year 9 Acatl

Days:

Cipactli (Alligator)

9 3 10 4 11 5 12 6 13 7 (13)**1** 8 2 9 3 10 4 11

Ehecatl (Wind)

10 4 11 5 12 6 13 7 *1* 8 2 9 3 10 4 11 5 12

Calli (House)

11 5 12 6 13 7 *1* 8 2 9 3 10 4 11 5 12 6 13

Cuetzpalin (Lizard)

12 6 13 7 *1* 8 2 9 3 10 4 11 5 12 6 13 7 *1*

Coatl (Snake)

13 7 *1* 8 2 9 3 10 4 11 5 12 6 13 7 *1* 8 2

Miquiztli (Death)

1 8 2 9 3 10 4 11 5 12 6 13 7 *1* 8 2 9 3

Mazatl (Deer)

2 9 3 10 4 11 5 12 6 13 7 *1* 8 2 9 3 10 4

Tochtli (Rabbit)

3 10 4 11 5 12 6 13 7 *1* 8 2 9 3 10 4 11 5

Atl (Water)

4 11 5 12 6 13 7 *1* 8 2 9 3 10 4 11 5 12 6

Itzcuintli (Dog)

5 12 6 13 7 *1* 8 2 9 3 10 4 11 5 12 6 13 7

Ozomatli (Monkey)

6 13 7 *1* 8 2 9 3 10 4 11 5 12 6 13 7 *1* 8

Malinalli (Grass)

7 *1* 8 2 9 3 10 4 11 5 12 6 13 7 *1* 8 2 9

Acatl (Reed)

8 2 9 3 10 4 11 5 12 6 13 7 *1* 8 2 9 3 10

Ocelotl (Jaguar)

9 3 10 4 11 5 12 6 13 7 *1* 8 2 9 3 10 4 11

Quauhtli (Eagle)

10 4 11 5 12 6 13 7 *1* 8 2 9 3 10 4 11 5 12

Cozcaquauhtli (Vulture)

11 5 12 6 13 7 *1* 8 2 9 3 10 4 11 5 12 6 13

Ollin (Motion)

12 6 13 7 *1* 8 2 9 3 10 4 11 5 12 6 13 7 *1*

Tecpatl (Flint)

13 7 *1* 8 2 9 3 10 4 11 5 12 6 13 7 *1* 8 2

Quiahuitl (Rain)

1 8 2 9 3 10 4 11 5 12 6 13 7 *1* 8 2 9 3

Xochitl (Flower)

2 9 3 10 4 11 5 12 6 13 7 *1* 8 2 9 3 10 4

Five Remaining Days of Year 9 Acatl:
Cipactli	5
Ehecatl	6
Calli	7
Cuetzpalin	8
Coatl	9

Tonalpohualli 13 (Day 1 Alligator) occurs in Year 9 Reed. The *trecenas* are:

1. 1 Death	8. 1 Motion	15. 1 Rabbit	22. 1 Rain
2. 1 Rain	9. 1 Dog	16. 1 Alligator	23. 1 Grass
3. 1 Grass	10. 1 House	17. 1 Jaguar	24. 1 Snake
4. 1 Snake	11. 1 Vulture	18. 1 Deer	25. 1 Flint
5. 1 Flint	12. 1 Water	19. 1 Flower	26. 1 Monkey
6. 1 Monkey	13. 1 Wind	20. 1 Reed	27. 1 Lizard
7. 1 Lizard	14. 1 Eagle	21. 1 Death	28. 1 Motion

The next year (10 Tecpatl) begins with Day 10 Miquiztli.

Days:

Miquiztli (Death)

10 4 11 5 12 6 13 7 *1* 8 2 9 3 10 4 11 5 12

Mazatl (Deer)

11 5 12 6 13 7 *1* 8 2 9 3 10 4 11 5 12 6 13

Tochtli (Rabbit)

12 6 13 7 *1* 8 2 9 3 10 4 11 5 12 6 13 7 *1*

Atl (Water)

13 7 *1* 8 2 9 3 10 4 11 5 12 6 13 7 *1* 8 2

Itzcuintli (Dog)

1 8 2 9 3 10 4 11 5 12 6 13 7 *1* 8 2 9 3

Ozomatli (Monkey)

2 9 3 10 4 11 5 12 6 13 7 *1* 8 2 9 3 10 4

Malinalli (Grass)

3 10 4 11 5 12 6 13 7 *1* 8 2 9 3 10 4 11 5

Acatl (Reed)

4 11 5 12 6 13 7 *1* 8 2 9 3 10 4 11 5 12 6

Ocelotl (Jaguar)

5 12 6 13 7 *1* 8 2 9 3 10 4 11 5 12 6 13 7

Quauhtli (Eagle)

6 13 7 *1* 8 2 9 3 10 4 11 5 12 6 13 7 *1* 8

Cozcaquauhtli (Vulture)

7 *1* 8 2 9 3 10 4 11 5 12 6 13 7 *1* 8 2 9

Ollin (Motion)

8 2 9 3 10 4 11 5 12 6 13 7 *1* 8 2 9 3 10

Tecpatl (Flint)

9 3 10 4 11 5 12 6 13 7 *1* 8 2 9 3 10 4 11

Quiahuitl (Rain)

10 4 11 5 12 6 13 7 *1* 8 2 9 3 10 4 11 5 12

Xochitl (Flower)

11 5 12 6 13 7 *1* 8 2 9 3 10 4 11 5 12 6 13

Cipactli (Alligator)

12 6 13 7 (14)**1** 8 2 9 3 10 4 11 5 12 6 13 7 (15)**1**

Ehecatl (Wind)

13 7 *1* 8 2 9 3 10 4 11 5 12 6 13 7 *1* 8 2

Calli (House)

1 8 2 9 3 10 4 11 5 12 6 13 7 *1* 8 2 9 3

Cuetzpalin (Lizard)

2 9 3 10 4 11 5 12 6 13 7 *1* 8 2 9 3 10 4

Coatl (Snake)

3 10 4 11 5 12 6 13 7 *1* 8 2 9 3 10 4 11 5

Five Remaining Days of Year 10 Tecpatl: Miquiztli   6

Mazatl   7

Tochtli   8

Atl   9

Itzcuintli   10

Tonalpohuallis 14 and 15 (Days 1 Alligator) occur in Year 10 Flint. The *trecenas* are:

1. 1 Dog	8. 1 Alligator	15. 1 Grass	22. 1 House
2. 1 House	9. 1 Jaguar	16. 1 Snake	23. 1 Vulture
3. 1 Vulture	10. 1 Deer	17. 1 Flint	24. 1 Water
4. 1 Water	11. 1 Flower	18. 1 Monkey	25. 1 Wind
5. 1 Wind	12. 1 Reed	19. 1 Lizard	26. 1 Eagle
6. 1 Eagle	13. 1 Death	20. 1 Motion	27. 1 Rabbit
7. 1 Rabbit	14. 1 Rain	21. 1 Dog	28. 1 Alligator

The next year (11 Calli) begins with Day 11 Ozomatli.

11. Year 11 Calli

Days:

Ozomatli (Monkey)

11 5 12 6 13 7 *1* 8 2 9 3 10 4 11 5 12 6 13

Malinalli (Grass)

12 6 13 7 *1* 8 2 9 3 10 4 11 5 12 6 13 7 *1*

Acatl (Reed)

13 7 *1* 8 2 9 3 10 4 11 5 12 6 13 7 *1* 8 2

Ocelotl (Jaguar)

1 8 2 9 3 10 4 11 5 12 6 13 7 *1* 8 2 9 3

Quauhtli (Eagle)

2 9 3 10 4 11 5 12 6 13 7 *1* 8 2 9 3 10 4

Cozcaquauhtli (Vulture)

3 10 4 11 5 12 6 13 7 *1* 8 2 9 3 10 4 11 5

Ollin (Motion)

4 11 5 12 6 13 7 *1* 8 2 9 3 10 4 11 5 12 6

Tecpatl (Flint)

5 12 6 13 7 *1* 8 2 9 3 10 4 11 5 12 6 13 7

Quiahuitl (Rain)

6 13 7 *1* 8 2 9 3 10 4 11 5 12 6 13 7 *1* 8

Xochitl (Flower)

7 *1* 8 2 9 3 10 4 11 5 12 6 13 7 *1* 8 2 9

Cipactli (Alligator)

8 2 9 3 10 4 11 5 12 6 13 7 (16)**1** 8 2 9 3 10

Ehecatl (Wind)

9 3 10 4 11 5 12 6 13 7 *1* 8 2 9 3 10 4 11

Calli (House)

10 4 11 5 12 6 13 7 *1* 8 2 9 3 10 4 11 5 12

Cuetzpalin (Lizard)

11 5 12 6 13 7 *1* 8 2 9 3 10 4 11 5 12 6 13

Coatl (Snake)

12 6 13 7 *1* 8 2 9 3 10 4 11 5 12 6 13 7 *1*

Miquiztli (Death)

13 7 *1* 8 2 9 3 10 4 11 5 12 6 13 7 *1* 8 2

Mazatl (Deer)

1 8 2 9 3 10 4 11 5 12 6 13 7 *1* 8 2 9 3

Tochtli (Rabbit)

2 9 3 10 4 11 5 12 6 13 7 *1* 8 2 9 3 10 4

Atl (Water)

3 10 4 11 5 12 6 13 7 *1* 8 2 9 3 10 4 11 5

Itzcuintli (Dog)

4 11 5 12 6 13 7 *1* 8 2 9 3 10 4 11 5 12 6

Five Remaining Days of Year 11 Calli:

Ozomatli	7
Malinalli	8
Acatl	9
Ocelotl	10
Quauhtli	11

Tonalpohualli 16 (Day 1 Alligator) occurs in Year 11 House. The *trecenas* are:

1. 1 Jaguar	8. 1 Snake	15. 1 Vulture	22. 1 Deer
2. 1 Deer	9. 1 Flint	16. 1 Water	23. 1 Flower
3. 1 Flower	10. 1 Monkey	17. 1 Wind	24. 1 Reed
4. 1 Reed	11. 1 Lizard	18. 1 Eagle	25. 1 Death
5. 1 Death	12. 1 Motion	19. 1 Rabbit	26. 1 Rain
6. 1 Rain	13. 1 Dog	20. 1 Alligator	27. 1 Grass
7. 1 Grass	14. 1 House	21. 1 Jaguar	28. 1 Snake

The next year (12 Tochtli) begins with Day 12 Cozcaquauhtli.

12. Year 12 Tochtli

Days:

Cozcaquauhtli (Vulture)

12 6 13 7 *1* 8 2 9 3 10 4 11 5 12 6 13 7 *1*

Ollin (Motion)

13 7 *1* 8 2 9 3 10 4 11 5 12 6 13 7 *1* 8 2

Tecpatl (Flint)

1 8 2 9 3 10 4 11 5 12 6 13 7 *1* 8 2 9 3

Quiahuitl (Rain)

2 9 3 10 4 11 5 12 6 13 7 *1* 8 2 9 3 10 4

Xochitl (Flower)
3 10 4 11 5 12 6 13 7 *1* 8 2 9 3 10 4 11 5
Cipactli (Alligator)
4 11 5 12 6 13 7 (17)**1** 8 2 9 3 10 4 11 5 12 6

Ehecatl (Wind)
5 12 6 13 7 *1* 8 2 9 3 10 4 11 5 12 6 13 7
Calli (House)
6 13 7 *1* 8 2 9 3 10 4 11 5 12 6 13 7 *1* 8
Cuetzpalin (Lizard)
7 *1* 8 2 9 3 10 4 11 5 12 6 13 7 *1* 8 2 9
Coatl (Snake)
8 2 9 3 10 4 11 5 12 6 13 7 *1* 8 2 9 3 10
Miquiztli (Death)
9 3 10 4 11 5 12 6 13 7 *1* 8 2 9 3 10 4 11

Mazatl (Deer)
10 4 11 5 12 6 13 7 *1* 8 2 9 3 10 4 11 5 12
Tochtli (Rabbit)
11 5 12 6 13 7 *1* 8 2 9 3 10 4 11 5 12 6 13
Atl (Water)
12 6 13 7 *1* 8 2 9 3 10 4 11 5 12 6 13 7 *1*
Itzcuintli (Dog)
13 7 *1* 8 2 9 3 10 4 11 5 12 6 13 7 *1* 8 2
Ozomatli (Monkey)
1 8 2 9 3 10 4 11 5 12 6 13 7 *1* 8 2 9 3

Malinalli (Grass)
2 9 3 10 4 11 5 12 6 13 7 *1* 8 2 9 3 10 4
Acatl (Reed)
3 10 4 11 5 12 6 13 7 *1* 8 2 9 3 10 4 11 5
Ocelotl (Jaguar)
4 11 5 12 6 13 7 *1* 8 2 9 3 10 4 11 5 12 6
Quauhtli (Eagle)
5 12 6 13 7 *1* 8 2 9 3 10 4 11 5 12 6 13 7

Five Remaining Days of Year 12 Tochtli:	Cozcaquauhtli	8
	Ollin	9
	Tecpatl	10
	Quiahuitl	11
	Xochitl	12

Tonalpohualli 17 (Day 1 Alligator) occurs in Year 12 Rabbit. The *trecenas* are:

1. 1 Flint	8. 1 Water	15. 1 Flower	22. 1 Monkey
2. 1 Monkey	9. 1 Wind	16. 1 Reed	23. 1 Lizard
3. 1 Lizard	10. 1 Eagle	17. 1 Death	24. 1 Motion

4. 1 Motion	11. 1 Rabbit	18. 1 Rain	25. 1 Dog
5. 1 Dog	12. 1 Alligator	19. 1 Grass	26. 1 House
6. 1 House	13. 1 Jaguar	20. 1 Snake	27. 1 Vulture
7. 1 Vulture	14. 1 Deer	21. 1 Flint	28. 1 Water

The next year (13 Acatl) begins with Day 13 Cipactli.

13. Year 13 Acatl

Days:

Cipactli (Alligator)

13 7 (18)**1** 8 2 9 3 10 4 11 5 12 6 13 7 (19)**1** 8 2

Ehecatl (Wind)

1 8 2 9 3 10 4 11 5 12 6 13 7 *1* 8 2 9 3

Calli (House)

2 9 3 10 4 11 5 12 6 13 7 *1* 8 2 9 3 10 4

Cuetzpalin (Lizard)

3 10 4 11 5 12 6 13 7 *1* 8 2 9 3 10 4 11 5

Coatl (Snake)

4 11 5 12 6 13 7 *1* 8 2 9 3 10 4 11 5 12 6

Miquiztli (Death)

5 12 6 13 7 *1* 8 2 9 3 10 4 11 5 12 6 13 7

Mazatl (Deer)

6 13 7 *1* 8 2 9 3 10 4 11 5 12 6 13 7 *1* 8

Tochtli (Rabbit)

7 *1* 8 2 9 3 10 4 11 5 12 6 13 7 *1* 8 2 9

Atl (Water)

8 2 9 3 10 4 11 5 12 6 13 7 *1* 8 2 9 3 10

Itzcuintli (Dog)

9 3 10 4 11 5 12 6 13 7 *1* 8 2 9 3 10 4 11

Ozomatli (Monkey)

10 4 11 5 12 6 13 7 *1* 8 2 9 3 10 4 11 5 12

Malinalli (Grass)

11 5 12 6 13 7 *1* 8 2 9 3 10 4 11 5 12 6 13

Acatl (Reed)

12 6 13 7 *1* 8 2 9 3 10 4 11 5 12 6 13 7 *1*

Ocelotl (Jaguar)

13 7 *1* 8 2 9 3 10 4 11 5 12 6 13 7 *1* 8 2

Quauhtli (Eagle)

1 8 2 9 3 10 4 11 5 12 6 13 7 *1* 8 2 9 3

Cozcaquauhtli (Vulture)

2 9 3 10 4 11 5 12 6 13 7 *1* 8 2 9 3 10 4

Ollin (Motion)
3 10 4 11 5 12 6 13 7 *1* 8 2 9 3 10 4 11 5
Tecpatl (Flint)
4 11 5 12 6 13 7 *1* 8 2 9 3 10 4 11 5 12 6
Quiahuitl (Rain)
5 12 6 13 7 *1* 8 2 9 3 10 4 11 5 12 6 13 7
Xochitl (Flower)
6 13 7 *1* 8 2 9 3 10 4 11 5 12 6 13 7 *1* 8

Five Remaining Days of Year 13 Acatl:

Cipactli	9
Ehecatl	10
Calli	11
Cuetzpalin	12
Coatl	13

Tonalpohuallis 18 and 19 (Days 1 Alligator) occur in Year 13 Reed. The *trecenas* are:

1. 1 Wind	8. 1 Reed	15. 1 Lizard	22. 1 Eagle
2. 1 Eagle	9. 1 Death	16. 1 Motion	23. 1 Rabbit
3. 1 Rabbit	10. 1 Rain	17. 1 Dog	24. 1 Alligator
4. 1 Alligator	11. 1 Grass	18. 1 House	25. 1 Jaguar
5. 1 Jaguar	12. 1 Snake	19. 1 Vulture	26. 1 Deer
6. 1 Deer	13. 1 Flint	20. 1 Water	27. 1 Flower
7. 1 Flower	14. 1 Monkey	21. 1 Wind	28. 1 Reed

The next year (1 Tecpatl) begins with Day 1 Miquiztli.

14. Year 1 Tecpatl

Days:
Miquiztli (Death)
1 8 2 9 3 10 4 11 5 12 6 13 7 *1* 8 2 9 3

Mazatl (Deer)
2 9 3 10 4 11 5 12 6 13 7 *1* 8 2 9 3 10 4
Tochtli (Rabbit)
3 10 4 11 5 12 6 13 7 *1* 8 2 9 3 10 4 11 5
Atl (Water)
4 11 5 12 6 13 7 *1* 8 2 9 3 10 4 11 5 12 6
Itzcuintli (Dog)
5 12 6 13 7 *1* 8 2 9 3 10 4 11 5 12 6 13 7
Ozomatli (Monkey)
6 13 7 *1* 8 2 9 3 10 4 11 5 12 6 13 7 *1* 8

Malinalli (Grass)
7 *1* 8 2 9 3 10 4 11 5 12 6 13 7 *1* 8 2 9
Acatl (Reed)
8 2 9 3 10 4 11 5 12 6 13 7 *1* 8 2 9 3 10

Ocelotl (Jaguar)
9 3 10 4 11 5 12 6 13 7 *1* 8 2 9 3 10 4 11
Quauhtli (Eagle)
10 4 11 5 12 6 13 7 *1* 8 2 9 3 10 4 11 5 12
Cozcaquauhtli (Vulture)
11 5 12 6 13 7 *1* 8 2 9 3 10 4 11 5 12 6 13

Ollin (Motion)
12 6 13 7 *1* 8 2 9 3 10 4 11 5 12 6 13 7 *1*
Tecpatl (Flint)
13 7 *1* 8 2 9 3 10 4 11 5 12 6 13 7 *1* 8 2
Quiahuitl (Rain)
1 8 2 9 3 10 4 11 5 12 6 13 7 *1* 8 2 9 3
Xochitl (Flower)
2 9 3 10 4 11 5 12 6 13 7 *1* 8 2 9 3 10 4
Cipactli (Alligator)
3 10 4 11 5 12 6 13 7 (20)1 8 2 9 3 10 4 11 5

Ehecatl (Wind)
4 11 5 12 6 13 7 *1* 8 2 9 3 10 4 11 5 12 6
Calli (House)
5 12 6 13 7 *1* 8 2 9 3 10 4 11 5 12 6 13 7
Cuetzpalin (Lizard)
6 13 7 *1* 8 2 9 3 10 4 11 5 12 6 13 7 *1* 8
Coatl (Snake)
7 *1* 8 2 9 3 10 4 11 5 12 6 13 7 *1* 8 2 9

Five Remaining Days of Year 1 Tecpatl:

Miquiztli	10
Mazatl	11
Tochtli	12
Atl	13
Itzcuintli	*1*

Tonalpohualli 20 (Day 1 Alligator) occurs in Year 1 Flint. The *trecenas* are:

1. 1 Death	9. 1 Dog	17. 1 Jaguar	25. 1 Flint
2. 1 Rain	10. 1 House	18. 1 Deer	26. 1 Monkey
3. 1 Grass	11. 1 Vulture	19. 1 Flower	27. 1 Lizard
4. 1 Snake	12. 1 Water	20. 1 Reed	28. 1 Motion
5. 1 Flint	13. 1 Wind	21. 1 Death	29. 1 Dog
6. 1 Monkey	14. 1 Eagle	22. 1 Rain	
7. 1 Lizard	15. 1 Rabbit	23. 1 Grass	
8. 1 Motion	16. 1 Alligator	24. 1 Snake	

The next year (2 Calli) begins with Day 2 Ozomatli.

15. Year 2 Calli

Days:

Ozomatli (Monkey)
2 9 3 10 4 11 5 12 6 13 7 *1* 8 2 9 3 10 4

Malinalli (Grass)
3 10 4 11 5 12 6 13 7 *1* 8 2 9 3 10 4 11 5

Acatl (Reed)
4 11 5 12 6 13 7 *1* 8 2 9 3 10 4 11 5 12 6

Ocelotl (Jaguar)
5 12 6 13 7 *1* 8 2 9 3 10 4 11 5 12 6 13 7

Quauhtli (Eagle)
6 13 7 *1* 8 2 9 3 10 4 11 5 12 6 13 7 *1* 8

Cozcaquauhtli (Vulture)
7 *1* 8 2 9 3 10 4 11 5 12 6 13 7 *1* 8 2 9

Ollin (Motion)
8 2 9 3 10 4 11 5 12 6 13 7 *1* 8 2 9 3 10

Tecpatl (Flint)
9 3 10 4 11 5 12 6 13 7 *1* 8 2 9 3 10 4 11

Quiahuitl (Rain)
10 4 11 5 12 6 13 7 *1* 8 2 9 3 10 4 11 5 12

Xochitl (Flower)
11 5 12 6 13 7 *1* 8 2 9 3 10 4 11 5 12 6 13

Cipactli (Alligator)
12 6 13 7 (21)**1** 8 2 9 3 10 4 11 5 12 6 13 7 (22)**1**

Ehecatl (Wind)
13 7 *1* 8 2 9 3 10 4 11 5 12 6 13 7 *1* 8 2

Calli (House)
1 8 2 9 3 10 4 11 5 12 6 13 7 *1* 8 2 9 3

Cuetzpalin (Lizard)
2 9 3 10 4 11 5 12 6 13 7 *1* 8 2 9 3 10 4

Coatl (Snake)
3 10 4 11 5 12 6 13 7 *1* 8 2 9 3 10 4 11 5

Miquiztli (Death)
4 11 5 12 6 13 7 *1* 8 2 9 3 10 4 11 5 12 6

Mazatl (Deer)
5 12 6 13 7 *1* 8 2 9 3 10 4 11 5 12 6 13 7

Tochtli (Rabbit)
6 13 7 *1* 8 2 9 3 10 4 11 5 12 6 13 7 *1* 8

Atl (Water)
7 *1* 8 2 9 3 10 4 11 5 12 6 13 7 *1* 8 2 9

Itzcuintli (Dog)
8 2 9 3 10 4 11 5 12 6 13 7 *1* 8 2 9 3 10

Five Remaining Days of Year 2 Calli: Ozomatli   11
                                             Malinalli   12
                                             Acatl   13
                                             Ocelotl   *1*
                                             Quauhtli   2

Tonalpohuallis 21 and 22 (Days 1 Alligator) occur in Year 2 House. The *trecenas* are:

1. 1 House	8. 1 Jaguar	15. 1 Snake	22. 1 Vulture
2. 1 Vulture	9. 1 Deer	16. 1 Flint	23. 1 Water
3. 1 Water	10. 1 Flower	17. 1 Monkey	24. 1 Wind
4. 1 Wind	11. 1 Reed	18. 1 Lizard	25. 1 Eagle
5. 1 Eagle	12. 1 Death	19. 1 Motion	26. 1 Rabbit
6. 1 Rabbit	13. 1 Rain	20. 1 Dog	27. 1 Alligator
7. 1 Alligator	14. 1 Grass	21. 1 House	28. 1 Jaguar

The next year (3 Tochtli) begins with Day 3 Cozcaquauhtli.

16. Year 3 Tochtli

Days:

Cozcaquauhtli (Vulture)
3 10 4 11 5 12 6 13 7 *1* 8 2 9 3 10 4 11 5

Ollin (Motion)
4 11 5 12 6 13 7 *1* 8 2 9 3 10 4 11 5 12 6

Tecpatl (Flint)
5 12 6 13 7 *1* 8 2 9 3 10 4 11 5 12 6 13 7

Quiahuitl (Rain)
6 13 7 *1* 8 2 9 3 10 4 11 5 12 6 13 7 *1* 8

Xochitl (Flower)
7 *1* 8 2 9 3 10 4 11 5 12 6 13 7 *1* 8 2 9

Cipactli (Alligator)
8 2 9 3 10 4 11 5 12 6 13 7 (23)**1** 8 2 9 3 10

Ehecatl (Wind)
9 3 10 4 11 5 12 6 13 7 *1* 8 2 9 3 10 4 11

Calli (House)
10 4 11 5 12 6 13 7 *1* 8 2 9 3 10 4 11 5 12

Cuetzpalin (Lizard)
11 5 12 6 13 7 *1* 8 2 9 3 10 4 11 5 12 6 13

Coatl (Snake)
12 6 13 7 *1* 8 2 9 3 10 4 11 5 12 6 13 7 *1*

Miquiztli (Death)
13 7 *1* 8 2 9 3 10 4 11 5 12 6 13 7 *1* 8 2

Mazatl (Deer)
1 8 2 9 3 10 4 11 5 12 6 13 7 *1* 8 2 9 3

Tochtli (Rabbit)

2 9 3 10 4 11 5 12 6 13 7 *1* 8 2 9 3 10 4

Atl (Water)

3 10 4 11 5 12 6 13 7 *1* 8 2 9 3 10 4 11 5

Itzcuintli (Dog)

4 11 5 12 6 13 7 *1* 8 2 9 3 10 4 11 5 12 6

Ozomatli (Monkey)

5 12 6 13 7 *1* 8 2 9 3 10 4 11 5 12 6 13 7

Malinalli (Grass)

6 13 7 *1* 8 2 9 3 10 4 11 5 12 6 13 7 *1* 8

Acatl (Reed)

7 *1* 8 2 9 3 10 4 11 5 12 6 13 7 *1* 8 2 9

Ocelotl (Jaguar)

8 2 9 3 10 4 11 5 12 6 13 7 *1* 8 2 9 3 10

Quauhtli (Eagle)

9 3 10 4 11 5 12 6 13 7 *1* 8 2 9 3 10 4 11

Five Remaining Days of Year 3 Tochtli:

	Cozcaquauhtli	12
	Ollin	13
	Tecpatl	*1*
	Quiahuitl	2
	Xochitl	3

Tonalpohualli 23 (Day 1 Alligator) occurs in Year 3 Rabbit. The *trecenas* are:

1. 1 Deer	8. 1 Flint	15. 1 Water	22. 1 Flower
2. 1 Flower	9. 1 Monkey	16. 1 Wind	23. 1 Reed
3. 1 Reed	10. 1 Lizard	17. 1 Eagle	24. 1 Death
4. 1 Death	11. 1 Motion	18. 1 Rabbit	25. 1 Rain
5. 1 Rain	12. 1 Dog	19. 1 Alligator	26. 1 Grass
6. 1 Grass	13. 1 House	20. 1 Jaguar	27. 1 Snake
7. 1 Snake	14. 1 Vulture	21. 1 Deer	28. 1 Flint

The next year (4 Acatl) begins with day 4 Cipactli.

17. Year 4 Acatl

Days:

Cipactli (Alligator)

4 11 5 12 6 13 7 (24)**1** 8 2 9 3 10 4 11 5 12 6

Ehecatl (Wind)

5 12 6 13 7 *1* 8 2 9 3 10 4 11 5 12 6 13 7

Calli (House)

6 13 7 *1* 8 2 9 3 10 4 11 5 12 6 13 7 *1* 8

Cuetzpalin (Lizard)

7 *1* 8 2 9 3 10 4 11 5 12 6 13 7 *1* 8 2 9

Coatl (Snake)

8	2	9	3	10	4	11	5	12	6	13	7	*1*	8	2	9	3	10		

Miquiztli (Death)

9	3	10	4	11	5	12	6	13	7	*1*	8	2	9	3	10	4	11

Mazatl (Deer)

10	4	11	5	12	6	13	7	*1*	8	2	9	3	10	4	11	5	12

Tochtli (Rabbit)

11	5	12	6	13	7	*1*	8	2	9	3	10	4	11	5	12	6	13

Atl (Water)

12	6	13	7	*1*	8	2	9	3	10	4	11	5	12	6	13	7	*1*

Itzcuintli (Dog)

13	7	*1*	8	2	9	3	10	4	11	5	12	6	13	7	*1*	8	2

Ozomatli (Monkey)

1	8	2	9	3	10	4	11	5	12	6	13	7	*1*	8	2	9	3

Malinalli (Grass)

2	9	3	10	4	11	5	12	6	13	7	*1*	8	2	9	3	10	4

Acatl (Reed)

3	10	4	11	5	12	6	13	7	*1*	8	2	9	3	10	4	11	5

Ocelotl (Jaguar)

4	11	5	12	6	13	7	*1*	8	2	9	3	10	4	11	5	12	6

Quauhtli (Eagle)

5	12	6	13	7	*1*	8	2	9	3	10	4	11	5	12	6	13	7

Cozcaquauhtli (Vulture)

6	13	7	*1*	8	2	9	3	10	4	11	5	12	6	13	7	*1*	8

Ollin (Motion)

7	*1*	8	2	9	3	10	4	11	5	12	6	13	7	*1*	8	2	9

Tecpatl (Flint)

8	2	9	3	10	4	11	5	12	6	13	7	*1*	8	2	9	3	10

Quiahuitl (Rain)

9	3	10	4	11	5	12	6	13	7	*1*	8	2	9	3	10	4	11

Xochitl (Flower)

10	4	11	5	12	6	13	7	*1*	8	2	9	3	10	4	11	5	12

Five Remaining Days of Year 4 Acatl:

Cipactli	13
Ehecatl	*1*
Calli	2
Cuetzpalin	3
Coatl	4

Tonalpohualli 24 (Day 1 Alligator) occurs in Year 4 Reed. The *trecenas* are:

1. 1 Monkey	8. 1 Wind	15. 1 Death	22. 1 Motion
2. 1 Lizard	9. 1 Eagle	16. 1 Rain	23. 1 Dog
3. 1 Motion	10. 1 Alligator	17. 1 Grass	24. 1 House

4. 1 Dog	11. 1 Jaguar	18. 1 Snake	25. 1 Vulture
5. 1 House	12. 1 Deer	19. 1 Flint	26. 1 Rabbit
6. 1 Vulture	13. 1 Flower	20. 1 Monkey	27. 1 Water
7. 1 Water	14. 1 Reed	21. 1 Lizard	28. 1 Wind

The next year (5 Tecpatl) begins with Day 5 Miquiztli.

18. Year 5 Tecpatl

Days:

Miquiztli (Death)

5   12   6   13   7   *1*   8   2   9   3   10   4   11   5   12   6   13   7

Mazatl (Deer)

6   13   7   *1*   8   2   9   3   10   4   11   5   12   6   13   7   *1*   8

Tochtli (Rabbit)

7   *1*   8   2   9   3   10   4   11   5   12   6   13   7   *1*   8   2   9

Atl (Water)

8   2   9   3   10   4   11   5   12   6   13   7   *1*   8   2   9   3   10

Itzcuintli (Dog)

9   3   10   4   11   5   12   6   13   7   *1*   8   2   9   3   10   4   11

Ozomatli (Monkey)

10   4   11   5   12   6   13   7   *1*   8   2   9   3   10   4   11   5   12

Malinalli (Grass)

11   5   12   6   13   7   *1*   8   2   9   3   10   4   11   5   12   6   13

Acatl (Reed)

12   6   13   7   *1*   8   2   9   3   10   4   11   5   12   6   13   7   *1*

Ocelotl (Jaguar)

13   7   *1*   8   2   9   3   10   4   11   5   12   6   13   7   *1*   8   2

Quauhtli (Eagle)

1   8   2   9   3   10   4   11   5   12   6   13   7   *1*   8   2   9   3

Cozcaquauhtli (Vulture)

2   9   3   10   4   11   5   12   6   13   7   *1*   8   2   9   3   10   4

Ollin (Motion)

3   10   4   11   5   12   6   13   7   *1*   8   2   9   3   10   4   11   5

Tecpatl (Flint)

4   11   5   12   6   13   7   *1*   8   2   9   3   10   4   11   5   12   6

Quiahuitl (Rain)

5   12   6   13   7   *1*   8   2   9   3   10   4   11   5   12   6   13   7

Xochitl (Flower)

6   13   7   *1*   8   2   9   3   10   4   11   5   12   6   13   7   *1*   8

Cipactli (Alligator)

7   (25)**1**   8   2   9   3   10   4   11   5   12   6   13   7   (26)**1**   8   2   9

Ehecatl (Wind)

8 2 9 3 10 4 11 5 12 6 13 7 *1* 8 2 9 3 10

Calli (House)

9 3 10 4 11 5 12 6 13 7 *1* 8 2 9 3 10 4 11

Cuetzpalin (Lizard)

10 4 11 5 12 6 13 7 *1* 8 2 9 3 10 4 11 5 12

Coatl (Snake)

11 5 12 6 13 7 *1* 8 2 9 3 10 4 11 5 12 6 13

Five Remaining Days of Year 5 Tecpatl: Miquiztli   *1*
                                                      Mazatl   2
      Tochtli   3
      Atl   4
      Itzcuintli   5

Tonalpohuallis 25 and 26 (Days 1 Alligator) occur in Year 5 Flint. The *trecenas* are:

1. 1 Eagle	8. 1 Death	15. 1 Motion	22. 1 Rabbit
2. 1 Rabbit	9. 1 Rain	16. 1 Dog	23. 1 Alligator
3. 1 Alligator	10. 1 Grass	17. 1 House	24. 1 Jaguar
4. 1 Jaguar	11. 1 Snake	18. 1 Vulture	25. 1 Deer
5. 1 Deer	12. 1 Flint	19. 1 Water	26. 1 Flower
6. 1 Flower	13. 1 Monkey	20. 1 Wind	27. 1 Reed
7. 1 Reed	14. 1 Lizard	21. 1 Eagle	28. 1 Death

The next year (6 Calli) begins with Day 6 Ozomatli.

19. Year 6 Calli

Days:

Ozomatli (Monkey)

6 13 7 *1* 8 2 9 3 10 4 11 5 12 6 13 7 *1* 8

Malinalli (Grass)

7 *1* 8 2 9 3 10 4 11 5 12 6 13 7 *1* 8 2 9

Acatl (Reed)

8 2 9 3 10 4 11 5 12 6 13 7 *1* 8 2 9 3 10

Ocelotl (Jaguar)

9 3 10 4 11 5 12 6 13 7 *1* 8 2 9 3 10 4 11

Quauhtli (Eagle)

10 4 11 5 12 6 13 7 *1* 8 2 9 3 10 4 11 5 12

Cozcaquauhtli (Vulture)

11 5 12 6 13 7 *1* 8 2 9 3 10 4 11 5 12 6 13

Ollin (Motion)

12 6 13 7 *1* 8 2 9 3 10 4 11 5 12 6 13 7 *1*

Tecpatl (Flint)

13 7 *1* 8 2 9 3 10 4 11 5 12 6 13 7 *1* 8 2

Quiahuitl (Rain)
1 8 2 9 3 10 4 11 5 12 6 13 7 *1* 8 2 9 3
Xochitl (Flower)
2 9 3 10 4 11 5 12 6 13 7 *1* 8 2 9 3 10 4
Cipactli (Alligator)
3 10 4 11 5 12 6 13 7 (27)**1** 8 2 9 3 10 4 11 5

Ehecatl (Wind)
4 11 5 12 6 13 7 *1* 8 2 9 3 10 4 11 5 12 6
Calli (House)
5 12 6 13 7 *1* 8 2 9 3 10 4 11 5 12 6 13 7
Cuetzpalin (Lizard)
6 13 7 *1* 8 2 9 3 10 4 11 5 12 6 13 7 *1* 8
Coatl (Snake)
7 *1* 8 2 9 3 10 4 11 5 12 6 13 7 *1* 8 2 9
Miquiztli (Death)
8 2 9 3 10 4 11 5 12 6 13 7 *1* 8 2 9 3 10

Mazatl (Deer)
9 3 10 4 11 5 12 6 13 7 *1* 8 2 9 3 10 4 11
Tochtli (Rabbit)
10 4 11 5 12 6 13 7 *1* 8 2 9 3 10 4 11 5 12
Atl (Water)
11 5 12 6 13 7 *1* 8 2 9 3 10 4 11 5 12 6 13
Itzcuintli (Dog)
12 6 13 7 *1* 8 2 9 3 10 4 11 5 12 6 13 7 *1*

Five Remaining Days of Year 6 Calli:

Ozomatli	2
Malinalli	3
Acatl	4
Ocelotl	5
Quauhtli	6

Tonalpohualli 27 (Day 1 Alligator) occurs in Year 6 House. The *trecenas* are:

1. 1 Rain	8. 1 Dog	15. 1 Alligator	22. 1 Grass
2. 1 Gras	9. 1 House	16. 1 Jaguar	23. 1 Snake
3. 1 Snake	10. 1 Vulture	17. 1 Deer	24. 1 Flint
4. 1 Flint	11. 1 Water	18. 1 Flower	25. 1 Monkey
5. 1 Monkey	12. 1 Wind	19. 1 Reed	26. 1 Lizard
6. 1 Lizard	13. 1 Eagle	20. 1 Death	27. 1 Motion
7. 1 Motion	14. 1 Rabbit	21. 1 Rain	28. 1 Dog

The next year (7 Tochtli) begins with Day 7 Cozcaquauhtli.

Days:

Cozcaquauhtli (Vulture)

7 *1* 8 2 9 3 10 4 11 5 12 6 13 7 *1* 8 2 9

Ollin (Motion)

8 2 9 3 10 4 11 5 12 6 13 7 *1* 8 2 9 3 10

Tecpatl (Flint)

9 3 10 4 11 5 12 6 13 7 *1* 8 2 9 3 10 4 11

Quiahuitl (Rain)

10 4 11 5 12 6 13 7 *1* 8 2 9 3 10 4 11 5 12

Xochitl (Flower)

11 5 12 6 13 7 *1* 8 2 9 3 10 4 11 5 12 6 13

Cipactli (Alligator)

12 6 13 7 (28)**1** 8 2 9 3 10 4 11 5 12 6 13 7 (29)**1**

Ehecatl (Wind)

13 7 *1* 8 2 9 3 10 4 11 5 12 6 13 7 *1* 8 2

Calli (House)

1 8 2 9 3 10 4 11 5 12 6 13 7 *1* 8 2 9 3

Cuetzpalin (Lizard)

2 9 3 10 4 11 5 12 6 13 7 *1* 8 2 9 3 10 4

Coatl (Snake)

3 10 4 11 5 12 6 13 7 *1* 8 2 9 3 10 4 11 5

Miquiztli (Death)

4 11 5 12 6 13 7 *1* 8 2 9 3 10 4 11 5 12 6

Mazatl (Deer)

5 12 6 13 7 *1* 8 2 9 3 10 4 11 5 12 6 13 7

Tochtli (Rabbit)

6 13 7 *1* 8 2 9 3 10 4 11 5 12 6 13 7 *1* 8

Atl (Water)

7 *1* 8 2 9 3 10 4 11 5 12 6 13 7 *1* 8 2 9

Itzcuintli (Dog)

8 2 9 3 10 4 11 5 12 6 13 7 *1* 8 2 9 3 10

Ozomatli (Monkey)

9 3 10 4 11 5 12 6 13 7 *1* 8 2 9 3 10 4 11

Malinalli (Grass)

10 4 11 5 12 6 13 7 *1* 8 2 9 3 10 4 11 5 12

Acatl (Reed)

11 5 12 6 13 7 *1* 8 2 9 3 10 4 11 5 12 6 13

Ocelotl (Jaguar)

12 6 13 7 *1* 8 2 9 3 10 4 11 5 12 6 13 7 *1*

Quauhtli (Eagle)

13 7 *1* 8 2 9 3 10 4 11 5 12 6 13 7 *1* 8 2

Five Remaining Days of Year 7 Tochtli: Cozcaquauhtli   3
                                       Ollin   4
                                       Tecpatl   5
                                       Quiahuitl   6
                                       Xochitl   7

Tonalpohuallis 28 and 29 (Days 1 Alligator) occur in Year 7 Rabbit. The *trecenas* are:

1. 1 House	8. 1 Jaguar	15. 1 Snake	22. 1 Vulture
2. 1 Vulture	9. 1 Deer	16. 1 Flint	23. 1 Water
3. 1 Water	10. 1 Flower	17. 1 Monkey	24. 1 Wind
4. 1 Wind	11. 1 Reed	18. 1 Lizard	25. 1 Eagle
5. 1 Eagle	12. 1 Death	19. 1 Motion	26. 1 Rabbit
6. 1 Rabbit	13. 1 Rain	20. 1 Dog	27. 1 Alligator
7. 1 Alligator	14. 1 Grass	21. 1 House	28. 1 Jaguar

The next year (8 Acatl) begins with Day 8 Cipactli.

21. Year 8 Acatl

Days:

Cipactli (Alligator)
8   2   9   3   10   4   11   5   12   6   13   7   (30)1   8   2   9   3   10

Ehecatl (Wind)
9   3   10   4   11   5   12   6   13   7   *1*   8   2   9   3   10   4   11

Calli (House)
10   4   11   5   12   6   13   7   *1*   8   2   9   3   10   4   11   5   12

Cuetzpalin (Lizard)
11   5   12   6   13   7   *1*   8   2   9   3   10   4   11   5   12   6   13

Coatl (Snake)
12   6   13   7   *1*   8   2   9   3   10   4   11   5   12   6   13   7   *1*

Miquiztli (Death)
13   7   *1*   8   2   9   3   10   4   11   5   12   6   13   7   *1*   8   2

Mazatl (Deer)
1   8   2   9   3   10   4   11   5   12   6   13   7   *1*   8   2   9   3

Tochtli (Rabbit)
2   9   3   10   4   11   5   12   6   13   7   *1*   8   2   9   3   10   4

Atl (Water)
3   10   4   11   5   12   6   13   7   *1*   8   2   9   3   10   4   11   5

Itzcuintli (Dog)
4   11   5   12   6   13   7   *1*   8   2   9   3   10   4   11   5   12   6

Ozomatli (Monkey)
5   12   6   13   7   *1*   8   2   9   3   10   4   11   5   12   6   13   7

Malinalli (Grass)
6   13   7   *1*   8   2   9   3   10   4   11   5   12   6   13   7   *1*   8

Acatl (Reed)
7 *1* 8 2 9 3 10 4 11 5 12 6 13 7 *1* 8 2 9
Ocelotl (Jaguar)
8 2 9 3 10 4 11 5 12 6 13 7 *1* 8 2 9 3 10
Quauhtli (Eagle)
9 3 10 4 11 5 12 6 13 7 *1* 8 2 9 3 10 4 11
Cozcaquauhtli (Vulture)
10 4 11 5 12 6 13 7 *1* 8 2 9 3 10 4 11 5 12

Ollin (Motion)
11 5 12 6 13 7 *1* 8 2 9 3 10 4 11 5 12 6 13
Tecpatl (Flint)
12 6 13 7 *1* 8 2 9 3 10 4 11 5 12 6 13 7 *1*
Quiahuitl (Rain)
13 7 *1* 8 2 9 3 10 4 11 5 12 6 13 7 *1* 8 2
Xochitl (Flower)
1 8 2 9 3 10 4 11 5 12 6 13 7 *1* 8 2 9 3

Five Remaining Days of Year 8 Acatl: Cipactli   4
                                        Ehecatl   5
                                        Calli   6
                                        Cuetzpalin   7
                                        Coatl   8

Tonalpohualli 30 (Day 1 Alligator) occurs in Year 8 Reed. The *trecenas* are:

1. 1 Deer	8. Flint	15. 1 Water	22. 1 Flower
2. 1 Flower	9. 1 Monkey	16. 1 Wind	23. 1 Reed
3. 1 Reed	10. 1 Lizard	17. 1 Eagle	24. 1 Death
4. 1 Death	11. 1 Motion	18. 1 Rabbit	25. 1 Rain
5. 1 Rain	12. 1 Dog	19. 1 Alligator	26. 1 Grass
6. 1 Grass	13. 1 House	20. 1 Jaguar	27. 1 Snake
7. 1 Snake	14. 1 Vulture	21. 1 Deer	28. 1 Flint

The next year (9 Tecpatl) begins with Day 9 Miquiztli.

22. Year 9 Tecpatl

Days:
Miquiztli (Death)
9 3 10 4 11 5 12 6 13 7 *1* 8 2 9 3 10 4 11

Mazatl (Deer)
10 4 11 5 12 6 13 7 *1* 8 2 9 3 10 4 11 5 12
Tochtli (Rabbit)
11 5 12 6 13 7 *1* 8 2 9 3 10 4 11 5 12 6 13
Atl (Water)
12 6 13 7 *1* 8 2 9 3 10 4 11 5 12 6 13 7 *1*

Itzcuintli (Dog)
13 7 *1* 8 2 9 3 10 4 11 5 12 6 13 7 *1* 8 2
Ozomatli (Monkey)
1 8 2 9 3 10 4 11 5 12 6 13 7 *1* 8 2 9 3

Malinalli (Grass)
2 9 3 10 4 11 5 12 6 13 7 *1* 8 2 9 3 10 4
Acatl (Reed)
3 10 4 11 5 12 6 13 7 *1* 8 2 9 3 10 4 11 5
Ocelotl (Jaguar)
4 11 5 12 6 13 7 *1* 8 2 9 3 10 4 11 5 12 6
Quauhtli (Eagle)
5 12 6 13 7 *1* 8 2 9 3 10 4 11 5 12 6 13 7
Cozcaquauhtli (Vulture)
6 13 7 *1* 8 2 9 3 10 4 11 5 12 6 13 7 *1* 8

Ollin (Motion)
7 *1* 8 2 9 3 10 4 11 5 12 6 13 7 *1* 8 2 9
Tecpatl (Flint)
8 2 9 3 10 4 11 5 12 6 13 7 *1* 8 2 9 3 10
Quiahuitl (Rain)
9 3 10 4 11 5 12 6 13 7 *1* 8 2 9 3 10 4 11
Xochitl (Flower)
10 4 11 5 12 6 13 7 *1* 8 2 9 3 10 4 11 5 12
Cipactli (Alligator)
11 5 12 6 13 7 (31)**1** 8 2 9 3 10 4 11 5 12 6 13

Ehecatl (Wind)
12 6 13 7 *1* 8 2 9 3 10 4 11 5 12 6 13 7 *1*
Calli (House)
13 7 *1* 8 2 9 3 10 4 11 5 12 6 13 7 *1* 8 2
Cuetzpalin (Lizard)
1 8 2 9 3 10 4 11 5 12 6 13 7 *1* 8 2 9 3
Coatl (Snake)
2 9 3 10 4 11 5 12 6 13 7 *1* 8 2 9 3 10 4

Five Remaining Days of Year 9 Tecpatl:
Miquiztli	5
Mazatl	6
Tochtli	7
Atl	8
Itzcuintli	9

Tonalpohualli 31 (Day 1 Alligator) occurs in Year 9 Flint. The *trecenas* are:

1. 1 Monkey	8. 1 Wind	15. 1 Reed	22. 1 Lizard
2. 1 Lizard	9. 1 Eagle	16. 1 Death	23. 1 Motion
3. 1 Motion	10. 1 Rabbit	17. 1 Rain	24. 1 Dog

4. 1 Dog	11. 1 Alligator	18. 1 Grass	25. 1 House
5. 1 House	12. 1 Jaguar	19. 1 Snake	26. 1 Vulture
6. 1 Vulture	13. 1 Deer	20. 1 Flint	27. 1 Water
7. 1 Water	14. 1 Flower	21. 1 Monkey	28. 1 Wind

The next year (10 Calli) begins with Day 10 Ozomatli.

23. Year 10 Calli

Days:

Ozomatli (Monkey)
10 4 11 5 12 6 13 7 *1* 8 2 9 3 10 4 11 5 12

Malinalli (Grass)
11 5 12 6 13 7 *1* 8 2 9 3 10 4 11 5 12 6 13

Acatl (Reed)
12 6 13 7 *1* 8 2 9 3 10 4 11 5 12 6 13 7 *1*

Ocelotl (Jaguar)
13 7 *1* 8 2 9 3 10 4 11 5 12 6 13 7 *1* 8 2

Quauhtli (Eagle)
1 8 2 9 3 10 4 11 5 12 6 13 7 *1* 8 2 9 3

Cozcaquauhtli (Vulture)
2 9 3 10 4 11 5 12 6 13 7 *1* 8 2 9 3 10 4

Ollin (Motion)
3 10 4 11 5 12 6 13 7 *1* 8 2 9 3 10 4 11 5

Tecpatl (Flint)
4 11 5 12 6 13 7 *1* 8 2 9 3 10 4 11 5 12 6

Quiahuitl (Rain)
5 12 6 13 7 *1* 8 2 9 3 10 4 11 5 12 6 13 7

Xochitl (Flower)
6 13 7 *1* 8 2 9 3 10 4 11 5 12 6 13 7 *1* 8

Cipactli (Alligator)
7 (32)**1** 8 2 9 3 10 4 11 5 12 6 13 7 (33)**1** 8 2 9

Ehecatl (Wind)
8 2 9 3 10 4 11 5 12 6 13 7 *1* 8 2 9 3 10

Calli (House)
9 3 10 4 11 5 12 6 13 7 *1* 8 2 9 3 10 4 11

Cuetzpalin (Lizard)
10 4 11 5 12 6 13 7 *1* 8 2 9 3 10 4 11 5 12

Coatl (Snake)
11 5 12 6 13 7 *1* 8 2 9 3 10 4 11 5 12 6 13

Miquiztli (Death)
12 6 13 7 *1* 8 2 9 3 10 4 11 5 12 6 13 7 *1*

Mazatl (Deer)
13 7 *1* 8 2 9 3 10 4 11 5 12 6 13 7 *1* 8 2
Tochtli (Rabbit)
1 8 2 9 3 10 4 11 5 12 6 13 7 *1* 8 2 9 3
Atl (Water)
2 9 3 10 4 11 5 12 6 13 7 *1* 8 2 9 3 10 4
Itzcuintli (Dog)
3 10 4 11 5 12 6 13 7 *1* 8 2 9 3 10 4 11 5

Five Remaining Days of Year 10 Calli: Ozomatli 6
    Malinalli 7
    Acatl 8
    Ocelotl 9
    Quauhtli 10

Tonalpohuallis 32 and 33 (Days 1 Alligator) occur in Year 10 House. The *trecenas* are:

1. 1 Eagle	8. 1 Death	15. 1 Motion	22. 1 Rabbit
2. 1 Rabbit	9. 1 Rain	16. 1 Dog	23. 1 Alligator
3. 1 Alligator	10. 1 Grass	17. 1 House	24. 1 Jaguar
4. 1 Jaguar	11. 1 Snake	18. 1 Vulture	25. 1 Deer
5. 1 Deer	12. 1 Flint	19. 1 Water	26. 1 Flower
6. 1 Flower	13. 1 Monkey	20. 1 Wind	27. 1 Reed
7. 1 Reed	14. 1 Lizard	21. 1 Eagle	28. 1 Death

The next year (11 Tochtli) begins with Day 11 Cozcaquauhtli.

24. Year 11 Tochtli

Days:
Cozcaquauhtli (Vulture)
11 5 12 6 13 7 *1* 8 2 9 3 10 4 11 5 12 6 13

Ollin (Motion)
12 6 13 7 *1* 8 2 9 3 10 4 11 5 12 6 13 7 *1*
Tecpatl (Flint)
13 7 *1* 8 2 9 3 10 4 11 5 12 6 13 7 *1* 8 2
Quiahuitl (Rain)
1 8 2 9 3 10 4 11 5 12 6 13 7 *1* 8 2 9 3
Xochitl (Flower)
2 9 3 10 4 11 5 12 6 13 7 *1* 8 2 9 3 10 4
Cipactli (Alligator)
3 10 4 11 5 12 6 13 7 (34)**1** 8 2 9 3 10 4 11 5

Ehecatl (Wind)
4 11 5 12 6 13 7 *1* 8 2 9 3 10 4 11 5 12 6
Calli (House)
5 12 6 13 7 *1* 8 2 9 3 10 4 11 5 12 6 13 7

Cuetzpalin (Lizard)

6   13   7   *1*   8   2   9   3   10   4   11   5   12   6   13   7   *1*   8

Coatl (Snake)

7   *1*   8   2   9   3   10   4   11   5   12   6   13   7   *1*   8   2   9

Miquiztli (Death)

8   2   9   3   10   4   11   5   12   6   13   7   *1*   8   2   9   3   10

Mazatl (Deer)

9   3   10   4   11   5   12   6   13   7   *1*   8   2   9   3   10   4   11

Tochtli (Rabbit)

10   4   11   5   12   6   13   7   *1*   8   2   9   3   10   4   11   5   12

Atl (Water)

11   5   12   6   13   7   *1*   8   2   9   3   10   4   11   5   12   6   13

Itzcuintli (Dog)

12   6   13   7   *1*   8   2   9   3   10   4   11   5   12   6   13   7   *1*

Ozomatli (Monkey)

13   7   *1*   8   2   9   3   10   4   11   5   12   6   13   7   *1*   8   2

Malinalli (Grass)

1   8   2   9   3   10   4   11   5   12   6   13   7   *1*   8   2   9   3

Acatl (Reed)

2   9   3   10   4   11   5   12   6   13   7   *1*   8   2   9   3   10   4

Ocelotl (Jaguar)

3   10   4   11   5   12   6   13   7   *1*   8   2   9   3   10   4   11   5

Quauhtli (Eagle)

4   11   5   12   6   13   7   *1*   8   2   9   3   10   4   11   5   12   6

Five Remaining Days of Year 11 Tochtli:

Cozcaquauhtli	7
Ollin	8
Tecpatl	9
Quiahuitl	10
Xochitl	11

Tonalpohualli 34 (Day 1 Alligator) occurs in Year 11 Rabbit. The *trecenas* are:

1. 1 Rain	8. 1 Dog	15. 1 Alligator	22. 1 Grass
2. 1 Grass	9. 1 House	16. 1 Jaguar	23. 1 Snake
3. 1 Snake	10. 1 Vulture	17. 1 Deer	24. 1 Flint
4. 1 Flint	11. 1 Water	18. 1 Flower	25. 1 Monkey
5. 1 Monkey	12. 1 Wind	19. 1 Reed	26. 1 Lizard
6. 1 Lizard	13. 1 Eagle	20. 1 Death	27. 1 Motion
7. 1 Motion	14. 1 Rabbit	21. 1 Rain	28. 1 Dog

The next year (12 Acatl) begins with Day 12 Cipactli.

25. Year 12 Acatl

Days:
Cipactli (Alligator)
12 6 13 7 (35)**1** 8 2 9 3 10 4 11 5 12 6 13 7 (36)**1**

Ehecatl (Wind)
13 7 *1* 8 2 9 3 10 4 11 5 12 6 13 7 *1* 8 2

Calli (House)
1 8 2 9 3 10 4 11 5 12 6 13 7 *1* 8 2 9 3

Cuetzpalin (Lizard)
2 9 3 10 4 11 5 12 6 13 7 *1* 8 2 9 3 10 4

Coatl (Snake)
3 10 4 11 5 12 6 13 7 *1* 8 2 9 3 10 4 11 5

Miquiztli (Death)
4 11 5 12 6 13 7 *1* 8 2 9 3 10 4 11 5 12 6

Mazatl (Deer)
5 12 6 13 7 *1* 8 2 9 3 10 4 11 5 12 6 13 7

Tochtli (Rabbit)
6 13 7 *1* 8 2 9 3 10 4 11 5 12 6 13 7 *1* 8

Atl (Water)
7 *1* 8 2 9 3 10 4 11 5 12 6 13 7 *1* 8 2 9

Itzcuintli (Dog)
8 2 9 3 10 4 11 5 12 6 13 7 *1* 8 2 9 3 10

Ozomatli (Monkey)
9 3 10 4 11 5 12 6 13 7 *1* 8 2 9 3 10 4 11

Malinalli (Grass)
10 4 11 5 12 6 13 7 *1* 8 2 9 3 10 4 11 5 12

Acatl (Reed)
11 5 12 6 13 7 *1* 8 2 9 3 10 4 11 5 12 6 13

Ocelotl (Jaguar)
12 6 13 7 *1* 8 2 9 3 10 4 11 5 12 6 13 7 *1*

Quauhtli (Eagle)
13 7 *1* 8 2 9 3 10 4 11 5 12 6 13 7 *1* 8 2

Cozcaquauhtli (Vulture)
1 8 2 9 3 10 4 11 5 12 6 13 7 *1* 8 2 9 3

Ollin (Motion)
2 9 3 10 4 11 5 12 6 13 7 *1* 8 2 9 3 10 4

Tecpatl (Flint)
3 10 4 11 5 12 6 13 7 *1* 8 2 9 3 10 4 11 5

Quiahuitl (Rain)
4 11 5 12 6 13 7 *1* 8 2 9 3 10 4 11 5 12 6

Xochitl (Flower)
5 12 6 13 7 *1* 8 2 9 3 10 4 11 5 12 6 13 7

Five Remaining Days of Year 12 Acatl: Cipactli   8
 Ehecatl   9
 Calli   10
 Cuetzpalin   11
 Coatl   12

Tonalpohuallis 35 and 36 (Days 1 Alligator) occur in Year 12 Reed. The *trecenas* are:

1. 1 House	8. 1 Jaguar	15. 1 Snake	22. 1 Vulture
2. 1 Vulture	9. 1 Deer	16. 1 Flint	23. 1 Water
3. 1 Water	10. 1 Flower	17. 1 Monkey	24. 1 Wind
4. 1 Wind	11. 1 Reed	18. 1 Lizard	25. 1 Eagle
5. 1 Eagle	12. 1 Death	19. 1 Motion	26. 1 Rabbit
6. 1 Rabbit	13. 1 Rain	20. 1 Dog	27. 1 Alligator
7. 1 Alligator	14. 1 Grass	21. 1 House	28. 1 Jaguar

The next year (13 Tecpatl) begins with Day 13 Miquiztli.

26. Year 13 Tecpatl

Days:

Miquiztli (Death)
13 7 *1* 8 2 9 3 10 4 11 5 12 6 13 7 *1* 8 2

Mazatl (Deer)
1 8 2 9 3 10 4 11 5 12 6 13 7 *1* 8 2 9 3

Tochtli (Rabbit)
2 9 3 10 4 11 5 12 6 13 7 *1* 8 2 9 3 10 4

Atl (Water)
3 10 4 11 5 12 6 13 7 *1* 8 2 9 3 10 4 11 5

Itzcuintli (Dog)
4 11 5 12 6 13 7 *1* 8 2 9 3 10 4 11 5 12 6

Ozomatli (Monkey)
5 12 6 13 7 *1* 8 2 9 3 10 4 11 5 12 6 13 7

Malinalli (Grass)
6 13 7 *1* 8 2 9 3 10 4 11 5 12 6 13 7 *1* 8

Acatl (Reed)
7 *1* 8 2 9 3 10 4 11 5 12 6 13 7 *1* 8 2 9

Ocelotl (Jaguar)
8 2 9 3 10 4 11 5 12 6 13 7 *1* 8 2 9 3 10

Quauhtli (Eagle)
9 3 10 4 11 5 12 6 13 7 *1* 8 2 9 3 10 4 11

Cozcaquauhtli (Vulture)
10 4 11 5 12 6 13 7 *1* 8 2 9 3 10 4 11 5 12

Ollin (Motion)
11 5 12 6 13 7 *1* 8 2 9 3 10 4 11 5 12 6 13

Tecpatl (Flint)

12 6 13 7 *1* 8 2 9 3 10 4 11 5 12 6 13 7 *1*

Quiahuitl (Rain)

13 7 *1* 8 2 9 3 10 4 11 5 12 6 13 7 *1* 8 2

Xochitl (Flower)

1 8 2 9 3 10 4 11 5 12 6 13 7 *1* 8 2 9 3

Cipactli (Alligator)

2 9 3 10 4 11 5 12 6 13 7 (37)**1** 8 2 9 3 10 4

Ehecatl (Wind)

3 10 4 11 5 12 6 13 7 *1* 8 2 9 3 10 4 11 5

Calli (House)

4 11 5 12 6 13 7 *1* 8 2 9 3 10 4 11 5 12 6

Cuetzpalin (Lizard)

5 12 6 13 7 *1* 8 2 9 3 10 4 11 5 12 6 13 7

Coatl (Snake)

6 13 7 *1* 8 2 9 3 10 4 11 5 12 6 13 7 *1* 8

Five Remaining Days in Year 13 Tecpatl: Miquiztli   9
                                           Mazatl   10
                                           Tochtli   11
                                           Atl   12
                                           Itzcuintli 13

Tonalpohualli 37 (Day 1 Alligator) occurs in Year 13 Flint. The *trecenas* are:

1. 1 Deer	8. 1 Flint	15. 1 Water	22. 1 Flower
2. 1 Flower	9. 1 Monkey	16. 1 Wind	23. 1 Reed
3. 1 Reed	10. 1 Lizard	17. 1 Eagle	24. 1 Death
4. 1 Death	11. 1 Motion	18. 1 Rabbit	25. 1 Rain
5. 1 Rain	12. 1 Dog	19. 1 Alligator	26. 1 Grass
6. 1 Grass	13. 1 House	20. 1 Jaguar	27. 1 Snake
7. 1 Snake	14. 1 Vulture	21. 1 Deer	28. 1 Flint

The next year (1 Calli) begins with day 1 Ozomatli.

27. Year 1 Calli

Days:

Ozomatli (Monkey)

1 8 2 9 3 10 4 11 5 12 6 13 7 *1* 8 2 9 3

Malinalli (Grass)

2 9 3 10 4 11 5 12 6 13 7 *1* 8 2 9 3 10 4

Acatl (Reed)

3 10 4 11 5 12 6 13 7 *1* 8 2 9 3 10 4 11 5

Ocelotl (Jaguar)

4 11 5 12 6 13 7 *1* 8 2 9 3 10 4 11 5 12 6

Quauhtli (Eagle)

5 12 6 13 7 *1* 8 2 9 3 10 4 11 5 12 6 13 7

Cozcaquauhtli (Vulture)

6 13 7 *1* 8 2 9 3 10 4 11 5 12 6 13 7 *1* 8

Ollin (Motion)

7 *1* 8 2 9 3 10 4 11 5 12 6 13 7 *1* 8 2 9

Tecpatl (Flint)

8 2 9 3 10 4 11 5 12 6 13 7 *1* 8 2 9 3 10

Quiahuitl (Rain)

9 3 10 4 11 5 12 6 13 7 *1* 8 2 9 3 10 4 11

Xochitl (Flower)

10 4 11 5 12 6 13 7 *1* 8 2 9 3 10 4 11 5 12

Cipactli (Alligator)

11 5 12 6 13 7 (38)**1** 8 2 9 3 10 4 11 5 12 6 13

Ehecatl (Wind)

12 6 13 7 *1* 8 2 9 3 10 4 11 5 12 6 13 7 *1*

Calli (House)

13 7 *1* 8 2 9 3 10 4 11 5 12 6 13 7 *1* 8 2

Cuetzpalin (Lizard)

1 8 2 9 3 10 4 11 5 12 6 13 7 *1* 8 2 9 3

Coatl (Snake)

2 9 3 10 4 11 5 12 6 13 7 *1* 8 2 9 3 10 4

Miquiztli (Death)

3 10 4 11 5 12 6 13 7 *1* 8 2 9 3 10 4 11 5

Mazatl (Deer)

4 11 5 12 6 13 7 *1* 8 2 9 3 10 4 11 5 12 6

Tochtli (Rabbit)

5 12 6 13 7 *1* 8 2 9 3 10 4 11 5 12 6 13 7

Atl (Water)

6 13 7 *1* 8 2 9 3 10 4 11 5 12 6 13 7 *1* 8

Itzcuintli (Dog)

7 *1* 8 2 9 3 10 4 11 5 12 6 13 7 *1* 8 2 9

Five Remaining Days of Year 1 Calli:

Ozomatli	10
Malinalli	11
Acatl	12
Ocelotl	13
Quauhtli	*1*

Tonalpohualli 38 (Day 1 Alligator) occurs in Year 1 House. The *trecenas* are:

1. 1 Monkey	8. 1 Wind	15. 1 Reed	22. 1 Lizard
2. 1 Lizard	9. 1 Eagle	16. 1 Death	23. 1 Motion
3. 1 Motion	10. 1 Rabbit	17. 1 Rain	24. 1 Dog

4. 1 Dog	11. 1 Alligator	18. 1 Grass	25. 1 5. House
5. 1 House	12. 1 Jaguar	19. 1 Snake	26. 1 Vulture
6. 1 Vulture	13. 1 Deer	20. 1 Flint	27. 1 Water
7. 1 Water	14. 1 Flower	21. 1 Monkey	28. 1 Wind
			29. 1 Eagle

The next year (2 Tochtli) begins with Day 2 Cozcaquauhtli.

28. Year 2 Tochtli

Days:

Cozcaquauhtli (Vulture)

2 9 3 10 4 11 5 12 6 13 7 *1* 8 2 9 3 10 4

Ollin (Motion)

3 10 4 11 5 12 6 13 7 *1* 8 2 9 3 10 4 11 5

Tecpatl (Flint)

4 11 5 12 6 13 7 *1* 8 2 9 3 10 4 11 5 12 6

Quiahuitl (Rain)

5 12 6 13 7 *1* 8 2 9 3 10 4 11 5 12 6 13 7

Xochitl (Flower)

6 13 7 *1* 8 2 9 3 10 4 11 5 12 6 13 7 *1* 8

Cipactli (Alligator)

7 (39)**1** 8 2 9 3 10 4 11 5 12 6 13 7 (40)**1** 8 2 9

Ehecatl (Wind)

8 2 9 3 10 4 11 5 12 6 13 7 *1* 8 2 9 3 10

Calli (House)

9 3 10 4 11 5 12 6 13 7 *1* 8 2 9 3 10 4 11

Cuetzpalin (Lizard)

10 4 11 5 12 6 13 7 *1* 8 2 9 3 10 4 11 5 12

Coatl (Snake)

11 5 12 6 13 7 *1* 8 2 9 3 10 4 11 5 12 6 13

Miquiztli (Death)

12 6 13 7 *1* 8 2 9 3 10 4 11 5 12 6 13 7 *1*

Mazatl (Deer)

13 7 *1* 8 2 9 3 10 4 11 5 12 6 13 7 *1* 8 2

Tochtli (Rabbit)

1 8 2 9 3 10 4 11 5 12 6 13 7 *1* 8 2 9 3

Atl (Water)

2 9 3 10 4 11 5 12 6 13 7 *1* 8 2 9 3 10 4

Itzcuintli (Dog)

3 10 4 11 5 12 6 13 7 *1* 8 2 9 3 10 4 11 5

Ozomatli (Monkey)

4 11 5 12 6 13 7 *1* 8 2 9 3 10 4 11 5 12 6

Malinalli (Grass)

5 12 6 13 7 *1* 8 2 9 3 10 4 11 5 12 6 13 7

Acatl (Reed)

6 13 7 *1* 8 2 9 3 10 4 11 5 12 6 13 7 *1* 8

Ocelotl (Jaguar)

7 *1* 8 2 9 3 10 4 11 5 12 6 13 7 *1* 8 2 9

Quauhtli (Eagle)

8 2 9 3 10 4 11 5 12 6 13 7 *1* 8 2 9 3 10

Five Remaining Days of Year 2 Tochtli: Cozcaquauhtli   11
                                   Ollin   12
                                   Tecpatl   13
                                   Quiahuitl   *1*
                                   Xochitl   2

Tonalpohuallis 39 and 40 (Days 1 Alligator) occur in Year 2 Rabbit. The *trecenas* are:

1. 1 Rabbit	8. 1 Rain	15. 1 Dog	22. 1 Alligator
2. 1 Alligator	9. 1 Grass	16. 1 House	23. 1 Jaguar
3. 1 Jaguar	10. 1 Snake	17. 1 Vulture	24. 1 Deer
4. 1 Deer	11. 1 Flint	18. 1 Water	25. 1 Flower
5. 1 Flower	12. 1 Monkey	19. 1 Wind	26. 1 Reed
6. 1 Reed	13. 1 Lizard	20. 1 Eagle	27. 1 Death
7. 1 Death	14. 1 Motion	21. 1 Rabbit	28. 1 Eagle

The next year (3 Acatl) begins with Day 3 Cipactli.

29. Year 3 Acatl

Days:

Cipactli (Alligator)

3 10 4 11 5 12 6 13 7 (41)**1** 8 2 9 3 10 4 11 5

Ehecatl (Wind)

4 11 5 12 6 13 7 *1* 8 2 9 3 10 4 11 5 12 6

Calli (House)

5 12 6 13 7 *1* 8 2 9 3 10 4 11 5 12 6 13 7

Cuetzpalin (Lizard)

6 13 7 *1* 8 2 9 3 10 4 11 5 12 6 13 7 *1* 8

Coatl (Snake)

7 *1* 8 2 9 3 10 4 11 5 12 6 13 7 *1* 8 2 9

Miquiztli (Death)

8 2 9 3 10 4 11 5 12 6 13 7 *1* 8 2 9 3 10

Mazatl (Deer)

9 3 10 4 11 5 12 6 13 7 *1* 8 2 9 3 10 4 11

Tochtli (Rabbit)

10 4 11 5 12 6 13 7 *1* 8 2 9 3 10 4 11 5 12

Atl (Water)
11 5 12 6 13 7 *1* 8 2 9 3 10 4 11 5 12 6 13
Itzcuintli (Dog)
12 6 13 7 *1* 8 2 9 3 10 4 11 5 12 6 13 7 *1*
Ozomatli (Monkey)
13 7 *1* 8 2 9 3 10 4 11 5 12 6 13 7 *1* 8 2

Malinalli (Grass)
1 8 2 9 3 10 4 11 5 12 6 13 7 *1* 8 2 9 3
Acatl (Reed)
2 9 3 10 4 11 5 12 6 13 7 *1* 8 2 9 3 10 4
Ocelotl (Jaguar)
3 10 4 11 5 12 6 13 7 *1* 8 2 9 3 10 4 11 5
Quauhtli (Eagle)
4 11 5 12 6 13 7 *1* 8 2 9 3 10 4 11 5 12 6
Cozcaquauhtli (Vulture)
5 12 6 13 7 *1* 8 2 9 3 10 4 11 5 12 6 13 7

Ollin (Motion)
6 13 7 *1* 8 2 9 3 10 4 11 5 12 6 13 7 *1* 8
Tecpatl (Flint)
7 *1* 8 2 9 3 10 4 11 5 12 6 13 7 *1* 8 2 9
Quiahuitl (Rain)
8 2 9 3 10 4 11 5 12 6 13 7 *1* 8 2 9 3 10
Xochitl (Flower)
9 3 10 4 11 5 12 6 13 7 *1* 8 2 9 3 10 4 11

Five Remaining Days of Year 3 Reed:

Cipactli	12
Ehecatl	13
Calli	*1*
Cuetzpalin	2
Coatl	3

Tonalpohualli 41 (Day 1 Alligator) occurs in Year 3 Reed. The *trecenas* are:

1. 1 Grass	8. 1 House	15. 1 Jaguar	22. 1 Snake
2. 1 Snake	9. 1 Vulture	16. 1 Deer	23. 1 Flint
3. 1 Flint	10. 1 Water	17. 1 Flower	24. 1 Monkey
4. 1 Monkey	11. 1 Wind	18. 1 Reed	25. 1 Lizard
5. 1 Lizard	12. 1 Eagle	19. 1 Death	26. 1 Motion
6. 1 Motion	13. 1 Rabbit	20. 1 Rain	27. 1 Dog
7. 1 Dog	14. 1 Alligator	21. 1 Grass	28. 1 House

The next year (4 Tecpatl) begins with Day 4 Miquiztli.

Days:

Miquiztli (Death)

4 11 5 12 6 13 7 *1* 8 2 9 3 10 4 11 5 12 6

Mazatl (Deer)

5 12 6 13 7 *1* 8 2 9 3 10 4 11 5 12 6 13 7

Tochtli (Rabbit)

6 13 7 *1* 8 2 9 3 10 4 11 5 12 6 13 7 *1* 8

Atl (Water)

7 *1* 8 2 9 3 10 4 11 5 12 6 13 7 *1* 8 2 9

Itzcuintli (Dog)

8 2 9 3 10 4 11 5 12 6 13 7 *1* 8 2 9 3 10

Ozomatli (Monkey)

9 3 10 4 11 5 12 6 13 7 *1* 8 2 9 3 10 4 11

Malinalli (Grass)

10 4 11 5 12 6 13 7 *1* 8 2 9 3 10 4 11 5 12

Acatl (Reed)

11 5 12 6 13 7 *1* 8 2 9 3 10 4 11 5 12 6 13

Ocelotl (Jaguar)

12 6 13 7 *1* 8 2 9 3 10 4 11 5 12 6 13 7 *1*

Quauhtli (Eagle)

13 7 *1* 8 2 9 3 10 4 11 5 12 6 13 7 *1* 8 2

Cozcaquauhtli (Vulture)

1 8 2 9 3 10 4 11 5 12 6 13 7 *1* 8 2 9 3

Ollin (Motion)

2 9 3 10 4 11 5 12 6 13 7 *1* 8 2 9 3 10 4

Tecpatl (Flint)

3 10 4 11 5 12 6 13 7 *1* 8 2 9 3 10 4 11 5

Quiahuitl (Rain)

4 11 5 12 6 13 7 *1* 8 2 9 3 10 4 11 5 12 6

Xochitl (Flower)

5 12 6 13 7 *1* 8 2 9 3 10 4 11 5 12 6 13 7

Cipactli (Alligator)

6 13 7 (42)**1** 8 2 9 3 10 4 11 5 12 6 13 7 (43)**1** 8

Ehecatl (Wind)

7 *1* 8 2 9 3 10 4 11 5 12 6 13 7 *1* 8 2 9

Calli (House)

8 2 9 3 10 4 11 5 12 6 13 7 *1* 8 2 9 3 10

Cuetzpalin (Lizard)

9 3 10 4 11 5 12 6 13 7 *1* 8 2 9 3 10 4 11

Coatl (Snake)

10 4 11 5 12 6 13 7 *1* 8 2 9 3 10 4 11 5 12

Five Remaining Days of Year 4 Tecpatl: Miquiztli 13
                                                           Mazatl *1*
                                                             Tochtli 2
                                                             Atl 3
                                                          Itzcuintli 4

Tonalpohuallis 42 and 43 (Days 1 Alligator) occur in Year 4 Flint. The *trecenas* are:

1. 1 Vulture	8. 1 Deer	15. 1 Flint	22. 1 Water
2. 1 Water	9. 1 Flower	16. 1 Monkey	23. 1 Wind
3. 1 Wind	10. 1 Reed	17. 1 Lizard	24. 1 Eagle
4. 1 Eagle	11. 1 Death	18. 1 Motion	25. 1 Rabbit
5. 1 Rabbit	12. 1 Rain	19. 1 Dog	26. 1 Alligator
6. 1 Alligator	13. 1 Grass	20. 1 House	27. 1 Jaguar
7. 1 Jaguar	14. 1 Snake	21. 1 Vulture	28. 1 Deer

The next year (5 Calli) begins with Day 5 Ozomatli.

31. Year 5 Calli

Days:

Ozomatli (Monkey)

5 12 6 13 7 *1* 8 2 9 3 10 4 11 5 12 6 13 7

Malinalli (Grass)

6 13 7 *1* 8 2 9 3 10 4 11 5 12 6 13 7 *1* 8

Acatl (Reed)

7 *1* 8 2 9 3 10 4 11 5 12 6 13 7 *1* 8 2 9

Ocelotl (Jaguar)

8 2 9 3 10 4 11 5 12 6 13 7 *1* 8 2 9 3 10

Quauhtli (Eagle)

9 3 10 4 11 5 12 6 13 7 *1* 8 2 9 3 10 4 11

Cozcaquauhtli (Vulture)

10 4 11 5 12 6 13 7 *1* 8 2 9 3 10 4 11 5 12

Ollin (Motion)

11 5 12 6 13 7 *1* 8 2 9 3 10 4 11 5 12 6 13

Tecpatl (Flint)

12 6 13 7 *1* 8 2 9 3 10 4 11 5 12 6 13 7 *1*

Quiahuitl (Rain)

13 7 *1* 8 2 9 3 10 4 11 5 12 6 13 7 *1* 8 2

Xochitl (Flower)

1 8 2 9 3 10 4 11 5 12 6 13 7 *1* 8 2 9 3

Cipactli (Alligator)

2 9 3 10 4 11 5 12 6 13 7 (44)**1** 8 2 9 3 10 4

Ehecatl (Wind)

3 10 4 11 5 12 6 13 7 *1* 8 2 9 3 10 4 11 5

Calli (House)
4 11 5 12 6 13 7 *1* 8 2 9 3 10 4 11 5 12 6
Cuetzpalin (Lizard)
5 12 6 13 7 *1* 8 2 9 3 10 4 11 5 12 6 13 7
Coatl (Snake)
6 13 7 *1* 8 2 9 3 10 4 11 5 12 6 13 7 *1* 8
Miquiztli (Death)
7 *1* 8 2 9 3 10 4 11 5 12 6 13 7 *1* 8 2 9

Mazatl (Deer)
8 2 9 3 10 4 11 5 12 6 13 7 *1* 8 2 9 3 10
Tochtli (Rabbit)
9 3 10 4 11 5 12 6 13 7 *1* 8 2 9 3 10 4 11
Atl (Water)
10 4 11 5 12 6 13 7 *1* 8 2 9 3 10 4 11 5 12
Itzcuintli (Dog)
11 5 12 6 13 7 *1* 8 2 9 3 10 4 11 5 12 6 13

Five Remaining Days of Year 5 Calli:	Ozomatli	*1*
	Malinalli	2
	Acatl	3
	Ocelotl	4
	Quauhtli	5

Tonalpohualli 44 (Day 1 Alligator) occurs in Year 5 House. The *trecenas* are:

1. 1 Flower	8. 1 Monkey	15. 1 Wind	22. 1 Reed
2. 1 Reed	9. 1 Lizard	16. 1 Eagle	23. 1 Death
3. 1 Death	10. 1 Motion	17. 1 Rabbit	24. 1 Rain
4. 1 Rain	11. 1 Dog	18. 1 Alligator	25. 1 Grass
5. 1 Grass	12. 1 House	19. 1 Jaguar	26. 1 Snake
6. 1 Snake	13. 1 Vulture	20. 1 Deer	27. 1 Flint
7. 1 Flint	14. 1 Water	21. 1 Flower	28. 1 Monkey

The next year (6 Tochtli) begins with Day 6 Cozcaquauhtli.

32. Year 6 Tochtli

Days:
Cozcaquauhtli (Vulture)
6 13 7 *1* 8 2 9 3 10 4 11 5 12 6 13 7 *1* 8

Ollin (Motion)
7 *1* 8 2 9 3 10 4 11 5 12 6 13 7 *1* 8 2 9
Tecpatl (Flint)
8 2 9 3 10 4 11 5 12 6 13 7 *1* 8 2 9 3 10
Quiahuitl (Rain)
9 3 10 4 11 5 12 6 13 7 *1* 8 2 9 3 10 4 11

Xochitl (Flower)
10 4 11 5 12 6 13 7 *1* 8 2 9 3 10 4 11 5 12
Cipactli (Alligator)
11 5 12 6 13 7 (45)1 8 2 9 3 10 4 11 5 12 6 13
Ehecatl (Wind)
12 6 13 7 *1* 8 2 9 3 10 4 11 5 12 6 13 7 *1*
Calli (House)
13 7 *1* 8 2 9 3 10 4 11 5 12 6 13 7 *1* 8 2
Cuetzpalin (Lizard)
1 8 2 9 3 10 4 11 5 12 6 13 7 *1* 8 2 9 3
Coatl (Snake)
2 9 3 10 4 11 5 12 6 13 7 *1* 8 2 9 3 10 4
Miquiztli (Death)
3 10 4 11 5 12 6 13 7 1 8 2 9 3 10 4 11 5

Mazatl (Deer)
4 11 5 12 6 13 7 *1* 8 2 9 3 10 4 11 5 12 6
Tochtli (Rabbit)
5 12 6 13 7 *1* 8 2 9 3 10 4 11 5 12 6 13 7
Atl (Water)
6 13 7 *1* 8 2 9 3 10 4 11 5 12 6 13 7 *1* 8
Itzcuintli (Dog)
7 *1* 8 2 9 3 10 4 11 5 12 6 13 7 *1* 8 2 9
Ozomatli (Monkey)
8 2 9 3 10 4 11 5 12 6 13 7 *1* 8 2 9 3 10

Malinalli (Grass)
9 3 10 4 11 5 12 6 13 7 *1* 8 2 9 3 10 4 11
Acatl (Reed)
10 4 11 5 12 6 13 7 *1* 8 2 9 3 10 4 11 5 12
Ocelotl (Jaguar)
11 5 12 6 13 7 *1* 8 2 9 3 10 4 11 5 12 6 13
Quauhtli (Eagle)
12 6 13 7 *1* 8 2 9 3 10 4 11 5 12 6 13 7 *1*

Five Remaining Days of Year 6 Tochtli: Cozcaquauhtli   2
                                          Ollin   3
                                          Tecpatl   4
                                          Quiahuitl   5
                                          Xochitl   6

Tonalpohualli 45 (Day 1 Alligator) occurs in Year 6 Rabbit. The *trecenas* are:

1. 1 Lizard	8. 1 Eagle	15. 1 Death	22. 1 Motion
2. 1 Motion	9. 1 Rabbit	16. 1 Rain	23. 1 Dog
3. 12 Dog	10. 1 Alligator	17. 1 Grass	24. 1 House

4. 1 House	11. 1 Jaguar	18. 1 Snake	25. 1 Vulture
5. 1 Vulture	12. 1 Deer	19. 1 Flint	26. 1 Water
6. 1 Water	13. 1 Flower	20. 1 Monkey	27. 1 Wind
7. 1 Wind	14. 1 Reed	21. 1 Lizard	28. 1 Eagle

The next year (7 Acatl) begins with Day 7 Cipactli.

33. Year 7 Acatl

Days:

Cipactli (Alligator)
7 (46)**1** 8 2 9 3 10 4 11 5 12 6 13 7 (47)**1** 8 2 9

Ehecatl (Wind)
8 2 9 3 10 4 11 5 12 6 13 7 *1* 8 2 9 3 10

Calli (House)
9 3 10 4 11 5 12 6 13 7 *1* 8 2 9 3 10 4 11

Cuetzpalin (Lizard)
10 4 11 5 12 6 13 7 *1* 8 2 9 3 10 4 11 5 12

Coatl (Snake)
11 5 12 6 13 7 *1* 8 2 9 3 10 4 11 5 12 6 13

Miquiztli (Death)
12 6 13 7 *1* 8 2 9 3 10 4 11 5 12 6 13 7 *1*

Mazatl (Deer)
13 7 *1* 8 2 9 3 10 4 11 5 12 6 13 7 *1* 8 2

Tochtli (Rabbit)
1 8 2 9 3 10 4 11 5 12 6 13 7 *1* 8 2 9 3

Atl (Water)
2 9 3 10 4 11 5 12 6 13 7 *1* 8 2 9 3 10 4

Itzcuintli (Dog)
3 10 4 11 5 12 6 13 7 *1* 8 2 9 3 10 4 11 5

Ozomatli (Monkey)
4 11 5 12 6 13 7 *1* 8 2 9 3 10 4 11 5 12 6

Malinalli (Grass)
5 12 6 13 7 *1* 8 2 9 3 10 4 11 5 12 6 13 7

Acatl (Reed)
6 13 7 *1* 8 2 9 3 10 4 11 5 12 6 13 7 *1* 8

Ocelotl (Jaguar)
7 *1* 8 2 9 3 10 4 11 5 12 6 13 7 *1* 8 2 9

Quauhtli (Eagle)
8 2 9 3 10 4 11 5 12 6 13 7 *1* 8 2 9 3 10

Cozcaquauhtli (Vulture)
9 3 10 4 11 5 12 6 13 7 *1* 8 2 9 3 10 4 11

Ollin (Motion)

10 4 11 5 12 6 13 7 *1* 8 2 9 3 10 4 11 5 12

Tecpatl (Flint)

11 5 12 6 13 7 *1* 8 2 9 3 10 4 11 5 12 6 13

Quiahuitl (Rain)

12 6 13 7 *1* 8 2 9 3 10 4 11 5 12 6 13 7 *1*

Xochitl (Flower)

13 7 *1* 8 2 9 3 10 4 11 5 12 6 13 7 *1* 8 2

Five Remaining Days of Year 7 Acatl: Cipactli   3
                                        Ehecatl   4
                                        Calli   5
                                        Cuetzpalin   6
                                        Coat   7

Tonalpohuallis 46 and 47 (Days 1 Alligator) occur in Year 7 Reed. The *trecenas* are:

1. 1 Rabbit	8. 1 Rain	15. 1 Dog	22. 1 Alligator
2. 1 Alligator	9. 1 Grass	16. 1 House	23. 1 Jaguar
3. 1 Jaguar	10. 1 Snake	17. 1 Vulture	24. 1 Deer
4. 1 Deer	11. 1 Flint	18. 1 Water	25. 1 Flower
5. 1 Flower	12. 1 Monkey	19. 1 Wind	26. 1 Reed
6. 1 Reed	13. 1 Lizard	20. 1 Eagle	27. 1 Death
7. 1 Death	14. 1 Motion	21. 1 Rabbit	28. 1 Rain

The next year (8 Tecpatl) begins with Day 8 Miquiztli.

34. Year 8 Tecpatl

Days:

Miquiztli (Death)

8 2 9 3 10 4 11 5 12 6 13 7 *1* 8 2 9 3 10

Mazatl (Deer)

9 3 10 4 11 5 12 6 13 7 *1* 8 2 9 3 10 4 11

Tochtli (Rabbit)

10 4 11 5 12 6 13 7 1 8 2 9 3 10 4 11 5 12

Atl (Water)

11 5 12 6 13 7 *1* 8 2 9 3 10 4 11 5 12 6 13

Itzcuintli (Dog)

12 6 13 7 *1* 8 2 9 3 10 4 11 5 12 6 13 7 *1*

Ozomatli (Monkey)

13 7 *1* 8 2 9 3 10 4 11 5 12 6 13 7 *1* 8 2

Malinalli (Grass)

1 8 2 9 3 10 4 11 5 12 6 13 7 *1* 8 2 9 3

Acatl (Reed)

2 9 3 10 4 11 5 12 6 13 7 *1* 8 2 9 3 10 4

Ocelotl (Jaguar)

3 10 4 11 5 12 6 13 7 *1* 8 2 9 3 10 4 11 5

Quauhtli (Eagle)

4 11 5 12 6 13 7 *1* 8 2 9 3 10 4 11 5 12 6

Cozcaquauhtli (Vulture)

5 12 6 13 7 *1* 8 2 9 3 10 4 11 5 12 6 13 7

Ollin (Motion)

6 13 7 *1* 8 2 9 3 10 4 11 5 12 6 13 7 *1* 8

Tecpatl (Flint)

7 *1* 8 2 9 3 10 4 11 5 12 6 13 7 *1* 8 2 9

Quiahuitl (Rain)

8 2 9 3 10 4 11 5 12 6 13 7 *1* 8 2 9 3 10

Xochitl (Flower)

9 3 10 4 11 5 12 6 13 7 *1* 8 2 9 3 10 4 11

Cipactli (Alligator)

10 4 11 5 12 6 13 7 (48)**1** 8 2 9 3 10 4 11 5 12

Ehecatl (Wind)

11 5 12 6 13 7 *1* 8 2 9 3 10 4 11 5 12 6 13

Calli (House)

12 6 13 7 *1* 8 2 9 3 10 4 11 5 12 6 13 7 *1*

Cuetzpalin (Lizard)

13 7 *1* 8 2 9 3 10 4 11 5 12 6 13 7 *1* 8 2

Coatl (Snake)

1 8 2 9 3 10 4 11 5 12 6 13 7 *1* 8 2 9 3

Five Remaining Days of Year 8 Tecpatl: Miquiztli 4
                                                      Mazatl 5
                                                      Tochtli 6
                                                      Atl 7
                                                      Itzcuintli 8

Tonalpohualli 48 (Day 1 Alligator) occurs in Year 8 Flint. The *trecenas* are:

1. 1 Grass	8. 1 House	15. 1 Jaguar	22. 1 Snake
2. 1 Snake	9. 1 Vulture	16. 1 Deer	23. 1 Flint
3. 1 Flint	10. 1 Water	17. 1 Flower	24. 1 Monkey
4. 1 Monkey	11. 1 Wind	18. 1 Reed	25. 1 Lizard
5. 1 Lizard	12. 1 Eagle	19. 1 Death	26. 1 Motion
6. 1 Motion	13. 1 Rabbit	20. 1 Rain	27. 1 Dog
7. 1 Dog	14. 1 Alligator	21. 1 Grass	28. 1 House

The next year (9 Calli) begins with Day 9 Ozomatli.

35. Year 9 Calli

Days:

Ozomatli (Monkey)

9 3 10 4 11 5 12 6 13 7 *1* 8 2 9 3 10 4 11

Malinalli (Grass)

10 4 11 5 12 6 13 7 *1* 8 2 9 3 10 4 11 5 12

Acatl (Reed)

11 5 12 6 13 7 *1* 8 2 9 3 10 4 11 5 12 6 13

Ocelotl (Jaguar)

12 6 13 7 *1* 8 2 9 3 10 4 11 5 12 6 13 7 *1*

Quauhtli (Eagle)

13 7 *1* 8 2 9 3 10 4 11 5 12 6 13 7 *1* 8 2

Cozcaquauhtli (Vulture)

1 8 2 9 3 10 4 11 5 12 6 13 7 *1* 8 2 9 3

Ollin (Motion)

2 9 3 10 4 11 5 12 6 13 7 *1* 8 2 9 3 10 4

Tecpatl (Flint)

3 10 4 11 5 12 6 13 7 *1* 8 2 9 3 10 4 11 5

Quiahuitl (Rain)

4 11 5 12 6 13 7 *1* 8 2 9 3 10 4 11 5 12 6

Xochitl (Flower)

5 12 6 13 7 *1* 8 2 9 3 10 4 11 5 12 6 13 7

Cipactli (Alligator)

6 13 7 (49)**1** 8 2 9 3 10 4 11 5 12 6 13 7 (50)**1** 8

Ehecatl (Wind)

7 *1* 8 2 9 3 10 4 11 5 12 6 13 7 *1* 8 2 9

Calli (House)

8 2 9 3 10 4 11 5 12 6 13 7 *1* 8 2 9 3 10

Cuetzpalin (Lizard)

9 3 10 4 11 5 12 6 13 7 *1* 8 2 9 3 10 4 11

Coatl (Snake)

10 4 11 5 12 6 13 7 *1* 8 2 9 3 10 4 11 5 12

Miquiztli (Death)

11 5 12 6 13 7 *1* 8 2 9 3 10 4 11 5 12 6 13

Mazatl (Deer)

12 6 13 7 *1* 8 2 9 3 10 4 11 5 12 6 13 7 *1*

Tochtli (Rabbit)

13 7 *1* 8 2 9 3 10 4 11 5 12 6 13 7 *1* 8 2

Atl (Water)

1 8 2 9 3 10 4 11 5 12 6 13 7 *1* 8 2 9 3

Itzcuintli (Dog)

2 9 3 10 4 11 5 12 6 13 7 *1* 8 2 9 3 10 4

Five Remaining Days in Year 9 Calli: Ozomatli   5
                                         Malinalli   6
                                         Acatl   7
                                         Ocelotl   8
                                         Quauhtli   9

Tonalpohuallis 49 and 50 (Days 1 Alligator) occur in Year 9 House. The *trecenas* are:

1. 1 Vulture	8. 1 Deer	15. 1 Flint	22. 1 Water
2. 1 Water	9. 1 Flower	16. 1 Monkey	23. 1 Wind
3. 1 Wind	10. 1 Reed	17. 1 Lizard	24. 1 Eagle
4. 1 Eagle	11. 1 Death	18. 1 Motion	25. 1 Rabbit
5. 1 Rabbit	12. 1 Rain	19. 1 Dog	26. 1 Alligator
6. 1 Alligator	13. 1 Grass	20. 1 House	27. 1 Jaguar
7. 1 Jaguar	14. 1 Snake	21. 1 Vulture	28. 1 Deer

The next year (10 Tochtli) begins with Day 10 Cozcaquauhtli.

36. Year 10 Tochtli

Days:

Cozcaquauhtli (Vulture)
10 4 11 5 12 6 13 7 *1* 8 2 9 3 10 4 11 5 12

Ollin (Motion)
11 5 12 6 13 7 *1* 8 2 9 3 10 4 11 5 12 6 13

Tecpatl (Flint)
12 6 13 7 *1* 8 2 9 3 10 4 11 5 12 6 13 7 *1*

Quiahuitl (Rain)
13 7 *1* 8 2 9 3 10 4 11 5 12 6 13 7 *1* 8 2

Xochitl (Flower)
1 8 2 9 3 10 4 11 5 12 6 13 7 *1* 8 2 9 3

Cipactli (Alligator)
2 9 3 10 4 11 5 12 6 13 7 (51)1 8 2 9 3 10 4

Ehecatl (Wind)
3 10 4 11 5 12 6 13 7 *1* 8 2 9 3 10 4 11 5

Calli (House)
4 11 5 12 6 13 7 *1* 8 2 9 3 10 4 11 5 12 6

Cuetzpalin (Lizard)
5 12 6 13 7 *1* 8 2 9 3 10 4 11 5 12 6 13 7

Coatl (Snake)
6 13 7 *1* 8 2 9 3 10 4 11 5 12 6 13 7 *1* 8

Miquiztli (Death)
7 *1* 8 2 9 3 10 4 11 5 12 6 13 7 *1* 8 2 9

Mazatl (Deer)
8 2 9 3 10 4 11 5 12 6 13 7 *1* 8 2 9 3 10

Tochtli (Rabbit)
9   3   10   4   11   5   12   6   13   7   *1*   8   2   9   3   10   4   11
Atl (Water)
10   4   11   5   12   6   13   7   *1*   8   2   9   3   10   4   11   5   12
Itzcuintli (Dog)
11   5   12   6   13   7   *1*   8   2   9   3   10   4   11   5   12   6   13
Ozomatli (Monkey)
12   6   13   7   *1*   8   2   9   3   10   4   11   5   12   6   13   7   *1*

Malinalli (Grass)
13   7   *1*   8   2   9   3   10   4   11   5   12   6   13   7   *1*   8   2
Acatl (Reed)
1   8   2   9   3   10   4   11   5   12   6   13   7   *1*   8   2   9   3
Ocelotl (Jaguar)
2   9   3   10   4   11   5   12   6   13   7   *1*   8   2   9   3   10   4
Quauhtli (Eagle)
3   10   4   11   5   12   6   13   7   *1*   8   2   9   3   10   4   11   5

Five Remaining Days in Year 10 Tochtli: Cozcaquauhtli   6
                                           Ollin   7
                                           Tecpatl   8
                                           Quiahuitl   9
                                           Xochitl   10

Tonalpohualli 51 (Day 1 Alligator) occurs in Year 10 Rabbit. The *trecenas* are:

1. 1 Flower	8. 1 Monkey	15. 1 Wind	22. 1 Reed
2. 1 Reed	9. 1 Lizard	16. 1 Eagle	23. 1 Death
3. 1 Death	10. 1 Motion	17. 1 Rabbit	24. 1 Rain
4. 1 Rain	11. 1 Dog	18. 1 Alligator	25. 1 Grass
5. 1 Grass	12. 1 House	19. 1 Jaguar	26. 1 Snake
6. 1 Snake	13. 1 Vulture	20. 1 Deer	27. 1 Flint
7. 1 Flint	14. 1 Water	21. 1 Flower	28. 1 Monkey

The next year (11 Acatl) begins with Day 11 Cipactli.

37. Year 11 Acatl

Days:
Cipactli (Alligator)
11   5   12   6   13   7   (52)**1**   8   2   9   3   10   4   11   5   12   6   13

Ehecatl (Wind)
12   6   13   7   *1*   8   2   9   3   10   4   11   5   12   6   13   7   *1*
Calli (House)
13   7   *1*   8   2   9   3   10   4   11   5   12   6   13   7   *1*   8   2
Cuetzpalin (Lizard)
1   8   2   9   3   10   4   11   5   12   6   13   7   *1*   8   2   9   3

Coatl (Snake)
2 9 3 10 4 11 5 12 6 13 7 *1* 8 2 9 3 10 4
Miquiztli (Death)
3 10 4 11 5 12 6 13 7 *1* 8 2 9 3 10 4 11 5

Mazatl (Deer)
4 11 5 12 6 13 7 *1* 8 2 9 3 10 4 11 5 12 6
Tochtli (Rabbit)
5 12 6 13 7 *1* 8 2 9 3 10 4 11 5 12 6 13 7
Atl (Water)
6 13 7 *1* 8 2 9 3 10 4 11 5 12 6 13 7 *1* 8
Itzcuintli (Dog)
7 *1* 8 2 9 3 10 4 11 5 12 6 13 7 *1* 8 2 9
Ozomatli (Monkey)
8 2 9 3 10 4 11 5 12 6 13 7 *1* 8 2 9 3 10

Malinalli (Grass)
9 3 10 4 11 5 12 6 13 7 *1* 8 2 9 3 10 4 11
Acatl (Reed)
10 4 11 5 12 6 13 7 *1* 8 2 9 3 10 4 11 5 12
Ocelotl (Jaguar)
11 5 12 6 13 7 *1* 8 2 9 3 10 4 11 5 12 6 13
Quauhtli (Eagle)
12 6 13 7 *1* 8 2 9 3 10 4 11 5 12 6 13 7 *1*
Cozcaquauhtli (Vulture)
13 7 *1* 8 2 9 3 10 4 11 5 12 6 13 7 *1* 8 2

Ollin (Motion)
1 8 2 9 3 10 4 11 5 12 6 13 7 *1* 8 2 9 3
Tecpatl (Flint)
2 9 3 10 4 11 5 12 6 13 7 *1* 8 2 9 3 10 4
Quiahuitl (Rain)
3 10 4 11 5 12 6 13 7 *1* 8 2 9 3 10 4 11 5
Xochitl (Flower)
4 11 5 12 6 13 7 *1* 8 2 9 3 10 4 11 5 12 6

Five Remaining Days of Year 11 Acatl:

Cipactli	7
Ehecatl	8
Calli	9
Cuetzpalin	10
Coatl	11

Tonalpohualli 52 (Day 1 Alligator) occurs in Year 11 Reed. The *trecenas* are:

1. 1 Lizard	8. 1 Eagle	15. 1 Death	22. 1 Motion
2. 1 Motion	9. 1 Rabbit	16. 1 Rain	23. 1 Dog
3. 1 Dog	10. 1 Alligator	17. 1 Grass	24. 1 House

4. 1 House	11. 1 Jaguar	18. 1 Snake	25. 1 Vulture
5. 1 Vulture	12. 1 Deer	19. 1 Flint	26. 1 Water
6. 1 Water	13. 1 Flower	20. 1 Monkey	27. 1 Wind
7. 1 Wind	14. 1 Reed	21. 1 Lizard	28. 1 Eagle

The next year (12 Tecpatl) begins with Day 12 Miquiztli.

38. Year 12 Tecpatl

Days:

Miquiztli (Death)
12 6 13 7 *1* 8 2 9 3 10 4 11 5 12 6 13 7 *1*

Mazatl (Deer)
13 7 *1* 8 2 9 3 10 4 11 5 12 6 13 7 *1* 8 2

Tochtli (Rabbit)
1 8 2 9 3 10 4 11 5 12 6 13 7 *1* 8 2 9 3

Atl (Water)
2 9 3 10 4 11 5 12 6 13 7 *1* 8 2 9 3 10 4

Itzcuintli (Dog)
3 10 4 11 5 12 6 13 7 *1* 8 2 9 3 10 4 11 5

Ozomatli (Monkey)
4 11 5 12 6 13 7 *1* 8 2 9 3 10 4 11 5 12 6

Malinalli (Grass)
5 12 6 13 7 *1* 8 2 9 3 10 4 11 5 12 6 13 7

Acatl (Reed)
6 13 7 *1* 8 2 9 3 10 4 11 5 12 6 13 7 *1* 8

Ocelotl (Jaguar)
7 *1* 8 2 9 3 10 4 11 5 12 6 13 7 *1* 8 2 9

Quauhtli (Eagle)
8 2 9 3 10 4 11 5 12 6 13 7 *1* 8 2 9 3 10

Cozcaquauhtli (Vulture)
9 3 10 4 11 5 12 6 13 7 *1* 8 2 9 3 10 4 11

Ollin (Motion)
10 4 11 5 12 6 13 7 *1* 8 2 9 3 10 4 11 5 12

Tecpatl (Flint)
11 5 12 6 13 7 *1* 8 2 9 3 10 4 11 5 12 6 13

Quiahuitl (Rain)
12 6 13 7 *1* 8 2 9 3 10 4 11 5 12 6 13 7 *1*

Xochitl (Flower)
13 7 *1* 8 2 9 3 10 4 11 5 12 6 13 7 *1* 8 2

Cipactli (Alligator)
(53)**1** 8 2 9 3 10 4 11 5 12 6 13 7 (54)**1** 8 2 9 3

Ehecatl (Wind)

2 9 3 10 4 11 5 12 6 13 7 *1* 8 2 9 3 10 4

Calli (House)

3 10 4 11 5 12 6 13 7 *1* 8 2 9 3 10 4 11 5

Cuetzpalin (Lizard)

4 11 5 12 6 13 7 *1* 8 2 9 3 10 4 11 5 12 6

Coatl (Snake)

5 12 6 13 7 *1* 8 2 9 3 10 4 11 5 12 6 13 7

Five Remaining Days of Year 12 Tecpatl:

Miquiztli	8
Mazatl	9
Tochtli	10
Atl	11
Itzcuintli	12

Tonalpohuallis 53 and 54 (Days 1 Alligator) occur in Year 12 Flint. The *trecenas* are:

1. 1 Rabbit	8. 1 Rain	15. 1 Dog	22. 1 Alligator
2. 1 Alligator	9. 1 Grass	16. 1 House	23. 1 Jaguar
3. 1 Jaguar	10. 1 Snake	17. 1 Vulture	24. 1 Deer
4. 1 Deer	11. 1 Flint	18. 1 Water	25. 1 Flower
5. 1 Flower	12. 1 Monkey	19. 1 Wind	26. 1 Reed
6. 1 Reed	13. 1 Lizard	20. 1 Eagle	27. 1 Death
7. 1 Death	14. 1 Motion	21. 1 Rabbit	28. 1 Rain

The next year (13 Calli) begins with Day 13 Ozomatli.

39. Year 13 Calli

Days:

Ozomatli (Monkey)

13 7 *1* 8 2 9 3 10 4 11 5 12 6 13 7 *1* 8 2

Malinalli (Grass)

1 8 2 9 3 10 4 11 5 12 6 13 7 *1* 8 2 9 3

Acatl (Reed)

2 9 3 10 4 11 5 12 6 13 7 *1* 8 2 9 3 10 4

Ocelotl (Jaguar)

3 10 4 11 5 12 6 13 7 *1* 8 2 9 3 10 4 11 5

Quauhtli (Eagle)

4 11 5 12 6 13 7 *1* 8 2 9 3 10 4 11 5 12 6

Cozcaquauhtli (Vulture)

5 12 6 13 7 *1* 8 2 9 3 10 4 11 5 12 6 13 7

Ollin (Motion)

6 13 7 *1* 8 2 9 3 10 4 11 5 12 6 13 7 *1* 8

Tecpatl (Flint)

7 *1* 8 2 9 3 10 4 11 5 12 6 13 7 *1* 8 2 9

Quiahuitl (Rain)

8   2   9   3   10   4   11   5   12   6   13   7   *1*   8   2   9   3   10

Xochitl (Flower)

9   3   10   4   11   5   12   6   13   7   *1*   8   2   9   3   10   4   11

Cipactli (Alligator)

10   4   11   5   12   6   13   7   (55)**1**   8   2   9   3   10   4   11   5   12

Ehecatl (Wind)

11   5   12   6   13   7   *1*   8   2   9   3   10   4   11   5   12   6   13

Calli (House)

12   6   13   7   *1*   8   2   9   3   10   4   11   5   12   6   13   7   *1*

Cuetzpalin (Lizard)

13   7   *1*   8   2   9   3   10   4   11   5   12   6   13   7   *1*   8   2

Coatl (Snake)

1   8   2   9   3   10   4   11   5   12   6   13   7   *1*   8   2   9   3

Miquiztli (Death)

2   9   3   10   4   11   5   12   6   13   7   *1*   8   2   9   3   10   4

Mazatl (Deer)

3   10   4   11   5   12   6   13   7   *1*   8   2   9   3   10   4   11   5

Tochtli (Rabbit)

4   11   5   12   6   13   7   *1*   8   2   9   3   10   4   11   5   12   6

Atl (Water)

5   12   6   13   7   *1*   8   2   9   3   10   4   11   5   12   6   13   7

Itzcuintli (Dog)

6   13   7   *1*   8   2   9   3   10   4   11   5   12   6   13   7   *1*   8

Five Remaining Days of Year 13 Calli:

Ozomatli	9
Malinalli	10
Acatl	11
Ocelotl	12
Quauhtli	13

Tonalpohualli 55 (Day 1 Alligator) occurs in Year 13 House. The *trecenas* are:

1. 1 Grass	8. 1 House	15. 1 Jaguar	22. 1 Snake
2. 1 Snake	9. 1 Vulture	16. 1 Deer	23. 1 Flint
3. 1 Flint	10. 1 Water	17. 1 Flower	24. 1 Monkey
4. 1 Monkey	11. 1 Wind	18. 1 Reed	25. 1 Lizard
5. 1 Lizard	12. 1 Eagle	19. 1 Death	26. 1 Motion
6. 1 Motion	13. 1 Rabbit	20. 1 Rain	27. 1 Dog
7. 1 Dog	14. 1 Alligator	21. 1 Grass	28. 1 House

The next year (1 Tochtli) begins with Day 1 Cozcaquauhtli.

Days:

Cozcaquauhtli (Vulture)

1 8 2 9 3 10 4 11 5 12 6 13 7 *1* 8 2 9 3

Ollin (Motion)

2 9 3 10 4 11 5 12 6 13 7 *1* 8 2 9 3 10 4

Tecpatl (Flint)

3 10 4 11 5 12 6 13 7 *1* 8 2 9 3 10 4 11 5

Quiahuitl (Rain)

4 11 5 12 6 13 7 *1* 8 2 9 3 10 4 11 5 12 6

Xochitl (Flower)

5 12 6 13 7 *1* 8 2 9 3 10 4 11 5 12 6 13 7

Cipactli (Alligator)

6 13 7 (56)**1** 8 2 9 3 10 4 11 5 12 6 13 7 (57)**1** 8

Ehecatl (Wind)

7 *1* 8 2 9 3 10 4 11 5 12 6 13 7 *1* 8 2 9

Calli (House)

8 2 9 3 10 4 11 5 12 6 13 7 *1* 8 2 9 3 10

Cuetzpalin (Lizard)

9 3 10 4 11 5 12 6 13 7 *1* 8 2 9 3 10 4 11

Coatl (Snake)

10 4 11 5 12 6 13 7 *1* 8 2 9 3 10 4 11 5 12

Miquiztli (Death)

11 5 12 6 13 7 *1* 8 2 9 3 10 4 11 5 12 6 13

Mazatl (Deer)

12 6 13 7 *1* 8 2 9 3 10 4 11 5 12 6 13 7 *1*

Tochtli (Rabbit)

13 7 *1* 8 2 9 3 10 4 11 5 12 6 13 7 *1* 8 2

Atl (Water)

1 8 2 9 3 10 4 11 5 12 6 13 7 *1* 8 2 9 3

Itzcuintli (Dog)

2 9 3 10 4 11 5 12 6 13 7 *1* 8 2 9 3 10 4

Ozomatli (Monkey)

3 10 4 11 5 12 6 13 7 *1* 8 2 9 3 10 4 11 5

Malinalli (Grass)

4 11 5 12 6 13 7 *1* 8 2 9 3 10 4 11 5 12 6

Acatl (Reed)

5 12 6 13 7 *1* 8 2 9 3 10 4 11 5 12 6 13 7

Ocelotl (Jaguar)

6 13 7 *1* 8 2 9 3 10 4 11 5 12 6 13 7 *1* 8

Quauhtli (Eagle)

7 *1* 8 2 9 3 10 4 11 5 12 6 13 7 *1* 8 2 9

Five Remaining Days of Year 1 Tochtli: Cozcaquauhtli   10
                                                   Ollin   11
                                                   Tecpatl   12
                                                   Quiahuitl   13
                                                   Xochitl   *1*

Tonalpohuallis 56 and 57 (Days 1 Alligator) occur in Year 1 Rabbit. The *trecenas* are:

1. 1 Vulture	8. 1 Deer	15. 1 Flint	22. 1 Water
2. 1 Water	9. 1 Flower	16. 1 Monkey	23. 1 Wind
3. 1 Wind	10. 1 Reed	17. 1 Lizard	24. 1 Eagle
4. 1 Eagle	11. 1 Death	18. 1 Motion	25. 1 Rabbit
5. 1 Rabbit	12. 1 Rain	19. 1 Dog	26. 1 Alligator
6. 1 Alligator	13. 1 Grass	20. 1 House	27. 1 Jaguar
7. 1 Jaguar	14. 1 Snake	21. 1 Vulture	28. 1 Deer
			29. 1 Flower

The next year (2 Acatl) begins with Day 2 Cipactli.

41. Year 2 Acatl

Days:
Cipactli (Alligator)
2 9 3 10 4 11 5 12 6 13 7 (58)**1** 8 2 9 3 10 4

Ehecatl (Wind)
3 10 4 11 5 12 6 13 7 *1* 8 2 9 3 10 4 11 5
Calli (House)
4 11 5 12 6 13 7 *1* 8 2 9 3 10 4 11 5 12 6
Cuetzpalin (Lizard)
5 12 6 13 7 *1* 8 2 9 3 10 4 11 5 12 6 13 7
Coatl (Snake)
6 13 7 *1* 8 2 9 3 10 4 11 5 12 6 13 7 *1* 8
Miquiztli (Death)
7 *1* 8 2 9 3 10 4 11 5 12 6 13 7 *1* 8 2 9

Mazatl (Deer)
8 2 9 3 10 4 11 5 12 6 13 7 *1* 8 2 9 3 10
Tochtli (Rabbit)
9 3 10 4 11 5 12 6 13 7 *1* 8 2 9 3 10 4 11
Atl (Water)
10 4 11 5 12 6 13 7 *1* 8 2 9 3 10 4 11 5 12
Itzcuintli (Dog)
11 5 12 6 13 7 *1* 8 2 9 3 10 4 11 5 12 6 13
Ozomatli (Monkey)
12 6 13 7 *1* 8 2 9 3 10 4 11 5 12 6 13 7 *1*

Malinalli (Grass)

13 7 *1* 8 2 9 3 10 4 11 5 12 6 13 7 *1* 8 2

Acatl (Reed)

1 8 2 9 3 10 4 11 5 12 6 13 7 *1* 8 2 9 3

Ocelotl (Jaguar)

2 9 3 10 4 11 5 12 6 13 7 *1* 8 2 9 3 10 4

Quauhtli (Eagle)

3 10 4 11 5 12 6 13 7 *1* 8 2 9 3 10 4 11 5

Cozcaquauhtli (Vulture)

4 11 5 12 6 13 7 *1* 8 2 9 3 10 4 11 5 12 6

Ollin (Motion)

5 12 6 13 7 *1* 8 2 9 3 10 4 11 5 12 6 13 7

Tecpatl (Flint)

6 13 7 *1* 8 2 9 3 10 4 11 5 12 6 13 7 *1* 8

Quiahuitl (Rain)

7 *1* 8 2 9 3 10 4 11 5 12 6 13 7 *1* 8 2 9

Xochitl (Flower)

8 2 9 3 10 4 11 5 12 6 13 7 *1* 8 2 9 3 10

Five Remaining Days of Year 2 Acatl:

Cipactli	11
Ehecatl	12
Calli	13
Cuetzpalin	*1*
Coatl	2

Tonalpohualli 58 (Day 1 Alligator) occurs in Year 2 Reed. The *trecenas* are:

1. 1 Reed	8. 1 Lizard	15. 1 Eagle	22. 1 Death
2. 1 Death	9. 1 Motion	16. 1 Rabbit	23. 1 Rain
3. 1 Rain	10. 1 Dog	17. 1 Alligator	24. 1 Grass
4. 1 Grass	11. 1 House	18. 1 Jaguar	25. 1 Snake
5. 1 Snake	12. 1 Vulture	19. 1 Deer	26. 1 Flint
6. 1 Flint	13. 1 Water	20. 1 Flower	27. 1 Monkey
7. 1 Monkey	14. 1 Wind	21. 1 Reed	28. 1 Lizard

The next year (3 Tecpatl) begins with Day 3 Miquiztli.

42. Year 3 Tecpatl

Days:

Miquiztli (Death)

3 10 4 11 5 12 6 13 7 *1* 8 2 9 3 10 4 11 5

Mazatl (Deer)

4 11 5 12 6 13 7 *1* 8 2 9 3 10 4 11 5 12 6

Tochtli (Rabbit)

5 12 6 13 7 *1* 8 2 9 3 10 4 11 5 12 6 13 7

Atl (Water)
6 13 7 *1* 8 2 9 3 10 4 11 5 12 6 13 7 *1* 8
Itzcuintli (Dog)
7 *1* 8 2 9 3 10 4 11 5 12 6 13 7 *1* 8 2 9
Ozomatli (Monkey)
8 2 9 3 10 4 11 5 12 6 13 7 *1* 8 2 9 3 10

Malinalli (Grass)
9 3 10 4 11 5 12 6 13 7 *1* 8 2 9 3 10 4 11
Acatl (Reed)
10 4 11 5 12 6 13 7 *1* 8 2 9 3 10 4 11 5 12
Ocelotl (Jaguar)
11 5 12 6 13 7 *1* 8 2 9 3 10 4 11 5 12 6 13
Quauhtli (Eagle)
12 6 13 7 *1* 8 2 9 3 10 4 11 5 12 6 13 7 *1*
Cozcaquauhtli (Vulture)
13 7 *1* 8 2 9 3 10 4 11 5 12 6 13 7 *1* 8 2

Ollin (Motion)
1 8 2 9 3 10 4 11 5 12 6 13 7 *1* 8 2 9 3
Tecpatl (Flint)
2 9 3 10 4 11 5 12 6 13 7 *1* 8 2 9 3 10 4
Quiahuitl (Rain)
3 10 4 11 5 12 6 13 7 *1* 8 2 9 3 10 4 11 5
Xochitl (Flower)
4 11 5 12 6 13 7 *1* 8 2 9 3 10 4 11 5 12 6
Cipactli (Alligator)
5 12 6 13 7 (59)1 8 2 9 3 10 4 11 5 12 6 13 7

Ehecatl (Wind)
6 13 7 *1* 8 2 9 3 10 4 11 5 12 6 13 7 *1* 8
Calli (House)
7 *1* 8 2 9 3 10 4 11 5 12 6 13 7 *1* 8 2 9
Cuetzpalin (Lizard)
8 2 9 3 10 4 11 5 12 6 13 7 *1* 8 2 9 3 10
Coatl (Snake)
9 3 10 4 11 5 12 6 13 7 *1* 8 2 9 3 10 4 11

Five Remaining Days of Year 3 Tecpatl: Miquiztli 12
                                        Mazatl   13
                                        Tochtli   *1*
                                        Atl   2
                                        Itzcuintli 3

Tonalpohualli 59 (Day 1 Alligator) occurs in Year 3 Flint. The *trecenas* are:

1. 1 Motion	8. 1 Rabbit	15. 1 Eagle	22. 1 Dog
2. 1 Dog	9. 1 Alligator	16. 1 Grass	23. 1 House
3. 1 House	10. 1 Jaguar	17. 1 Snake	24. 1 Vulture
4. 1 Vulture	11. 1 Deer	18. 1 Flint	25. 1 Water
5. 1 Water	12. 1 Flower	19. 1 Monkey	26. 1 Wind
6. 1 Wind	13. 1 Reed	20. 1 Lizard	27. 1 Eagle
7. 1 Eagle	14. 1 Death	21. 1 Motion	28. 1 Rabbit

The next year (4 Calli) begins with Day 4 Ozomatli.

43. Year 4 Calli

Days:

Ozomatli (Monkey)

4 11 5 12 6 13 7 *1* 8 2 9 3 10 4 11 5 12 6

Malinalli (Grass)

5 12 6 13 7 *1* 8 2 9 3 10 4 11 5 12 6 13 7

Acatl (Reed)

6 13 7 *1* 8 2 9 3 10 4 11 5 12 6 13 7 *1* 8

Ocelotl (Jaguar)

7 *1* 8 2 9 3 10 4 11 5 12 6 13 7 *1* 8 2 9

Quauhtli (Eagle)

8 2 9 3 10 4 11 5 12 6 13 7 *1* 8 2 9 3 10

Cozcaquauhtli (Vulture)

9 3 10 4 11 5 12 6 13 7 *1* 8 2 9 3 10 4 11

Ollin (Motion)

10 4 11 5 12 6 13 7 *1* 8 2 9 3 10 4 11 5 12

Tecpatl (Flint)

11 5 12 6 13 7 *1* 8 2 9 3 10 4 11 5 12 6 13

Quiahuitl (Rain)

12 6 13 7 *1* 8 2 9 3 10 4 11 5 12 6 13 7 *1*

Xochitl (Flower)

13 7 *1* 8 2 9 3 10 4 11 5 12 6 13 7 *1* 8 2

Cipactli (Alligator)

(60)**1** 8 2 9 3 10 4 11 5 12 6 13 7 (61)**1** 8 2 9 3

Ehecatl (Wind)

2 9 3 10 4 11 5 12 6 13 7 *1* 8 2 9 3 10 4

Calli (House)

3 10 4 11 5 12 6 13 7 *1* 8 2 9 3 10 4 11 5

Cuetzpalin (Lizard)

4 11 5 12 6 13 7 *1* 8 2 9 3 10 4 11 5 12 6

Coatl (Snake)

5 12 6 13 7 *1* 8 2 9 3 10 4 11 5 12 6 13 7

Miquiztli (Death)

6 13 7 *1* 8 2 9 3 10 4 11 5 12 6 13 7 *1* 8

Mazatl (Deer)

7 *1* 8 2 9 3 10 4 11 5 12 6 13 7 *1* 8 2 9

Tochtli (Rabbit)

8 2 9 3 10 4 11 5 12 6 13 7 *1* 8 2 9 3 10

Atl (Water)

9 3 10 4 11 5 12 6 13 7 *1* 8 2 9 3 10 4 11

Itzcuintli (Dog)

10 4 11 5 12 6 13 7 *1* 8 2 9 3 10 4 11 5 12

Five Remaining Days of Year 4 House: Ozomatli   13
                                        Malinalli   *1*
                                        Acatl   2
                                        Ocelotl   3
                                        Quauhtli   4

Tonalpohuallis 60 and 61 (Days 1 Alligator) occur in Year 4 House. The *trecenas* are:

1. 1 Alligator	8. 1 Grass	15. 1 House	22. 1 Jaguar
2. 1 Jaguar	9. 1 Snake	16. 1 Vulture	23. 1 Deer
3. 1 Deer	10. 1 Flint	17. 1 Water	24. 1 Flower
4. 1 Flower	11. 1 Monkey	18. 1 Wind	25. 1 Reed
5. 1 Reed	12. 1 Lizard	19. 1 Eagle	26. 1 Death
6. 1 Death	13. 1 Motion	20. 1 Rabbit	27. 1 Rain
7. 1 Rain	14. 1 Dog	21. 1 Alligator	28. 1 Grass

The next year (5 Tochtli) begins with Day 5 Cozcaquauhtli.

44. Year 5 Tochtli

Days:

Cozcaquauhtli (Vulture)

5 12 6 13 7 *1* 8 2 9 3 10 4 11 5 12 6 13 7

Ollin (Motion)

6 13 7 *1* 8 2 9 3 10 4 11 5 12 6 13 7 *1* 8

Tecpatl (Flint)

7 *1* 8 2 9 3 10 4 11 5 12 6 13 7 *1* 8 2 9

Quiahuitl (Rain)

8 2 9 3 10 4 11 5 12 6 13 7 *1* 8 2 9 3 10

Xochitl (Flower)

9 3 10 4 11 5 12 6 13 7 *1* 8 2 9 3 10 4 11

Cipactli (Alligator)

10 4 11 5 12 6 13 7 (62)**1** 8 2 9 3 10 4 11 5 12

Ehecatl (Wind)

11 5 12 6 13 7 *1* 8 2 9 3 10 4 11 5 12 6 13

Calli (House)
12 6 13 7 *1* 8 2 9 3 10 4 11 5 12 6 13 7 *1*

Cuetzpalin (Lizard)
13 7 *1* 8 2 9 3 10 4 11 5 12 6 13 7 *1* 8 2

Coatl (Snake)
1 8 2 9 3 10 4 11 5 12 6 13 7 *1* 8 2 9 3

Miquiztli (Death)
2 9 3 10 4 11 5 12 6 13 7 *1* 8 2 9 3 10 4

Mazatl (Deer)
3 10 4 11 5 12 6 13 7 *1* 8 2 9 3 10 4 11 5

Tochtli (Rabbit)
4 11 5 12 6 13 7 *1* 8 2 9 3 10 4 11 5 12 6

Atl (Water)
5 12 6 13 7 *1* 8 2 9 3 10 4 11 5 12 6 13 7

Itzcuintli (Dog)
6 13 7 *1* 8 2 9 3 10 4 11 5 12 6 13 7 *1* 8

Ozomatli (Monkey)
7 *1* 8 2 9 3 10 4 11 5 12 6 13 7 *1* 8 2 9

Malinalli (Grass)
8 2 9 3 10 4 11 5 12 6 13 7 *1* 8 2 9 3 10

Acatl (Reed)
9 3 10 4 11 5 12 6 13 7 *1* 8 2 9 3 10 4 11

Ocelotl (Jaguar)
10 4 11 5 12 6 13 7 *1* 8 2 9 3 10 4 11 5 12

Quauhtli (Eagle)
11 5 12 6 13 7 *1* 8 2 9 3 10 4 11 5 12 6 13

Five Remaining Days of Year 5 Tochtli:

Cozcaquauhtli	*1*
Ollin	2
Tecpatl	3
Quiahuitl	4
Xochitl	5

Tonalpohualli 62 (Day 1 Alligator) occurs in Year 5 House. The *trecenas* are:

1. 1 Snake	8. 1 Vulture	15. 1 Deer	22. 1 Flint
2. 1 Flint	9. 1 Water	16. 1 Flower	23. 1 Monkey
3. 1 Monkey	10. 1 Wind	17. 1 Reed	24. 1 Lizard
4. 1 Lizard	11. 1 Eagle	18. 1 Death	25. 1 Motion
5. 1 Motion	12. 1 Rabbit	19. 1 Rain	26. 1 Dog
6. 1 Dog	13. 1 Alligator	20. 1 Grass	27. 1 House
7. 1 House	14. 1 Jaguar	21. 1 Snake	28. 1 Vulture

The next year (6 Acatl) begins with Day 6 Cipactli.

45. Year 6 Acatl

Days:
Cipactli (Alligator)
6 13 7 (63)1 8 2 9 3 10 4 11 5 12 6 13 7 (64)1 8

Ehecatl (Wind)
7 *1* 8 2 9 3 10 4 11 5 12 6 13 7 *1* 8 2 9

Calli (House)
8 2 9 3 10 4 11 5 12 6 13 7 *1* 8 2 9 3 10

Cuetzpalin (Lizard)
9 3 10 4 11 5 12 6 13 7 *1* 8 2 9 3 10 4 11

Coatl (Snake)
10 4 11 5 12 6 13 7 *1* 8 2 9 3 10 4 11 5 12

Miquiztli (Death)
11 5 12 6 13 7 *1* 8 2 9 3 10 4 11 5 12 6 13

Mazatl (Deer)
12 6 13 7 *1* 8 2 9 3 10 4 11 5 12 6 13 7 *1*

Tochtli (Rabbit)
13 7 *1* 8 2 9 3 10 4 11 5 12 6 13 7 *1* 8 2

Atl (Water)
1 8 2 9 3 10 4 11 5 12 6 13 7 *1* 8 2 9 3

Itzcuintli (Dog)
2 9 3 10 4 11 5 12 6 13 7 *1* 8 2 9 3 10 4

Ozomatli (Monkey)
3 10 4 11 5 12 6 13 7 *1* 8 2 9 3 10 4 11 5

Malinalli (Grass)
4 11 5 12 6 13 7 *1* 8 2 9 3 10 4 11 5 12 6

Acatl (Reed)
5 12 6 13 7 *1* 8 2 9 3 10 4 11 5 12 6 13 7

Ocelotl (Jaguar)
6 13 7 *1* 8 2 9 3 10 4 11 5 12 6 13 7 *1* 8

Quauhtli (Eagle)
7 *1* 8 2 9 3 10 4 11 5 12 6 13 7 *1* 8 2 9

Cozcaquauhtli (Vulture)
8 2 9 3 10 4 11 5 12 6 13 7 *1* 8 2 9 3 10

Ollin (Motion)
9 3 10 4 11 5 12 6 13 7 *1* 8 2 9 3 10 4 11

Tecpatl (Flint)
10 4 11 5 12 6 13 7 *1* 8 2 9 3 10 4 11 5 12

Quiahuitl (Rain)
11 5 12 6 13 7 *1* 8 2 9 3 10 4 11 5 12 6 13

Xochitl (Flower)
12 6 13 7 *1* 8 2 9 3 10 4 11 5 12 6 13 7 *1*

Five Remaining Days of Year 6 Acatl: Cipactli   2
    Ehecatl   3
    Calli   4
    Cuetzpalin   5
    Coatl   6

Tonalpohuallis 63 and 64 (Days 1 Alligator) occur in Year 6 Reed. The *trecenas* are:

1. 1 Water	8. 1 Flower	15. 1 Monkey	22. 1 Wind
2. 1 Wind	9. 1 Reed	16. 1 Lizard	23. 1 Eagle
3. 1 Eagle	10. 1 Death	17. 1 Motion	24. 1 Rabbit
4. 1 Rabbit	11. 1 Rain	18. 1 Dog	25. 1 Alligator
5. 1 Alligator	12. 1 Grass	19. 1 House	26. 1 Jaguar
6. 1 Jaguar	13. 1 Snake	20. 1 Vulture	27. 1 Deer
7. 1 Deer	14. 1 Flint	21. 1 Water	28. 1 Flower

The next year (7 Tecpatl) begins with Day 7 Miquiztli.

46. Year 7 Tecpatl

Days:

Miquiztli (Death)
7 *1* 8 2 9 3 10 4 11 5 12 6 13 7 *1* 8 2 9

Mazatl (Deer)
8 2 9 3 10 4 11 5 12 6 13 7 *1* 8 2 9 3 10

Tochtli (Rabbit)
9 3 10 4 11 5 12 6 13 7 *1* 8 2 9 3 10 4 11

Atl (Water)
10 4 11 5 12 6 13 7 *1* 8 2 9 3 10 4 11 5 12

Itzcuintli (Dog)
11 5 12 6 13 7 *1* 8 2 9 3 10 4 11 5 12 6 13

Ozomatli (Monkey)
12 6 13 7 *1* 8 2 9 3 10 4 11 5 12 6 13 7 *1*

Malinalli (Grass)
13 7 *1* 8 2 9 3 10 4 11 5 12 6 13 7 *1* 8 2

Acatl (Reed)
1 8 2 9 3 10 4 11 5 12 6 13 7 *1* 8 2 9 3

Ocelotl (Reed)
2 9 3 10 4 11 5 12 6 13 7 *1* 8 2 9 3 10 4

Quauhtli (Eagle)
3 10 4 11 5 12 6 13 7 *1* 8 2 9 3 10 4 11 5

Cozcaquauhtli (Vulture)
4 11 5 12 6 13 7 *1* 8 2 9 3 10 4 11 5 12 6

Ollin (Motion)
5 12 6 13 7 *1* 8 2 9 3 10 4 11 5 12 6 13 7

Tecpatl (Flint)
6 13 7 *1* 8 2 9 3 10 4 11 5 12 6 13 7 *1* 8
Quiahuitl (Rain)
7 *1* 8 2 9 3 10 4 11 5 12 6 13 7 *1* 8 2 9
Xochitl (Flower)
8 2 9 3 10 4 11 5 12 6 13 7 *1* 8 2 9 3 10
Cipactli (Alligator)
9 3 10 4 11 5 12 6 13 7 (65)**1** 8 2 9 3 10 4 11

Ehecatl (Wind)
10 4 11 5 12 6 13 7 *1* 8 2 9 3 10 4 11 5 12
Calli (House)
11 5 12 6 13 7 *1* 8 2 9 3 10 4 11 5 12 6 13
Cuetzpalin (Lizard)
12 6 13 7 *1* 8 2 9 3 10 4 11 5 12 6 13 7 *1*
Coatl (Snake)
13 7 *1* 8 2 9 3 10 4 11 5 12 6 13 7 *1* 8 2

Five Remaining Days of Year 7 Tecpatl: Miquiztli   3
                                         Mazatl   4
                                         Tochtli   5
                                         Atl   6
                                         Itzcuintli   7

Tonalpohualli 65 (Day 1 Alligator) occurs in Year 7 Flint. The *trecenas* are:

1. 1 Reed	8. 1 Lizard	15. 1 Eagle	22. 1 Death
2. 1 Death	9. 1 Motion	16. 1 Rabbit	23. 1 Rain
3. 1 Rain	10. 1 Dog	17. 1 Alligator	24. 1 Grass
4. 1 Grass	11. 1 House	18. 1 Reed	25. 1 Snake
5. 1 Snake	12. 1 Vulture	19. 1 Deer	26. 1 Motion
6. 1 Flint	13. 1 Water	20. 1 Flower	27. 1 Monkey
7. 1 Monkey	14. 1 Wind	21. 1 Reed	28. 1 Lizard

The next year (8 Calli) beings with Day 8 Ozomatli.

47. Year 8 Calli

Days:
Ozomatli (Monkey)
8 2 9 3 10 4 11 5 12 6 13 7 *1* 8 2 9 3 10

Malinalli (Grass)
9 3 10 4 11 5 12 6 13 7 *1* 8 2 9 3 10 4 11
Acatl (Reed)
10 4 11 5 12 6 13 7 *1* 8 2 9 3 10 4 11 5 12
Ocelotl (Jaguar)
11 5 12 6 13 7 *1* 8 2 9 3 10 4 11 5 12 6 13

Quauhtli (Eagle)

12 6 13 7 *1* 8 2 9 3 10 4 11 5 12 6 13 7 *1*

Cozcaquauhtli (Vulture)

13 7 *1* 8 2 9 3 10 4 11 5 12 6 13 7 *1* 8 2

Ollin (Motion)

1 8 2 9 3 10 4 11 5 12 6 13 7 *1* 8 2 9 3

Tecpatl (Flint)

2 9 3 10 4 11 5 12 6 13 7 *1* 8 2 9 3 10 4

Quiahuitl (Rain)

3 10 4 11 5 12 6 13 7 *1* 8 2 9 3 10 4 11 5

Xochitl (Flower)

4 11 5 12 6 13 7 *1* 8 2 9 3 10 4 11 5 12 6

Cipactli (Alligator)

5 12 6 13 7 (66)**1** 8 2 9 3 10 4 11 5 12 6 13 7

Ehecatl (Wind)

6 13 7 *1* 8 2 9 3 10 4 11 5 12 6 13 7 *1* 8

Calli (House)

7 *1* 8 2 9 3 10 4 11 5 12 6 13 7 *1* 8 2 9

Cuetzpalin (Lizard)

8 2 9 3 10 4 11 5 12 6 13 7 *1* 8 2 9 3 10

Coatl (Snake)

9 3 10 4 11 5 12 6 13 7 *1* 8 2 9 3 10 4 11

Miquiztli (Death)

10 4 11 5 12 6 13 7 *1* 8 2 9 3 10 4 11 5 12

Mazatl (Deer)

11 5 12 6 13 7 *1* 8 2 9 3 10 4 11 5 12 6 13

Tochtli (Rabbit)

12 6 13 7 *1* 8 2 9 3 10 4 11 5 12 6 13 7 *1*

Atl (Water)

13 7 *1* 8 2 9 3 10 4 11 5 12 6 13 7 *1* 8 2

Itzcuintli (Dog)

1 8 2 9 3 10 4 11 5 12 6 13 7 *1* 8 2 9 3

Five Remaining Days of Year 8 Calli:	Ozomatli	4
	Malinalli	5
	Acatl	6
	Ocelotl	7
	Quauhtli	8

Tonalpohualli 66 (Day 1 Alligator) occurs in Year 8 House. The *trecenas* are:

1. 1 Motion	8. 1 Rabbit	15. 1 Rain	22. 1 Dog
2. 1 Dog	9. 1 Alligator	16. 1 Grass	23. 1 House
3. 1 House	10. 1 Jaguar	17. 1 Snake	24. 1 Vulture

4. 1 Vulture	11. 1 Deer	18. 1 Flint	25. 1 Water
5. 1 Water	12. 1 Flower	19. 1 Monkey	26. 1 Wind
6. 1 Wind	13. 1 Reed	20. 1 Lizard	27. 1 Eagle
7. 1 Eagle	14. 1 Death	21. 1 Motion	28. 1 Rabbit

The next year (9 Tochtli) begins with Day 9 Cozcaquauhtli.

48. Year 9 Tochtli

Days:

Cozcaquauhtli (Vulture)

9　3　10　4　11　5　12　6　13　7　*1*　8　2　9　3　10　4　11

Ollin (Motion)

10　4　11　5　12　6　13　7　*1*　8　2　9　3　10　4　11　5　12

Tecpatl (Flint)

11　5　12　6　13　7　*1*　8　2　9　3　10　4　11　5　12　6　13

Quiahuitl (Rain)

12　6　13　7　*1*　8　2　9　3　10　4　11　5　12　6　13　7　*1*

Xochitl (Flower)

13　7　*1*　8　2　9　3　10　4　11　5　12　6　13　7　*1*　8　2

Cipactli (Alligator)

(67)**1**　8　2　9　3　10　4　11　5　12　6　13　7　(68)**1**　8　2　9　3

Ehecatl (Wind)

2　9　3　10　4　11　5　12　6　13　7　*1*　8　2　9　3　10　4

Calli (House)

3　10　4　11　5　12　6　13　7　*1*　8　2　9　3　10　4　11　5

Cuetzpalin (Lizard)

4　11　5　12　6　13　7　*1*　8　2　9　3　10　4　11　5　12　6

Coatl (Snake)

5　12　6　13　7　*1*　8　2　9　3　10　4　11　5　12　6　13　7

Miquiztli (Death)

6　13　7　*1*　8　2　9　3　10　4　11　5　12　6　13　7　*1*　8

Mazatl (Deer)

7　*1*　8　2　9　3　10　4　11　5　12　6　13　7　*1*　8　2　9

Tochtli (Rabbit)

8　2　9　3　10　4　11　5　12　6　13　7　*1*　8　2　9　3　10

Atl (Water)

9　3　10　4　11　5　12　6　13　7　*1*　8　2　9　3　10　4　11

Itzcuintli (Dog)

10　4　11　5　12　6　13　7　*1*　8　2　9　3　10　4　11　5　12

Ozomatli (Monkey)

11　5　12　6　13　7　*1*　8　2　9　3　10　4　11　5　12　6　13

Malinalli (Grass)

12 6 13 7 *1* 8 2 9 3 10 4 11 5 12 6 13 7 *1*

Acatl (Reed)

13 7 *1* 8 2 9 3 10 4 11 5 12 6 13 7 *1* 8 2

Ocelotl (Jaguar)

1 8 2 9 3 10 4 11 5 12 6 13 7 *1* 8 2 9 3

Quauhtli (Eagle)

2 9 3 10 4 11 5 12 6 13 7 *1* 8 2 9 3 10 4

Five Remaining Days of Year 9 Tochtli:

Cozcaquauhtli	5
Ollin	6
Tecpatl	7
Quiahuitl	8
Xochitl	9

Tonalpohuallis 67 and 68 (Days 1 Alligator) occur in Year 9 Rabbit. The *trecenas* are:

1. 1 Alligator	8. 1 Grass	15. 1 House	22. 1 Jaguar
2. 1 Jaguar	9. 1 Snake	16. 1 Vulture	23. 1 Deer
3. 1 Deer	10. 1 Flint	17. 1 Water	24. 1 Flower
4. 1 Flower	11. 1 Monkey	18. 1 Wind	25. 1 Reed
5. 1 Reed	12. 1 Lizard	19. 1 Eagle	26. 1 Death
6. 1 Death	13. 1 Motion	20. 1 Rabbit	27. 1 Rain
7. 1 Rain	14. 1 Dog	21. 1 Alligator	28. 1 Grass

The next year (10 Acatl) begins with Day 10 Cipactli.

49. Year 10 Acatl

Days:

Cipactli (Alligator)

10 4 11 5 12 6 13 7 (69)1 8 2 9 3 10 4 11 5 12

Ehecatl (Wind)

11 5 12 6 13 7 *1* 8 2 9 3 10 4 11 5 12 6 13

Calli (House)

12 6 13 7 *1* 8 2 9 3 10 4 11 5 12 6 13 7 *1*

Cuetzpalin (Lizard)

13 7 *1* 8 2 9 3 10 4 11 5 12 6 13 7 *1* 8 2

Coatl (Snake)

1 8 2 9 3 10 4 11 5 12 6 13 7 *1* 8 2 9 3

Miquiztli (Death)

2 9 3 10 4 11 5 12 6 13 7 *1* 8 2 9 3 10 4

Mazatl (Deer)

3 10 4 11 5 12 6 13 7 *1* 8 2 9 3 10 4 11 5

Tochtli (Rabbit)

4 11 5 12 6 13 7 *1* 8 2 9 3 10 4 11 5 12 6

Atl (Water)

5 12 6 13 7 *1* 8 2 9 3 10 4 11 5 12 6 13 7

Itzcuintli (Dog)

6 13 7 *1* 8 2 9 3 10 4 11 5 12 6 13 7 *1* 8

Ozomatli (Monkey)

7 *1* 8 2 9 3 10 4 11 5 12 6 13 7 *1* 8 2 9

Malinalli (Grass)

8 2 9 3 10 4 11 5 12 6 13 7 *1* 8 2 9 3 10

Acatl (Reed)

9 3 10 4 11 5 12 6 13 7 *1* 8 2 9 3 10 4 11

Ocelotl (Jaguar)

10 4 11 5 12 6 13 7 *1* 8 2 9 3 10 4 11 5 12

Quauhtli (Eagle)

11 5 12 6 13 7 *1* 8 2 9 3 10 4 11 5 12 6 13

Cozcaquauhtli (Vulture)

12 6 13 7 *1* 8 2 9 3 10 4 11 5 12 6 13 7 *1*

Ollin (Motion)

13 7 *1* 8 2 9 3 10 4 11 5 12 6 13 7 *1* 8 2

Tecpatl (Flint)

1 8 2 9 3 10 4 11 5 12 6 13 7 *1* 8 2 9 3

Quiahuitl (Rain)

2 9 3 10 4 11 5 12 6 13 7 *1* 8 2 9 3 10 4

Xochitl (Flower)

3 10 4 11 5 12 6 13 7 *1* 8 2 9 3 10 4 11 5

Five Remaining Days of Year 10 Acatl:

Cipactli	6
Ehecatl	7
Calli	8
Cuetzpalin	9
Coatl	10

Tonalpohualli 69 (Day 1 Alligator) occurs in Year 10 Reed. The *trecenas* are:

1. 1 Snake	8. 1 Vulture	15. 1 Deer	22. 1 Flint
2. 1 Flint	9. 1 Water	16. 1 Flower	23. 1 Monkey
3. 1 Monkey	10. 1 Wind	17. 1 Reed	24. 1 Lizard
4. 1 Lizard	11. 1 Eagle	18. 1 Death	25. 1 Motion
5. 1 Motion	12. 1 Rabbit	19. 1 Rain	26. 1 Dog
6. 1 Dog	13. 1 Alligator	20. 1 Grass	27. 1 House
7. 1 House	14. 1 Jaguar	21. 1 Snake	28. 1 Vulture

The next year (11 Tecpatl) begins with Day 11 Miquiztli.

Days:

Miquiztli (Death)

| 11 | 5 | 12 | 6 | 13 | 7 | *1* | 8 | 2 | 9 | 3 | 10 | 4 | 11 | 5 | 12 | 6 | 13 |

Mazatl (Deer)

| 12 | 6 | 13 | 7 | *1* | 8 | 2 | 9 | 3 | 10 | 4 | 11 | 5 | 12 | 6 | 13 | 7 | *1* |

Tochtli (Rabbit)

| 13 | 7 | *1* | 8 | 2 | 9 | 3 | 10 | 4 | 11 | 5 | 12 | 6 | 13 | 7 | *1* | 8 | 2 |

Atl (Water)

| *1* | 8 | 2 | 9 | 3 | 10 | 4 | 11 | 5 | 12 | 6 | 13 | 7 | *1* | 8 | 2 | 9 | 3 |

Itzcuintli (Dog)

| 2 | 9 | 3 | 10 | 4 | 11 | 5 | 12 | 6 | 13 | 7 | *1* | 8 | 2 | 9 | 3 | 10 | 4 |

Ozomatli (Monkey)

| 3 | 10 | 4 | 11 | 5 | 12 | 6 | 13 | 7 | *1* | 8 | 2 | 9 | 3 | 10 | 4 | 11 | 5 |

Malinalli (Grass)

| 4 | 11 | 5 | 12 | 6 | 13 | 7 | *1* | 8 | 2 | 9 | 3 | 10 | 4 | 11 | 5 | 12 | 6 |

Acatl (Reed)

| 5 | 12 | 6 | 13 | 7 | *1* | 8 | 2 | 9 | 3 | 10 | 4 | 11 | 5 | 12 | 6 | 13 | 7 |

Ocelotl (Jaguar)

| 6 | 13 | 7 | *1* | 8 | 2 | 9 | 3 | 10 | 4 | 11 | 5 | 12 | 6 | 13 | 7 | *1* | 8 |

Quauhtli (Eagle)

| 7 | *1* | 8 | 2 | 9 | 3 | 10 | 4 | 11 | 5 | 12 | 6 | 13 | 7 | *1* | 8 | 2 | 9 |

Cozcaquauhtli (Vulture)

| 8 | 2 | 9 | 3 | 10 | 4 | 11 | 5 | 12 | 6 | 13 | 7 | *1* | 8 | 2 | 9 | 3 | 10 |

Ollin (Motion)

| 9 | 3 | 10 | 4 | 11 | 5 | 12 | 6 | 13 | 7 | *1* | 8 | 2 | 9 | 3 | 10 | 4 | 11 |

Tecpatl (Flint)

| 10 | 4 | 11 | 5 | 12 | 6 | 13 | 7 | *1* | 8 | 2 | 9 | 3 | 10 | 4 | 11 | 5 | 12 |

Quiahuitl (Rain)

| 11 | 5 | 12 | 6 | 13 | 7 | *1* | 8 | 2 | 9 | 3 | 10 | 4 | 11 | 5 | 12 | 6 | 13 |

Xochitl (Flower)

| 12 | 6 | 13 | 7 | *1* | 8 | 2 | 9 | 3 | 10 | 4 | 11 | 5 | 12 | 6 | 13 | 7 | *1* |

Cipactli (Alligator)

| 13 | 7 | (70)**1** | 8 | 2 | 9 | 3 | 10 | 4 | 11 | 5 | 12 | 6 | 13 | 7 | (71)**1** | 8 | 2 |

Ehecatl (Wind)

| *1* | 8 | 2 | 9 | 3 | 10 | 4 | 11 | 5 | 12 | 6 | 13 | 7 | *1* | 8 | 2 | 9 | 3 |

Calli (House)

| 2 | 9 | 3 | 10 | 4 | 11 | 5 | 12 | 6 | 13 | 7 | *1* | 8 | 2 | 9 | 3 | 10 | 4 |

Cuetzpalin (Lizard)

| 3 | 10 | 4 | 11 | 5 | 12 | 6 | 13 | 7 | *1* | 8 | 2 | 9 | 3 | 10 | 4 | 11 | 5 |

Coatl (Snake)

| 4 | 11 | 5 | 12 | 6 | 13 | 7 | *1* | 8 | 2 | 9 | 3 | 10 | 4 | 11 | 5 | 12 | 6 |

Five Remaining Days of Year 11 Tecpatl: Miquiztli   7

Mazatl   8

Tochtli   9

Atl   10

Itzcuintli   11

Tonalpohuallis 70 and 71 (Days 1 Alligator) occur in Year 11 Flint. The *trecenas* are:

1. 1 Water	8. 1 Flower	15. 1 Monkey	22. 1 Wind
2. 1 Wind	9. 1 Reed	16. 1 Lizard	23. 1 Eagle
3. 1 Eagle	10. 1 Death	17. 1 Motion	24. 1 Rabbit
4. 1 Rabbit	11. 1 Rain	18. 1 Dog	25. 1 Alligator
5. 1 Alligator	12. 1 Grass	19. 1 House	26. 1 Jaguar
6. 1 Jaguar	13. 1 Snake	20. 1 Vulture	27. 1 Deer
7. 1 Deer	14. 1 Flint	21. 1 Water	28. 1 Flower

The next year (12 Calli) begins with Day 12 Ozomatli.

51. Year 12 Calli

Days:

Ozomatli (Monkey)

12 6 13 7 *1* 8 2 9 3 10 4 11 5 12 6 13 7 *1*

Malinalli (Grass)

13 7 *1* 8 2 9 3 10 4 11 5 12 6 13 7 *1* 8 2

Acatl (Reed)

1 8 2 9 3 10 4 11 5 12 6 13 7 *1* 8 2 9 3

Ocelotl (Jaguar)

2 9 3 10 4 11 5 12 6 13 7 *1* 8 2 9 3 10 4

Quauhtli (Eagle)

3 10 4 11 5 12 6 13 7 *1* 8 2 9 3 10 4 11 5

Cozcaquauhtli (Vulture)

4 11 5 12 6 13 7 *1* 8 2 9 3 10 4 11 5 12 6

Ollin (Motion)

5 12 6 13 7 *1* 8 2 9 3 10 4 11 5 12 6 13 7

Tecpatl (Flint)

6 13 7 *1* 8 2 9 3 10 4 11 5 12 6 13 7 *1* 8

Quiahuitl (Rain)

7 *1* 8 2 9 3 10 4 11 5 12 6 13 7 *1* 8 2 9

Xochitl (Flower)

8 2 9 3 10 4 11 5 12 6 13 7 *1* 8 2 9 3 10

Cipactli (Alligator)

9 3 10 4 11 5 12 6 13 7 (72)**1** 8 2 9 3 10 4 11

Ehecatl (Wind)

10 4 11 5 12 6 13 7 *1* 8 2 9 3 10 4 11 5 12

Calli (House)
11 5 12 6 13 7 *1* 8 2 9 3 10 4 11 5 12 6 13
Cuetzpalin (Lizard)
12 6 13 7 *1* 8 2 9 3 10 4 11 5 12 6 13 7 *1*
Coatl (Snake)
13 7 *1* 8 2 9 3 10 4 11 5 12 6 13 7 *1* 8 2
Miquiztli (Death)
1 8 2 9 3 10 4 11 5 12 6 13 7 *1* 8 2 9 3

Mazatl (Deer)
2 9 3 10 4 11 5 12 6 13 7 *1* 8 2 9 3 10 4
Tochtli (Rabbit)
3 10 4 11 5 12 6 13 7 *1* 8 2 9 3 10 4 11 5
Atl (Water)
4 11 5 12 6 13 7 *1* 8 2 9 3 10 4 11 5 12 6
Itzcuintli (Dog)
5 12 6 13 7 *1* 8 2 9 3 10 4 11 5 12 6 13 7

Five Remaining Days of Year 12 Calli: Ozomatli   8
                                          Malinalli   9
                                          Acatl   10
                                          Ocelotl   11
                                          Quauhtli   12

Tonalpohualli 72 (Day 1 Alligator) occurs in Year 12 House. The *trecenas* are:

1. 1 Reed	8. 1 Lizard	15. 1 Eagle	22. 1 Death
2. 1 Death	9. 1 Motion	16. 1 Rabbit	23. 1 Rain
3. 1 Rain	10. 1 Dog	17. 1 Alligator	24. 1 Grass
4. 1 Grass	11. 1 House	18. 1 Jaguar	25. 1 Snake
5. 1 Snake	12. 1 Vulture	19. 1 Deer	26. 1 Flint
6. 1 Flint	13. 1 Water	20. 1 Flower	27. 1 Monkey
7. 1 Monkey	14. 1 Wind	21. 1 Reed	28. 1 Lizard

The next and last year (13 Tochtli) begins with Day 13 Cozcaquauhtli.

52. Year 13 Tochtli

Days:
Cozcaquauhtli (Vulture)
13 7 *1* 8 2 9 3 10 4 11 5 12 6 13 7 *1* 8 2

Ollin (Motion)
1 8 2 9 3 10 4 11 5 12 6 13 7 *1* 8 2 9 3
Tecpatl (Flint)
2 9 3 10 4 11 5 12 6 13 7 *1* 8 2 9 3 10 4
Quiahuitl (Rain)
3 10 4 11 5 12 6 13 7 *1* 8 2 9 3 10 4 11 5

Xochitl (Flower)
4 11 5 12 6 13 7 *1* 8 2 9 3 10 4 11 5 12 6

Cipactli (Alligator)
5 12 6 13 7 (73)**1** 8 2 9 3 10 4 11 5 12 6 13 7

Ehecatl (Wind)
6 13 7 *1* 8 2 9 3 10 4 11 5 12 6 13 7 *1* 8

Calli (House)
7 *1* 8 2 9 3 10 4 11 5 12 6 13 7 *1* 8 2 9

Cuetzpalin (Lizard)
8 2 9 3 10 4 11 5 12 6 13 7 *1* 8 2 9 3 10

Coatl (Snake)
9 3 10 4 11 5 12 6 13 7 *1* 8 2 9 3 10 4 11

Miquiztli (Death)
10 4 11 5 12 6 13 7 *1* 8 2 9 3 10 4 11 5 12

Mazatl (Deer)
11 5 12 6 13 7 *1* 8 2 9 3 10 4 11 5 12 6 13

Tochtli (Rabbit)
12 6 13 7 *1* 8 2 9 3 10 4 11 5 12 6 13 7 *1*

Atl (Water)
13 7 *1* 8 2 9 3 10 4 11 5 12 6 13 7 *1* 8 2

Itzcuintli (Dog)
1 8 2 9 3 10 4 11 5 12 6 13 7 *1* 8 2 9 3

Ozomatli (Monkey)
2 9 3 10 4 11 5 12 6 13 7 *1* 8 2 9 3 10 4

Malinalli (Grass)
3 10 4 11 5 12 6 13 7 *1* 8 2 9 3 10 4 11 5

Acatl (Reed)
4 11 5 12 6 13 7 *1* 8 2 9 3 10 4 11 5 12 6

Ocelotl (Jaguar)
5 12 6 13 7 *1* 8 2 9 3 10 4 11 5 12 6 13 7

Quauhtli (Eagle)
6 13 7 *1* 8 2 9 3 10 4 11 5 12 6 13 7 *1* 8

Five Remaining Days of Year 13 Tochtli: Cozcaquauhtli 9
                                          Ollin   10
                                          Tecpatl   11
                                          Quiahuitl   12
                                          Xochitl   13

Tonalpohualli 73, the last (Day 1 Alligator), occurs in Year 13 Rabbit. The *trecenas* are:

1. 1 Motion   8. 1 Rabbit   15. 1 Rain   22. 1 Dog
2. 1 Dog   9. 1 Alligator   16. 1 Grass   23. 1 House
3. 1 House   10. 1 Jaguar   17. 1 Snake   24. 1 Vulture

4. 1 Vulture	11. 1 Deer	18. 1 Flint	25. 1 Water
5. 1 Water	12. 1 Flower	19. 1 Monkey	26. 1 Wind
6. 1 Wind	13. 1 Reed	20. 1 Lizard	27. 1 Eagle
7. 1 Eagle	14. 1 Death	21. 1 Motion	28. 1 Rabbit

The 52-year calendar of vague solar years combined with the 73 cycles of Augural days is concluded. The next year begins the cycles anew with Year 1 Reed (Acatl) and Day 1 Alligator (Cipactli).

Notes

Chapter 1

1. Peter Martyr's epitaph:

   > *Rerum Aetate Nostra Gestarum*
   > *Et Novi Orbis Ignoti Hactenus*
   > *Illustratori Petro Martyri Mediolanensi*
   > *Caesaro Senatori*
   > *Qui, Patria Relicta*
   > *Bella Gertanatensi Miles Interfuit*
   > *Mox Urbe Capta, Primum Canonico*
   > *Deinde Priori Hujus Ecclesiae*
   > *Decanus Et Capitulum*
   > *Carissimo Collegae Posuerre Sepulchrum*
   > *Anno MDXXVI.*

2. Peter Martyr notes the discovery of the potato (Volume 1:113) and the incredibly poisonous manchineel tree, or death apple, *Hippomane mancinella*, family Euphorbiaceae (Volume 1:211). He is precise and amazingly thorough in his cataloging of New World phenomenology and creatures.

3. Martyr's translator, Francis MacNutt (D'Angleria 1912, 1:238), remarks in his fourth note: "The man may have been a Peruvian or of the civilized plateau people of Cundinamarca. Wiener, in his interesting work, *Perou et Bolivie*, studies the Peruvian system of writing." However, this indigenous man was likely from Panama (Boone 2000:3).

4. Codex Aubin No. 20 is folded into eighths. "Not all the hide codices were folded screenfold style. Some may have been folded horizontally and vertically, as a napkin, and others may have been rolled" (Boone 2000:23).

5. Concerning "erased and reused," Codex Selden (3135A) is entirely a palimpsest painted over an older, erased document. Codex Zouche-Nuttall shows signs of multiple erasures and reworking, especially on the so-called reverse document (Pages 42–84).

Chapter 2

1. I have been unable to find this quotation in MacNutt's 1912 translation of Peter Martyr's *De orbe novo*.
2. Edna St. Vincent Millay, "Renascence," in *Renascence and Other Poems*, www .Bartleby.com/131/, 1999.
3. "Other images" can also mean nonpictorial items such as letters, words, and hieroglyphs.

Chapter 3

1. Jansen and Pérez Jiménez do not seem to recognize the War from Heaven nor the location of the event.

Chapter 4

1. However, Caso (1984, 2:266a) says: "era una hija de ♂ Viento 'Aquila de peder- nales' y de alguna de sus espossas ♀ 5 Hierba 'Venda de perlas' o ♀ 10 Aguila 'Quetzales-telaraña.'"
2. Translation mine.

Chapter 5

1. In the Colonial Period Codex Selden, Lady Six Monkey's name change via change of female garment occurs after a journey through the earth (Selden 6-III) and after she becomes a warrior (Pages 7-IV through 8-III). In Codex Zouche-Nuttall, Lady Three Flint Elder's name change occurs after the Jaltepec ceremonies and after she gives birth to Lady Three Flint Younger. Subsequently, Three Flint Elder journeys beneath the earth. In the Selden passage, no specific subterranean activities are dis- played for Lady Six Monkey; in Zouche-Nuttall, the underworld ceremonies appear in detail.

Chapter 7

1. The codex shows six dots, not five, so there is an error.

Chapter 8

1. The A-O sign looks Zapotec in style. On Zouche-Nuttall Page 33b, ♂ Seven Rain Xipe presides over the marriage of ♂ Five Flower (a Zapotec) and ♀ 4 Rabbit at Mitla.

Bibliography

Adelhofer, Otto

1974. *Codex Vindobonensis Mexicanus I: Vollständige Faksimile-Ausgabe im Originalformat: History and Description of the Manuscript.* Codices selecti phototypice impressi Volume 5. Graz, Austria: Akademische Druck- u. Verlagsanstalt.

Aguilar-Moreno, Manuel

2007. "Aztec Art." www.famsi.org/research/aguilar/Aztec_Art.pdf.

Blanton, Richard E., Gary M. Fineman, Stephen A. Kowaleski, and Linda M. Nicholas

1999. *Ancient Oaxaca.* Cambridge: Cambridge University Press.

Boone, Elizabeth Hill

2000. *Stories in Red and Black: Pictorial Histories of the Aztecs and Mixtecs.* Austin: University of Texas Press.

2007. *Cycles of Time and Meaning in the Mexican Books of Fate.* Austin: University of Texas Press.

Brumfiel, Elizabeth

1989. "Factional Competition in Complex Society." In *Domination and Resistance,* ed. Daniel Miller, Michael Rowlands, and Christopher Tilley, 127–139. London: Unwin Hyman.

Brundage, Burr Cartwright

1979. *The Fifth Sun: Aztec Gods, Aztec World.* Austin: University of Texas Press.

Burgoa, Francisco de

1934[1670]. *Palestra historial.* Publicaciones, vol. 24. Mexico City: Archivo General de la Nación.

Burland, C. A.

1957. "Ancient Mexican Documents in Great Britain." *Man* 57 (May): 76–77.

Byland, Bruce, and John M.D. Pohl

1994. *In the Realm of 8 Deer: The Archaeology of the Mixtec Codices.* Norman: University of Oklahoma Press.

Caso, Alfonso

1949. *El mapa de Teozacoalco*. Mexico City: Editorial Cultura.

1950. "Explicación del Reverso del Codex Vindobonensis Mexicanus I." In *Sobre-tiro de la Memoria del Colegio Nacional* 5(5). Mexico City: El Colegio Nacional de México.

1960. *Interpretation of the Codex Bodley 2858*. Translated by Ruth Morales and revised by John Paddock. Mexico City: Sociedad Mexicana de Antropología.

1964. *Interpretation of the Codex Selden 3135(A.2)*. Translated by Jacinto Quirarte. Revised by John A. Paddock. Mexico City: Sociedad Mexicana de Antropología.

1966. *Interpretation of the Codex Colombino*. Mexico City: Sociedad Mexicana de Antropología.

1971. "Calendrical Systems of Central Mexico." In *Handbook of Middle American Indians*, Robert Wauchope, General Editor, Vol. 10, 333–348. Archaeology of Northern Mesoamerica Series, Part One, Gordon F. Elkholm and Ignacio Bernal, Volume Editors. Austin: University of Texas Press.

1984. *Reyes y reinos de la mixteca*. 2 vols. Mexico City: Fondo de Cultura Económica.

1998. *The Map of Teozacoalco*. Translated by Manuel Aguilar and Claudia Alarcón, Workbook for the Long Workshop of the Texas Meetings at the University of Texas, Austin, Department of Art and Art History.

Clark, Cooper J.

1912. *The Story of "Eight Deer" in Codex Colombino*. London: Taylor and Francis.

D'Angleria, Peter Martyr

1912[1533]. *De rebus oceanicus and orbe novo decadas tres*. Francis Augustine Mac-Nutt, translator. New York: G. P. Putnam's Sons.

Davies, Nigel

1977. *The Toltecs Until the Fall of Tula*. The Civilization of the American Indian Series. Norman and London: University of Oklahoma Press. Reprinted 1987.

Davies, Paul

1995. *About Time: Einstein's Unfinished Revolution*. A Touchstone Book. New York, London, Toronto, Sydney, Tokyo, Singapore: Simon & Schuster.

Diehl, Richard A.

1984. *Tula: The Toltec Capital of Ancient Mexico*. London: Thames and Hudson.

Durán, Diego

1977. *Book of the Gods and Rites and the Ancient Calendar*. Translated and edited by Fernando Horcasitas and Doris Heyden. Foreword by Miguel León-Portilla. Norman: University of Oklahoma Press.

Evans, Susan Toby

2004. *Ancient Mexico and Central America: Archaeology and Culture History*. London: Thames and Hudson.

Flannery, Kent, and Joyce Marcus

1996. *Zapotec Civilization*. London: Thames and Hudson.

Furst, Jill Leslie

1978a. *Codex Vindobonensis Mexicanus I: A Commentary*. Publication Number 4. Albany: Institute for Mesoamerican Studies, State University of New York at Albany.

1978b. "The Life and Times of ♂ 8 Wind 'Flinted Eagle': A Commentary on the First Seven Pages of the 'Obverse' of *Codex Zouche-Nuttall*." *Alcheringa/Ethnopoetics* 4(1): 2–37.

1979. "The Old Gods on the Obverse of Codex Vindobonensis Mexicanus I." Ph.D. diss., University of New Mexico. Ann Arbor, MI: University Microfilms International.

Hamann, Byron

2002. "The Social Life of Pre-Sunrise Things." *Indigenous Mesoamerican Archaeology* 43(1): 351.

Hartig, Otto

1910. "Peter Martyr d'Anghiera." In *Catholic Encyclopedia*, Vol. 9. New York: Robert Appleton and Company. http://www.newadvent.org/cathen/09740a.htm.

Jansen, Maarten

1990. "The Search for History in Mixtec Codices." *Ancient Mesoamerica* 1(1): 99–112.

Jansen, Maarten, and G. A. Pérez Jiménez

2005. *Codex Bodley: A Painted Chronicle from the Mixtec Highlands, Mexico*. Treasures from the Bodleian Library. Oxford: Bodleian Library, University of Oxford.

Joyce, Authur A., Andrew G. Workinger, Byron Hamann, Peter Keroefges, Maxine Oland, and Stacie M. King

2004. "Lord 8 Deer 'Jaguar Claw' and the Land of the Sky: The Archaeology and History of Tututepec." *Latin American Antiquity* 15(3): 273–297.

Klein, Cecelia F.

1993. "Teocuitlatl, 'Divine Excrement': The Significance of 'Holy Shit' in Ancient Mexico." *Art Journal: Scatological Art* 52(3) (Autumn): 20–27.

Klein, Cecelia F., Eulogio Guzmán, Elisa C. Mandell, and Maya Stanfield-Mazzi

2002. "The Role of Shamanism in Mesoamerican Art: A Reassessment." *Current Anthropology* 43(3): 383–419.

Long, Richard C. E.

1926.　"The Zouche Codex." *The Journal of the Royal Anthropological Institute of Great Britain and Ireland* (London) 56 (July–December): 239–258.

McCloud, Scott

1993.　*Understanding Comics: The Invisible Art.* New York: HarperCollins.

Millay, Edna St. Vincent

1945.　*Collected Lyrics.* New York and London: Harper and Brothers.

Miller, Arthur

1975.　Introduction to the Dover Edition of *The Codex Nuttall: A Picture Manuscript from Ancient Mexico.* Edited by Zelia Nuttall, with new introductory text by Arthur G. Miller. New York: Dover Publications.

Millon, Rene

1988.　"Where Do They All Come From? The Provenance of the Wagner Murals from Teotihuacan." In *Feathered Serpents and Flowering Trees: Reconstructing the Murals of Teotihuacan,* ed. Kathleen Berrin, 78–113. Seattle: University of Washington Press.

Monaghan, John

1990.　"Performance and the Structure of the Mixtec Codices." *Ancient Mesoamerica* (Cambridge University Press) 1(1): 133–140.

Moreno García, Pilar, and Marta Torres Santo Domingo

2008.　The *"Biblioteca Histórica"* (Historical Library) of the Universidad Complutense de Madrid and Its Travel Book Collection. Translated by Icíar Muguerza López. World Library and Information Congress (IFLA), Quebec, 02/07/2008. http://www.ifla.org/IV/ifla74/index.htm.

Nicholson, H. B.

2001.　*Topiltzin Quetzalcoatl: The Once and Future Lord of the Toltecs.* Boulder: University Press of Colorado. Originally published 1966.

Nicholson, Irene

1985.　*Mexican and Central American Mythology.* Library of the World's Myths and Legends. New York: Peter Bedrick Books. Originally published 1967.

Nuttall, Zelia Maria Magdalena

1902.　Introduction to *Codex Nuttall: Facsimile of an Ancient Mexican Codex Belonging to Lord Zouche of Harynworth, England.* Cambridge: Peabody Museum of American Archaeology and Ethnology, Harvard University.

Paddock, John

1985.　"Tezcatlipoca in Oaxaca." *Ethnohistory* 32(4): 309–325.

1985.　"Covert Content in Codices Borgia and Nuttall." *Ethos* 13(4): 358–380.

Pohl, John M.D.

1991.   *Aztec, Mixtec and Zapotec Armies.* Illustrated by Angus McBride. London: Osprey Publishing.

1994.   *The Politics of Symbolism in the Mixtec Codices.* Nashville, TN: Vanderbilt University Publications in Anthropology.

2002.   *Narrative Art, Craft Production, and Gift Economy in Postclassic Oaxaca and Related Areas of Mexico: Workbook for the Advanced Mixtec Class.* Mixtec Workshop at the Maya Meetings at Austin, University of Texas, March 10–16. Austin: Department of Art and Art History, University of Texas.

Rabin, Emily

1979.   "The War of Heaven in Codices Zouche-Nuttall and Bodley: A Preliminary Study." *Actes du XLII Congrés International des Américanistes* (Paris: ICA) 7: 171–182.

Reilly, F. Kent, III

1995.   "Art, Ritual, and Rulership in the Olmec World." In *The Olmec World: Ritual and Rulership,* by Michael Coe, et al., 27–47. Princeton, NJ: The Art Museum, Princeton University.

Renfrew, Colin, and Paul Bahn

2004.   *Archaeology: Theories, Methods, and Practice.* London: Thames and Hudson.

Smith, Mary Elizabeth

1963.   "The Codex Colombino: A Document of the South Coast of Oaxaca." *Tlalocan* 4(3): 276–288.

1973.   *Picture Writing from Ancient Southern Mexico: Mixtec Place Signs and Maps.* Civilization of the American Indian Series. Norman: University of Oklahoma Press.

Stark, Barbara

n.d.   Proyecto Arqueológico La Mixtequilla. Archaeology.asu.edu/vm/meso america/PALM/PALM_pub.html.

Steele, Barbara Fitzsimmons

1997.   "Cave Rituals in Oaxaca, Mexico." Paper presented at the 1997 Convention of the Society for American Archaeology, Nashville, Tennessee.

Stephens, John Lloyd

1969[1841].   *Incidents of Travel in Central America, Chiapas and Yucatan, with 111 Illustrations in Two Volumes.* Volume 1. New York: Dover Publications.

Stross, Brian

2006.   "Maize in Word and Image in Southeastern Mesoamerica." In *Histories of Maize,* ed. John Staller, Robert Tykot, and Bruce Benz, 578–599. Waltham, MA: Academic Press (Elsevier).

Taube, Karl

1986. "The Writing Systems of Ancient Teotihuacan." *Ancient America* 1: 85, 88.

Tedlock, Dennis

1985. *Popul Vuh: The Definitive Version of the Mayan Book of the Dawn of Life and the Glories of Gods and Kings.* A Touchstone Book. New York: Simon & Schuster.

Toorians, Lauran.

1983. "Some Light in the Dark Century of Codex Vindobonensis Mexicanus I." *Codices manuscripti* (Vienna) 9(1): 26–29.

1984. "Codex Vindobonensis Mexicanus I, Its History Completed." *Codices manuscripti* (Vienna) 10(3): 87–97.

Tozzer, Alfred M.

1933. "Obituary: Zelia Nuttall." *American Anthropologist* New Series 35(3): 475–482.

Troike, Nancy P.

1978. "Fundamental Changes in the Interpretations of the Mixtec Codices." *American Antiquity* 43(4): 553–568.

1987. Introduction to *Codex Zouche-Nuttall.* British Museum London (Add. MS. 39671). Vollständige Faksimile-Ausgabe des Codex im Originalformat. Graz, Austria: Akademische Druck- u. Verlagsanstalt.

Tyler, Stephen A.

1986. "Post-Modern Ethnography: From Document of the Occult to Occult Document." In *Writing Culture: The Poetics and Politics of Ethnography*, ed. James Clifford and George E. Marcus, 122–140. Berkeley: University of California Press.

Williams, Robert Lloyd

1991. "Codex Zouche-Nuttall 'Obverse': Summary of Contents." In *Texas Notes on Precolumbian Art, Writing and Culture* 20–24 (September). CHAAAC, Department of Art, University of Texas, Austin.

2004. "The Aztec/Mixtec Calendar." Unpublished manuscript.

2006. "The History of Lord Eight Wind of Suchixtlan: A Chronological Analysis and Commentary on Codex Zouche-Nuttall, Pages One through Eight." Master's thesis, Texas State University-San Marcos.

2009. *Lord Eight Wind of Suchixtlan and the Heroes of Ancient Oaxaca: Reading History in the Codex Zouche-Nuttall.* Austin: University of Texas Press.

Williams, Robert Lloyd, Rex Kuntz, and Timothy Albright

1993. "Eight Deer Plays Ball Again: Notes on a New Codiacal Cognate. In: *Texas Notes on Precolumbian Art, Writing, and Culture* 50 (March). CHAAAC, Department of Art, University of Texas, Austin.

Undated Electronic Documents

Undated. Jamaica National Heritage Trust. Our Lady of Perpetual Help/St. Ann. Data on Peter Martyr d'Angleria, Italy. http://www.jnht.com/heritage_site.php?id=91.

Undated. "Peter Martyr d'Anghiera." *Wikipedia the Free Encyclopedia.* http://en.wikipedia.org/wiki/Peter_Martyr_d'Anghiera.

Index

Italic page numbers refer to figures and tables.

Eagle Warriors, 51, 52
Earthquake Hill, 171
effigy heads, 121
Eight Death, Lord, 174
Eight Deer, Lady, 129
Eight Deer Jaguar Claw, Lord: assassination of, 151; assassination of Lord Twelve Motion and the Siege of Hua Chino, 212, 215; Battle in the Sky and Eight Deer becomes Sun God Lord, 46, 203, 204–209, 214; birth and death of, 146; and ceremonies, 123, 157, 160, 162, 173–174, 210; Chalcatongo Event, 151, 157, 160, 161, 162, 163, 164; and childhood military career, 152, 155, 156–157, 159–160, 164; and communication with the dead, 34, 142; conference with 112 Lords, 176, 195; conquests with Tolteca/Chichimeca, 174; death of, 221; genealogy of, 12, 99, 102, 103, 132, 133, 150, 220–221; and Hua Chino, 23, 45, 81, 214–215; and Lady Nine Reed, 170–174; and Lady Six Monkey, 151; and Lord Eight Wind, 140; as lord of Tilantongo, 174; as lord of Tututepec, 123, 146, 150, 157, 160, 161–164, 231; and Lord Twelve Motion, 32, 156, 157, 160, 163, 171, 172, 176, 195, 205, 209, 210; and Lord Two Rain, 44; and Oracle of the Dead at Chalcatongo, 34, 45, 151, 160, 161, 162, 163, 169, 231; and parentage statement, 152, 155, 164; peregrinations from Tilantongo and ceremonies and conquests with Toltecs, 195–197, 200–201, 203; political biography of, 14, 31, 32, 45, 53, 99, 139, 142, 149, 150, 156, 221, 230; Sun God nose ornament, 209, 212; territorial expansions of Tututepec hegemony, 150, 164, 166, 169; Toltec Alliance, 15, 103, 140, 150, 172–174, 195–197,

200–201, 203; Toltec nose ornament, 164, 174, 209, 212; transition to Tututepec, 157
Eight House, Lady, 94, 96
Eight Lizard, Lady, 51, 53
Eight Snake, Lord, 174
Eight Wind Eagle Flints of Suchixtlan, Lord: and Apoala, 141; biography of, 32, 33, 39, 40–41, 52, 53, 54–55, 115, 142, 148; birth of, 70, 141; death of, 44, 88; family of, 42–44, 51, 53, 143; introduction of, 35–36, 37, 39, 51, 127, 139, 143; lack of precedent ancestry, 139; as lineage founder, 42–43, 53–54, 115, 118, 132, 140, 144, 218, 231; mummy of, 34, 44, 45, 46, 53, 140, 142; and sacred plants, 37–39, 143; and Yucuñudahui, 30, 143
El Baúl Stela, Guatemala, 27
Eleven Alligator, Lord, 79
Eleven Caves Hill, Holy Tree Ceremony, 157, 160
Eleven Snake, Lady, 129
Eleven Snake, Lord, 209
Eleven Water, Lady, 101, 102, 155, 156
Eleven Wind, Lord, 23, 29, 45, 220, 229–230
Epiclassic Period, 138, 148
events: forward progression of, 124, 126, 139; and Mesoamerican calendar, 27; and reading order, 31–32, 39

FAMSI (Foundation for the Advancement of Mesoamerican Studies, Inc.), 16
fire-drilling bundle, 73, 118, 144
fire-drilling paraphernalia complex, 74, 79, 80, 96, 118, 129, 144
Fire Serpent Ballcourt, 69, 70, 74, 80, 81, 118
Fire Serpent Hill, 204, 207, 212
Five Alligator, Lord: biography of, 101–103; and Council of Four, 101, 103;

death of, 161, 162; families of, 32, 101, 102, 152, 155; marriages of, 101, 102, 132–133, 152, 156; parents of, 99, 101; and third story of Codex Zouche-Nuttall, 140

Five Beans Town, 169

Five Caves Island Town, 204

Five Death, Lady, 129

Five Deer, Lady, 48–49, 52

Five Dog, Lord, 79, 103–104

Five Flower, Lord: apotheosis of, 73, 78, 91, 123, 144; and ceremonies, 70, 72, 74, 77–78, 144; and founding story, 67, 139; and Lady Eight Lizard, 51, 53; and Lady Three Flint Elder, 65, 66, 67, 71, 77–78, 91, 139, 144, 148; and Lady Three Flint Younger, 76; and processions, 68, 69, 70

Five Flower at Zaachila, Lord, 106, 127, 145

Five Jaguar, Lady, 81

Five Motion, Lord, 99

Five Reed, Lady, 81, 90, 95, 97–98

Five Snake, Lady, 74

Five Vulture, Lord, 74

Five Wind, Lord, 118, 119, 142

Fondo de Cultura Económica, Mexico City, 20

Four Alligator, Lord: and fire-drilling-bundle cult, 144; and Lady One Death, 81, 89, 90, 91, 94; and Lord Twelve Wind Smoke-Eye, 79; parents of, 129

Four Death, Lord, 72, 91, 122, 123

Four Deer, Lord, 72, 91, 122, 123

Four House, Lord, 74, 87–88, 90, 140

Four Jaguar, Lady, 90

Four Jaguar, Lord, 68

Four Jaguar the Toltec, Lord: ambassadors of, 162; in ballcourt, 212; and bird-decapitation sacrifice, 174; with gift, 212; and Lord Eight Deer Jaguar Claw, 164, 170, 171, 173, 197,

205, 209, 212; and Sun God, 208; in Toltec-style canoe, 204

Four Lizard, Lord, 94, 96

Four Motion, Lord, 41, 73, 129, 140, 207

Four Rabbit, Lord, 81, 90, 95

Four Rabbit at Mitla, Lady, 106, 145, 162

Four Rain, Lord, 96

Four Snake, Lord: and bird sacrifice, 41; and ceremonies, 118, 129; insignia of, 130; and Lady One Death, 90; parents of, 127, 129; and processions, 120–121, 127–128; as sacrificial victim, 123; and third story of Codex Zouche-Nuttall, 140

Four Wind, Lord, 12, 151, 197, 214, 229, 230, 231

Furst, Jill Leslie, 9, 14, 130, 170

García, Luis Reyes, 20

grass knots, 38, 121, 169

grass mats, 38–39, 79, 89, 117, 121, 123, 169, 197

Gregorian calendar, 28

Hearts Temple, 123

Hua Chino (Red-and-White bundle): lineage of, 81; and Lord Eight Deer Jaguar Claw, 23, 45, 81, 212, 215; as polity, 90; siege of, 212, 215; temple of, 229; Tilantongo's political rivalry with, 81, 95, 142, 161; and Wasp Hill, 95

human sacrifice: and Lady Six Monkey, 229; and Lord Eight Deer Jaguar Claw, 206, 215; and Lord Four Jaguar, 68; and Lord Nine Flower, 196; and Lord Nine Wind Quetzalcoatl, 122, 123, 128; Martyr d'Anghera on, 3; and War from Heaven, 41; and Xipe-Totec, 130–131

Imperial Library of Vienna, 13

Incense and Plumes Plains, 205

Mixteca/Puebla art style, 138

Mixtec calendar: and AD eras, *29*; and calendar as memory, 28–29; complete Mixtec/Aztec calendar, 247–320; cycle correspondences, 246; cycle of 260 days (*tonalpohualli*), 236–238; and Julian calendar dates, 28, 54; and Lord Five Alligator, 155; occurrence of 260-day sacred calendars in 365-day Mixtec solar calendar, 234–235; pictogram tableaux connected by chronological markers in, 25, 27; schematic of Aztec/Mixtec calendar, 233

Mixtec manuscripts: Caso Andrade on, 17–18; in Europe, 11, 15, 18–19; and history, 21–23, 34, 218–231; and occulted information, 231; pictogram tableaux in, 25; Pohl on, 9, 16. *See also* Codex Bodley; Codex Colombino-Becker I Fragments (Codex Alfonso Caso); Codex Selden; Codex Vindobonensis Mexicanus I; Codex Zouche-Nuttall

Mixtec people: chronological perspective of history, 147–148; deities of, 130; and Lord Seven Rain, 131; lords of, 176, 195; and Toltecs, 53, 55; and Zapotecs, 39

Mixtec pictogram documents: Adelhofer on, 11–12; corrections and erasures in, 31, 149; and dates as written metaphor, 147; juxtaposition of pictorial and other images, 22, 322n3; mnemonic nature of, 11, 21, 22, 28–29, 218, 231; motion picture analogy, 22; narrative structure of, 21, 22–23, 25; reading order of, 25–26; sequential progression of images, 22; and transmission of historical knowledge, 11, 21–22; vertical or horizontal bands of linear text in, 25–26. *See also* pictogram tableaux

Mixtequilla, 12, 18

Monte Albán, 148

Monte Albán I phase, 27

Monte Negro, 94, 95, 96, 97, 140

Montezuma II: library of, 11, 12, 15, 18

Mouth Mountain, 162

mummies: and communication with the dead, 34, 44, 45, 53; Lord Eight Wind, 34, 44, 45, 46, 53, 140, 142; Lord Two Rain Twenty Jaguars, 34, 45–46, 142, 215; mummy-bundling ceremonies, 41, 97, 142–143, 212; Parliament of Mummies, 44–46

myth history, 21

Naked Woman with Wrinkled Abdomen Hill, 209

narrative structure: and boustrophedon, 152; of Codex Zouche-Nuttall, 16, 23, 29–30; of Codex Zouche-Nuttall (Obverse), 33–34, 46, 116, 139–142, 144, 152; and concordant narratives, 23; of Mixtec pictogram documents, 21, 22–23, 25; of open writing, 1; and reciters, 88

New World indigenous books: construction of, 4–5, 15; contents of, 5; documentation of, 1, 4–7; types of, 5–6. *See also* indigenous New World writing

New World indigenous peoples, 3, 12. *See also specific peoples*

Nicholson, H. B., 138

Nine Alligator, Lady, 118, 119, 142, 155

Nine Alligator, Lord, 73, 79

Nine Eagle, Lady, 102, 152, 156

Nine Flower, Lord: birth of, 102, 156; and ceremonies, 73; and human sacrifice, 196; and Lord Eight Deer Jaguar Claw, 173; and processions, 79; as sacrifice victim, 204, 207, 212

Nine Grass, Lady. *See* Oracle of the Dead at Chalcatongo

Nine House, Lady, 96

ditions, 21. *See also* performers and performances; reciters

Peabody Museum, Harvard, 9, 10, 19, 20, 170
Pérez Jiménez, G. A., 28, 102, 322n1
performers and performances: and conflation in presentation, 151, 231; and flexibility in reading order, 39, 46–47, 126; of indigenous history, 21, 22–23, 28, 218; and narrative structure, 29–30; and two-page sections, 46
Peter Martyr Church, Sevilla la Nueva, Jamaica, 3
Peter the Martyr of Verona, 2
Phillip II (king of Spain), 12
pictogram tableaux: chronological markers in, 25, 27, 36; and concordant narratives, 23; and conflation, 151, 231; corrections and erasures in, 31; Mixteca/Puebla art style, 138; in Mixtec manuscripts, 25; as mnemonic devices, 28, 139, 151, 218; open writing as, 1; reading order of, 27, 30, 32. *See also* Mixtec pictogram documents
Place Where the Sky Is Held Up, 204
Plume Sun Plain, 207
poetry, 21–22
Pohl, John M.D.: on Ayuta/Atoyaquillo, 100; on Codex Zouche-Nuttall Page 15, 70; on Lord Eight Deer Jaguar Claw, 163; and Mixtec chronology, 28, 246; on Mixtec manuscripts, 9, 16; on Mixtec pictogram documents, 22; on Tilantongo, 103
Popocatépetl, 68
Proyecto Arqueológico La Mixtequilla, 12

Quetzal Hill, 49

Rabbit Hill, 96
Rabin, Emily, 28

Rain God effigy, 121, 141, 205
Rain God Town, 160
reading techniques: and boustrophedon, 15, 25, 26, 32, 46, 115, 116, 139, 145, 149, 150, 152, 159, 201, 214–215; and calendar as memory, 28–39; circular reading order, 36, 133; and Codex Zouche-Nuttall, 26–27; and Codex Zouche-Nuttall (Reverse), 150; and footpaths, 115, 116, 117, 124, 126, 128, 138, 139, 145, 149; and occulted data, 29–30, 36–37, 116, 117, 126, 151, 221, 230, 231; and similarity of dates, 36; and subtle techniques of scribes, 31–32; and visual stop, 117
reciters: and chronology, 29; and conflation in presentation, 151, 231; and pictogram tableaux as mnemonic devices, 28, 139, 151, 218; and subtle techniques of scribes, 26, 31–32, 88; and two-page sections, 46
Relaciones Geográficas, 17
Ribera, 6
Rising Ñuu, 207
River of the Tree, 49

Sacrificed Cormorant Hill and Town, 166
San Pedro Jicayán, 67
Sawyer, Johann, 37
Sayutepec, 116, 117, 122–124, 145, 146–147
Schönberg, Nikolaus, 13
scribal strategies: and corrections and erasure, 31, 133; distinguishing dates and names, 33, 117; and folding out to omit data, 33, 39; and Mixtec calendar usage, 27, 28; and reading order, 26, 31, 32; and retrospective writing, 94, 142; subtle techniques, 26, 31–32, 88; and Time's Arrow, 29–30, 36; and visual creativity, 116
Serpent Ballcourt, 144

Two Reed, Lord, 68
Two Spindles Town, 157
Two Stalks Hill, 166

Venus staff, 74, 79, 80, 89, 124, 174
Venus Staff Hill, 166
Veracruz, Mexico, 12, 18

War from Heaven narrative: beginning
of, 30, 86, 148; and Codex Zouche-
Nuttall, Document 1 (Obverse) Pages
3–4, 23, 35, 36, 39, 40–42, 115; ending of, 76, 89, 140, 141, 143, 148; folding out to omit data, 33, 39, 66, 94,
115–116; and Mixtec chronology, 28,
322n1; and plant bundles, 86–87; and
postwar chronology, *146*; and reading order, 29–30, 36, 37; War with
the Stone Men, 35, 40, 42, 87–88,
127, 148; War with the Striped Men,
35, 40–41, 42, 88–89; Wasp Hill destroyed in, 31, 76, 78, 81, 90, 95, 144
Wasp Hill: dynastic territory of, 47, 90;
and footpath, 115; and Lady One
Death, 81, 90, 91, 141, 144; lineage of,
33, 76, 77, 78, 81, 86, 90, 94, 95, 97,
139, 144, 145; royal temple of, 74, 79,
80, 145; and Tilantongo, 94, 95, 145;

and War from Heaven, 31, 76, 78,
81, 90, 95, 144; and Zapotecs, 148
water creatures, 204
Water Top Hill, 166
Weeping Man Town, 203
White Flint Hill, 89
White Hill, 166
White Olla Hill, 166
Widmanstetter, Johann Albrecht, 13
Wilhelm IV of Saxe-Weimar, 13

Xipe-Totec (deity), 130–131
Xochimilca, 53

Yanhuitlán, 116
Year 1 Reed, and Mesoamerican calendar, 27
Year 1 Reed Day 1 Alligator, as metaphor
for "beginning," 47, 54, 234
Yucuñudahui (Rain God Hill), 30, 37, 38,
39, 89, 143

Zaachila, genealogies, 105–106
Zapotecs: and Codex Zouche-Nuttall, 16;
dynasties of, 148; and Mixtec calendar, 155; and Mixtec lords of Teozacoalco, 145; and Mixtec people, 39
Zuazo, Juan Ruiz, 107

Turn to end of book to begin reading the codex.

Codex Zouche-Nuttall (reverse), Page 84. © The Trustees of the British Museum.

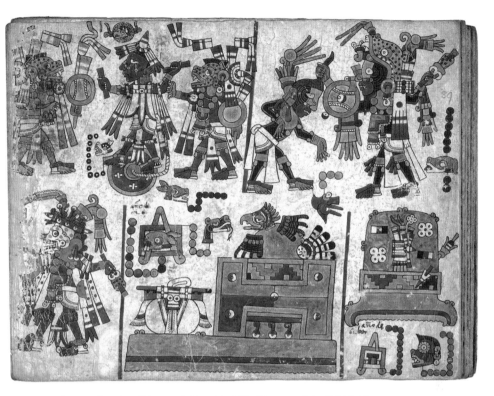

Codex Zouche-Nuttall (reverse), Page 83. © The Trustees of the British Museum.

Codex Zouche-Nuttall (reverse), Page 82. © The Trustees of the British Museum.

Codex Zouche-Nuttall (reverse), Page 81. © The Trustees of the British Museum.

Codex Zouche-Nuttall (reverse), Page 80. © The Trustees of the British Museum.

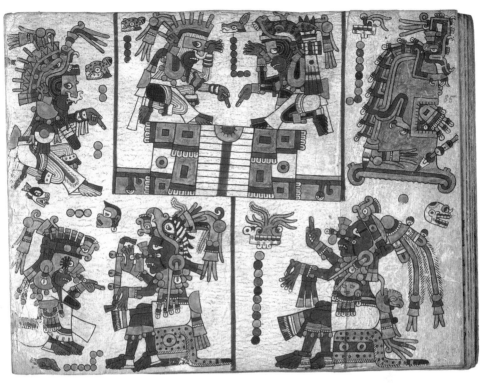

Codex Zouche-Nuttall (reverse), Page 79. © The Trustees of the British Museum.

Codex Zouche-Nuttall (reverse), Page 78. © The Trustees of the British Museum.

Codex Zouche-Nuttall (reverse), Page 77. © The Trustees of the British Museum.

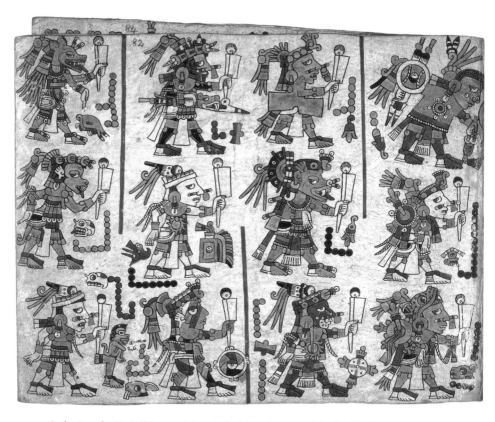

Codex Zouche-Nuttall (reverse), Page 76b. © The Trustees of the British Museum.

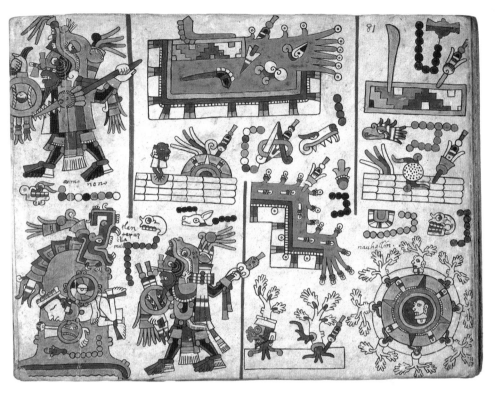

Codex Zouche-Nuttall (reverse), Page 76a. © The Trustees of the British Museum.

Codex Zouche-Nuttall (reverse), Page 75. © The Trustees of the British Museum.

Codex Zouche-Nuttall (reverse), Page 74. © The Trustees of the British Museum.

Codex Zouche-Nuttall (reverse), Page 73. © The Trustees of the British Museum.

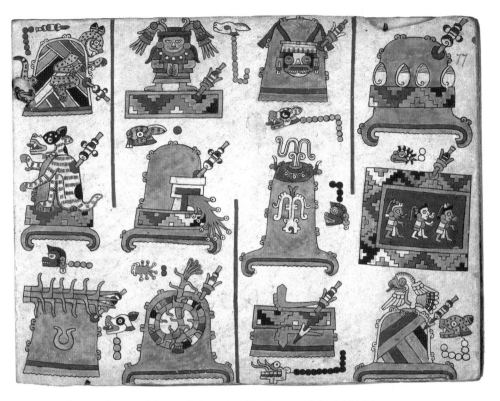

Codex Zouche-Nuttall (reverse), Page 72. © The Trustees of the British Museum.

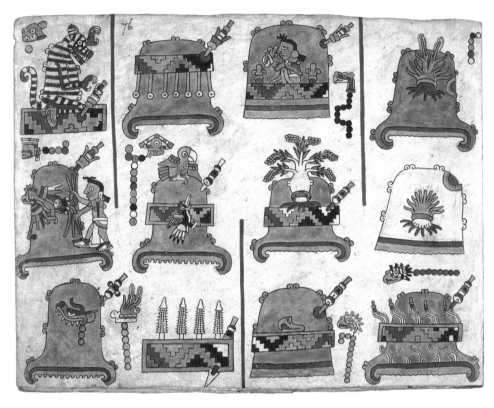

Codex Zouche-Nuttall (reverse), Page 71. © The Trustees of the British Museum.

Codex Zouche-Nuttall (reverse), Page 70. © The Trustees of the British Museum.

Codex Zouche-Nuttall (reverse), Page 69. © The Trustees of the British Museum.

Codex Zouche-Nuttall (reverse), Page 68. © The Trustees of the British Museum.

Codex Zouche-Nuttall (reverse), Page 67. © The Trustees of the British Museum.

Codex Zouche-Nuttall (reverse), Page 66. © The Trustees of the British Museum.

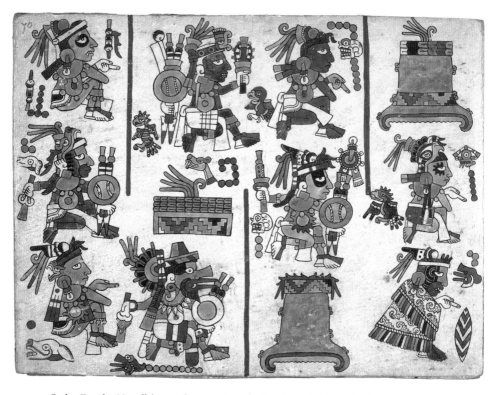

Codex Zouche-Nuttall (reverse), Page 65. © The Trustees of the British Museum.

Codex Zouche-Nuttall (reverse), Page 64. © The Trustees of the British Museum.

Codex Zouche-Nuttall (reverse), Page 63. © The Trustees of the British Museum.

Codex Zouche-Nuttall (reverse), Page 62. © The Trustees of the British Museum.

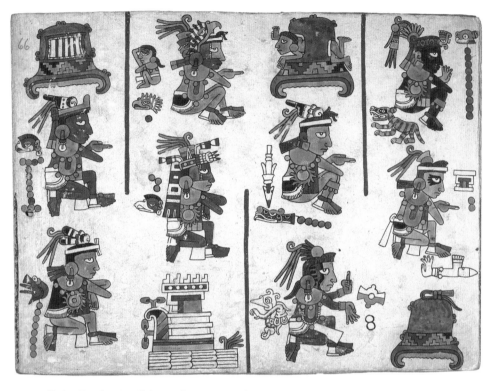

Codex Zouche-Nuttall (reverse), Page 61. © The Trustees of the British Museum.

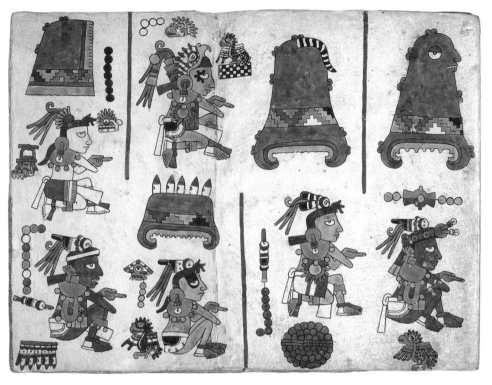

Codex Zouche-Nuttall (reverse), Page 60. © The Trustees of the British Museum.

Codex Zouche-Nuttall (reverse), Page 59. © The Trustees of the British Museum.

Codex Zouche-Nuttall (reverse), Page 58. © The Trustees of the British Museum.

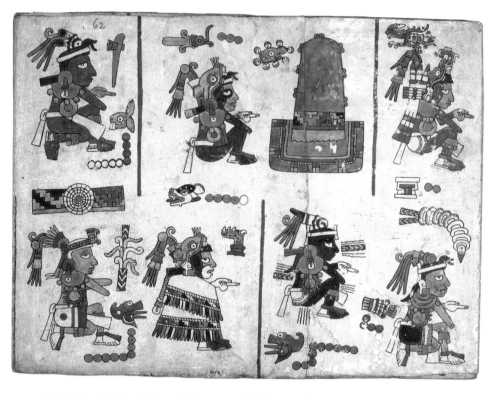

Codex Zouche-Nuttall (reverse), Page 57. © The Trustees of the British Museum.

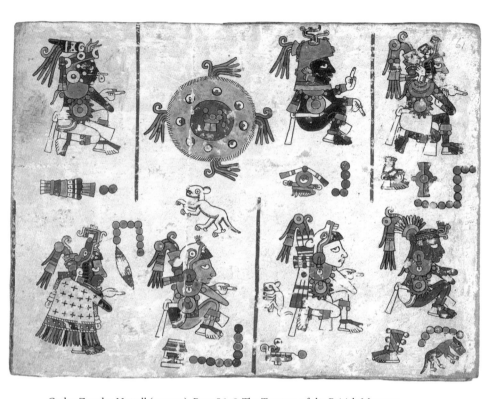

Codex Zouche-Nuttall (reverse), Page 56. © The Trustees of the British Museum.

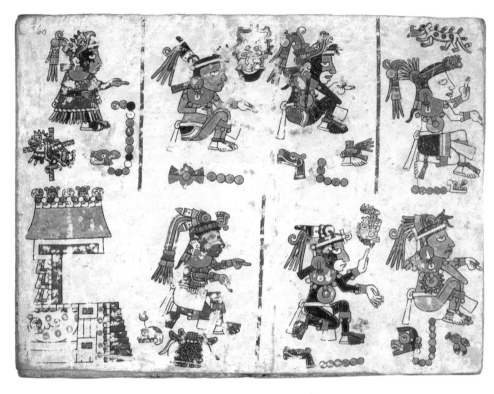

Codex Zouche-Nuttall (reverse), Page 55. © The Trustees of the British Museum.

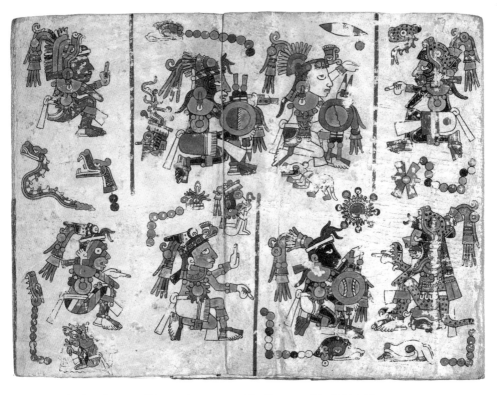

Codex Zouche-Nuttall (reverse), Page 54. © The Trustees of the British Museum.

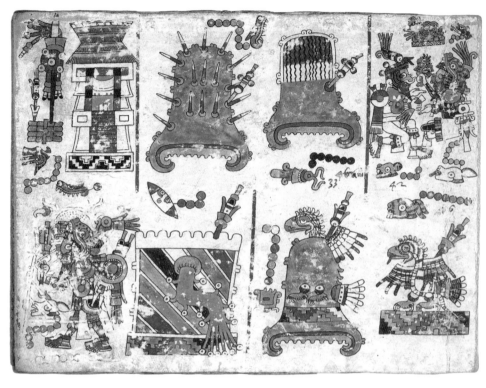

Codex Zouche-Nuttall (reverse), Page 53. © The Trustees of the British Museum.

Codex Zouche-Nuttall (reverse), Page 52. © The Trustees of the British Museum.

Codex Zouche-Nuttall (reverse), Page 51. © The Trustees of the British Museum.

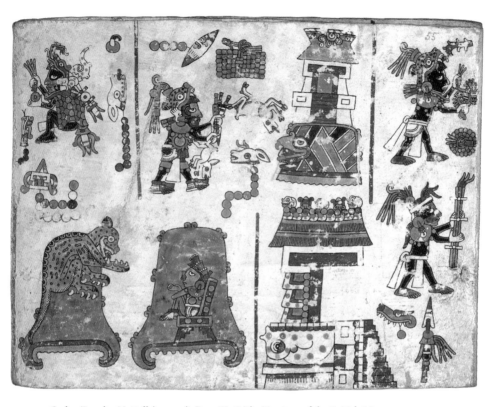

Codex Zouche-Nuttall (reverse), Page 50. © The Trustees of the British Museum.

Codex Zouche-Nuttall (reverse), Page 49. © The Trustees of the British Museum.

Codex Zouche-Nuttall (reverse), Page 48. © The Trustees of the British Museum.

Codex Zouche-Nuttall (reverse), Page 47. © The Trustees of the British Museum.

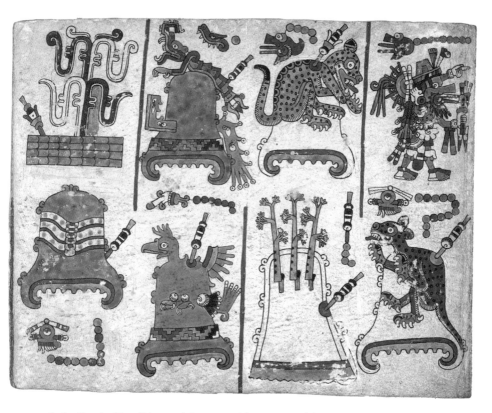

Codex Zouche-Nuttall (reverse), Page 46. © The Trustees of the British Museum.

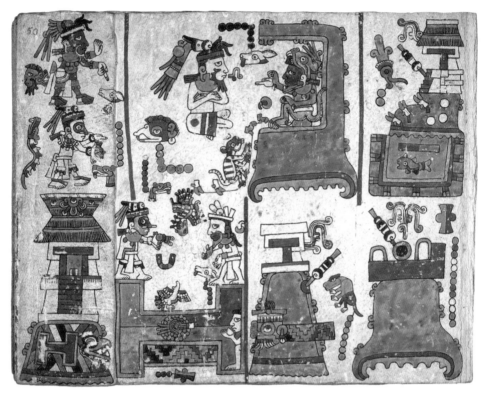

Codex Zouche-Nuttall (reverse), Page 45. © The Trustees of the British Museum.

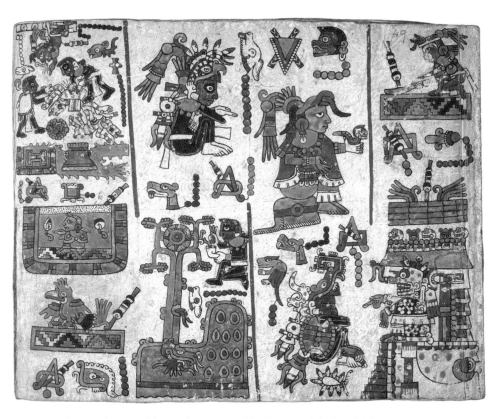

Codex Zouche-Nuttall (reverse), Page 44. © The Trustees of the British Museum.

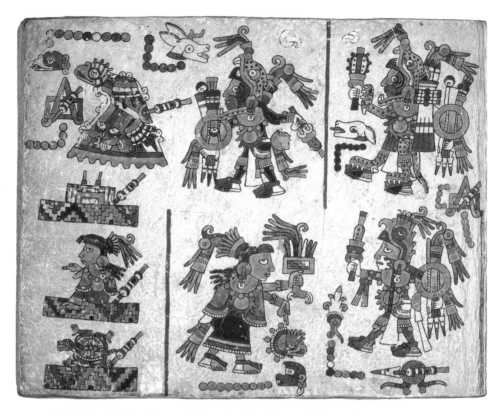

Codex Zouche-Nuttall (reverse), Page 43. © The Trustees of the British Museum.

Codex Zouche-Nuttall (reverse), Page 42. © The Trustees of the British Museum.

Codex Zouche-Nuttall (obverse), Page 41. © The Trustees of the British Museum.

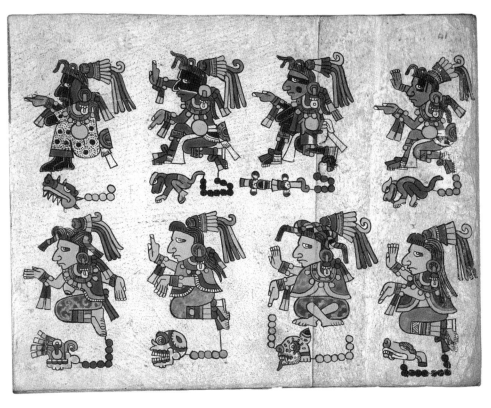

Codex Zouche-Nuttall (obverse), Page 40. © The Trustees of the British Museum.

Codex Zouche-Nuttall (obverse), Page 39. © The Trustees of the British Museum.

Codex Zouche-Nuttall (obverse), Page 38. © The Trustees of the British Museum.

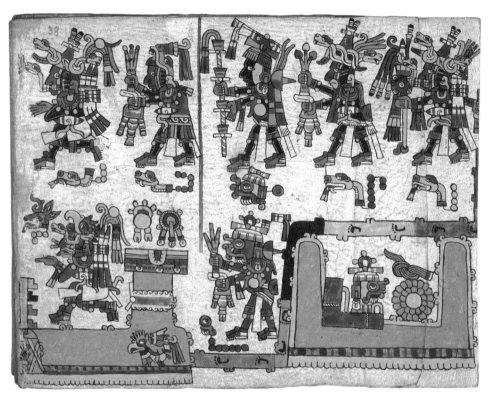

Codex Zouche-Nuttall (obverse), Page 37. © The Trustees of the British Museum.

Codex Zouche-Nuttall (obverse), Page 36. © The Trustees of the British Museum.

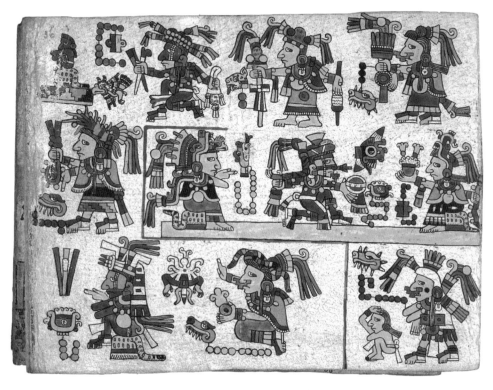

Codex Zouche-Nuttall (obverse), Page 35. © The Trustees of the British Museum.

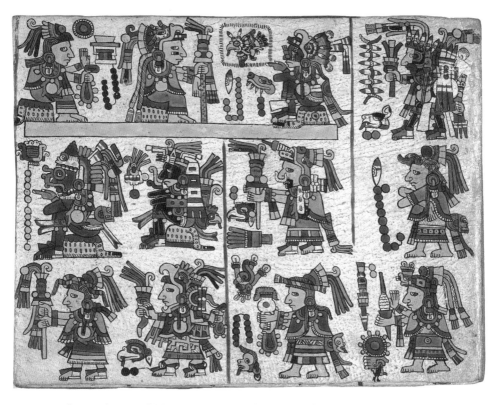

Codex Zouche-Nuttall (obverse), Page 34. © The Trustees of the British Museum.

Codex Zouche-Nuttall (obverse), Page 33. © The Trustees of the British Museum.

Codex Zouche-Nuttall (obverse), Page 32. © The Trustees of the British Museum.

Codex Zouche-Nuttall (obverse), Page 31. © The Trustees of the British Museum.

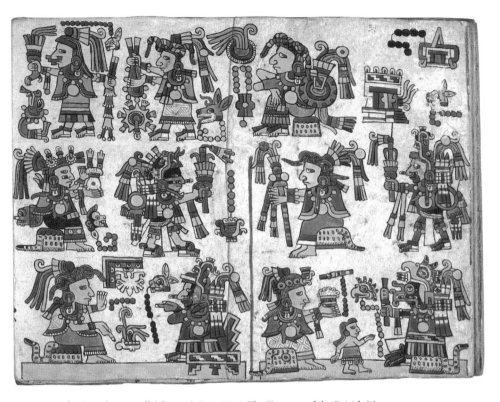

Codex Zouche-Nuttall (obverse), Page 30. © The Trustees of the British Museum.

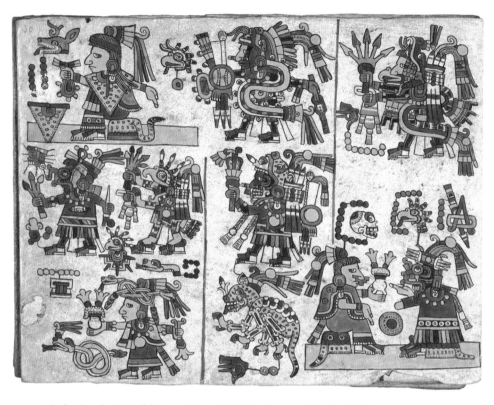

Codex Zouche-Nuttall (obverse), Page 29. © The Trustees of the British Museum.

Codex Zouche-Nuttall (obverse), Page 28. © The Trustees of the British Museum.

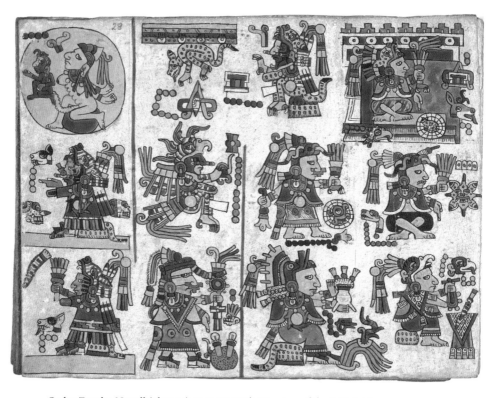

Codex Zouche-Nuttall (obverse), Page 27. © The Trustees of the British Museum.

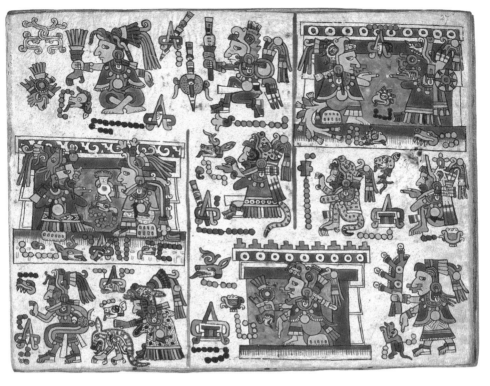

Codex Zouche-Nuttall (obverse), Page 26. © The Trustees of the British Museum.

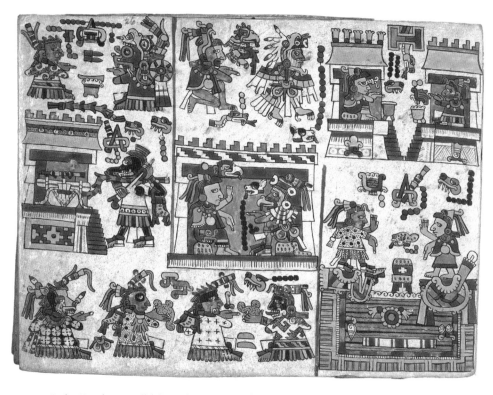

Codex Zouche-Nuttall (obverse), Page 25. © The Trustees of the British Museum.

Codex Zouche-Nuttall (obverse), Page 24. © The Trustees of the British Museum.

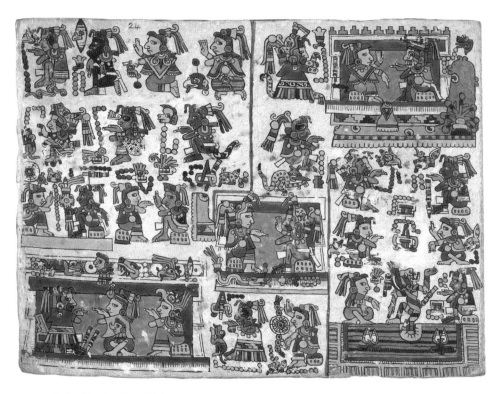

Codex Zouche-Nuttall (obverse), Page 23. © The Trustees of the British Museum.

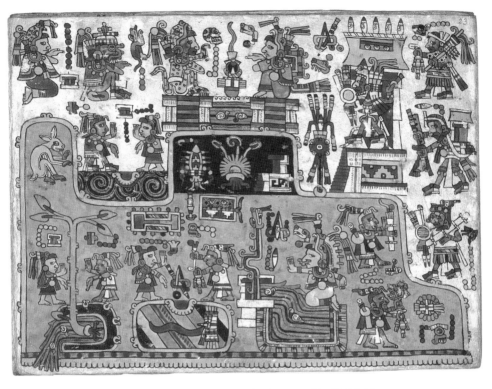

Codex Zouche-Nuttall (obverse), Page 22. © The Trustees of the British Museum.

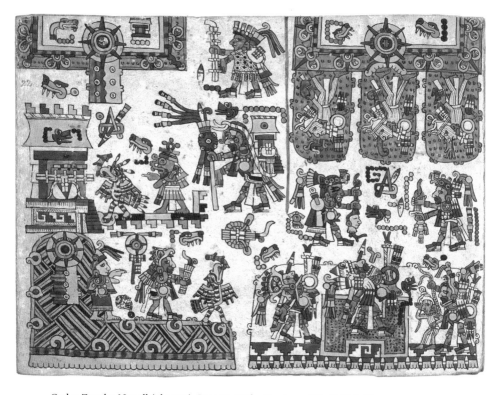

Codex Zouche-Nuttall (obverse), Page 21. © The Trustees of the British Museum.

Codex Zouche-Nuttall (obverse), Page 20. © The Trustees of the British Museum.

Codex Zouche-Nuttall (obverse), Page 19b. © The Trustees of the British Museum.

Codex Zouche-Nuttall (obverse), Page 19a. © The Trustees of the British Museum.

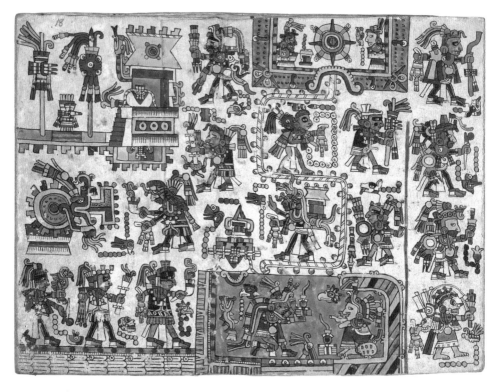

Codex Zouche-Nuttall (obverse), Page 18. © The Trustees of the British Museum.

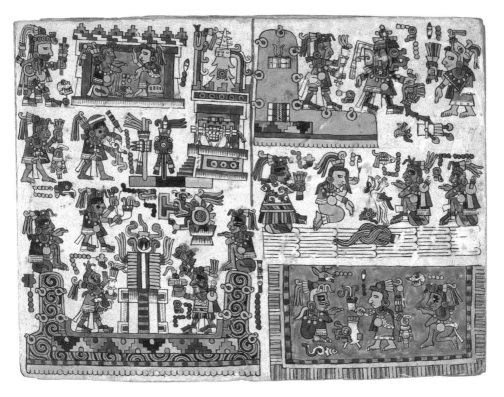

Codex Zouche-Nuttall (obverse), Page 17. © The Trustees of the British Museum.

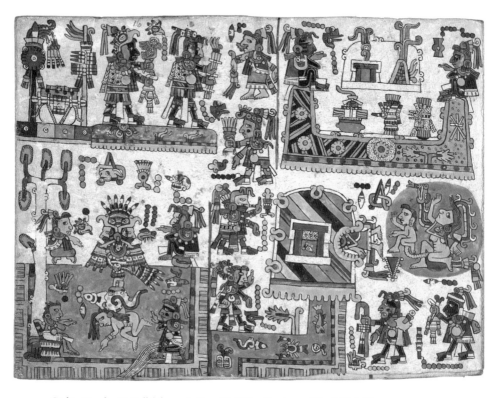

Codex Zouche-Nuttall (obverse), Page 16. © The Trustees of the British Museum.

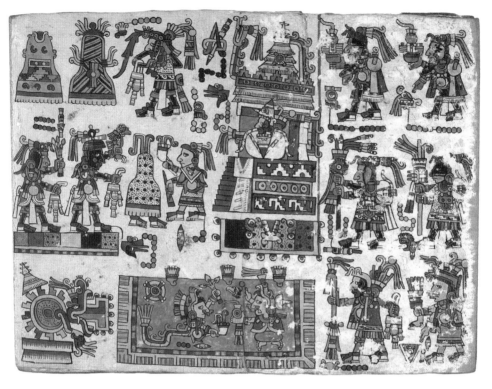

Codex Zouche-Nuttall (obverse), Page 15. © The Trustees of the British Museum.

Codex Zouche-Nuttall (obverse), Page 14. © The Trustees of the British Museum.

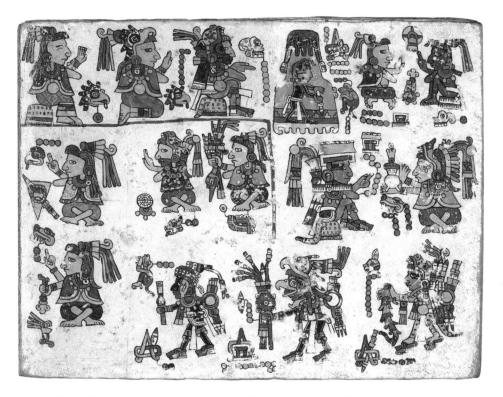

Codex Zouche-Nuttall (obverse), Page 13. © The Trustees of the British Museum.

Codex Zouche-Nuttall (obverse), Page 12. © The Trustees of the British Museum.

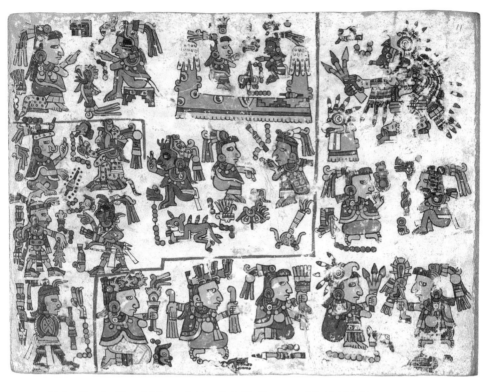

Codex Zouche-Nuttall (obverse), Page 11. © The Trustees of the British Museum.

Codex Zouche-Nuttall (obverse), Page 10. © The Trustees of the British Museum.

Codex Zouche-Nuttall (obverse), Page 9. © The Trustees of the British Museum.

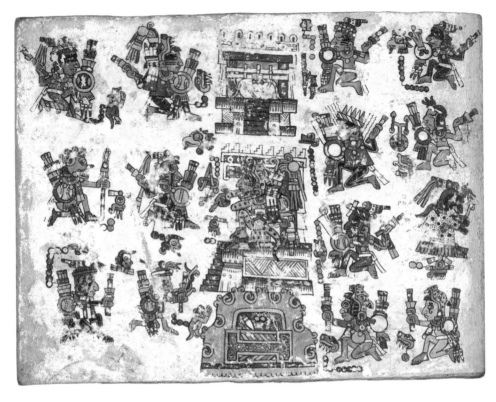

Codex Zouche-Nuttall (obverse), Page 8. © The Trustees of the British Museum.

Codex Zouche-Nuttall (obverse), Page 7. © The Trustees of the British Museum.

Codex Zouche-Nuttall (obverse), Page 6. © The Trustees of the British Museum.

Codex Zouche-Nuttall (obverse), Page 5. © The Trustees of the British Museum.

Codex Zouche-Nuttall (obverse), Page 4. © The Trustees of the British Museum.

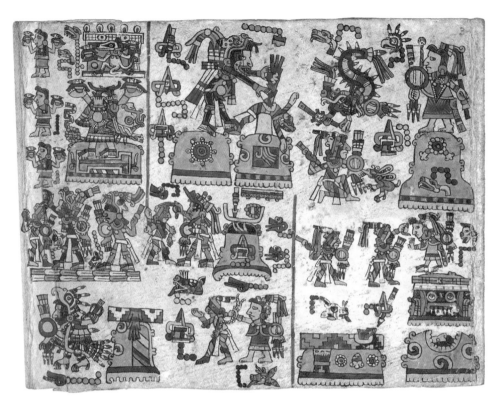

Codex Zouche-Nuttall (obverse), Page 3. © The Trustees of the British Museum.

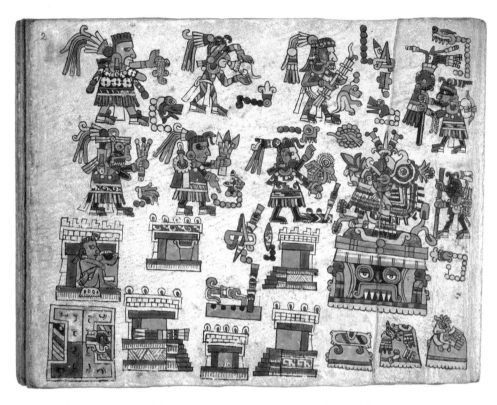

Codex Zouche-Nuttall (obverse), Page 2. © The Trustees of the British Museum.